The Dark Side of
Risk Management

FT Prentice Hall

FINANCIAL TIMES

In an increasingly competitive world, we believe it's quality of thinking that will give you the edge – an idea that opens new doors, a technique that solves a problem, or an insight that simply makes sense of it all. The more you know, the smarter and faster you can go.

That's why we work with the best minds in business and finance to bring cutting-edge thinking and best learning practice to a global market.

Under a range of leading imprints, including *Financial Times Prentice Hall*, we create world-class print publications and electronic products bringing our readers knowledge, skills and understanding, which can be applied whether studying or at work.

To find out more about Pearson Education publications, or tell us about the books you'd like to find, you can visit us at **www.pearsoned.co.uk**

PEARSON
Education

The Dark Side of Risk Management

How People Frame Decisions in Financial Markets

LUCA CELATI

An imprint of **Pearson Education**

London · New York · Toronto · Sydney · Tokyo · Singapore · Hong Kong · Cape Town
New Delhi · Madrid · Paris · Amsterdam · Munich · Milan

Pearson Education Limited

Edinburgh Gate
Harlow CM20 2JE
Tel: +44 (0)1279 623623
Fax: +44 (0)1279 431059
Website: www.pearsoned.co.uk

First published in Great Britain in 2004

The right of Luca Celati to be identified as author of this work has been asserted
by him in accordance with the Copyright, Designs and Patents Act 1988.

ISBN 0 273 66346 1

British Library Cataloguing-in-Publication Data
A catalogue record for this book is available from the British Library

Library of Congress Cataloging-in-Publication Data

Celati, Luca.
   The dark side of risk management : how people frame decisions in financial markets /
Luca Celati.
      p. cm.
   Includes bibliographical references and index.
   ISBN 0-273-66346-1 (hbk.)
      1. Investments--Psychological aspects. 2. Finance--Psychological aspects. 3. Risk
management. 4. Investments--Decision making. I. Title.

HG415.15.C45 2004
332'.01'9--dc22   2004047099

10 9 8 7 6 5 4 3 2 1
08 07 06 05 04

This publication is designed to provide accurate and authoritative information in regard to the
subject matter covered. It is sold with the understanding that neither the authors nor the publisher
is engaged in rendering legal, investing, or any other professional service. If legal advice or other
expert assistance is required, the service of a competent professional person should be sought.

The publisher and contributors make no representation, express or implied, with regard to the accuracy
of the information contained in this book and cannot accept any responsibility or liability for any errors
or omissions that it may contain.

The opinions of Luca Celati are not necessarily the opinions of Abraxas Capital Management.

Typeset in 10/13 pt ITC Garamond Light by 30
Printed and bound by Biddles, King's Lynn, UK

The publisher's policy is to use paper manufactured from sustainable forests.

To my beloved wife Laura and our wonderful children

Contents

Contents

PART II

Practice

PART III

Going forward

Foreword

In an increasingly complex financial world where the use and application of derivatives are now commonplace, the role of risk management has taken on a greater significance in all trading organizations. All through the hierarchy, from support personnel, traders, managers, and risk personnel to the Board, key decisions are being made in ever shorter time spans based on pre-assembled information with little time to think through the myriad assumptions that are built in. Even if you have the information, do you really know what to do with it?

In order to answer this basic question, legions of consultants and IT specialists have labelled as 'risk management' the provision of information, rather than its content or how it is used in decision-making. In my own experience as a trader and then as a manager, I have learned to be sceptical of over-engineered solutions and black-box answers.

As an end-user, I would contend that risk management in its truest form is mostly an art that addresses decision-making, rather than a quantitative or IT science of how to run risk reporting.

Regardless of technology or products or the phase of the economic cycle, the biggest risk lies in traders' and decision-makers' heads rather than in their trades. The latter, rather than the former, is where today's widely accepted 'best practices' in risk management spend the overwhelming portion of time and resources. Yet human failure and neglect are the driving force of most of the risk disasters we have witnessed over the past decade. It should make one seriously question whether the risk industry is pursuing the 80/20 principle the wrong way around. This devastating charge, led by this book and its exploration of the Dark Side, is supported by a thoroughly documented list of human biases and their consequences.

Based on the common mantra of independence, most will assume that risk managers are serving exclusively the Boards of their organizations and that their job will be mostly to guard against evil and greedy traders. As a matter of fact, the best risk managers are those who can best balance their responsibilities towards Boards and traders. What is the point of having someone who is 'independent' but has no clue what a trading desk is aiming for?

A better awareness of the Dark Side is also where the biggest opportunity for a quantum leap in our understanding of risk lies. This book paves the way for a more intelligent and less mechanical approach to risk by putting the individual frames of risk back on centre stage. Pretending to 'solve' the problem by putting rules and frameworks around the individual is the easier and generally favoured route in the short term. Unsurprisingly, many books and consultants make a brisk business out of those 'solutions', which exacerbate organizations' dysfunctional bureaucracy in the long term, making them less agile and responsive and exposing them even further to human biases.

Many risk management books claim to offer definitive answers with their elegant quantitative and statistical models. This book exposes the many unwelcome practical effects of standard financial theory assumptions. Then, the persistent and pervasive nature of human biases is the only certainty that remains to be reckoned with. There is no shortage of challenges in today's financial markets. Few can be more daunting than facing one's own and admitting to them as the first step towards personal and professional growth. And that is the innovative angle in risk management that this book provides. While there are many books about the quantitative side of risk management and the behavioural aspects of finance, this book is unique in that it links these two areas in a manner that is practical and yet interesting to follow and read.

T.J. Lim

T.J. Lim is a Partner of NewSmith Capital Partners, an Investment Management and Corporate Advisory Partnership headquartered in London, UK. Previously, he was the Head of International Debt at Merrill Lynch, co-Head of Global Markets at Dresdner Kleinwort Benson and a member of the management board, and Global Head of FX and Fixed Income Derivatives at UBS in London.

Preface

Men plan and God laughs.
(*Talmudic saying*)

Why I wrote this book

First as a trader and then as a risk manager, I have often been amazed at seeing the market's persistent ability to baffle any human attempt to control it. This book is about the many psychological issues that surround trading and their practical consequences. That's a marked shift in emphasis from other excellent books on this topic and the broad field of behavioural finance. Rather than concentrating entirely on the theory, empirical studies and academic debates, this book intends to make the topic more accessible for people who want to roll up their sleeves and get their hands dirty. Most risk practitioners know that people and processes – also relying mostly on people – account for the lion's share of operational risk. Isn't it time to start looking at the *causes* of people's behaviour rather than just measuring its *effects*?

The theme of accidents resulting from human error is not new. Conversely, the extent to which the consequences of financial risk disasters spread across time and geographical borders is unprecedented. This is a logical consequence of the massive impact of globalization, technology and leverage. This book attempts to fill the void that exists between risk management, widely regarded as a quantitative discipline, and recent insights from behavioural sciences and cognitive psychology. It is my genuine hope that it will lay the foundations for more targeted studies to help practitioners on the vast array of issues that it covers.

Why should you read this book and what sets it apart from others on the topic?

This book differs from other excellent publications on the area of human behaviours in finance and investing in three ways. It is the first book:

- to illustrate the consequences of behavioural finance in risk management, the area of institutions that is mandated with optimizing risk-adjusted performance;

- to introduce psychometric testing tools in a book on finance and risk management;
- to emphasize practical applications in the daily risk and trading reality, rather than theoretical or academic issues.

What you will learn from this book

You will:

- develop a better understanding of the beliefs, assumptions and context dependence that surround your decisions. You trade probabilities, not prices, and those probabilities reflect your beliefs, assumptions and psychology. The state of mind – resourceful or not – into which you put yourself ultimately determines how successful you will become;
- learn that biases can actually perform some useful functions, provided that you know the right context with which you will pair them;
- see how pervasive human biases are in driving questionable decisions not only for individuals but also for the organizations and systems of which they are members;
- realize how human failure – rather than models, markets or defaults – is the common feature in all the major risk disasters and financial panics of the last 20 years and why top managers never learn their lesson.

Acknowledgements

When I set about writing this book, I knew that it would be virtually impossible to go one-on-one against such a daunting topic alone. The feedback, encouragement and support that many individuals from different walks of life provided proved a decisive factor.

As you will find out, *The Dark Side of Risk Management* is very much a journey of introspection and personal growth – topics that seldom top the list of formal finance training and experience. Accordingly, first and foremost, I would like to thank Gilles Dufour, a Paris-based professional Executive Coach for the active interest and support he provided throughout this project, and in particular for the chapter he wrote on personal growth. Chapter 12 is indeed a critical step in understanding and outgrowing one's biases and effectively addresses the Dark Side of Risk Management.

Gilles was trained as an Executive Coach in NY, London and Paris, and started his coaching practice in 1999. His firm GD-Conseil (www.gd-conseil.com) has been successful in establishing key relationships with clients such as Géodis, L'Oréal, Natexis Banque Populaire, Oddo, and the PPR group (FNAC, CFAO). GD-Conseil focuses on executive coaching, team coaching and leadership development programs. Gilles specializes in developing effective professional relationships, enhancing communication skills, and implementing effective time management. A certified Yoga teacher, he also helps align physical health with professional objectives.

Gilles holds a BS from Supelec, a leading French Engineering College where he graduated in 1985; he also has a MS in Entrepreneurship from HEC. He then worked for 10 years in the Capital Markets departments of various investment banks (JP Morgan, Paribas and Deutsche Bank). During that time, he also served as a Director to Business Objects, the world's leading provider of enterprise business intelligence.

Much of the credit for the birth of this book also belongs to Joe Tanega, first for encouraging me so hard to press forward with it and secondly for working phenomenally hard on the editing of chapters 4 through 8.

Establishing and improving the connectivity between the insights from academia and the real world of trading is very much at the heart of this book. Drawing from disparate sources of cutting-edge research in different but related fields helped me immensely in making their insights more accessible to readers. I am thankful for the interest and support that the following academics provided to this project (names are, of course, not in order of importance):

- Dr John A. Johnson of the University of Pennsylvania, and Dr Lewis R. Goldberg and his team at the Oregon Research Institute, for helping me meet the challenge of introducing psychometric tools into a risk and finance book by adapting the tests provided on the IPIP.org web site;

- Professors Stephen Morris and Hyun Song Shin for their work on game theory applications in finance and risk management;

- Professors Fenton O'Crevy and Nigel Nicholson for their research on the behaviour of traders and their managers;

- Professor Hersh Shefrin, the Mario L. Belotti Professor of Finance at the Leavey School of Business, Santa Clara University, for his many useful comments;

- Professor John R. Nofsinger, of Washington State University, for his helpful feedback and enthusiastic support of the project.

In addition, several individuals, friends and colleagues have enthusiastically spent a substantial amount of their precious spare time reviewing various drafts of the book. Amongst others, I am most indebted to Dr Roger Becker of Life Science Consulting, Mario Borrelli of Banca Nazionale del Lavoro, Alex Frick, Rüdiger Holzammer of RedHerring, T.J. Lim of NewSmith Financial Solutions, Marie Menendez of Moody's Investor Services, Professor Avinash Persaud of GAM, Raman Sharma, Konstantin von Schweinitz of DRKW and Garret Thunen for the thorough review that they provided and how they helped clarify my concepts and their explanation in the book.

With respect to Pearson Education, I would like to extend my thanks to Benjamin Roberts, Kate Salkilld, Paula Devine and Richard Stagg. Without their hard work and dedication, it would have been impossible to meet the tight schedule that was set for the project.

Last but not least, my wife Laura and my children Paolo and Marco deserve special appreciation for their unwavering support and forgoing the countless weekends that I spent on this project.

The publishers would like to thank the following for permission to reproduce copyright material:

Professor John A. Johnson of Pennsylvania State University, and Dr Lewis R. Goldberg and his team at the Oregon Research Institute for the IPIP Questionnaire in Appendix A; Springer-Verlag and Professor Manfred Zimmerman for use of Table 2.1: Bandwidth of the sensory systems, reprinted from *Human Physiology*, 2nd ed., Manfred Zimmerman, 'The nervous system in the context of Info Theory', R.F. Schmidt and G. Thews (eds), Springer-Verlag, 1989, translation of *Physiologie des Menschen*, 23rd ed, p. 172; Penguin Books Ltd for use of Table 2.2: Media Bandwidth, from *The User Illusion: Cutting Consciousness Down to Size*, by Tor Nørretranders, translated by Jonathan Sydenham (Viking, 1998), copyright © 1991 Tor Nørretranders, translation copyright © 1998 Jonathan Sydenham; Alan Richmond, and www.eluzions.com, for Figs. 2.2: Lines and dots, 2.3: The cube, 2.10: Vase, 2.12: Lines; Dr Penny Fidler (At-Bristol, www.youramazingbrain.org) for Figs 2.8: Monsters (copyright © Cecilia Slack), 2.5: Spiral, 2.7: Bristol Café Wall, 2.4: Female Figure, 2.6: Geometric Shapes; Dr Eric H. Chudler for Fig. 2.11: Dots; Doubleday, a division of Random House, Inc., for use of text reprinted from *Decision Traps*, by J. Edward Russo and Paul J.H.

Schoemaker, copyright © 1989 J. Edward Russo and Paul J.H. Schoemaker; The Econometric Society for use of text reprinted from 'Prospect Theory – An Analysis of Decision under Risk', by Daniel Kahneman and Amos Tversky, *Econometrica*, 1979; Kluwer Academic/Plenum Publishers for use of Fig. 4.1: Utility chart according to prospect theory and conventional theory, reprinted from 'Cumulative prospect theory', by Amos Tversky and Daniel Kahneman, *Journal of Risk and Uncertainty*, 1992; John Wiley & Sons Limited for use of text reprinted from 'Mental Accounting Matters', by R.H. Thaler, *Journal of Behavioural Decision-Making*, 12, 1999, copyright © 1999 John Wiley & Sons Limited; Heldref Publications for use of Table 5.2: Judgment of relative frequency for selected pairs of lethal events, reprinted from 'Rating the risks', by P. Slovic, B. Fischhoff and S. Lichtenstein, *Environment*, 21(3), 1979, copyright © 1979 Heldref Publications; McGraw-Hill Education for text reprinted from S. Plous, *Psychology of Judgement and Decision Making*, McGraw-Hill, 1993, copyright © 1993 The McGraw-Hill Companies; John Wiley & Sons, Inc. for use of text reprinted from B. Fischhoff, 'For those condemned to study the past: Reflections on historical judgment', in R.A Schweder and D.W. Fiske (eds), *New Directions for Methodology of Social and Behavioural Science*, Jossey-Bass, 1980, copyright © 1980 John Wiley & Sons, Inc., reprinted by permission of John Wiley and Sons, Inc.; Springer-Verlag for use of Table 6.1: How different organizational cultures handle safety information, reprinted from R. Westrum, 'Cultures with requisite imagination', in J. Wise, D. Hopkin and P. Stager (eds), *Verification and Validation of Complex Systems*, Springer-Verlag, 1980; Stephen Morris and H.S. Shin for use of Table 6.2: The various actors' behaviours and the Thai baht peg, and text, all reprinted from 'Risk management with interdependent choice', *Oxford Review of Economic Policy*, Autumn, 1999 (reprinted in *Financial Stability Review*, Bank of England, November, 1999), and 'Unique equilibrium in a model of self-fulfilling currency attacks', *American Economic Review*, 88; Elsevier for use of Fig. 7.6: Price ratio between Royal Dutch and Shell stocks, reprinted from *Journal of Financial Economics*, 53(2), 1999, K. Froot, 'How are stock prices affected by the location of trade?', pp. 189–216, copyright © 1999 with permission from Elsevier; Professor Avinash Persaud for use of material drawn from his lecture, entitled 'Where have all the risks gone', given at Gresham College, London, in November, 2002; Elsevier for use of Fig. 8.1: Prospect theory and trading managers' behaviour, reprinted from *Accounting, Organizations and Society*, 27($\frac{1}{2}$), 2002, P. Willman *et al*, 'Trader's tales: Agency, manager behaviour and loss aversion in investment banking', pp. 85–98, copyright © 2002 with permission from Elsevier; Elsevier for use of text reprinted from *Journal of Economic Psychology*, 23, 2002, J.M.E. Pennings, 'Pulling the trigger or not: Factors affecting behaviour of initiating a position in derivative markets', pp. 263–78, copyright © 2002 with permission from Elsevier; Professor Alex Frino for use of text reprinted from 'The propensity for local traders in futures markets to ride losses: Evidence of irrational or rational behaviour?', draft paper, University of Sydney; McGraw-Hill Education for use of Table 10.1: A hit parade of mishaps, reprinted from L. Cunningham, *Outsmarting the Smart Money*, McGraw-Hill, 2002, copyright © 2002 The McGraw-Hill Companies; Pearson Education for use of Table 10.2: Effect of leverage from reverse repos on portfolio return when interest rates increase 2.75% during the year, reprinted from J. Norfsinger, *Investment*

Blunders of the Rich and Famous, © 2003, p. 218. Reprinted by permission of Pearson Education, Inc., Upper Saddle River, New Jersey; Village Modial/Pearson Éducation France for use of Fig. 12.2: The five phases of change, reprinted from G.D. Carton, *Eloge du changement*, p. 212, copyright © 1999 Ed. Village Mondial; Professor Lázló Merö for use of Fig. A3.2: Bluffing, reprinted from L. Merö, *Moral Calculations*, Copernicus, Springer-Verlag, 1998; Perseus Books Group for use of text reprinted from D. Dörner, The Logic of Failure, copyright © 1996 Perseus Books, Addison-Wesley.

PART I

Theory

If you do not know who you are, markets are an expensive place to find out.

(Adam Smith)

CHAPTER 1

Throwing down the gauntlet

Wanted, men for a hazardous journey. Low wages, intense cold, long months of darkness and constant risks. Return uncertain.

(E. Shackleton, 1900, insertion in a London newspaper)

7±2:

- Rationality in finance and risk management? Oh, yeah!

- What is in it for you?

- Practical applications, not academic disputes

- It begins inside you

- What the book is and what it is not

- Structure of the book

1.1 The punchline: what's in it for you?

OK, you may have already heard it, people are not as rational as they claim to be, but then, you may think, so what? If you work in an investment bank or in any trading room, the question above, magically embodied by your bonus expectations, is likely to top the list. Well, let's face it, your emotional state has quite a bearing on your performance and your bonus. Does that arouse your interest?

This is the key question of this book: How aware are you and your organization of the frames, assumptions and beliefs that underpin your thoughts, analyses and decisions? Such awareness of the process and its weaknesses is far more elusive than people think.

What will you get out of this book? The good news is that there are tools to reach a higher level of awareness, better decisions and split-second, unconscious execution. You can too. Over time, these translate into fewer mistakes, better performance and (no, it hasn't been forgotten!) a larger bonus. In ancient Japan, samurai warriors were legendary for pairing the two attributes of awareness and flawless, lightning-fast execution. Many traders and decision-makers do the opposite and get into trouble. That is, they pay insufficient attention to the process and the battle terrain – and then freeze when it's time for the execution.

The bad news is that all of this is exclusively your responsibility. Nobody else can be responsible for the inner workings of your mind. What you make out of the tools provided in this book is solely up to you. This book is not going to provide another trust-me cookie-cutter decision-making crutch for you. You'd better get rid of the crutch.

1.2 The issue and its sub-themes

In few areas has the human sub-conscious as deep an impact on performance as in trading. Accordingly, many professional traders manage their emotional state actively and keep a close look on how it affects their decisions. Despite emotional intelligence becoming a buzzword, however, most organizations struggle to manage such emotional discipline and be aware of how their members feel. Simply put, how could a large bank or trading room possibly run an 'emotional audit' when there are no standards or benchmarks available for this emotional risk? As modern financial services providers become increasingly complex, the distortions caused by flawed decisions are magnified accordingly.

No one can deny the impact and sophistication achieved by the risk management industry over the last 20 years in meeting the classic management request for more information, both in finance and outside it. The main thesis of this book is that these very achievements have opened a gap between the *availability* and the *use* of information. Imagine that a bank and its management are portrayed as a car and its driver. Then, efforts have focused overwhelmingly on the former rather than on the latter. Within the financial risk management industry, comparatively limited attention has been put into understanding *how* information is applied and how aware management and traders are of their own limitations in processing it.

This general theme is articulated in this book as follows:

- Regardless of their honesty in admitting it, people are far less rational than they believe themselves to be. That is the trump card that behavioural finance, a recent area of modern financial theory, has been using in leading the charge against the assumptions of conventional modern finance and its well-known efficient market hypothesis (EMH).

- Conversely, conventional economics has recognized the importance of human emotions only recently.[1] Relying largely on the assumptions of conventional economics, modern finance has not attributed much weight to psychology and human behaviours. The same applies to modern risk management, a relatively new discipline that has developed over the last 20 years as a by-product of the explosive financial innovation driven by technology and derivative products.

- As a matter of fact, human emotions, biases and frames surrounding problems and information play a critical and poorly understood role in risk and top management decisions. Context dependence plays a critical role in affecting supposedly 'rational' and 'objective' decisions.

- In the context of financial risk management issues, most attention – whether inside a bank or in the academic and empirical studies surrounding it – targets the measurement and information production activities rather than the decision-making processes that use them. It is the latter's cognitive and behavioural issues – rather than the former – that drive individual and group decisions.

- People problems that were superficially labelled as 'mismanagement' have been at the root of all major crises and financial risk management disasters in the last 15 years. The system, model or infrastructure issues blamed by subsequent studies were amongst the symptoms and effects of these disasters, rather than their ultimate cause. As a result, the behavioural and cognitive lessons have not been completely learned. Then, it is hardly surprising that other major crises keep happening and losses follow.

- No generally accepted metrics exist to measure thinking styles and biases in financial decision-making either at individual or organizational level. Consistent with a basic risk management principle, you cannot manage what you cannot measure. Accordingly, this prevents most banks from measuring and managing an excessive exposure to selected mental dimensions and biases in their operations and activities.

- Modern risk management largely neglects the interdependence between decision-makers. The assumption of individual decision-making without any regard for others is another drawn from conventional economics. In practice, people are far more interdependent. This is at the root of higher order beliefs. Tribal-like herd instincts in people management further reinforce concentration of thinking styles and mental frames in the organization.

- External constituencies, such as rating agencies, regulators, analysts and investors (which also consist of individuals), exhibit these behavioural biases and reflect them in their risk assessments of banks.

---

[1] The conventional economics assumptions of rational decision-making and no impact of human emotions reigned unchallenged since the days of Adam Smith until the early 1970s. Then, empirical studies by psychologists Daniel Kahneman and Amos Tversky started showing the importance of human biases in a variety of behaviours. This was especially true with respect to attitudes towards risk and uncertainty. The gist of their conclusions is illustrated later, in Chapter 4. As a tribute to the growing importance of human behaviours, Daniel Kahneman won the Nobel Prize in Economics in 2002. It should come as no surprise that not only individual human behaviours but also the interaction between people was unexplored until the development of modern game theory in the 1950s.

1.3 Not another behavioural finance book

There are already at least half a dozen excellent books on behavioural finance and how people's biases affect investment decisions, all of which deserve great respect. So, what is the rationale for another book? For sure, behavioural finance and cognitive psychology have given a great service to finance in attributing to human behaviours the importance that they deserve. At the same time, coming from the trading room himself, the Author sees considerable opportunity for making these insights more accessible to people who should rely on them in their countless assumptions, decisions and trades, first and foremost the brave souls in the trading room. This book will not lay any claim to absolute perfection. Facilitating the understanding for end-users is far more important. Simply put, this book is for people who want to get their hands dirty, rather than as a classy conversation topic to impress market counterparts and investors at the golf club or over tea. The stakes from the potential applications of increased awareness of one's emotions and biases are simply too high to ignore.

In that respect, and in the discussion of many topics, the book is deliberately controversial – a price worth paying if it helps people in their day-to-day reality. By the way, the search for absolute 'right' answers is also a human fallacy, the binary 'right-or-wrong' bias described later, in Chapter 5.

The following four areas deserve greater attention than they have previously been given:

- the psychological risk factor in risk management;
- focus on practical issues and cases rather than on academic skirmishes;
- dealing with one's biases is not as hopeless as commonly believed;
- the introduction of some applications of psychometric testing to understand biases before attempting to manage them.

The next four sections explain these points in greater detail.

1.3.1 Risk management meets behavioural finance

This book studies the risk management issues created by human emotions and behaviours. To date, investment management has been the main arena in which behavioural finance has been challenging the EMH and its mean-variance optimization (MVO) assumptions. Probably due to the far lower transparency in performance evaluation metrics and limited outside disclosure, little attention has been paid to the consequences of implicit – and distorted – MVO thinking *inside* financial institutions. This applies particularly to risk management, one of the key areas mandated with managing risk-return trade-offs between the various internal and external constituencies of a modern financial institution. Aside from their traditional disaster-prevention role, these groups now manage risk capital and in this respect face similar challenges to their investment management counterparts. Increasing competition and more stringent outside disclosure have put additional emphasis on risk capital optimization as a mission of modern risk management teams. In short, avoiding disasters is no longer enough. These extra responsibilities, while making the job far more exciting, mean that modern risk managers have to face many of the same behavioural issues as their money-management counterparts.

What makes this topic especially interesting is how Wall Street's notoriously strong egos magnify traditional decision-making issues inside an organization. An impressive body of studies in behavioural finance and cognitive psychology over the last 20 years has confirmed the existence and consistency of these human biases. Not much has been done to even measure – let alone manage – them. Accordingly, while recent emphasis[2] – last but not least by regulators – on the area of operational risk has underscored how the human element is responsible for at least two-thirds of operational losses, these statistics are nothing but the ex-post effects of a deeper problem.

In a similar fashion, well-publicized studies of risk management problems at Orange County, Metallgesellschaft, Barings, LTCM, Enron, Allfirst and others have investigated mostly the limitations in technology, organizational infrastructure and models supporting the trading operation. By comparison, not much time was spent on the issues of the people involved. The *real* problems lie in the faulty way in which people receive, frame and process information when making their decisions and, worse, how little they learn from their mistakes. Maintaining and reinforcing a state of denial on how little people really know about themselves – let alone the world that surrounds them – compounds the problem further.

The behavioural revolution can benefit risk management in major ways. Over time, the use of the psychometric tools that this book introduces can be used to develop a more thorough understanding of the behavioural drivers of performance. This in turn can provide new criteria to allocate risk capital based on the psychological composition of a population of risk-takers.

1.3.2 Focus on real-life cases rather than on academic skirmishes

This book aims to provide some practical – albeit by no means perfect – guidelines and thought processes to use inside a financial institution. By that, we typically mean a bank with a trading room, dealmakers and risk managers, the latter looking at market risk, credit risk or both. What happens inside the decision-makers' heads – rather than the sophistication of the tools they use – is the prime concern here. There is more than enough work to do on the thought process *including making sure there is an active and critical one*. That makes a moot point out of any theoretical discussions on the need to use a fourth or a second generation hedging or pricing model in a specific situation. Strangely, most analyses of major risk problems in recent years conclude with recommendations that pursue exactly the opposite route. Has Value-at-Risk (VaR) been used inappropriately in the most recent crisis? We should then hire outside consultants to explain it. And, while we are at it, let's install a more powerful Monte-Carlo simulation engine!

---

[2] See, amongst others, the 2002 RMA OpRisk Poll (www.rmahq.org), which attributed 64% and 25% of the causes of operational risk to processes and people, respectively (Loewenton, 2003). In his insightful book *Managing the Risk of Organizational Accidents* (p. 42), Reason (1997) provides other evidence of human failures accounting for about 80% of accident causes. See also the study by MIT professor R. John Hansman on confusion in aircrafts in D. Hughes, 'Incidents reveal mode confusion. Automated cockpits special report part 1', *Aviation Week and Space Technology*, 30 January 1995, p.5. According to this study, confusion and other human errors account for over 80% of problem instances, including accidents.

Understanding and addressing these human decision-making limitations in risk management is what this book is about. Rehashing other debates between EMH and behavioural finance researchers would not add much value for people who trade and manage risk on a daily basis. Readers who are interested in behavioural finance books on investment management and the frequent skirmishes between their authors and EMH supporters can find excellent references in the Further reading section and consult them directly.

One may argue that the 'average' bank – regardless of its definition – does not suffer from these biases and issues and may even find surveys confirming this hypothesis. Even if this was true, that does not cancel the magnitude of disasters that made the headlines at 'average' banks over the last few years.

These horror stories did happen. Choosing to label them as 'aberrations' or 'biases' is pure semantics. In the case of banks, the arguments about how sophisticated the tools should be or what causes their theoretical limitations largely misses the point. Rather, the major issue is how passively and inappropriately standard risk and finance tools are often used. The quest for more information or for more sophisticated models is often a crutch for top management's inability to process existing information or decide upon it. Eliminating the need for that crutch by understanding the problem at its roots is what really matters.

Biases are hardly an academic matter. As a matter of fact, finance professionals ignore their serious consequences at their own peril. Consistently with its practical orientation, the book will show in Chapter 10 how human failure has always been the consistent theme underlying a series of well-known financial risk management problems. Finance professionals are hardly alone, since these pervasive human traits go well beyond the frontiers of finance. That will be shown in the series of real-life risk disasters discussed in Chapter 11.

1.3.3 Biases, not yet a completely lost battle

This is yet a third aspect in which this book explores a different dimension from standard behavioural finance arguments. Behavioural finance offers more descriptions of human biases than help in dealing with them. It argues that they are here to stay and all that one can do is accept them and limit the number of decisions, as many of them will likely be wrong.

In many instances, this is likely to hold. In others, however, there may be some positive facets of biases that are worth exploring. If you are a trader and lean towards extrapolation bias,[3] you'd better limit your activity to trending markets only. Otherwise, you risk being eaten alive in markets that move sideways. In other words, we are conditioned to believe that biases are inherently and only 'bad'. Recall the following quote from William Shakespeare:

> *There is nothing inherently good or bad, but thinking it makes it so.*

---

[3] That is, you tend to form your expectation on future prices by projecting based on the past ones. By doing this, you are undervaluing new information and overvaluing historical data.

Every bias that you have performs some useful function for you and you have to decode it and understand it before you try to reprogramme it. Since most decisions are context-dependent, you simply have to develop a deeper understanding of those situations in which the negative side-effects of one's biases will be curbed. A prudent trader, for instance, will risk underperforming more aggressive ones in the short term but will hope to outlive them through adverse phases. His expected reward is to continue to trade thanks to the lower draw-downs that he will likely suffer over time. The answer for him is not to become more aggressive but to seek different market conditions to suit his temperament.

1.3.4 Applications of psychometric testing

This will probably be one of the most controversial areas of the book, as this topic seldom crosses paths with finance. Yet, basic risk management states that you cannot understand what you do not measure. Psychometric testing has been around for over 30 years and this book will show and use some of the tools out there. You have nothing to lose and much to gain from knowing a little bit more about yourself and how you make your decisions. Chapter 8 shows the huge gap between the processes that banks label as 'people manage-ment' and a thorough understanding of the psychological drivers of performance. Based on the empirical evidence at most financial institutions, one should conclude that human resources 'management' is mostly an accounting exercise over headcount and costs. Financial institutions have a great opportunity to harness the brainpower of their staff. The concentration of bright, motivated individuals in the financial services industry is simply a phenomenally under-utilized resource. This is a big black hole that the industry ought to look into soon or else leave the task of asking them to do so to regulators.

1.4 Denial dies hard

To be fair, there is some awareness of how people's biases interfere with risk management decisions. Overconfidence, however, is a pervasive human trait and this will not be the first or the last book to show it (see Chapter 4). Denial of the human element of risk manage-ment is a much simpler – and, in the short term, cheaper – choice than studying and tackling the problem head-on. Chapter 13 illustrates this problem and the violent disagree-ment that some will probably display towards some of the remarks in this book.

1.5 It begins inside you

A major goal of this book is to stimulate some healthy debate inside your organization and – more importantly – inside YOU. Organizations are nothing but a reflection of the personali-ties of their leaders and staff. As inside, so outside, what is inside is what gets out: first of all, if you wish to improve the decision-making processes in your organization, you must develop a greater awareness of the weaknesses that you and others around you display when processsing information and making decisions. The brutal truth is that you have to put forth actions rather than words. Leaders are the first ones who have to embody the change. This book is not about providing yet another crutch.

In the wake of the most recent risk management disasters, some have advocated more articulated lines of accountability or different organizational set-ups. Once again, making the corporate protective shields thicker or more sophisticated does not change what goes on in the hearts and minds of decision-makers. In the auto analogy used earlier in this chapter, no degree of sophistication in the engine, brakes or instruments can make up for a drunk or blind driver (and there is ample empirical evidence to show that humans *are* probability-blind.) Only a quantum leap will get the job done and the path towards it is by no means easy or safe. Staring at individual and corporate fears, facing them and moving on is what that quantum leap is about.

1.6   What this book is and what it is not

As the human brain cannot be codified in a set of mechanical rules and algorithms, it is important to establish what this book does NOT offer. It is NOT:

- a sure-fire way to make money;
- another forum for theoretical skirmishes;
- a popular management fad;
- a set of formulae to price and hedge risks.

Conversely, this book aims to:

- generate a better awareness of how it is wrong to treat risk management as a purely analytical and logical process. This widespread view underestimates the impact of psychological issues on risk decisions;
- explain practical ways to bring the 'right side of the brain' issues back to centre stage when risk decisions are involved;
- clarify how politically correct groupthink and common wisdom leads an organization to assume major long-term risks in return for short-term benefits;
- set the record straight to achieve a more orthodox disclosure or human risk and discipline inside and outside an organization.

It is important to rehearse the first two points and underscore what this book is *not*. Lack of behavioural finance-driven arbitrage activity is often used as an argument by its critics, and particularly by many EMH supporters. This book is more about a philosophy and a mind-set than about repeating what you already know, so it requires an open mind. Continuing with the auto analogy, having a reasonable understanding of the challenges of driving in fog or on ice does not propel the car forward but is still a necessary skill to possess. Being aware of how little we actually know and understanding how many implicit assumptions, shortcuts and mental frames we use in our decisions is a necessary – but not sufficient – ingredient to do business.

1.7 Who should read this book

The issues explored in this book belong to the common ground between a variety of disciplines. Key amongst them are:

- behavioural and modern finance;

- risk management;

- cognitive psychology;

- a bit of group and game theory.

The complexity and specialized nature of these topics assume a basic understanding of these subjects. That makes this book more suitable to an intermediate/advanced risk practitioner – not just the staff in a risk management/risk control team but the top management above them and the traders surrounding them. These ultimate clients of a modern risk management team should be the first to become aware of the bias in their decisions. It is sometimes said that information provided by risk management matters only inasmuch as the changes in behaviours it drives. Then, no success criterion is more relevant than helping these actors make sounder decisions. Risk is a pervasive theme in a financial institution, so it would not make sense to drive this revolution in the isolated silo of a risk management team. Few are willing to fund purely academic efforts anyway.

1.8 About the author

This book reflects my real-life experience at leading international merchant banks and the biases that I acquired while working there. Readers must forgive some references to my personal work experience in trading, derivatives and risk management over the last 15 years. I consider myself lucky to have been involved in the industry during such an unprecedented wave of financial innovation. I claim no exemption from the biases described in this book and some of my views will likely reflect them. Three professional phases were particularly important in shaping them:

- four years as a proprietary trader in illiquid sovereign bonds and currencies at Bankers Trust in London;

- four years as the loan portfolio manager and credit positioning trader at Bankers Trust in New York;

- six years in risk management, three as the global head of risk management at the debt division of Dresdner Kleinwort Wasserstein (DRKW) in London. My other risk management experiences have been as a consultant and now in my current position as chief investment officer at Abraxas Capital Management, a hedge fund based in London.

Much of the thrust behind this book must be ascribed to an eye-opening behavioural finance seminar and workshop that I attended in London in November 1999, during which I was able to see a devastating demonstration of human overconfidence. Specifically, the 17 workshop participants were asked to rate their driving skills relative to the average driver. I found myself as one of only three participants who rated themselves 'average'. This is perfectly aligned with the empirical results that are usually found when this question is asked (see Chapter 4). If that is how educated investment professionals rate their skills in a normal activity such as driving, I thought, guess what they must think of their professional skills in investing![4]

After such a major lesson, I have spent the last four years applying behavioural tools to risk management. The approach is not antithetic to the standard toolkit that is normally used to quantify risk. Rather, my point is simply that a behavioural overlay should exist for the conventional tools. While extremely interesting, most books on behavioural finance are generally written by academics rather than traders or risk managers. By targeting human behaviours and their risk consequences, this book addresses a major blind spot in risk management and fills a void between this discipline and behavioural studies.

1.9 Structure of the book

The vast territory covered by this book presents a major challenge. Contrary to the topics in other risk management texts, human behaviour is almost impossible to deal with in watertight compartments. Dealing with the issues sequentially may work well with books that are chock-full of equations but not as satisfactorily with human issues. All this increases the risk of losing the path. In short, you and your biases are the key actors in this story of risk and how it is framed. In the various chapters, you will see the following jigsaw. This visual arrangement of the book's topics aims to facilitate the reader's navigation through the book.

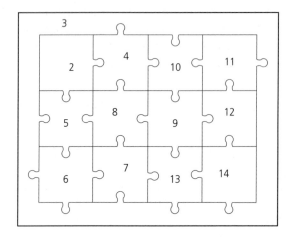

---

[4] This is referred to as the Lake Wobegon syndrome, after the fictional rural Minnesota community in which *all* children are above average.

This book is organized as follows:

- Part I provides the theory that underpins the frame of risk concept.

  - Chapter 2, on psychometric testing, will allow you to get some information on your thought and decision-making processes. No quiz can provide you with certainties and this one is no exception. It can help you, however, to understand how some key aspects of your personality affect your risk decisions. As even major well-established tests do not escape controversy, extreme caution is imperative when evaluating the results of this test. This is a bike rather than a spaceship and should be taken as such. Nevertheless, great potential exists to develop psychometric tests targeted to the trading and risk industry. This test must be viewed as just a stone thrown in the pond that may eventually give birth to a deeper and more appropriate way of evaluating people and the risks that they involve. This chapter also shows some of the modalities that people routinely use in their daily activities and decision-making and the associated physiology. Contrary to what the daily work routine may induce one to expect, there is hardly any uniformity in the mental programmes and strategies that people employ to perform their duties. And there are no better or worse programmes, only different programmes that will achieve different results.

  - Chapter 3 will define the frames of risk concept and provide the conceptual framework for the discussion in the following chapters.

  - Chapter 4 will summarize some of the principles of conventional modern finance and how many assumptions are relaxed – or conveniently ignored – in the real world. In practice, people are not nearly as rational as they appear and make more mistakes than their egos are willing to honestly admit. Behavioural finance has shed a lot of light on these phenomena, which were previously labelled 'aberrations'.

  - Based on the framework set out in the two preceding chapters, Chapter 5 explores the most important individual biases.

  - Chapter 6 is about group frames of risk and game theory. Modern finance and risk management have borrowed from standard economics the assumption of decision-making independent of other actors. As a matter of fact, we are not alone and we'd better take into serious account how the interdependence with others influences our supposedly rational decisions. Modern game theory adds another insight on the effects of human and group interaction and how this further affects rational decision-making.

- Part II provides a perspective on the real world, the main actors and their different and often conflicting biases.

  - Chapter 7 illustrates several frames of risk examples in trading and risk management. This will show how information can be twisted and distorted to provide the basis – or the excuse – for supposedly 'rational' decisions.

  - As one of the major sources of risk in the organization and the risk manager's main counterpart, the trader is the first figure to be introduced. Chapter 8 provides a robust set of empirical studies on trader behaviour. The correlation between behaviour and performance increases the stakes significantly and makes these frames of risk of utmost importance.

- The risk manager is the main area of attention in this book and one of the actors who best embodies the contradictions between modern finance and reality. Chapter 9 studies the behaviours of risk managers and of the other actors inside and outside their organizations.

- Chapter 10, on a series of risk disasters and panics and their behavioural roots, shows the catastrophic effects of human neglect in finance.

- Chapter 11 uses a series of major real-world accidents to illustrate how financial managers are not alone in making poor risk assessments. There is a frightening similarity in the behaviours that lead to mishaps.

■ Part III attempts to provide a further reality check to the frame of risk concept. Is there anything that one can do to actively manage them? How would that be reflected in a risk conversation with some typical trading room characters? What are the main charges that could be moved against it and against this book? And, last but not least, what can one do about biases?

- As the author believes that the individual is at the roots of biases, any steps have to begin there. Accordingly, Chapter 12 dwells on the individual, his or her career and financial objectives and what kind of soul search is necessary before one looks at the organization. The institutional point of view and specific do's and don'ts for both individuals and groups follow. The chapter offers some practical steps to address the many behavioural issues analysed in the previous chapters.

- Chapter 13 is about the opposition and some of the charges that will likely be moved against this book.

- The recap of the major action points is in the epilogue.

For those readers who are interested in skimming through the book quickly, each chapter begins with a summary of the 7 ± 2 most important points, an abstract and the related implications. This way, you have the option of jumping to the areas in which you are most interested very quickly and revisit other sections later.

Let's begin the frames journey!

CHAPTER 2

Your information risk processing

The real voyage of discovery consists not in seeing new landscapes, but in having new eyes.

(Marcel Proust)

7±2:

- The questionnaire
- Your information processing apparatus
- The key representational systems
- Limits in human information processing and the 7±2 rule
- Some fun with our 'reality'

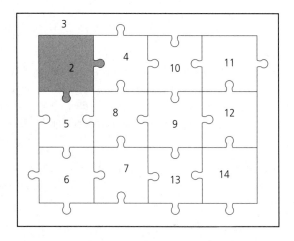

Abstract

To put the 'It Begins Inside You' motto into practice, no point could be more important than yourself in commencing the journey into the framing of risk. This chapter kicks off with the questionnaire, a set of questions to help you recognize your own frames in dealing with information and making decisions. The Disclaimer section explains why questionnaire, rather than test, was chosen to denote this set of questions.

Later on, this chapter provides a very broad overview of what is going on inside that risk processing computer that is the brain and what the surrounding physiology is. As was the case with interpretation of the questionnaire results, caution is essential when drawing conclusions from this chapter. The human risk machine is way too complex to be explained in one chapter or even in an entire encyclopedia. This chapter, however, may spark your curiosity to explore the topic in greater detail to learn more about yourself and how you process information. That would already be a very worthy achievement for this modest piece on the topic.

Implications: Before jumping to make decisions, do yourself a favour and try to understand what information you are selecting and discarding to get there. The same applies to judging other people's decisions. Lack of understanding of people's differences in processing information is often behind people's inability to work together effectively.

2.1 About the questionnaire – a disclaimer

Psychology and behavioural sciences have been recognized only recently as relevant factors in the field of economics, let alone finance. It is hardly surprising, then, to witness the large divide between the field of finance on the one side and psychometric tests for personality assessment on the other.

This book is deliberately controversial in several respects and the application of psychometric tools is one of them. Some of these tools have been around, in some cases, for decades, yet there is considerable controversy and scepticism about their application. In the context of this book, about risk and trading decisions, there are at least five major issues to be aware of when using these tools:

■ *Need for scientific validation*. There do not seem to be any widely accepted validated tests for the risk and finance profession because there is no such thing as a standard in the field.

■ *Validation can only be achieved with respect to performance*. The careful safeguard of performance information at large banks is completely necessary and understandable. However, the acid validation test would be to assess correlations between psychometric dimensions revealed by tests and actual performance. Empirical evidence of the use of psychometric tools in the continuous assessment of people – meaning not just in the hiring phase – in the trading industry is scant at best. That is one of the messages of Chapter 8. Simply put, performance is evaluated based on one's profit and loss (P&L), sometimes taking into account the level of limit and risk capital usage and, occasionally, adjusting for some market benchmark of performance. The impact of one's psychometric dimensions is nowhere on the map.

- *'Dog chasing its tail' between scientific validation and establishment of a standard psychometric test in finance.* Given the difficulties above, it is hardly surprising to witness the lack of a generally accepted psychometric standard in the trading industry. The latter requires prior validation and vice versa.

- *Need for a standard.* The issue above exists also in reverse. Without scientific validation, there is no standard test to point to. So, there you have a dog chasing its tail.

- *Misuses and abuses are possible,* as is the case with any tool. In such a sensitive area, there are major confidentiality and legal issues to reckon with.

This is a huge challenge but one has to start somewhere. The choice fell on a test called IPIP that is freely available on the internet. The results of this tool present a satisfactory correlation with other established standard tests – such as Myers-Briggs™, NEO-PI™ and JPI™. The set of questions will be labelled as 'questionnaire' instead of 'test' to underscore the extreme caution that is necessary when venturing into this largely uncharted terrain.

Nobody could be so naive as to think that a single questionnaire can provide an accurate or comprehensive picture of your personality. Accordingly, the results are presented 'as is' and no responsibility is assumed for any loss or adverse consequence that you might incur as a result of their interpretation. The same applies for the uses and confidentiality surrounding this sensitive topic. By taking this test or imparting it to others, you assume complete responsibility for any subsequent interpretation, use or breach of confidentiality associated with its results. Let me underscore that the use of a qualified professional psychologist is imperative before you take any serious step or decision following this questionnaire's results. These tools can be powerful in revealing some personality traits of yourself or your subordinates that you may not be comfortable with or even aware of. The potential for incorrect use is there, too.

My very modest contribution is just a set of questions, which were deliberately labelled as 'questionnaire' instead of 'test' to underscore their largely experimental status in the world of risk and trading. You should ask these about yourself and other people that you interact with. This is just a low-resolution, and by no means conclusive, snapshot of some aspects of your personality and has to be viewed as such. Then, if you become intrigued by the topic and want to delve deeper, you can hire a professional psychologist and take some of the other standard tests.

This book leans towards practical applications. Consistently with this principle, the author feels strongly that an 80/20 solution is preferable to doing nothing for years until a scientifically proven test for trading and risk professionals becomes available.

In short, this questionnaire is just a simple way to provide you with some feedback on yourself and show you the great potential of some of these tools out there. I lay no claim to this questionnaire becoming the absolute reference standard in the field.

It is my genuine hope that this book will help to break the watertight compartments that still exist between the worlds of trading and psychology. Later on in this book, a series of risk disasters in Chapters 10 and 11 will show how the human side of risk management is just too costly to ignore. There is no doubt that other professional psychologists could pick up from these questions to craft better sets that can be validated to qualify as a specialized test for the financial services industry. In turn, these results could be used to study correlations with performance and become an important driver of risk capital.

2.2 Questionnaire instructions

Please complete the questionnaire in Appendix A, section one. Answer every question by choosing a figure ranging between 1 (strongly disagree) and 5 (strongly agree). Whether you are taking the questionnaire on a discretionary basis or someone is imparting it to you, you should answer every question honestly. Should these answers be used against you unfairly, you will get the ultimate answer on the opportunity to change boss and, possibly, employer.

Please be aware that the use of the questionnaire is subject to the terms and conditions set forth by IPIP, who provide this tool on the internet and have kindly granted permission to use it in this book.

Section two of Appendix A provides a scoresheet and an explanation of the answers. If you are interested in comparing your results with the average profiles of those who have taken the questionnaire until December 2003, please contact the author on info@riskandregret.com.

2.3 Briefly on your brain, information processing and physiology

One cannot begin the discussion of our body's information management process without looking at the brain first. The web in our brain cortex is made up of tens of billions of cells, each weaving thousands (about 10,000, to be precise) of connections with other cells. These connections – called synapses – result in the electro-chemical interaction between cells. Synapses are formed from very early childhood as a result of our various experiences. For instance, risk-taking attitudes formed in our teens do not change much thereafter.

Each experience will develop a particular pattern of synapses. While scientists know that synapses contribute to specific behaviours, they cannot quantify the precise contribution of these cell connections.

A particular area of the cortex, the prefrontal cortex, is located about $1\frac{1}{2}$ centimetres (1") behind the eyes and becomes especially active when we make intellectual decisions. Under these circumstances, there is a sudden increase in the blood and oxygen flows to the brain.

In the simple experiment of counting backward from 50 to zero, for instance, blood flow increased by 27 per cent (Cohen, 2001). The body secretes adrenalin and the heartbeat soars. That's how the workings of the brain respond to an emergency 'fight-or-flight' situation.

Cerebral blood flows and the closely associated oxygen metabolism of the brain absorb a large proportion of the body's energy resources. These activities can account for as much as one-fifth of one's energy consumption. In particular, thought processes alone can account for a 10 per cent increase in the brain's oxygen metabolism (Roland *et al*, 1987). This is far above other important cerebral activities such as sensing or movement. The measurement of blood flows, pioneered by Larssen *et al* (1977) since the 1960s, made it possible to recognize which parts of the brain were active.

Not all thought processes account for the same amount of blood circulation and use of energy. For instance, visualization activities are more engaging than mental arithmetic or rhyming (Roland & Friberg, 1985; Friberg & Roland, 1988). Likewise, conversation leads to a greater increase in cerebral blood circulation than mere reporting.

2.4 Your information channels and their limitations

Your eyes, ears and physical kinesthetic perceptions are the main tools that the brain uses to collect information. According to some studies, between 70 and 90 per cent of all the cues that one picks up are mostly visual. Another 10–20 per cent are auditory and the balance is kinesthetic.

It is natural for one to think that these representations refer to the actual act of seeing, hearing or feeling. This is not necessary. The mere act of visualizing something or imagining the sound, smell, or feeling associated with something is a way to access a specific sensory system.

The language and analogies that one uses reveal much of one's favourite representation system. Let's look at some examples for each of these sensory systems:

- *Visual*: Your eyes account for most of the cues that the brain receives. The several observations and studies on the topic can only provide a range, rather than an exact figure. However, the next section will show that the intensity of stimuli from the eyes, measured in bits per second, outnumbers the impulses from the skin, the second largest source, by a factor of ten. The visual cues matter not only in the receipt of the image itself but also in the *way* in which it is received. Different intensities, colours, intermittencies and so on will indeed make the impact of images more or less vivid.

- *Auditory*: This refers to hearing, voices and sounds, another major source of information. In this case, the intensity will vary depending on the tempo of the stimulus, the presence of interruptions, its location and other features. Martial arts masters, for instance, are legendary for their ability to recognize the direction from which a threat or weapon may come even when they are blindfolded.

■ *Kinesthetic*: How else could one label the feelings that one experiences and summarizes in expressions such as 'gut feeling' or 'it weighs on me'? This has more to do with a particular feeling of the body, such as warmth, discomfort, pressure and so on. Again, this manifests itself in various degrees of intensity.

Note that these systems are not used only in connection with actual images, sounds or feelings, but also with respect to imaginary situations. Our brain's ability to travel across time and space is indeed one of the most powerful resources that Mother Nature has equipped us with. If you picture your brain as a powerful computer, you could easily imagine most if not all of its memory being engaged by the situation, set of thoughts or issues at hand. At the same time, the computer also has a large 'hard disk' of situations, instances and other resources that are stored in the memory and that can be accessed at will.

In addition to having a favourite system, people create certain sequences to represent reality – regardless of whether it is actual or not – to themselves. The first representation system that they adopt is usually the main and most powerful one. Starting from a different angle, the secondary one will generally reinforce the message of the first. People's response to various situations will then simply be dictated by the various representational sequences that they employ under a variety of situations. That's where your responsibility comes into play. While you cannot choose the situations that life throws at you, you can definitely pick the states to adopt in your response to them. In the context of this book, if you can decode your response into the combination of representational sequences that risk and trading involve, you will find it easier and quicker to recognize more and less resourceful states and understand what your body and physiology are trying to tell you.

2.4.1 The human bandwidth bottleneck

Borrowing from communications and network technology, *human bandwidth* is the phrase used to indicate mankind's information processing capabilities. By now, the limitations of the brain relative to the human sensory apparatus are well documented. This information bottleneck lies at the root of management's inability to turn more information into better decisions. Bandwidth limitations, when combined with increasing amounts and frequency of information, set the conditions for making more mistakes. In these situations, the brain copes with information overload by resorting to more heuristics, shortcuts and categorizations. Not all of these rules of thumb work. This, in turn, makes errors more likely. Chapter 5 explains the most common heuristics that people use.

The generic 'information overload' label is often used to explain these human information processing problems. But what are the specific issues that make humans unable to avoid or limit the effects of information overload?

Comprehensive research on human limitations in an information-processing capacity has been available for almost half a century and is best summarized by George Miller's seminal paper *The Magical Number Seven Plus or Minus Two* (1955). The span of absolute judgment and the storage capacity of immediate memory impose severe limitations on the amount of information that we are able to receive, process, and remember. One copes with this information bottleneck mostly by organizing the input stimuli simultaneously into several dimensions and successively into a sequence of *chunks*. In communication jargon, this process is termed *recoding*.

There are limits to how far one can stretch. Based on a series of previous experiments by other psychologists, Miller (1955) observed the following aspects of human information processing and the number of items that could be retained in memory:

- the span of absolute judgment (such as rating the position of points along a rating scale);

- the span of attention (such as reporting how many dots are flashed on a screen);

- the span of immediate memory (such as remembering a list of numbers).

He concluded that all these activities could retain seven plus or minus two items. The human brain, however, uses a technique called *clustering* that categorizes words in groups (such as 'apple' and 'banana' both belong to the 'fruit' group). This mechanism can stretch human short-term memory to up to 15 abstract words instead of the conventional seven to nine.

The '7±2' used at the beginning of each chapter in this book is meant to honour Dr Miller's findings by using no more than that number of bullet points to summarize the highlights of each chapter.

These limitations show up in a variety of ways. Pollack & Ficks (1954) tested subjects on sounds by varying six different acoustic variables. They were: frequency, intensity, rate of interruption, on-time fraction, total duration, and spatial location. Each one of these six variables could assume any one of five different values. So they could present a total of 15,625 different tones. The listeners made a separate rating for each one of these six dimensions. Only about 150 different categories (slightly less than 1 per cent of the total) could be absolutely identified without error.

The internet has only exacerbated the limitations of human bandwidth. The following figures help understand the disproportionate imbalance between the processing capability of our brain relative to the main senses:

TABLE 2.1 ▥ Bandwidth of the sensory systems[5]

Sensory system	Total bandwidth (bits/second)	Conscious bandwidth (bits/second)
Eyes	10,000,000	40
Ears	100,000	30
Skin	1,000,000	5
Taste	1,000	1
Smell	100,000	1

[5] © 1989 Springer-Verlag. With thanks to Professor Zimmermann.

It is worth noting that these figures are additive. This means that the brain receives over 11 million bits per second from our sensory mechanisms. On average, subject to age, human bandwidth is approximately 16 bits per second. Bear in mind the sequence that is occurring in the human brain:

Impression → Consciousness → Expression

Consciousness consists largely of *discarded* information. This seems to be an evolutionary issue in that the brain (i.e., ourselves) would become totally overloaded, and eventually crazy, if it were fully conscious of all the information we are exposed to. Interestingly enough, it is this reduction filter in the central nervous system which is broadened by certain hallucinogenic drugs, e.g., alcohol, mescalin, LSD etc. Let me be provocative enough to state that this broadening is precisely what renders us creative. Needless to say, this is not an invitation to consume drugs. Rather it is the individual peculiarity of the filter's density which might determine a person's more creative or analytical capacities, aside from the intake of drugs. By this, I mean that consciousness is mostly about weeding out noise to create meaningful information. After all, who wouldn't prefer a carefully crafted one-sheet summary report to a thick computer printout? In this respect, despite consciousness's unmatched flexibility, at any given moment one is not conscious of much at all. Awareness of an experience implies that it has passed. An important case about advertisements in New Orleans in 1957 brought to centre stage the importance of subliminal messages and pre-conscious stimuli processes. 'Precon' was indeed the label chosen for the process, after the *preconscious* stimuli that it relied on. These were placed in advertising messages and movies. Despite the lack of conscious registration, the 'precon' messages carried sufficiently powerful influence to obtain the desired result.

Here are some other relevant examples adapted from Nørretranders (1998):

TABLE 2.2 ■ Media bandwidth

	Bandwidth
Television	>1,000,000 bps
Radio	>10,000 bps
Text read aloud	25 bps

Reproduced by permission of Penguin Books Ltd.

In an early study by Külpe (1904), it was shown that observers report more accurately on an attribute to which they are predisposed than on attributes to which they are not. By implication, this means that people who are better disposed towards incorporating information with their auditory system will struggle when information is presented to them in a different format, for instance graphs or videos. A brief note on the systems that people use to process information follows in the next section.

Let me provide another example of clustering. Please compare the following two spreadsheet cells:

1000000000000	1,000,000,000,000

The number on the right is formatted with commas separating the zeroes into groups of three. Most likely, you will find it more legible. This is because your brain has an easier time with the number divided into bits of three figures than in absorbing a 10-digit figure in one go. That is why, when presented with the number on the left, many will have to look at it more than once and count the zeroes. Simply put, their brain cannot categorize and is quickly overloaded. The same happens when you try to memorize a phone number. Without specific training, you will start falling behind after five or six figures because your brain cannot keep up.

Another case in point comes from the way in which the human mind processes images. If you have a reasonable understanding of DV video, you will know that DV movies consist of a series of images, called frames. There are normally between 9 and 25 frames per second in a DV movie. The movement that the mind perceives is an illusion, since each frame is indeed a still image. Also, it is not necessary for each frame to offer a superb image resolution, since the brain would not have time to capture it anyway. When you put the subject in front of an enlarged still picture, however, the brain has enough time to focus on its details and understand the differences in image quality, typically its resolution.

In short, the issues above imply that, no matter how sophisticated one's information system, there is an absolute constraint on how many items the brain can process at any one time. This may explain why senior decision-makers often outsource the management of more detailed information to junior colleagues and assistants. Aside from the increased staff costs, this alternative carries a subtle price, as the introduction of a process that depends on subordinates involves operational risk. It also relies to a critical extent on the commonality of communication styles across different levels of the organization.

There is a dilemma and apparent contradiction at play here. On the one hand, a manager should have colleagues and subordinates who communicate in the same style that he uses. On the other hand, he should encourage diversity of style amongst them to reduce potential herding behaviour and to curb his own aversion to cognitive dissonance, two biases that will be shown in Chapters 5 and 6 respectively. It does not take a genius to discover the order of priority that managers place on these two competing interests.

2.5 Your decision-making styles and motivations

Emphasis on a particular sense in capturing and framing information is not the only result of years of conditioning, successes and failures. Another, very important consequence is the development of a style and set of motivations to process and drive their decisions.

Let's suppose, for instance, that you have read in a newspaper or heard on the radio that the price of gold is increasing. You are wondering whether or not you should buy into the rally or sit it out until the next price dip. How do you decide what to do? And, even more important, why do you decide one way or another?

The latter question introduces the importance of motivations behind the decision. Which of the two basic instincts do you heed, greed or fear? A fear-driven investor may say: 'I have three kids to send to college and am a conservative investor in bonds. The prospect of soaring inflation scares me to death. Gold would act as a hedge against that risk'[6] Or: 'I am short gold, I'd better cover myself quickly.' Conversely, an investor motivated by greed, or its close relative, *hope*, may decide: 'I want to make a million dollars to buy myself a bigger house and a more powerful car', or: 'My gold position is still underwater relative to my original cost and this increase has cut my losses. Let's wait another little bit to sell to see if this increase brings me back to profit.'

Major differences also exist in the information set that is used to make a decision. This book argues that everybody, more or less, has a reference frame – a frame of risk – for their decisions. This manifests itself in two respects:

- *Internal versus external reference frame*. Some people are more prone to introspection and will seek answers in their own hearts, whereas others will mostly look around themselves.

- *Top down versus bottom up*. Professional investors who engage in asset allocation will be familiar with this distinction. In the context of one's personality, the former approach starts from a big picture of reality and then collects detailed information to fill the frame. The latter approach looks for details first and assembles the overall picture later.

This means that, if you are working with a 'big picture' type you'd better keep details to a bare minimum. His opinion is that detailed material is for lowly analysts anyway. However, a detail-orientated type will probably dismiss any discussion that starts from a big-picture angle as superficial rubbish with no real substance. The *order* in which information is presented is as important as the information itself. In our example, the order in which one may insert the details or the macro picture into the main body of the message or into an appendix depends on the counterpart that one faces.

Last, but not least, given the same picture, different pieces of information are salient, or relevant to people. Some may decide based on the elements that are consistent with the broad picture. We refer to them as *matchers*. Others, who can be labelled as *mis-matchers*, may go after bits of information that provide disconfirming evidence.

Matchers will tend to follow trends and stay with the general consensus. Mis-matchers will have a contrarian bias. It is easy to see how groupthink and peer pressure will tend to isolate mis-matchers in the context of group decisions or committees. In these settings, there is far more interest in getting decisions done no matter what than in listening to the mis-matchers' voice of caution. Yet, these are exactly the situations in which it is most important to listen to their concerns and observations on weaknesses in the general consensus view. Different issues arise from these two characters' trading styles:

---

[6] As bonds are made of a set of cashflows that are generally fixed, higher inflation in the future makes future cashflows less valuable, thereby hurting the bond's price. Floating-rate bonds were devised to offset this problem in a period of rising interest rates.

- *Matchers* are more versed in trend-following trades but will tend to overstay their trends and get complacent about their continuation. Their limits will have to be smaller than for a short-term momentum trader because they will be exposed to short-term volatility for longer periods of time. They are best managed with time-stops, where they are forced to reduce the position after a certain time period has elapsed.

- *Mis-matchers* excel at picking market turning points but will risk bleeding their capital away too quickly waiting for the day of reckoning when the market does finally change direction. Their limits should be small but flexible, so that they can progressively increase winning positions as the market moves in their favour.

2.6 Reality or frames? How do you interpret what you see?

The concluding section in this chapter offers you some examples on a variety of reference points and ways to look at information. At the same time, this should provide you with some fun.

You probably deem yourself to be fairly objective in analysing reality. But what do you really see? The examples in this section show how easy it is for you to automatically construct images. The answers are given in the footnotes to this chapter. As a demonstration of some widespread human tendencies, it is the ideal bridge between the individual frames discussed above and the next chapter's general framework on how risks are framed.

Look at the following figures. What do they show?[7]

FIGURE 2.1: Geometrical figures

---

[7] It is the word LIFT. Some readers may not have understood it due to some parts of the letters becoming confused with the white background.

Please count the number of black dots in this image.[8]

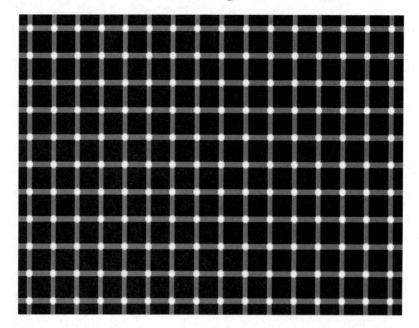

FIGURE 2.2 ■ Lines and dots

Look at the following picture. Is the dark grey dot inside the cube or outside?[9]

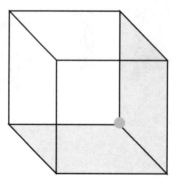

FIGURE 2.3 ■ The cube

---

[8] There are no black dots. This is called the *Hermann Illusion* and is due to the field covered by one's retina.
[9] The dot could be either inside or outside. The shading of two sides of the cube creates an illusion of perspective. This is called *Necker's Cube*, after the Swiss crystallographer Louis Albert Necker, who devised this illusion in 1832.

What does the following portrait show?[10]

FIGURE 2.4 ■ Female figure

What can you say about the following spiral?[11] Put your finger on the dark dot and try to follow the path to see where it leads you.

FIGURE 2.5 ■ Spiral

---

[10] It shows, at the same time, an old and a young woman.

[11] Despite the deceptive look, it is a set of circles, rather than a spiral. It is called *Fraser's Spiral*, after the author of this illusion.

What do you think the next figure portrays?[12]

FIGURE 2.6 ■ Geometric shapes

Are these lines straight or parallel?[13]

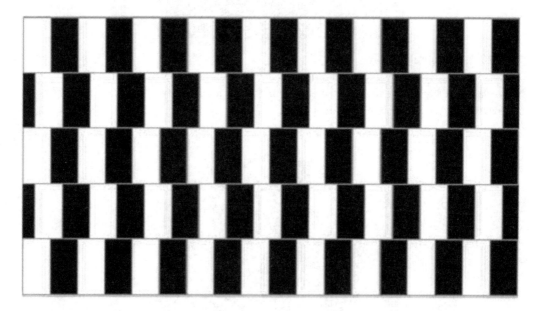

FIGURE 2.7 ■ Bristol café wall

[12] If you answered a triangle with the tips on top of three circles, you are in the majority. As a matter of fact, the triangle in this figure exists in your brain only! Your mind creates the imaginary lines connecting the tips and forming the triangle. This shows beyond doubt the brain's tendency to see patterns where there are none. This is called *Kanisza's Illusion* after its author.

[13] The lines are indeed parallel but the patterns deceive one into believing otherwise. This was spotted by Professor Richard Gregory and members of his lab whilst walking past a café in Bristol, United Kingdom.

What do you see? Is it a big monster chasing a little monster?[14]

FIGURE 2.8 ■ Monsters

What can you say about the slant in the two vertical lines?[15]

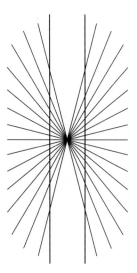

FIGURE 2.9 ■ Lines

---

[14] Take a closer look. The monsters are identical in size but the perspective of the corridor makes the more distant monster look larger.

[15] There is no slant; the two lines are perfectly parallel. This is called the *Hering Illusion*.

What does the following portray?[16]

FIGURE 2.10 ■ Vase

What can you say about the two circles surrounded by other circles in the following image?[17]

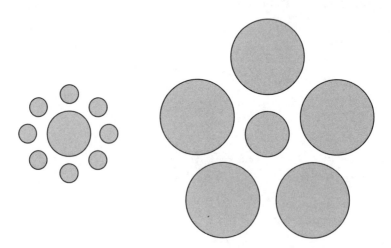

FIGURE 2.11 ■ Circles

---

[16] It shows simultaneously one vase and two female faces. This is called *Rubin's Vase*.
[17] Both circles are the same size. It is the surrounding circles that make the left circle appear larger than the right one. This is called the *Ebbinghaus Effect* or *Titchener-Ebbinghaus Illusion*. It offers a second-to-none example of context dependence.

What can you say about the horizontal lines in this picture?[18]

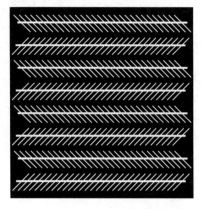

FIGURE 2.12 ■ Lines

Here comes another one. What can you say about the following three-pronged item?[19]

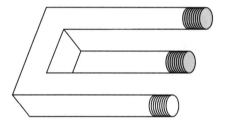

FIGURE 2.13 ■ Tool

In the visual domain, we are extremely sensitive to framing. Artists understand how to use the frame to find the contour line which has no name, and which the accurately represents the image they wish you to see. For our purposes, all the images you have just examined exhibit context dependence. They should make you think about how developed are your abilities to see, hear and feel more than one view, sound or feeling at a given point in time. The hard reality is that the brain is programmed to be in one state and one only at any given point in time.

---

[18] Another good example of how patterns create context dependence. The lines are perfectly parallel but the patterns that cross them lead you to believe otherwise. This is called *Zollner's Illusion*.
[19] The third prong, the one in the middle, does not exist.

Now suppose you saw only one meaningful picture in the figures above. Given your current abilities for discrimination, how might you be affected when viewing financial information? Are you really so sure the conclusions you draw are eminently straightforward?

The fact is that you have certain cognitive preferences that directly affect the way you interpret and transfer environmental noise into useful information about the world. You will see this point expanded in the account of individual biases in Chapter 5. The continuous bombardment of information conditions your expectations of events. Later on, in Chapter 7, frames will be expanded to introduce other types of information processing problems and practical examples from the trading industry will be provided.

Frames of risk: the concept

Everything you can imagine is real.

(Pablo Picasso)

7±2:

- The frame of risk broad concept
- The systemic frame of risk
- The organizational frame of risk
- The individual frame of risk

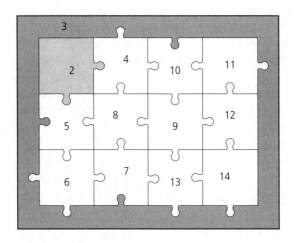

Abstract

Very few decisions, if any, are not context-dependent. This pervasive frame that surrounds decisions, of which people are often unaware, is at the heart of the endless series of mental shortcuts and assumptions that people normally use in their everyday life. This chapter is about the three major sets of frames of risk that are employed by individuals, their organizations and the systems of which they are members.

Implications: As every risk and problem can eventually be traced back to some human decision or assumption, frames of risk and biases are at the heart of every risk. That's why they have such a central position in this book.

3.1 Frames of risk[20] in decisions: one concept, multiple applications

In light of the strong emphasis that this book put on the individual in the previous chapter, you may be led to believe that this book is mostly about individual psychology. It is true that this text encourages you to explore the inner core of your personality, particularly, those aspects that have a direct bearing on your decision-making. That, however, is not the gist of the book. Far more interesting are the applications of people's decisions in a variety of settings.

The frame of risk theory deems bias to be the key element to explain people's behaviour. These tendencies are by no means confined to individual behaviour. Every entity, constituency, regulatory or political body that surrounds an individual and his organization is made up of people who, in turn, have their fair share of biases.

Throughout the book, individual bias will receive the lion's share of the attention. For all the politically correct talk of group and team decision-making, pulling the trigger is an individual pursuit. This is a corollary of the basic risk management principle of attributing each risk to a clearly identified owner who is responsible for it. Otherwise, the odds are good that this risk will result in some trouble at some point in time in the future.

This chapter explores the interaction between the individual and the other constituencies around him, which should help the reader to understand the next few chapters on frames of risk in theory and practice. Chapter 1 stated that our journey would always put the individual and his biases centre stage. This chapter shows how individual biases manifest themselves in groups, in the professional activities of the trader and the risk manager and in the behaviour of other actors in the trading drama. The closing chapters of the practice part of this book will then demonstrate some of the high-profile horror stories that flawed human decisions created.

---

[20] A considerable body of literature exists on cognitive frames in business and life. In their comprehensive *The Art of High-Stakes Decision-Making*, for instance, J. Keith Murnighan and John C. Mowen show as many as eight frames (engineering/technology, sales/marketing, production, political, legal, accounting, competitive, ethical) that managers can adopt in their decisions. Thus, 'risk frames' would be equally legitimate in the context of this book. The author has chosen the equivalent 'frame of risk' in order to avoid any confusion with the completely different meaning and context associated with the word 'frame' in risk management software. The term 'frame' in this book refers exclusively to the widely accepted definition of this term in cognitive psychology and decision-making with risk and uncertainty. No implicit or explicit reference is made to any other meaning that others may associate to this term.

3.2 Frames of risk definition

Finding a concept that would summarize the pervasiveness of psychological issues and show how these affect risk decisions was one of the major challenges during the preparation of this book. The issue is compounded by the very different approaches with which authors prepare books on risk issues on one side and psychological-behavioural topics on the other. Simply put, there was not much professional risk literature to use as a reference.

Cognitive psychologists are well accustomed with the 'frames' term, which emphasizes the context dependence that manifests itself so often in people's decisions. You have already encountered context dependence in the visual sphere when you were asked to comment on the figures in the last chapter.

'Risk' is also a well-known term that is associated with uncertainty. While most, especially outside the finance profession, will relate risk to 'loss', I would like to remain neutral and treat risk as exposure to *both* the upside and the downside. This is closer to the statistical definition of risk by quantitative practitioners, best embodied in the standard deviation of returns over a pre-set time horizon.

This is an important principle, since most people confuse *loss aversion* with *risk aversion*. If the latter applied, one would expect a consistent risk profile irrespective of one's expectations on future profits or losses. Conversely, as we shall see in the next chapter, a robust body of empirical evidence shows that people's risk preferences are far from consistent. Many investors, even those armed with years of professional experience, will call themselves risk averse when they are really averse only to losses. The very same professionals will then behave differently when there are some profits to lock in.

In short, the recurrent term 'frames of risk' used in this book means risk communication or decision that relies on context-dependent information. Throughout this book, you will see three general sets of frames of risk, referring to: the individual, his organization and the system to which he belongs.

Whenever someone faces uncertainty, frames of risk manifest themselves in five equally important aspects:

■ *Data gathering* This refers to the processes that collect raw data to be analysed in the decision. Which data will be collected is very much a function of what the decision-maker feels is important. For instance, a credit officer will look for a company's recent financial statements far more eagerly than for charts plotting the recent progress of the stock price. Conversely, a trader will be keener on the latter piece of information. In short, every decision-maker will have his own set of mental filters – his frames of risk – to weed out unimportant information.

■ *Information processing* Once the data is in, how is it processed? Again, this depends on the end-users' wishes. A credit office will probably look for a set of accounting ratios, whereas a trader will hunt for statistics.

■ *Process assumptions* This has to do with beliefs on how the problem/project at hand will behave in the future. Here, depending on the decision-maker's background, different aspects will become relevant. In the case of a bank owning a position in the corporate bond issued by a certain company, a trader will worry mostly about the price action in the next few days or weeks. A credit officer may – just as rationally – disregard a major drop in the value of that company's bonds and continue supporting the company if he expects it to remain financially viable.

■ *Decision-making style* As was seen in Chapter 2, people have different personalities and motivations. Inevitably, these affect the way in which they will approach issues, whether because they are motivated by fear instead of greed or because they tend to think in bottom-up rather than in top-down terms.

■ *Post-decision monitoring* The decision-maker's frame of risk on what is relevant will also influence his approach in tracking the progress of the decision's outcome. This may be one of the possible explanations of the problems and losses incurred by some major organizations (as will be shown in Chapter 10). Some of their relevant decision-makers did not see the risk as a large enough problem to track it with data and the best staff. When the problem finally erupted, decision-makers were often taken completely by surprise and simply did not know what to do.

3.3 At a glance

At the risk of oversimplifying reality, the following paragraphs provide a brief overview of the various levels at which frames of risk operate.

The individual is the oft-underestimated source of decisions and the ultimate source of risk. Several labels exist to categorize the various consequences of people's decisions, such as market risk, credit risk, legal risk and operational risk to name but a few. They all have one source: the human element. The following scheme has individual frames of risk and biases tower above the systemic and organizational spheres that are more often pursued in the discussion of risk management issues.

The intersection between the three areas, which is marked with an 'X' in Figure 3.1, shows the terrain in which an organization interacts with outside constituencies. All these are composed of individuals with their own frames of risk and those of the organizations or groups of which they are part. It will be extremely difficult – if not altogether impossible – to quantify or measure this complex interplay of biases in this region. Figure 3.1 shows three sets of actors in different positions:

■ *The outsiders* These are individuals, organizations and regulatory bodies that live on the fringes of the organization. They attempt to harmonize the organization's frames of risk with their own individual frames of risk and with those of the organizations to which they belong. An auditor, for instance, will make sure that the organization complies with accounting standards. A regulator will check that the organization complies with regulatory requirements. A stock market analyst will insist on disclosure to ensure comparability between the firm and others that he follows.

■ *The senior insiders* Typically an organization's Board of Directors and top management, those who are most exposed to contact with the outsiders and who bear the greatest responsibility for the frames of risk that the organization adopts *vis-à-vis* the outside environment.

■ *The other insiders* Typically individuals and groups who perform mostly internal functions and who are not among the organization's risk decision-makers.

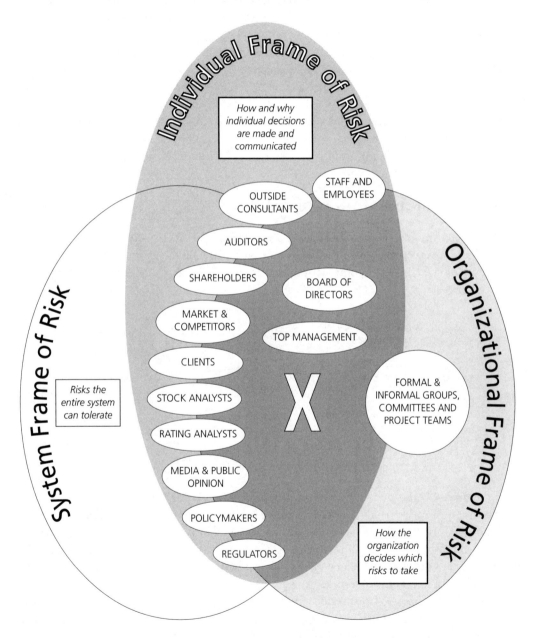

FIGURE 3.1 ■ Frames of risk applications at various levels

There is no dismissal of the importance of organizational or systemic risks. The smooth functioning of organized markets and the liquidity that they provide would be impossible to achieve without them. The issue is that organizations, political and regulatory bodies are ultimately the showpiece of the personality of those who manage them. Ignoring this basic principle, the financial services industry has nevertheless borrowed the top-down model of organization from the military sector and from the first organizational models of the industrial revolution. Constructing an organization around people – rather than forcing it upon them – is an exercise with few, if any, of the short-term payoffs that managers and shareholders crave.

Nevertheless, as basic textbook finance states, there is no such thing as a free lunch. Organizations do not escape this principle, as they involve a price of increasing complexity and, potentially, making markets' basic risk transfer mechanisms less transparent. All the three frames of risk outlined so far are closely related to the decreasing transparency of risk transfers. Complexity, one of the topics addressed in Chapter 7, is an issue that will surface most dramatically in the high-profile risk disasters of Chapters 10 and 11.

3.4 The systemic frame of risk

Depending on the biases of individuals and their groups, the environment that surrounds the firm and its incentives is fairly straightforward. With the increased scale of the stakes, macroeconomic stability becomes of paramount importance in the eyes of policymakers and opinion leaders.

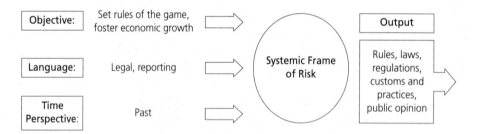

FIGURE 3.2 ■ The systemic frame of risk

Accordingly, risk language is nowhere on the map. After all, the job of policymakers is to set the boundaries, rather than to manage risk. The time perspective of constituencies surrounding the organization is towards the past. How could it be otherwise? Organizations provide only historical data – mostly financial statements. Only the past is the source for past abuses and problems which can then be dealt with by laws, rules and guidelines. These are the behaviours that the system intends to deter.

This has the unwelcome side effect of forcing what is essentially a legal and reporting/accounting language on organizations and the risks that they manage, which makes the process of risk communication (discussed in Chapter 6) crucial.

3.5 The organizational frame of risk

The balancing act between internal and external objectives and the garnering of resources to achieve them is what any organization is about. While complying with external rules of the game dictated by the system that surrounds it, the organization sets rules and standards for its staff. The more an organization's standards and principles are attuned to those of the individuals who work for it, the better the alignment and the greater the potential for staff growth, employee satisfaction and better performance.

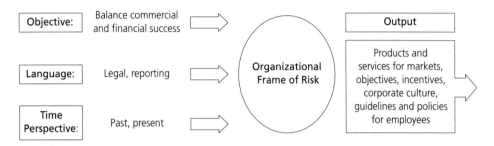

FIGURE 3.3 ■ The organizational frame of risk

In practice, such a perfect alignment seldom exists. There will always be a minority of people whose values and beliefs conflict with the views that prevail in the organization. Investment banks have been accustomed for years to intense turf wars between bankers and traders. While both categories may talk about risk and claim that benefiting the shareholder is their sole concern, the way they would like to steer the organization presents massive differences:

■ Bankers may see the firm's future in forging better customer relationships and committing more of the firm's capital to loans and granting credit. They hope to build goodwill to stand a better chance of winning business at some point in the future. They will view their trading colleagues as socially unsophisticated and as the source of volatility in revenues, hardly what stock market analysts want to see.

■ Traders, on the other hand, will ask for a larger slice of the risk capital pie for risk-taking activities based on market views. They will argue that the liquidity and mobility of their risk capital is unmatched and the immediate return generally above their banking colleagues. They will watch with suspicion any build-up in the organization's loan portfolios, a source of large losses when the economy suffers. In addition, they will often resent the different performance evaluation standards that are used for them and their banking colleagues. In the case of the latter, the organization will tend to be more patient in waiting for the return on capital to materialize.

Other categories of actors cut across product lines such as the above and play a relevant role in the organizational frame of risk. These are the teams or task forces mandated to perform significant projects for one or more areas inside the organization. These groups of individuals engage in an endless process of negotiation between their frames of risk, those of their fellow group co-workers and the rest of the organization.

In the same fashion as their systemic counterparts, organizations also tend to rely on past information to a considerable extent. Their clients and external constituencies only care about past performance information, and the organization does not want its competitors to get their hands on what the organization is doing now or in the future. Being live entities made up of individuals who take risks now and live and think in the present, organizations also have to remain attuned to their perspective.

3.6 The individual frame of risk

At the heart of the whole system, the individual and his decision-making are the ultimate source of risk and how it is managed in the organization.

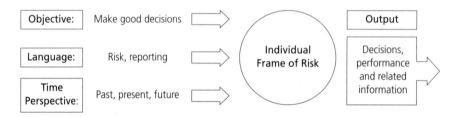

FIGURE 3.4 ■ The individual frame of risk

Another aspect worth examining is the striking difference in language and time perspective between the individual on the one side and the organization and system that surround him on the other. This has a major bearing on individual decisions and is in itself a significant source of issues for them.

As performance evaluation – for both an organization and its external constituencies – tends to look back, rather than forward, information flowing from individuals to their organizations and to outside constituencies complies. Risk language is one of the casualties of this process. The reality is that very little risk disclosure is required in today's financial statements. What is published for financial reporting or regulatory capital purposes, such as Value-at-Risk (VaR) figures during or at the end of a given period, also refers to the past, rather than to the future. That is *risk reporting*, rather than *risk management*. To talk about the latter, there must be a forward-looking orientation and an element of uncertainty.

Submerged between countless pieces of accounting language, real risk information has little way to be heard atop the organization, let alone outside it. By the time a regulator receives the information on the level of risk that an organization has incurred, say, one or two months ago, both the forward orientation of information and the element of uncertainty have disappeared. One is pretending to make *risk management* decisions with information *about past activity*. The longer the lag, the more meaningless the risk management label becomes! How is that for an understanding of the information that one uses? Do you really believe that using end-of-day VaR information that is, say, one week old can seriously qualify as risk management? At best, one may be able to guess that the present resembles the past and that current risk levels are close to those incurred in the past – assuming that the word 'management' has any meaning under such an assumption!

This is the paradox which individuals face when making decisions and taking risks. While the input has to be as up-to-date as possible, the output is always subject to the straitjackets of accounting and financial reporting. It is as if your day-to-day activity was conducted in Portuguese but your company, boss, regulator, analyst and so on could read and understand only Japanese. Then, as soon as you have carried out an activity, your next challenge becomes how to translate it and explain it in Japanese.

This difference in language and time orientation has profound consequences, as it does not always create the appropriate incentives. Decisions which may look uneconomical from a shareholder's value perspective and risk management perspective can indeed become perfectly justifiable when evaluated from an accounting viewpoint. For instance, reducing risk inventories just before reporting time makes perfect sense to beat the regulator but has no place in any EMH, theoretical finance or trading textbook. The incentives of window-dressing and dilution of market-to-market losses through some long-dated complicated transactions are questionable from an economic value point of view but incomprehensible in the context of the wrinkles of financial reporting.

This reporting-versus-economic frame of risk conflict creates a first important context for people's decisions. This theme will underpin several major biases for both individuals and groups. As such, it is the ideal bridge between the general application of frames of risk and individual biases.

That's the key topic of the next chapter.

CHAPTER 4

Behavioural finance and basic biases

Where is the wisdom that we have lost in knowledge?/ Where is the knowledge that we have lost in information?

(*T.S. Eliot*: Choruses from 'The Rock')

7±2:

- Modern finance relies on rationality assumptions from basic economics
- Heavy empirical evidence contrasts this proposition
- Human biases and frames heavily interfere in their decision-making
- Little attention has been paid to how emotions affect risk decisions
- The efficient market hypothesis and the behavioural finance challenge
- The basic individual biases
- After reading this book, the human side should become the *key risk* to watch, rather than just a peripheral aspect

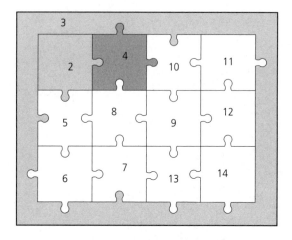

Abstract

Modern finance theory, which has laid the foundations for today's risk processes and quantitative models, implicitly assumes that people act rationally. Simply put, rational decision-making is at the heart of the EMH. Empirical evidence, however, devastates this proposition. While human biases precede and interfere with judgment, little attention has been given to how decision-makers use information from their risk processes and how much the framing of such information affects their decisions. This chapter provides an overview of the main issues affecting individual decisions and their risk consequences. After you finish this book, your risk awareness should benefit from treating the human and psychological side as *the* key risk issue, rather than just as a peripheral aspect.

The opening section of the chapter summarizes some of the arguments in modern finance between the EMH camp and the behavioural finance supporters. Rather than rehash the skirmishes, the focus is on an area of primary practical importance which is the *inappropriate use* of standard finance tools due to distorted human thought processes. The practitioner should be concerned with bringing under control those unconscious aspects of behaviour that underpin risk decisions. The following two sections analyse individual human biases and risk consequences in greater detail. Later, Chapters 10 and 11 show their effects in practice with a *hit parade* of market crashes and risk management disasters. One factor common to these disasters is unconscious human errors.

Implications: Regardless of how much you believe in fancy quantitative models and high-performance computers and people to run them, never underestimate the human weaknesses underlying them. Run periodic fire drills to push people outside of their comfort zone and vaccinate them with some stress before they experience it in the next crisis.

4.1 Academic anathemas

Much of the conceptual framework underpinning the models and assumptions of modern risk operations relies on fundamental principles of Modern Finance Theory ('MFT'). As risk-return optimization was the innovation that marked the birth of modern finance and revolutionized the entire trading industry, it is important to understand its assumptions. Many of these were retained when the pioneers started setting up modern risk management systems in the late 1980s. As time progressed, however, these assumptions became buried under the increasing complexity of the giant trading machines into which many entrepreneurial desks had evolved. Developments in behavioural studies and cognitive psychology brought fresh challenges to market efficiency principles. These developments outside the mainstream MFT blossomed into a new set of interdisciplinary studies that spanned economics, finance, behavioural sciences and psychology. Behavioural finance was born. The next two sub-sections provide a glimpse of these two schools of thought and some of their highlights.

There is little to be gained from rehashing the long-standing theoretical arguments of many excellent studies. The application, rather than the theory debates, is what this book is about. Excellent books and references are provided for those readers who wish to delve deeper in modern finance and behavioural theory.

4.2 The efficient market hypothesis (EMH)

Although modelling the financial markets remains one of the most challenging problems, significant progress in our understanding of how the markets work has come from a large and diverse body of research relying on a few premises of human rationality. The main body of conventional financial-economic theory goes under the name of Modern Finance Theory ('MFT'). This comes from a line of papers which generally make the same presumptions of human behaviour in rational decision-making. This includes such luminaries as Markowitz (1952, 1959) with mean-variance portfolio theory, Sharpe's (1964) asset pricing model with Lintner's (1965) and Merton's (1973) further elaborations, Black & Scholes's (1973) option pricing and hedging models, Ross's (1976) arbitrage pricing theory and Cox, Ingersoll & Ross's (1985) ideas on interest rates, to name but a few. MFT is a school of thought and the conceptual architecture of modern finance remains attractive as a model because of its simplicity of assumptions about human nature. The key assumptions of modern finance are:

■ *Risk and return symmetry* Investors would be willing to assume more risk only if compensated with additional expected return.

■ *Law of one price or 'No arbitrage condition'* The continuous activity of arbitrageurs would keep risk and expected return in line with each other. Arbitrages, when they occur, last only for a very brief period of time. Selling pressure would lower the price of those securities that are overpriced relative to their level of risk. Conversely, arbitrageurs would bid up the price of undervalued securities – also relative to their risk – until the price is fair. Based on their level of risk, some securities have prices that are not perfectly aligned with the fair price. The effect of these 'anomalies', however, is small.

■ *Investors are risk averse* All investors are – on balance – rational. Irrational investors exert a negligible effect on the market as a whole. If that effect has any significance, it cancels out the effect of other irrational investors.

■ *Complete markets* The arbitrage activity in the second bullet point above is assumed to face no limits in terms of risk capital available or institutional constraints of the market.

This symmetry between risk and return is the main principle of MFT and of market efficiency in general. The related popular expression 'there is no such thing as a free lunch' summarizes the ideal self-consistent dynamical state of a market resulting from continuous actions of traders (arbitrageurs) trying to outsmart each other to achieve a better risk-adjusted performance. In more elegant terms, this principle drives the so-called Efficient Market Hypothesis ('EMH').

One of the key aspects of Markowitz's models is that an investor could also optimize the risk-adjusted performance of his portfolio by choosing a blend of securities whose returns were only partially – or even negatively – correlated. Given a target return, he would choose the mix that would minimize the risk of his portfolio or, technically speaking, the mean variance of returns. This process is commonly referred to as 'mean-variance optimization' ('MVO').

4.3 The behavioural finance challenge

Behavioural sciences have long challenged the economic assumption of human rationality that is central to classic financial theory. Among these studies, Kahneman and Tversky in the 1970s and 1980s struck at the heart of conventional utility theory which underpins both economics and modern finance. Eventually, these insights were recognized with the 2002 Nobel Prize in Economics for Daniel Kahneman. In short, major biases were found to be both widespread and consistent. Individuals were by no means as rational and objective as standard economics and modern finance had assumed them to be. The next two sections analyse these individual biases and their consequences in some detail.

For now, these findings had the immediate effect of challenging key principles of MFT and would give birth to the new interdisciplinary field of behavioural finance. This new discipline would articulate the attack in several detailed studies on the effect of human biases in financial decisions. Key findings include:

- *Reference points* Individual decisions hinge to a considerable extent on mental reference points. For instance, someone who bought a stock at $10 and saw it rise to $100 and then drop to $50 would probably feel better than someone who bought the same stock at $75 before the rise and the successive fall in prices.

- *S-shaped utility curve* As a corollary to the previous point, one's utility functions are by no means as linear as conventional theory assumes. They adopt an S-shaped profile depending on an individual's reference point. That is the essence of prospect theory. Below the reference point, where the individual finds himself in a losing situation, the utility function takes a convex shape, encouraging a risk-seeking behaviour. In a favourable situation, the utility function becomes concave and increasingly risk-averse.

- *Mental accounting and anchoring* Mental accounting and substantial anchoring to past reference points affects buying and selling decisions, making them in no way as rational as modern finance would assume. Under- and overreaction to events and announcements follows.

- *No probability competence* Probability assessments by individuals are also plagued by substantial biases, due to a variety of factors. These include framing, mental shortcuts, neglect of conditional probabilities according to Bayesian theory, different assessment of events depending on whether they are viewed as a combination or not and the incorrect assessment of low-probability events.

- *Sub-optimal portfolios* Consistent with their above-mentioned mental accounting behaviour, investors seldom consider their portfolio as a whole but tend to break it down into a 'safe' and an 'aggressive' account. Contrary to MVO assumptions, this means that the correlations between these two layers are largely neglected. As a result, conventional modern finance would consider the resulting portfolio sub-optimal.

These major empirical findings have sparked ferocious debates in academia and beyond for over 15 years. The conventional modern finance camp has often disregarded these issues as aberrations. Their behavioural finance challengers have been amassing a growing body of empirical evidence from several markets. Neither school can be dismissed lightly. It is true, as EMH supporters argue, that surefire, risk-free arbitrages from behavioural finance have yet to be found.

The ebbs and flows of markets over the last 20 years – and particularly phenomena such as the 22 per cent one-day stock market crash of 1987 and the internet stock market bubble in the late 1990s – would hardly strike one as examples of rational decision-making. Indeed, behavioural finance theorists would argue that bubble phenomena can only be explained if one takes behavioural finance seriously. One could interpret instances such as the debacle of hedge fund long-term capital management from both points of view. The EMH camp may argue that even if behavioural issues existed, it is by no means risk-free to position against them. Their behavioural finance opponents could equally use these persistent biases and arbitrageurs' inability to correct them as the very demonstration of weakness in conventional finance theory.

The stakes in this debate are sky high, as the dramatic innovation in trading and investment management that has occurred over the last 20 years has relied heavily on the conceptual tools and theoretical framework developed by EMH. Enormous amounts of funds are managed and measured according to these metrics and criteria and changing them is neither easy nor painless. A change in investment management approach – for instance, by shifting funds under management from a manager who believes in EMH to one who subscribes to the behavioural finance camp – means significant flows of business and fees defecting from one approach to another. It is understandable, then, that many EMH-believing practitioners who have drafted the models and skills of MFT have powerful vested interests in clinging to their beliefs and dismiss the behavioural finance findings.

The major market crashes and risk management disasters that have occurred since the late 1980s are not, however, debatable. Their interpretation as a correction of inefficiencies (as the EMH camp may claim) or as the very demonstration of inefficient decision-making (as some behavioural finance supporters argue) is beside the point. This book offers a framework for the practitioner that goes beyond the mere listing of events and helps understand the *underlying behaviours* of the people involved, the ultimate causes of these misfortunes. Chapters 10 and 11 show the application of this framework in the analysis of a series of disasters in finance and beyond. To create a behavioural risk management framework, one has to understand the key behavioural biases first. The fundamental tendencies of people have deep ramifications into a large set of individual biases, which are explored in greater detail in Chapter 5.

4.4 Biases basics

Conversely, an impressive body of empirical evidence over the last 30 years from cognitive psychology and the behavioural sciences shows that humans are hardly the rational information device that MFT would have us believe. This is a far cry from a comprehensive list but it drives the point home. As many as 88 individual biases have been identified by some authors (Barach, 1996) and readers are welcome to consult the bibliography for a more in-depth analysis. Other important psychological issues relating to group behaviour should not be underestimated and are analysed in Chapter 6.

4.4.1 Overconfidence

This over-arching theme neither enjoys the same recognition in cognitive psychology nor deserves a technical term as the other biases that will be explained in the next sections. It is, however, the most remarkably consistent of all, particularly so amongst the bloated egos that populate the glamorous world of finance. As the common denominator of all human decision-making issues, this is where the discussion starts.

One clarification with respect to the overconfidence label is of paramount importance. Overconfidence does not mean making overly aggressive forecasts, as is routine practice in finance. This is a framing problem, since the word 'over' is commonly associated with 'too much' and may generate the false impression that this issue could be avoided just by making the next estimates more prudent or even *too* prudent. Rather, the term indicates humans' excessive faith in the information that they use in their decisions. In short, one simply overestimates the reliability of one's own knowledge and abilities.

As a practical demonstration, consider that a super-majority (usually over 75 per cent and up to 90 per cent) of drivers consider themselves to be above average. This is remarkably consistent in surveys across a wide spectrum of samples, structured according to education and geographical region (Näätänen and Summala, 1975; Svenson, 1981). Most feel they will live past 80 (Weinstein, 1980) and are less likely to be harmed by the products they use (Rethans, 1979).[21]

The following trivia quiz from Russo & Schoemaker (1989) (Table 4.1) will give you a chance to decide whether or not you are overconfident. For each of the following questions, write down a low and a high guess figure so that you have a 90 per cent confidence interval that the correct answer is located between the two. Attaining the 90 per cent mark means making exactly one mistake, no more, no less. Set the interval so that it is neither too narrow (overconfident estimate) nor too wide (underconfident guess).

TABLE 4.1 ■ Overconfidence

		90% confidence range	
		Low	*High*
1	Martin Luther King's age at death		
2	Length of the Nile River		
3	Number of countries that were members of OPEC		
4	Number of books in the Old Testament		
5	Diameter of the moon in miles		
6	Weight of an empty Boeing 747 in pounds		
7	Year in which Wolfgang Amadeus Mozart was born		
8	Gestation period (in days) of an Asian elephant		
9	Air distance from London to Tokyo		
10	Deepest (known) point in the oceans (in feet)		

From Decision Traps *by J. Edward Russo and Paul J.H. Schoemaker, copyright © 1989 by J. Edward Russo and Paul J.H. Schoemaker. Used by permission of Doubleday, a division of Random House, Inc.* [22]

[21] From Russo & Schoemaker (1989).

[22] Please also look for the related concept of Lake Wobegon syndrome in the Glossary.

The answers are given in the footnote below.[23] If, according to the test above, you are overconfident, relax. There is no need for justification or denial. After all, you are probably reading the book by yourself anyway and no one needs to know. You will likely find it some comfort to know that you have plenty of illustrious company. Despite the risk of being blamed for *hindsight bias*, which is discussed later on in the next chapter, a long list of examples from history this book includes in Appendix B. This should shed quite some light on how far off the mark even famous and educated people can be. By the way, if that list provides you with some comfort, that is yet another bias, called *herd behaviour* – but that is a story for group issues in Chapter 6.

4.4.2 Prospect theory

Among the various theories that have been proposed as an alternative to utility theory in conventional economics, prospect theory has had the deepest impact and most lasting effect. In developing its model of economic behaviour and decisions concerning risk and uncertainty, prospect theory borrows heavily from the behavioural sciences and cognitive psychology, thereby breaking down the silos of knowledge that separate these disciplines from economics.

The insensitivity to mental reference points was one of the key assumptions that MFT inherited from conventional utility theory. Consequently, a direct relationship should exist between risk and return. Indeed, even Markowitz (1952) had noticed the convex and concave sections of the curve. His, however, was an expectation model and could not realistically take that important intuition forward. Concave and convex utility functions would not see the light for the next quarter of a century. Later on, frame independence was going to become one of the key assumptions of the Modigliani–Miller approach to corporate finance.[24]

Pioneered by Daniel Kahneman and the late Amos Tversky (1979, 1992), prospect theory underscored the existence of an S-shaped curve in individual utility preferences. According to this curve, losses would encourage individuals to assume higher risks whereas gains would make them more risk-averse. Let's consider the following.

PROBLEM   1

Would you rather:
- take a bet that pays $4,000 80 per cent of the time and $0 (zero) 20 per cent of the time? or,
- take a bet that pays $3,000 all the time?

Studies show that 80 per cent of the subjects opt for the sure gain. Let's now flip the payoff.

---

[23] (1) 39 years; (2) 4,187 miles; (3) 13 countries; (4) 39 books; (5) 2,160 miles; (6) 390,000 pounds; (7) 1756; (8) 645 days; (9) 5,959 miles; (10) 36,198 feet.
[24] Merton Miller himself summarized this principle at a University of Chicago event in 1986: 'If you transfer a dollar from your right pocket to your left pocket, you are no wealthier. Franco (Modigliani) and I proved that rigorously.'

PROBLEM   2

Would you rather:

- take a bet in which you lose $4,000 80 per cent of the time and $0 (zero) 20 per cent of the time? or,
- take a bet in which you lose $3,000 all the time?

According to conventional utility theory, the answers to these two problems should be identical. After all, in the second problem, it would look rational to prefer a sure loss of $3,000 to an expected-value loss of $(0.8 \times \$4,000 + 0.2 \times 0 = \$3,200)$. Yet, only 8 per cent of the respondents accepted this alternative. The overwhelming majority, 92 per cent, opted to take the gamble.

Kahneman and Tversky offered their subjects another variation on this problem.

PROBLEM   3

Would you rather:

- take a bet that pays $3,000 90 per cent of the time and $0 (zero) 10 per cent of the time? or,
- take a bet that pays $6,000 45 per cent of the time and $0 (zero) in the remaining 55 per cent of the time?

Relative to Problem 1, the proportion of subjects who opted for the safer alternative (a) increased to 86 per cent. Let's look at the other side of the coin and ask the same questions about losses.

PROBLEM   4

Would you rather:

- take a bet in which you lose $3,000 90 per cent of the time and $0 (zero) 10 per cent of the time? or,
- take a bet in which you lose $6,000 45 per cent of the time and $0 (zero) in the remaining 55 per cent of the time?

Again, 92 per cent opted to take (b), the riskier alternative.

What is the lesson? When presented with a choice of gains, risk and uncertainty, subjects will prefer safer, smaller gains to larger but riskier gains – the more risk-averse behaviour. Conversely, choices involving losses will make subjects more risk-seeking and willing to prefer larger potential losses to a smaller, safer figure. This is the perfect opposite of the old trading and poker maxim of 'letting gains run and cutting losses quickly'. Risk aversion displayed in preferences increases further as the potential gains look more likely.

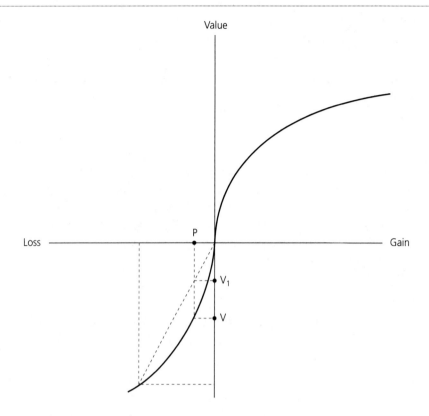

FIGURE 4.1 ▪ Utility chart according to prospect theory and conventional theory[25]

Figure 4.1 plots the S-shaped curve of prospect theory. The flex point coincides with the individual mental reference point.

The lower left quadrant in Figure 4.1 illustrates the different utility implications between conventional expected utility theory (plotted as a diagonal dashed line) and prospect theory (shown as a continuous curve). At any particular loss point P, the utility (V_1) on the vertical axis resulting from conventional theory is above the one (V) from prospect theory. In economics, this means that the cost incurred to achieve this latter utility V is higher. The equivalent in finance is a higher level of risk. The origin, where the two axes cross each other, is the subjects' reference point and the inflection point of the curve.

Yet more inconsistencies with conventional utility theory were found. In their landmark prospect theory article, Kahneman and Tversky also examined how shifts in probability – while keeping the payoff constant – would affect subjects' preferences. Recall from Problem 3 above that subjects were asked to choose between the two bets paying $3,000 or $6,000 respectively.

[25] Figure 4.1 from Tversky & Kahneman (1992), pp. 293–323.

PROBLEM   5

Would you rather:

- take a bet that pays $3,000 0.02 per cent of the time and $0 (zero) in the remaining time?, or
- take a bet that pays $6,000 0.01 per cent of the time and $0 (zero) in the remaining time?

Relative to Problem 3 above, subjects' preferences flipped, with 73 per cent opting for (b). The intuition is that whilst there is a possibility of winning, the probability is tiny. In these instances, most choose the larger potential gain. Notice that the ratio of probabilities between the alternatives (a) and (b) is the same for both problems: 2:1.

Interest in the problem of decisions under ignorance had existed long before Kahneman and Tversky's studies. Their conclusions on subjects' preferences were consistent with the *Ellsberg principle* that had been developed several years earlier, in 1961. The principle, which is named after its author, states that people prefer to bet on known rather than unknown probabilities. Here is his classic example.

Ellsberg's 'two-colour' problem

There are two urns, each containing red and black balls. Urn A contains an equal number of balls, 50, for each colour. Urn B contains 100 balls in an unknown proportion. Subjects can receive $100 or nothing depending on which ball is drawn. Which urn would you draw from?

What would you prefer? The answer is in the footnote below.[26]

Fox and Tversky (1991) investigated the pattern implied by the Ellsberg principle and found preferences that were consistent with it. Again, these preferences – labelled as the *principle of comparative ignorance* – were inconsistent with conventional utility theory.

This principle is illustrated by studies on subjects' ability to guess temperature ranges. These empirical studies underscored the importance of familiarity in driving subjects' preference for estimating the temperature of San Francisco over Istanbul. Arguably, temperature ranges are far less predictable in San Francisco and so is the probability of a successful estimate. Nevertheless, familiarity emerged as the dominant criterion and most opted to estimate the temperature in the US city. Heath and Tversky (1991) also showed that people often prefer a bet on an event in their area of competence over a bet on a matched-chance event, in spite of the fact that the probability is far more opaque with the former than with the latter.

---

[26] Most people prefer to draw from Urn A because they know the probabilities. This is inconsistent with conventional expected utility theory because it implies that the subjective probabilities are greater for Urn A than for the unknown urn and therefore do not add up to one for both urns.

The asymmetry in utility preferences postulated by prospect theory is at the root of many inconsistent behaviours observed in daily banking and trading practices. Part II of this book analyses at length many instances in which prospect theory consistently explains the decisions of the various actors involved in finance and investment banking. No actor in the risk and trading world or those closely associated with it – regulators, analysts, consultants, the media or the general public – can escape the ambit of prospect theory. A multitude of empirical studies have applied prospect theory to finance during the last 20 years. Key applications to portfolio management that will be shown in the following sections include various forms of so-called *mental accounting*, such as investors' preference for dividends over capital gains, the endowment effect and investors' management of winning and losing positions.

Chapter 5 delves deeper into these individual biases and the related theory and empirical studies.

Individual biases and risk consequences

Reality is merely an illusion, albeit a very persistent one.

(Albert Einstein)

7±2:

- Heuristics, judgmental biases and context dependence
- Representativeness and anchoring
- Biased probability assessments
- Self-preservation biases
- Sequential information processing bias
- Risk disorder syndrome (RDS)

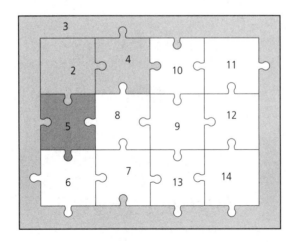

Abstract

Overconfidence and the emphasis on mental reference points postulated by prospect theory lie at the heart of many dangerously unconscious behaviours. These are embodied in a large set of individual psychological biases that create a context for mankind's supposedly rational decision-making.

Implications: Many decisions that one deems 'rational' do not qualify as such. They just 'feel' right. In the context of today's large trading organizations and the associated high stakes, the feel factor can have major consequences. It can never be completely eliminated, and it may even be desirable to retain it, but one has to be aware of it to manage it consciously.

5.1 The broad picture

Generally speaking, individual decisions concerning risk and uncertainty use quick rules of thumb and mental pictures to analyse a particular situation. These two categories are not as rigidly separated as the following lines may lead one to believe. The mental picture or frame that takes shape in one's subconscious may indeed – by virtue of its vividness – be used in analogy-driven thought processes, thereby contributing to an incorrect heuristic. The following lines and sections provide one possible view (and by no means the only one) of how individual biases are structured.

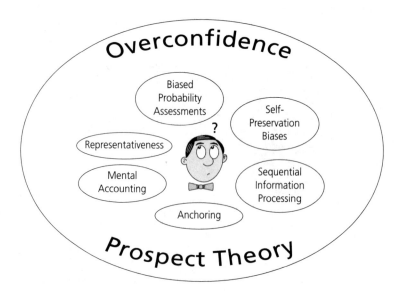

FIGURE 5.1 ■ The big picture of individual biases

Individual biases can be grouped as follows:

- Heuristics and judgmental biases, which lead individuals to use shortcuts, assumptions – consciously or not – and rules of thumb in their decisions. They include:
  - Representativeness and similarity bias
  - Anchoring and adjustment:
    (i) Status quo bias
    (ii) Under- and overreaction and conservatism
    (iii) Mean-reversion and prediction/extrapolation biases

- Framing and context dependence, whereby an individual creates a mental picture of a particular situation and uses it as a factor in his decision. This section focuses on specific displays of this behaviour. Features of this pattern are:
  - Mental accounting, loss aversion and endowment effect
  - Biased probability assessments:
    (i) Availability bias
    (ii) Base rates and Bayes
    (iii) Lotto bias and gambler's fallacy
  - Self-preservation bias:
    (i) Cognitive resonance and aversion to negative feedback loops
    (ii) Binary bias (right-or-wrong, Y/N, one state or another), aversion to ambiguity and perfectionism
    (iii) Selective attention bias
    (iv) Illusion of control
    (v) Self-attribution bias
    (vi) Hindsight/confirmation bias and regret management
  - Sequential information processing bias

5.2 Representativeness and anchoring

5.2.1 Representativeness and similarity bias

In a complex and dynamic world, it is very desirable – and all too human – to attempt to simplify and organize our information and knowledge in terms of categories, groups and analogies. Frequent probabilistic questions for decision-makers include:

- What is the probability that Object A belongs to the Class or Category B?
- What is the probability that Event A is generated from Process B?
- What is the probability that Process B will result in Event A?

One might define groups in terms of certain traits and view all members within that group as having a known and/or predictable behaviour. *Representativeness* (Kahneman & Tversky, 1972) is the art of comparing samples of a defined population with a larger population and drawing conclusions from such a comparison. The samples may include events, objects and processes. If A is defined as the sample and B as the larger population, then the A's are expected to be highly similar to their parent population of B's and to provide a fairly accurate and hopefully reliable representation of the characteristics in question. Such heuristic is used for judgment and prediction. This assumed similarity in the essential processes of both the sample and its parent population is based on the *connotative distance* between them and is also called *similarity bias*.

Consider the following situation:

Which of the following is most likely?

(a) A man is under 55 and has a heart attack.
(b) A man has a heart attack.
(c) A man smokes and has a heart attack.
(d) A man is over 55, smokes, and has a heart attack.

You can find the answer and the explanations in the footnote below.[27]

The probability assessments used in the representativeness heuristic suffer from major framing issues. These often undermine the conclusion drawn from them. You have already seen some of the effects of context dependence in the visual sphere in Chapter 2. Chapter 7 shows further applications to trading and risk management situations.

---

[27] The answer is (b), the man has a heart attack. Most people answer (d). Smoking and age, while increasing the chances of heart attack, cover only a subset of the population of heart attack victims, many of whom may be younger and non-smokers. Therefore, the probability of (d) must be lower, as (b) is further multiplied by two probability factors (respectively, smoking and being older than 55) that are both <1. The conjunction of probabilistic events cannot be more probable than any individual event. Instead, people use similarity to the prototype to guide their judgments. This explains what Kahneman and Tversky called *context dependence*, whereby the conclusion is strongly affected by the surrounding information.

5.2.2 Anchoring and adjustment

More information is always desirable, isn't it? Consider the following situation, which occurred in the United States in 1983, when the prime borrowing rate was 11 per cent (Russo & Schoemaker, 1989).

100 managers were asked: 'What is your best estimate of the prime interest rate six months from now?' The average answer was 10.90 per cent. The same question was put to a second group, but only after asking: 'Do you believe that six months from now the prime rate will be above or below 8 per cent?'

Would that question 'drag' the answer down? It did. The average answer was now 10.50 per cent, or 40 basis points below the first group's estimate. What about replacing the 8 per cent of the supplementary question with 14 per cent? You guessed it, a third group set their average estimate at 11.2 per cent, or 30 basis points above the first group's guess. What impact do you think the extra figure had on the respondents' guess?

Are you still sceptical? Then consider the following experiment, also by Russo and Schoemaker. At first, subjects were asked for the last three digits of their phone number. We will indicate those digits with the notation 'XYZ'. Then, the interviewer asked the subjects: 'I am going to add 400 to XYZ. Do you think Attila the Hun was defeated in Europe before or after (XYZ+400) AD?' Without being informed on the outcome of their previous answer, the subjects were then asked to guess in which year Attila was actually defeated. The correct answer was 451 AD. What about the subjects' answers? Just a bit higher. Let's look at the following table:

TABLE 5.1 ■ Phone numbers and Attila's defeat[28]

Range of the initial anchor (telephone number + 400)	Average estimate of the year of Attila's defeat
400 to 599	629
600 to 799	680
800 to 999	789
1000 to 1199	885
1200 to 1399	988

There is not much to add on what relationship exists between phone numbers and Attila! Yet, respondents attributed significant relevance to the information provided before the question and anchored themselves to it. Thereafter, they believed that the two figures were in some way related.

---

[28] From Russo & Schoemaker (1989), reprinted with permission.

Information overload and shortage of time make people more prone to anchoring. When no clear reference points are set in the decision-maker's mind, humans will be more likely to look for one to use as an anchor. If one is not readily available, they will probably grab the first one where some figures, statistics or other information suggest – or, more appropriately, make them believe – that a certain factor or piece of information is relevant.

Anchoring is recurrent in the business world, and the world of finance is no exception. A recent example of important anchors is offered by those new valuation metrics proposed by analysts to justify a stock price that appears sky high by traditional valuation standards. Do you remember the valuation of internet companies based on price-to-*subscription sales* ratios? Every projection about the future that relies to some extent on historical data also includes some degree of anchoring bias. As steering the organization wisely through future risks is at the very heart of risk management, this area is populated with strong visualizations of graphs and metrics anchoring biases par excellence. This is just part of the major problems facing contemporary risk managers discussed in Chapter 9. A substantial body of academic literature and empirical studies has focused on earning estimates by analysts and management and investors' post-announcement reactions. While very important, these studies are outside the main area of this book, which is risk management. Interested readers can find a more detailed analysis of these issues in the *Beyond Greed and Fear* and *Advances in Behavioural Finance* books cited in the bibliography.

Anchoring is not only an important heuristic but also a central theme of framing and of *re*framing. The latter is a technique developed in the United States by psychologists Bandler and Grinder in the 1970s that attempts to change patients' anchors. While a detailed account of their techniques is beyond the scope of this book, reframing is nevertheless an important aspect of financial and trading decision-making. Not surprisingly, limiting the effect of mental anchors is a perennial challenge of utmost importance for any trader. It is part of his discipline to understand how his favourite anchors affect his judgment. Anchors can indeed translate into major performance problems for traders if not managed consciously. Not sticking with a pre-set game plan and trade rationale can have disastrous consequences for any trader. This is discussed in Chapter 8.

5.2.3 Mental accounting and loss aversion bias

It is now time to look at some of the concrete applications of anchoring, mental reference points and prospect theory.

Mental accounting consists of looking at one's portfolio or one or more of its positions and adopting inconsistent decisions, as these decisions are based on separate mental pockets. Typical well-documented examples in the financial world are the treatment of income separate from capital gains or dividends, or decisions on selling one's winning stocks versus losers.

According to the Modigliani–Miller principle in corporate finance, investors should be indifferent between realizing income from capital gains or dividends. But are they? The absence of taxes was a critical assumption of that principle. In practice, most countries tax dividend income at a higher rate than capital gains. So, in after-tax terms, an investor should be better off with the latter. In practice, investors have a preference for dividends over capital gains (Shefrin & Statman, 1984). The rationale is that dividends are considered something 'extra', somewhat apart from one's nest egg. Selling an appreciated security, on the other hand, is associated with dipping into one's nest egg and evokes the associated guilt feelings.

Extensive empirical studies on investors' behaviour have explored the asymmetric loss aversion that was described as part of prospect theory. The general tendency to hold on to losing stocks and get rid of winners quickly has been defined as *disposition effect* (Shefrin & Statman, 1985). Further empirical evidence on the behaviour of retail investors follows in Section 8.4.1.

Two key explanations are offered:

▢ Investors prefer taking the odds of seeing their losing positions improve than taking a guaranteed loss. The latter is a form of pain, which the human brain is genetically predisposed to avoid at all costs, including the risk of taking *greater* pain later.

▢ The pain of losses is *two and a half times stronger* than the gratification of gains (Tversky & Kahneman, 1986; Luce & Fishburn, 1991; Luce, 2000).

Hedonic[29] *framing* is another variety of mental accounting. It involves segregating gains and integrating losses by presenting them, respectively, one at a time and as one block. Let's label the outcome of two events x and y respectively. $v(x)$ and $v(y)$ are the values corresponding to these two outcomes. According to hedonic framing:

$$v(x+y) \neq v(x) + v(y)$$

The expected utility principle of conventional economics is breached, since otherwise the two terms of the equation above would be equivalent. This means that the value that individuals attribute to events varies depending on their combinations and the context.

Thaler (1985) presents the following question: 'Who is happier, someone who wins two lotteries that pay $50 and $25 respectively, or someone who wins a single lottery paying $75?' About two-thirds of the subjects (64 per cent) say that the two-time winner is happier.

We can summarize the results so far into the following principles:

▢ Segregate gains (because the gain function is concave).

▢ Integrate losses (because the loss function is convex).

▢ Integrate smaller losses with larger gains (to offset loss aversion).

▢ Segregate small gains (silver linings) from larger losses (because the gain function is steepest at the origin, the utility of a small gain can exceed the utility of slightly reducing a large loss).

In practice, survey evidence (Thaler & Johnson, 1990) does not support the second of these principles, as subjects prefer experiencing losses one at a time. In addition, every loss was found to increase the sensitivity to the following loss. These empirical conclusions mean that loss aversion will be exacerbated even further relative to what prospect theory

---

[29] Hedonism is the philosophy that aims at the satisfaction of senses. 'Hedonic' then means 'of pleasure, relating to pleasure, or characterized by pleasure'.

states. Another critical implication for trading and risk management is, in Thaler's own words (1999):

> *... we should expect to see that some of the discretion inherent in any accounting system will be used to avoid to experience losses.*

Unfortunately, this warning on the dangerous incentives of combining accounting and loss experience has repeatedly fallen on deaf ears over the years. Chapters 7, 10 and 11 show how this often occurs in practice and the dire consequences.

The *sunk cost* bias (Thaler, 1980) is yet another display of mental accounting and loss aversion for which large organizations and projects are notorious. In this instance, a cost that was incurred in the past for a given project is used as a justification for engaging in sub-optimal projects in the future. Consider the following example:

EXAMPLE 5.1

Sunk cost bias

You have a £7 ticket to the movies, and on the way to the cinema you lose it.

- Suppose instead, you didn't have a ticket, but on the way there you lose £7 cash.
- Under which scenario are you more likely to buy a ticket when you get to the cinema?

Let's look at another similar situation:

EXAMPLE 5.2

Sunk cost bias

You have spent £20 for a ticket to watch your favourite football team's next away game, 40 miles from home. On the day of the game, there is a snowstorm. You drive to the game venue all the same, thinking that you would not have done it if those tickets had been complimentary.

In financial institutions and large organizations, some technology projects with long-term consequences dramatically demonstrate sunk cost bias. Often, the choice to continue with a sub-optimal development masks the need to avoid writing off the original project and cutting losses. As this process is repeated at several stages, the cost of fixing a flawed development mounts and the sunk cost bias strengthens further. Eventually, only a drastic event, such as a management change or a major crisis, forces the organization to face reality.

5.2.4 Endowment effect and status quo bias

The *endowment effect* (Thaler, 1980) concerns the different treatments of wealth depend-ing on its sources and the manner in which it was acquired. Consider the following example. Imagine two brothers who have similar spending habits and lifestyles and can both survive on £700 per month. Jack has £1,000 in his bank account. Tom has £700 and then wins £300 in the lottery. How much of the £300 should Tom stash away in the bank?

The sudden rise in wealth experienced by many investors in the 1990s thanks to the soaring values of their property and stock portfolios provides ample examples of the endowment effect. How much of this newfound wealth could they afford to spend? Maki & Palumbo (2001) investigated precisely this question in the United States by aggregating wealth and saving patterns from the Survey of Consumer Finances and the flow of funds accounts during the late 1990s. They found that those groups of households that benefited the most from the increase in equity prices – those with high incomes or who have achieved some college education – were also the groups that substantially decreased their rates of saving. Not surprisingly, these households also increased their rates of spending relative to 'regular' income to adjust their lifestyle to a higher perceived wealth.

Very similar to the endowment effect is the *status quo bias* (Samuelson & Zeckhauser, 1988), whereby a subject chooses inaction as the best way forward. For instance, someone who follows the financial markets and manages his own portfolio may have received a sudden inheritance of a portfolio of cash and securities from a deceased relative. Should that be merged into the original portfolio or treated separately? Samuelson and Zeckhauser concluded from field experiments that subjects who are presented with a range of alterna-tives will most likely select the one that is designated as the status quo. Another application of status quo bias is the case in which the original cost of a financial asset that one owns may be so remote or negligible that one mentally considers that asset to be worthless and does nothing about it. Consider the case of those who may have received stock options for free as part of their employment compensation, a popular pattern in the 1990s. They may do nothing to manage them *exactly* because they cost nothing, irrespective of the fact that their market value may be positive.

5.2.5 Other important anchoring biases

Anchoring by analysts, investors and management around earnings announcements is an important source of behavioural biases. Accordingly, it has received substantial attention in research and academic literature over the last 15 years. Hersh Shefrin's book *Beyond Greed and Fear* offers a comprehensive summary of the state of the art in these studies to those who are interested in further exploration.

The adjustment process in forecasts and the *conservatism* (Phillips & Edwards, 1966) that it displays are aspects of anchoring that are even more important for trading and risk manage-ment purposes. Investors' notorious habit of waiting too long to adjust their positions to trends is an example of such anchoring and under-adjustment once the trend changes. A large amount of ego-driven pride is on the line when it is time for anybody to acknowledge overshooting in the previous forecast. Some self-preservation bias, described later in this chapter, is involved as well. These tendencies, and the sense of frustration that they engender, become even more serious when there is an unexpected delay between response and effect. Examples are natural systems or thermostats, which operate on the principle of negative feedback control. Unexpected delays may mean the operator moves too late or too early. For example, piloting a simulated submarine the first time almost always leads to a crash to the bottom of the ocean because the operator moves at first too early and then too late to right the submersible.

Consider the following example from Edwards (1968):

> We have two urns containing 1,000 poker chips each. In Urn 1, 70 per cent of chips are red and 30 per cent blue. In Urn 2, the opposite applies (30 per cent blue, 70 per cent red). One of the urns is chosen randomly and a dozen chips are drawn from it: eight red chips and four blue chips. What are the chances (answer in per cent) that the chips came from Urn 1, the one mostly with red chips?

For now, simply jot down your answer. You can compare it to the answer and comments in the footnote below.[30]

Another tendency related to anchoring that few, if any, traders or strategic planners are exempt from is called *mean-reversion bias*. The former has buried many traders and risk managers who overused it. Stated in its most innocent form, mean-reversion bias means literally 'the trend will eventually have to return to the mean'. The fact that the 'mean' can be defined in a variety of ways, both in time span (weekly, monthly, daily and so on) and calculation mechanics (arithmetic, geometric, exponentially weighted, to name just a few of the most common types), is by no means a trivial or irrelevant detail. More often than not,

---

[30] If your figure came out between 70% and 80%, congratulations, it matches most people's estimate. This is yet another demonstration of how strong anchoring can be and how under-adjustment occurs. The correct answer, however, is 96.3%. Consider that there are two mutually exclusive hypotheses: Urn 1 and Urn 2, each with a prior probability of 0.5. This probability will be called p(1) and p(2), respectively. Without knowing anything else, the prior probability of drawing 8 red and 4 blue chips out of the 2,000-chip sample is 0.0002439. This will be called P(S). According to Bayesian statistics, the posterior probability of Urn 1 given the sequence S will be:

$$P(1|S) = \frac{P(S|1)}{P(S|1)} \times P(1)$$

$$P(S|1) = 0.000469774, \text{ so:}$$

$$P(1|S) = \frac{0.000469774}{0.0002439} \times 0.5 = 0.963$$

the 'mean' is what the subconscious makes the relevant person see. It is far from obvious that *the market will see the same mean*! Even more crucially, this thought process implicitly assumes that one's risk capital will outlast the length of time required for mean reversion to happen, which is again often not the case.

Those traders and forecasters who are trying to call tops and bottoms in security or foreign-exchange prices are succumbing to anchoring and mean-reversion biases. Simply put, their assessment of something as being 'cheap' or 'expensive' is relative to a previous price to which their subconscious is anchored. The same applies to those investors who have anchored themselves to high yields in the past, most notably in fixed-income securities. Smart salespersons who will offer them financial products of questionable credit quality or liquidity in return for high nominal yields will exploit exactly that anchor. In addition, mean-reversion assumptions (or hopes thereof) often degenerate into the gambler's fallacy, another serious problem in probability understanding and management. Section 5.3.3 analyses the law of small numbers associated with these misconceptions.

Prediction/extrapolation bias is also widespread in financial markets and is evidenced by the perennial human habit of engaging experts who claim they can help see the future. Tea leaves or fortune tellers anyone? Over-reliance on recent information is common. At best, the reliability of experts' forecasts must be taken with a rather large grain of salt.[31]

5.3 Biased probability assessments

5.3.1 Availability bias

Availability bias is perhaps the most prominent of cognitive frames. It can also be used as a heuristic in probability judgment and become a source of representativeness error. The availability bias uses information processed by the brain in a variety of ways. This section will analyse the most important ones, namely by:

- information retrieval
- information construction
- information simulation.

Availability bias by information retrieval uses events that are more vivid, more visual and sound more likely (or, simply, are not so scary that one sub-consciously shuts them out as extremely unlikely). The probability and frequency judgments used by this process rely on *associative distance*, the ease of availability of a given set of information. This differs from the similarity bias discussed in 5.2.1, as that bias relies instead on *connotative distance*.

---

[31] One of the experiments on analysts' overconfidence, performed by Kiell & Stephan (1997), asked a number of brokers to predict share and currency prices within a 90% confidence interval. Less than one-fourth (24%) of the 360 forecasts were right in comparison with the 90% required.

Consider the following study from Slovic, Fischhoff & Lichtenstein (1976). Forty-one causes of death, including disease, accidents, homicide, suicide and natural hazards, were used to ask questions of a large sample of students. Death probabilities for a randomly selected US resident ranged between 1×10^{-8} (botulism) to 8.5×10^{-3} (heart disease). 106 pairs of these causes were created and subjects were asked to indicate, for each pair, the more likely cause of death and the ratio of the greater to the lesser frequency.

Where the frequency ratios between the more and the less frequent event was below 2:1, the answers were poor. Table 5.2 compares the answers with the true ratio.

TABLE 5.2 ■ Judgment of relative frequency for selected pairs of lethal events

Less likely	More likely	True ratio	Geom. mean of judged ratios
Asthma	Firearm accident	1.20	11.00
Breast cancer	Diabetes	1.25	0.13
Lung	Stomach cancer	1.25	0.31
Leukaemia	Emphysema	1.49	0.58
Stroke	All cancer	1.57	21.00
All accidents	Stroke	1.85	0.04
Pregnancy	Appendicitis	2.00	0.10
Tuberculosis	Fire and flames	2.00	10.50
Emphysema	All accidents	5.19	2.69
Polio	Tornado	5.30	4.26
Drowning	Suicide	9.60	5.50
Tornado	Asthma	20.90	0.36
Syphilis	Homicide	46.00	31.70
Botulism	Lightning	52.00	0.30
Flood	Homicide	92.00	81.70
Syphilis	Diabetes	95.00	2.36
Botulism	Asthma	920.00	1.50
Excess cold	All cancer	982.00	1,490.00
Botulism	Emphysema	10,600.00	24.00

Events that are easy to remember or picture in one's mind appear more likely and increase their perceived frequency. The image of being eaten alive by a shark is an anchor that evokes primordial fears. The odds of dying that way are likely to be significantly overestimated in comparison to the health risks of being stung by a malaria-carrying mosquito. Likewise, those instances that appear often or vividly in films, television or newspapers are likely to seem more realistic, frequent and likely. Consistent with the principle of cognitive dissonance, which will be explained later in this chapter, our cognitive mechanisms are wired to avoid excessively intense pain. Events that are too frightening even to consider are shut off through a *denial* mechanism. Nuclear war or ecological catastrophes are cases in point.

With respect to the study above, accidents, cancer, botulism and tornadoes receive heavy media coverage and their frequency is significantly overstated. Asthma and diabetes, conversely, are seldom considered as causes of death by the media. Their frequency is underestimated. Diseases, which were thought to cause as many deaths as accidents, actually killed 16 times more. Death by stroke took 11 times the number of lives that were claimed by homicides every year, despite the latter being considered as likely a cause of death.

Slovic, Fischhoff & Lichtenstein (1979) summarized the biases emerging from this and other studies in Table 5.3.

TABLE 5.3 ■ Bias in judged frequency of death

Most overestimated	Most underestimated
All accidents	Smallpox vaccination
Motor vehicle accidents	Diabetes
Pregnancy, childbirth and abortion	Stomach cancer
Tornadoes	Lightning
Flood	Stroke
Botulism	Tuberculosis
All cancer	Asthma
Fire and flames	Emphysema
Venomous bite or sting	
Homicide	

A follow-up study by Combs & Slovic (1979) examined the news reporting of the causes of death on both coasts of the US. It found similar biases in both newspapers. Violent and catastrophic events such as accidents, tornadoes and fires were reported far more frequently than less spectacular but still statistically significant causes of death, such as disease. In spite of the 16:1 actual death ratio between disease and accidents mentioned previously, the latter were reported three times as frequently and deemed responsible for seven times the number of dead. Disease also caused 100 times the number of victims claimed by homicide every year, and yet articles about homicide were three times as frequent.

Laypeople are generally more prone to availability bias than experts, as the latter have been trained to use scientific risk, expressing it – in the case above – in terms of actual number of deaths. However, as Gigerenzer (2002) has shown, even doctors have great trouble understanding the precise meaning of risk statistics if they are not communicated in 'natural' frequency form. Exploiting availability bias in an audience is a very important skill for marketers and public prosecutors. Compare the level of detail and realism in the following statements:

- Jackson (the defendant) entered the house, killed the victim and, on his way out, hit a table.
- Jackson (the defendant) entered the house by *shattering the back door window*, found the victim and, *after repeatedly stabbing her, finished her off with a hammer* while she was lying on the ground in a *pool of blood*. On his way out, he stumbled into a table, knocking a bowl of *salsa on the white carpet*.

Recency bias is a subset of availability bias based on information retrieval. The importance of more recent information is in fact exaggerated in the decision-maker's mind. Many investors, both professional and not, are often susceptible to recency bias and over-react accordingly. Pulling out of the market after a large drop and projecting over-optimistically after a major rally are classic applications of recency bias.

The information retrieval process that triggers availability bias often attributes particular relevance to *salience*. This applies especially when the decision-maker faces a so-called *buridanic* choice, namely a situation in which he or she is unable to identify a strictly best option. Sometimes this may not be the objective situation but, rather, one generated by the weak principles used in the decision and/or by the decision-maker's lack of time. What is the tie-breaker in those situations? Contrary to the 'coin toss' problem-solving approach that decision theorists had assumed would be used, *salience* would become the dominant criterion. Empirical tests in supermarkets in the United Kingdom, for instance, have revealed that salience of functionally irrelevant features – such as, for instance, the 'yellowness' of a chicken's skin – would become the key decision criterion (Carpenter *et al*, 1994). In choosing from a row of identical items on a supermarket shelf, customers tended to take one in the middle, and in choosing from a set of equivalent routes, they opted for the most external one (Christenfeld, 1995).

The examples and studies above explain availability bias based on information *retrieval*. Availability bias can also be triggered by information *construction*. These functions use different areas of the brain. For instance, one may conceive the following question:

In the English language, which is higher, the probability that a word starts with the letter j or that j is the third letter (not counting words with less than four letters)?

Originally resulting only from the two classes of mental operations described above, retrieval and construction (Kahneman & Tversky, 1973), the availability heuristic was further enriched by a third process, the *simulation* heuristic (Kahneman & Tversky, 1979). The classic 'what if?' question that underpins simulations will likely strike a familiar note with those managers, traders and risk management practitioners to whom this book is primarily directed. Scenario construction and alterations are the most critical ingredients of any simulation and, not surprisingly, the main source of biases. Three kinds of these exist:

- an *Alice in Wonderland* (in Kahneman's and Tversky's own words) unrealistic mixture of fantasy and reality;

- neglect of conditional probabilities in scenario modifications. For instance, altering one of the scenario developments may depend on removing – or introducing – a prior event that had a very low probability. This issue is confirmed by empirical findings, too (Kahneman & Tversky, 1979);

- the *cross-country skier's downhill run bias* (again, according to Kahneman's and Tversky's own definition). Prior to brief downhill runs, cross-country skiers face long and laborious climbs. In making alterations, the preference for easier conditions often translates into scenario conditions that are excessively and unrealistically favourable.

Later chapters will show availability bias in practice. Media, as an expression of common opinion, is heavily affected by availability bias. The simulation heuristic – coupled with the lotto bias that will be described in later sections of this chapter – is a common source of risk management problems in practice. Chapter 9 digs deeper into these issues.

5.3.2 Bayes, base rates and probability misconceptions

Decisions-makers are always looking for ways to simplify the representation of complex problems and reduce them to smaller, more manageable sequential components. This attempt often results in oversimplification in two ways:

- *insensitivity to base rates and probabilities*, also called *conjunction fallacy* (Kahneman & Tversky, 1982) – that is, a tendency to overuse the cause–effect linear relationships in the event sequence and ignore the prior probabilities that preceded each stage;

- a *sequential processing bias* that considers each event as the result of only *one* cause and neglects multiple causes, interdependencies and correlations. The links between causes and effects are explained as one-to-one linear relationships. (Section 5.5 addresses this problem.)

Jumping to conclusions of the 'A leads to B which, in turn, causes C' variety based on a series of linear, unconditional relationships offers simplification, saves time and, as such, is of course appealing. The dark side of this approach is that it leads to major misrepresentations of the probabilities which, in turn, often generate wrong conclusions and decisions. This problem is similar to the issue of conservatism presented in 5.2.5 above from a mechanical computation point of view, as conditional probabilities are involved in both cases. Under conservatism, one does not adjust ex-post probabilities sufficiently as new information becomes available. In this case, one neglects conditional probability completely.

Consider, for instance, the following problem:

> You are the manager of a restaurant and are analysing the quality of service provided to customers. Feedback from market research tells you that you lose on average two-thirds of the customers when the food has been considered unsatisfactory. Overall, you are losing about 15 per cent of your customers. On average, the food that you serve is considered unsatisfactory about 10 per cent of the time. If a client is lost, what is the probability that the food that he has received is poor?

You can find the answer in the footnote below.[32]

The legal and medical fields are replete with such instances and the ugly consequences are easy to understand. During the controversial OJ Simpson trial in the US, the use of unconditional – as opposed to conditional – probabilities by talented lawyers attracted considerable attention (see Taleb, 2002).[33]

Still other major problems help to understand how sketchy human understanding of probabilities can become. Let's consider another example.

---

[32] The correct answer is 33.56%. Let X be the event 'poor food' and Y the event 'lose the client'. The prior belief is that $P(X)=0.1$. Also $P(Y|X)=0.667$. First, one has to calculate the unconditional probability of losing the client, $P(Y)$.

So, we have $P(Y)= P(Y|X) \times P(X) + P(Y|\text{not } X) \times P(\text{not } X) = 0.667 \times 0.1 + 0.15 \times 0.9 = 0.2017$.

We now use Bayes' Rule to calculate the posterior probability, $P(X|Y)$, of poor food given that a client has been lost. So:

$$P(Y \mid X) = \frac{P(Y \mid X)}{P(Y)} \times P(X)$$

$$P(X \mid Y) = \frac{0.667}{0.2017} \times 0.1 = 0.963$$

[33] In his brilliant book *Fooled by Randomness* (2002), Taleb has a section entitled 'Kafka in a Courtroom' that explains how the arguments used during the trial would generate absurd probabilities.

> Would you rather:
>
> (a) be right 90 per cent of the time with 50 observations?, or
>
> (b) be right 60 per cent of the time with a sample of 1,000 observations?

When analysing this objectively, (b) would be the more appropriate answer both from a statistical and a common sense standpoint. Unfortunately, one seldom has the luxuries of objectivity and time to think about further alternatives in the real world. Regardless of their definition, people are after results, which are generally associated with action. So, in spite of its statistical limitations, and likely *survivorship bias*, (a) provides a stronger illusion of certainty to support action. This bias is also called *insensitivity to sample size*. Other than for pure statistical naiveté, this bias can often be the symptom of ego involvement in achieving the 'solution' or 'result' 'no matter what it takes'. This tendency is the statistical facade of two key self-preservation biases, aversion to ambiguity and selective attention. They will be discussed under 'Binary biases, aversion to ambiguity and perfectionism' and 'Selective attention, confirmation bias and self-fulfilling prophecies' in 5.4.2 and 5.4.3 respectively.

5.3.3 Gambler's fallacy and lotto bias

Still other misconceptions about the meaning of chance and probability loom large. Let's analyse another question. When considering tosses of a fair coin for Heads (H) or Tails (T), which of the following sequences is most likely?

> (a) HHHHHH
>
> (b) HHHTTT
>
> (c) THHTHT

Answer (c) looks most likely, doesn't it? After all, it makes intuitive sense to expect outcomes to change often. And yet the answer is *none*. The probability is indeed $(\frac{1}{2})^6$, or 0.015625. You may think that a streak of equal outcomes increases the probability of an opposite outcome at the next toss. Unfortunately, examples such as this one do not feature enough tosses for the principle to apply.

This example shows the dangers of confusing *frequency* and *probability*. If the coin being flipped is fair, the probability of a certain outcome from each toss remains unchanged at $\frac{1}{2}$, regardless of the number of previous tosses and prior sequences of outcomes. *The coin has no memory*. That is why streaks with the same outcome can happen far more frequently and last far longer that one would expect. Only over a very large number of outcomes does the frequency in the number of outcomes converges towards the $\frac{1}{2}$ that one expects. This is yet another form of mental anchoring to the previous outcomes. Unlike the coin, the person who makes the toss does have memory and takes into some account the previous results. If one toss is to follow a streak of heads or tails, one expects mean-reversion to skew the odds in favour of the opposite outcome. The principle of increasing the stakes as the losing streak continues is called the *St Petersburgh's Paradox*, after the mathematician Daniel Bernoulli (1738), who formalized it mathematically. The paradox consists in the fact that someone should, in theory, be willing to pay infinity to join a game of doubling the stakes as the negative series of outcomes extends itself. In practice, it can be demonstrated that the maximum utility of the game is about twice as large as the initial stake (Kritzman, 2000). By doing so, one would take a tiny risk of incurring a catastrophic loss if the game draws on over a very large number of tosses.

A rudimentary rule of thumb called the *square root rule* can become invaluable in avoiding this mistake. This rule says that almost all of the variations from the expected mean should come within three times the square root of the mean. So, let us indicate with F the total number of flips and with H the expected number of heads. As the probability of either outcome, heads or tails, is $\frac{1}{2}$, one would normally expect the total number of heads to converge towards

$$H = F/2$$

The square root rule implies that:

$$H = \frac{F}{2} \pm 3\sqrt{\frac{F}{2}}$$

This means that, over 20 tosses, one would expect:

$$H = \frac{20}{2} \pm 3\sqrt{\frac{20}{2}} = 0 \pm 3\sqrt{10} = 10 \pm 9.49$$

The outcome can then range between zero and 20, that is, all heads or all tails. This means that even if, for instance, all heads had come out of the first 12 tosses, a gambler could hardly afford to bet safely on even *one* tail coming out!

Let us consider the expected range over 100 tosses:

$$H = \frac{100}{2} \pm 3\sqrt{\frac{100}{2}} = 50 \pm 3\sqrt{50} = 50 \pm 21.21$$

Even in this case, the number of heads can experience a substantial variability and range between 19 and 71!

The laws of large numbers and mean reversion are valid, however. Let us consider a substantially larger number of throws, for instance 10,000:

$$H = \frac{10,000}{2} \pm 3\sqrt{\frac{10,000}{2}} = 5,000 \pm 3\sqrt{10,000} = 5,000 \pm 300$$

Here, the number of heads ranges between 4,700 and 5,300.

Figure 5.2 shows how the law of large numbers *really* works. As you can see, the two curves representing the higher and lower Expected Value (EV) according to the square root rule converge to the expected 50 per cent figure only after a very large number of coin tosses.

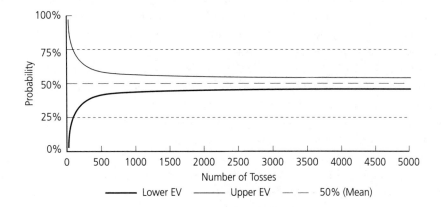

FIGURE 5.2 ■ The law of large numbers, reality and myth

In basic statistical terms, this means that, over the long haul, the standard deviation of outcomes becomes progressively smaller relative to the mean.

The square root rule is widely used in finance, and has seen one of its most important applications in the Basle Capital Adequacy Accords. Caution, however, is imperative. Its usefulness as a rule of thumb notwithstanding, even the square root rule tends to underestimate risk.[34]

Professional poker players are familiar with these issues, which, not by chance, are labelled *gambler's fallacy* or, occasionally, *lotto bias*. The fallacy consists of the distorted expectation that the law of large numbers – or mean reversion – will reassert itself and turn things in favour of the player before risk capital is exhausted. This also explains why pros use rigorous *position sizing* rules to keep their stakes within a very low percentage (usually up to 1 per cent) of their total risk capital over a series of runs.

While valid, the law of large numbers applies only over a *large* number of random events. *Law of small numbers* was indeed the term coined by Kahneman & Tversky (1971, 1974) to describe the outcome of empirical surveys carried out to test this belief in practice. Interested readers can find the detailed results in the related articles in the bibliography.

Needless to say, the gambler's fallacy leads to *gambler's ruin*. The latter has destroyed a very large number of traders, risk specialists and their managers. The irony lies exactly in the

---

[34] The rule cannot take into account the possibility of occasional 'jumps' in security prices over time. These mathematical discontinuities increase risk further. The underestimation of risk grows as the time horizon increases. (Danielsson and Zigrand, 2003).

overconfidence that a high level of education, experience and social recognition engender in risk and trading professionals relative to their less glamorous Las Vegas counterparts. This overconfidence, in turn, leads them to ignore basic position sizing rules.

It is worth bearing in mind that failure has far fewer fathers than success and trading is no exception. The traders destroyed by gambler's ruin who are mentioned amongst the risk disasters in Chapter 10 are only the handful of instances that became too large for their firms to hide. The trading industry has witnessed numerous disasters on a smaller scale that will never be known outside their institutions.

Professional risk managers can hardly consider themselves exempt from this bias. Over-reliance on VaR – with respect to rare catastrophic losses in high-volatility situations – is also an illustrious application of gambler's fallacy. Like the fair coin of the previous example, the statistical processes that generate the probability distributions – and ultimately the VaR – used by risk managers assume a total lack of memory. Markets, however, are ultimately made up of people and consequently do have some memory. The assumption that the markets have no memory and that asset prices move in a random walk – or as atomistic Brownian motion – underlies the rationalist school of modern finance theory (Bachelier, 1900). The practical import of this premise is that we should be very careful in looking at the face of randomness because we can attribute whatever we want to see in it. As Ramsey's law tells us, we can never ever really see randomness because as we approach closer and closer we start to see more and more patterns.

Underestimating highly unlikely events is also a recurrent tendency in normal daily life. Drivers know the consequences of not wearing a seat belt in case of accident and research confirmed it as early as the 1970s (Knapper, Cropley & Moore, 1976; Marzoni, 1971). Nevertheless, only a small percentage of drivers were found to be wearing them due to the low probability of having an accident[35] (Slovic, Fischhoff & Lichtenstein, 1978). For highly unlikely but high-severity risks, such as floods, Johnson et al (1993) found individuals heavily underinsured even when coverage was subsidized. According to Kunreuther (2001), individuals simplify their models of choice for unlikely events by thinking in binary zero or one terms. They will normally round off to zero the probability of small-likelihood events and think 'It won't happen to me' (see the related bias in Chapter 6). After disasters, the probability is rounded up to one according to the 'It will happen to me' school of thought. The vividness of the pain can also be viewed as an availability bias (see 5.3.1 earlier). There is another simple reason. Insurance premiums are an out-of-pocket cost, whereas the very unlikely costs of disaster are treated as an opportunity cost. And, as confirmed by Thaler (1980), out-of-pocket costs loom much larger.

[35] In 1978, the year of the study, Slovic, Fischhoff and Lichtenstein estimated that approximately 1 in every 3.5 million trips ended in a fatal accident and 1 in every 100,000 trips caused a disabling injury.

5.3.4 Hot-hand effect

Gambler's fallacy is the worst sort of misconception that people hold with respect to streaks, but hardly the only one. Another one is called the *hot-hand effect*, from the label that is attributed to basketball players after a series of successful shots. According to this biased belief, a series of positive or negative outcomes influences the following events, creating some meaningful correlation between successive events. If randomness holds, then these independent events should not be showing any statistically significant correlation. Popular sayings that 'success breeds success and failure breeds failure' reflect this belief.

Gilovich, Vallone & Tversky (1985) led a series of four studies to document the discrepancy between basketball players' and fans' *perceptions* of hot hand in shooting. These authors studied the performance of varsity, college and professional players, including the Philadelphia 76ers in 1980–81. In each case, they found no statistically significant differences in the probability of a successful shot regardless of the previous shot. Worse, such probability was shown to remain completely unaffected even if the previous *three* shots had been successful or not.

Albright (1993) led some second-generation hot-hand research on streaks in baseball, finding only a handful of isolated instances of players whose batting average would improve after successful streaks. Finally, a third wave of research by Albert & Bennett (2001) went back to basketball to look for some hot-hand effect for players across seasons, that is, whether success in one season could help predict a positive outcome in the following one. Even in this case, no evidence of a hot-hand effect emerged.

With their eternal quest for higher visibility and related power and compensation, trading and investment banking professionals actively attempt to generate and reinforce belief in a hot-hands effect in their institutions. Some empirical research has confirmed the existence of this in mutual funds (Hendricks, Patel & Zeckhauser, 1993; Carhart, 1997; Carpenter & Lynch, 1999) and in UK pension funds (Tonks, 2002).

5.4 Self-preservation biases

Pain avoidance and the quest for pleasure have been at the top of mankind's priority list since prehistoric times. In some aspects, such as binary and selective attention bias, today's professionals have much in common with their ancestors. Other tendencies, while aimed at the same goals, are more subtle and related to the psychological sense of security and comfort that humans crave. Both categories will be discussed in the following sections.

5.4.1 Aversion to cognitive dissonance and negative feedback loops

Once an opinion is formed in the human mind, it becomes the standard against which information and perceptions from the outside world will be viewed. Information that is not aligned to these views originates in cognitive dissonance and, as such, has its importance discounted quickly. The plain fact is that we have ears only for what we want and like to hear and eyes to see only what we want to see. In a previous chapter, we discussed how we in fact have preferred sensory representation systems and convincer sequences which delete or generalize certain information. Later on in this book, Chapter 6 shows how, in the context of large organizations, biases turned to noise reinforce prejudice. Simply put, it is natural to seek company in support of our opinions, as this is another facet of mankind's risk aversion. It takes some insight and a great deal of diligent effort to change our crude, inappropriate and insensitive frames of risk.

According to the theory of cognitive dissonance, people are usually motivated to reduce or avoid psychological inconsistencies (Plous, 1993). People experience cognitive dissonance when they simultaneously hold two thoughts that feel psychologically inconsistent, contradictory or incompatible (Festinger, 1957). In one experiment by Festinger & Carlsmith (1959), two groups of undergraduate students at Stanford University were divided into three groups. While all groups would perform some prosaic laboratory tasks involving tools, the first two would be paid, respectively, $1 and $20. They would thereafter tell one another that the tasks were enjoyable and provide the experimenters with the rating of the tasks. Pretending that he needed some replacements, the experimenter would then ask the subjects if they were willing to repeat the menial tasks for the same amount they had received before, $1 and $20 respectively. Another rating was requested. In this case, the $1 subjects rated the tasks as *more* enjoyable than the $20 subjects. This was explained as follows (Plous, 1993):

■ The $1 subjects were trying to avoid holding two conflicting views at the same time, namely:

 – The task was extremely boring.

 – For only $1, I (an honest person) told someone that the task was interesting and enjoyable.

■ The $20 subjects rated the tasks for what they were – a drudgery – because they felt they had already a good reason to manage the apparent cognitive dissonance, the extra $20 that they had received.

Later, the psychologist Daryl Bem (1972) offered other explanations for the test results based on *self-perception theory*. Unlike cognitive dissonance theory, this reconciles the findings of Festinger and Carlsmith by placing emphasis on the way people provide explanations of their own behaviour. Cognitive theory gives precedence to inner psychological conflict, claiming that it is the most important factor. Research to date has not yet been able to resolve these differences of opinion.

Predecisional dissonance, which as the term implies precedes choice, is perhaps the most commonly expected to occur but not the only type. *Postdecisional dissonance*, which relates to regret (see 5.4.6), also exists. Knox & Inkster (1968) found examples in horse racing, where betters would tweak the chances of winning on a horse *after* making a bet. Frankel & Doob (1968) applied a similar procedure to voters. Research on predecisional dissonance has targeted its influence on consumer behaviour (Doob, 1969).

Advertisers, movie producers and book publishers have learned how to tailor their offerings to suit current trends in public opinion. Producing something that is liable to generate cognitive dissonance may endanger future business if this dissonance is not pursued as part of a deliberate strategy. Occasionally, for instance, some advertisements rely on particularly repugnant and brutal images that offend our sensitivity or provoke moral outrage. While risky, this strategy generally aims to impress a brand or product in the minds of the target audience. The vividness of the images and situations presented obviously aims to generate availability bias by retrieval.

Cognitive resonance can leave an individual trader, desk or an entire organization exposed to sudden shocks and dislocations. As such, it is a subtle enemy to fight. Spotting the weak points in our own arguments and views means hard work, time and self-discipline. Few are lucky enough to apply all these three qualities on a consistent basis. Far more often, *denial* is the normal reaction to negative feedback – that is, expressed as disconfirming information or early objections to our opinions or actions. Ignoring such feedback and seeking refuge in one's own certainties and rationalizations is a common reaction that compounds the problems thereafter. Denial increases the volatility and deepens the discount of obtaining a full resolution of the initial problem.

5.4.2 Binary biases, aversion to ambiguity and perfectionism

The binary bias, that our actions should be judged in terms of wrong or right, probably originates from our parents and is then encouraged and reinforced at school and finally continues later on in our life at work and elsewhere. After all, viewing things in the digital, 'yes or no', 'black or white', 'good or bad', 'accept or reject' and so on, makes decisions simpler and quicker.

This lesson applies to virtually all fields of human experience and is actively sought in the trading and risk worlds, too. In the financial markets, however, seasoned traders apply this rule with a twist. The reality of 'right' or 'wrong' is no longer defined in *absolute* terms but *relative to a price*. This is a critical distinction that many ignore or neglect at their peril, since financial markets ultimately punish them with underperformance. This is one of the key reasons for the apparent inconsistency between a firm's reputation as a 'good company' and its subsequent underperformance. Indeed, empirical evidence supports the notion that *good companies make bad stocks* (Solt & Statman, 1989; Shefrin & Statman, 1995). For a more detailed account of these paradoxical tendencies in the financial markets, see Shefrin (2000).

Is the human mind able to cope with complex scenarios intuitively or does it always seek the pure certainty? Ockham's razor is great if you can at least count the variables. And when the variables are so elegantly defined then technology may help us calculate and visualize the unfolding of complex scenarios. This, however, solves only a small part of the initial problem. It takes effort and an open mind to see opposites and not just assume things fall into the categories of opposites.

Consider how difficult it is for someone who has not trained or learned how to be in two *different emotional states* at the same time. One may try to construct the feeling of being in two emotional states simultaneously, say 'sad and happy', but that is a far cry from actually experiencing it. The inability to feel in two states at the same time is indeed a human limitation. You have already experienced context dependence and the difficulty of seeing two points of view at the same time in the visual sphere when looking at the images in Chapter 2. Let's try other variations on the theme:

- Have you ever tried to be simultaneously depressed *and* joyful?

- Let's try with one's location bearings: How does it *feel* to be – at the same time – 58 per cent in Frankfurt and 42 per cent in Rome?

- Now, consider the problem over the time dimension. What would living one-third each in ancient Greece, the Italian Renaissance and in Napoleonic France feel like?

- It is not going to get any easier when dealing with two types of sound at once. Can you listen to a weak and a loud sound without the latter overriding the former?

Poor complexity management is the most immediate consequence of these shortcomings. Faced with complicated scenarios, humans seek to simplify reality by focusing – deliberately or not – on a more manageable subset. These *selective attention* and *sequential processing* biases are discussed, respectively, in the next section and later in 5.5.

5.4.3 Selective attention, confirmation bias and self-fulfilling prophecies

'Tunnel vision' is an oft-used phrase in the business world to denote a focused but somewhat restricted attention span. This tendency is one of the basic self-preservation instincts that mankind has likely inherited from the far less hospitable conditions in which our prehistoric forefathers found themselves. While the dangerous animals that they faced differ from today's risks, that basic fight-or-flee instinct that is built into mankind's genetic code still persists. Sub-consciously, this instinct can provide a useful service, as it forces the decision-maker to face the most critical problem at hand and disregard peripheral or relatively irrelevant issues.

It can – and often does – become dangerous if used excessively or if other less immediate issues are neglected for too long. The same applies when selective attention is not coupled with a sufficient awareness of the other issues that one chooses to de-prioritize as part of an overall strategy.

Selective attention bias is also often used to avoid cognitive dissonance by weeding out those sources of information that would call one's overall view into question. When this happens, the line between conscious behaviour and self-hypnosis becomes very thin indeed and the potential for self-delusion and self-fulfilling prophecies becomes significant. Recall the Ellsberg principle and prospect theory, which show that people have a natural tendency to accept bets close to their area of competence and familiarity. Selective attention bias and cognitive resonance, in turn, exaggerate these tendencies in practice. *Confirmation bias* is the term used to indicate fairly easy threshold conditions for testable hypotheses such that the hypothesis cannot be falsified under those conditions. Such easy-to-pass tests may lead to an *illusion of validity*, yet another bias.

Again, business and finance do not escape these biases. Leaving aside potential conflicts of interest generated by their firms' need to please corporate clients, analysts are known to look for what fits into their own sub-conscious perspective of the world (Hunter & Coggin, 1998). Excessively prudent business plans that rely on easy-to-beat targets are also an example of confirmation bias with respect to management ability.

Trading and risk management, with their quest for concise single-figure metrics into which risk reports can be aggregated, are also significantly exposed to these biases. Focusing attention on a single VaR figure without paying attention to the shape of the probability distribution around it can be lethal. Many option traders who have managed the hedging of their portfolio mainly for local moves have my sympathy for they no doubt have experienced the gut wrenching acceleration of major moves to remote areas of their portfolio. Let me urge many technical traders who see their systems achieve success too quickly in tests to be doubly careful, since this could raise the suspicion – if not the evidence – of some confirmation bias.

5.4.4 Illusion of control

While most would agree that in situations requiring skill, there is a causal link between behaviour and outcome, the presence of chance – or, as one would commonly say, luck – is the element that makes this link far more unstable in financial markets. Their outcomes are driven, to a considerable extent, by randomness. The presumption that one can control such outcomes is one of the most widespread and dangerous fallacies of the trading world. This illusion coalesces well with the self-attribution bias that is discussed in the next section, since the latter is fundamental in managing the asymmetry of attributing outcomes to skill or to bad luck. More often than not, self-attribution bias acts as a psychological option that follows illusion of control and implements it. The person suffering from an illusion of control might think, 'If things work out, I'm a hero. If they don't, then it's bad luck or someone else's fault.'

Modern technology and risk management – or, more precisely, the misunderstandings of opportunities which they have opened – are at least partly responsible for fostering and reinforcing the illusion of control in finance over the years. In this sense, modern risk managers face an important ethical question, as the overstated ability to control outcomes is often used to lay a (shaky) foundation for further expansion into larger volumes and more complicated products and markets. And regulators who require more sophisticated risk management technology may perversely be aiding and abetting this illusion even further by providing guidance which actually allows them to take more risk for less cost, which is one of the unintended consequences of the Basel II Accord.

While common sense would dictate that top management heed the advice of their risk chiefs, major psychological issues that have already been illustrated – such as aversion to cognitive dissonance and selective attention bias – cloud the picture. In short, one should not assume that getting the right ears to really listen *and* act upon the information can be accomplished without considerable entreaty.

A large body of literature has investigated the various motivations underpinning the illusion of control. Most studies share the conclusion that illusion of control is really about one's quest to master the surrounding environment. There is a broad range of psychological explanations:

- striving for superiority (Adler, 1930)
- need for competence (White, 1959)
- instinct to master (Hendrick, 1943).

Other empirical research has pursued more specific themes. These include beliefs in chance events such as coin tosses (Langer & Roth, 1975) or dice (Goffman, 1967; Henslin, 1967), illusions of control based on familiarity and choice (Langer, 1975), illusory and invisible correlations (Jennings, Amabile & Ross, 1982).

From both an organizational and an individual point of view, losing touch with one's limits is a major symptom of overconfidence that often paves the road to future disasters. The magnitude of resources managed by an organization acts as a magnifying glass for this behavioural problem and for its consequences. Being such a pervasive tendency, the illusion of control has been a central theme of behavioural surveys of traders. This will be one of the key topics when we come to examine the trader's behaviour in Chapter 8.

5.4.5 Self-attribution bias

Consistent with the standard theory, free lunches are not abundant in modern financial markets. Bloated egos and self-professed 'gurus', on the other hand, have never been in short supply. *Self-attribution bias*, the tendency to attribute successes to one's skills and failures to endogenous causes, should therefore come as no surprise. Amongst professionals, we would no doubt agree that in investment banking, self-attribution bias reaches peak intensity at the time when bonuses are discussed.

Management's statements and earnings announcements often betray self-attribution bias. Negative announcements after some major and apparently uncontrollable event are prime examples. For instance, the appreciation of a company's domestic currency is often used to justify poor earnings. However, few ever mention the opposite situation – domestic products becoming more competitive thanks to a depreciating currency – when trading conditions become more favourable. Another example comes from the wave of third-quarter earnings revisions in 2001 blaming the 11 September terrorist attack. Notwithstanding some effect on consumer confidence, one should question whether that dramatic event could be the sole cause of poor quarterly earnings.

Empirical research has confirmed the existence of this bias in various settings including: achievement of tasks (Davis & Davis, 1972; Feather, 1969; Fitch, 1970; Wolosin, Sherman & Till, 1973), teaching performance (Beckman, 1970; Freize & Weiner, 1971; Johnson, Feigenbaum & Weiby, 1964) and actors (Beckman, 1970; Gross, 1966; Polefka, 1965). Studies in finance have emphasized mainly the behaviour of analysts and their reliance on their own sources based on a self-attribution bias (Daniel, Hirschleifer & Subrahmanyam, 1998). Additional issues with respect to analysts will be discussed later in Chapter 9.

5.4.6 Hindsight bias and regret management

There is little that mankind would not do to defend and justify their own judgments and confirm their previous views after the fact. Ego attachment, again, is in the driver's seat here. Both in the military and in the financial spheres, one often hears the popular saying that 'generals prepare to fight the last war'. Fitting prior views to subsequent events or 'assigning higher probabilities retrospectively than during the experiment' are the very essence of the *hindsight bias* or *I-knew-it-all-along effect* (Plous, 1993).

According to Fischhoff (1980):

When we receive outcome knowledge, we immediately make sense out of it by integrating it into what we already know about the subject. Having made this reinterpretation, the reported outcome appears a more or less outgrowth of the reinterpreted situation. 'Making sense' out of what we are told about the past is, in turn, so natural that we may be unaware that outcome knowledge has had any effect on us ....
In trying to reconstruct our foresightful state of mind, we will remain anchored in our insightful perspective, leaving the reported outcome too likely looking.

When we look at events in this light, many outcomes do appear 'inevitable' in many respects, including:

■ the speed with which events have happened (Fischer, 1970);

■ a tendency to remember people as having been much more similar to their current selves than was actually the case (Yarrow, Campbell and Burton, 1970);

■ the bias underpinning some kinds of historiography (Barraclough, 1972);

■ the picture of participants in a given historical situation as being aware of the eventual consequences of their decisions (Fischer, 1970);

■ the posterior assessment of some experiments as becoming critical to decide some controversies in research (Lakatos, 1970).

A considerable body of research has used a broad spectrum of experimental techniques, response instructions and different groups to study hindsight biases in various settings. Their existence has been ascertained in elections (Leary, 1982; Synodinos, 1986), medical diagnoses (Arkes, Wortmann, Saville & Harkness, 1981), pregnancy tests (Pennington, Rutter, McKenna & Morley, 1980), buying decisions (Walster, 1967), games (Leary, 1981), assessments of strategic international negotiations (Fischhoff & Beyth, 1975) and other fields.

Hindsight bias is the nemesis common to anybody involved in developing projections and systems to manage future situations. Those traders who rely on technical analysis are classic victims of this tendency. Few match their elation after discovering some 'magic' system. Unfortunately the vicissitude of emotion parallels the subsequent brutal disillusionment that follows. With every failure, the resolute developer grinds out new conditions under which the selected technique or methodology works – this is a common reaction. This then becomes another instance of hindsight bias and is often intertwined with survivorship bias as discussed above. Related to hindsight bias is a substantial body of empirical research which focuses on belief perseverance in the face of empirical challenges. Ross & Anderson (1982) and Nisbett & Ross (1980) offer comprehensive overviews of these studies.

Within financial institutions, the primary area of interest of this book, traders are hardly alone in falling prey to this bias. Past successes are key ingredients of a food chain that serves many clients both inside and outside the organization. Allocating more capital and resources to past winners and withdrawing them from losers is a common practice in strategic planning and budgeting. It takes guts, after all, to argue against these practices which appear to be in keeping with the general belief that markets are unforgiving. However, keeping accurate written records that allow you to explicitly evaluate how past events may have turned out differently are simple acid tests against hindsight bias. A mere list of the reasons for particular outcomes will likely suffer from and reinforce its power.

Hindsight bias is not enough to put up a rearguard action against error. This is also a key feature of *regret*, which involves rethinking previous choices. Very important amongst these are those decisions in which *not* choosing was the preferred option. Research shows that people regret most the things that they did not do (Gilovich & Husted-Medvec, 1993). The intuition is that one can always find some good reason – after the fact – to justify past actions. Regret, and in particular the *fear of regret*, is a key psychological feeling that is very important in the context of risk management. Indeed, some highly respected risk practitioners consider the balancing act between risk and regret as the very essence of risk management (Dembo & Freeman, 1998). Conversely, the conventional quantitative view of risk management often neglects the importance of regret. This is dangerous. Chapter 9 illustrates how the fear of regret relates to the role of a contemporary risk manager.

5.4.7 Knowledge-equal-solution fallacy

Another facet of people's quest for comfort and security is the illusion that knowing and understanding a problem is equivalent to solving it. Many, especially in the professional setting, often fall prey to this kind of bias. This sentiment is further reinforced by ideas or statements such as 'the solution will be implemented', 'they will realize it' (who?) or 'the (Board, Committee, boss or other relevant authority) must approve it'. Unfortunately, knowledge is not synonymous with either action or solution. This fallacy may help explain why some banks, major dealers and investors mentioned in the risk disasters in Chapters 10 and 11 repeated the behavioural and practical mistakes from previous crises. Their awareness of the potential consequences of their flawed internal setup was necessary but by no means sufficient to prevent them from committing the same errors again and again.

5.5 Sequential information-processing bias

Sequential information processing can be considered a subset of selective attention bias, in that people just cut through the maze of relationships between cause and effect and choose to focus their attention on just one (or more) linear relationship(s). Cause and effect is often linked in a network of relationships and often interdependent. Predator–prey relationships in biology are an example of such an interdependent relationship. Simplifying cause/effect relationships is a naturally attractive way of managing complexity and saves time. Scientific research and processes have a natural inclination toward direct cause/effect links.

Networks and their issues have long been studied in the world of information systems. *Metcalfe's Law*, named after Ethernet and 3Com founder Bob Metcalfe, summarizes their importance. Originally designed for computer networks, this law states, using Metcalfe's own words:

> The power of the network increases exponentially by the number of computers connected to it. Therefore, every computer added to the network both uses it as a resource while adding resources in a spiral of increasing value and choice.

That means that the power of networks – expressed in terms of number of relationships, in which each computer has both a transmitting and a receiving relationship – grows as the square of the number of users. Just look at the following table:

TABLE 5.4 ■ Metcalfe's Law and computer networks

Number of users	Number of relationships
2	2
3	9
4	16
5	25

Metcalfe's Law is often associated with the more famous Moore's Law, coined by Intel co-founder Gordon Moore in the mid-1960s with respect to the processing power of micro-processors. Keeping cost constant, according to Moore's Law, such processing power doubles every 18 months.

Unfortunately, life and business are not as simple as one would like them to be. The oversimplification in the analysis that preceded decisions and actions soon becomes evident and unforeseen effects appear. These adverse effects are known as the *law of unintended consequences*. This bias is recurrent in large and complex organizations, as showing results quickly is often welcome and unintended consequences follow actions only with a lag. By that time, the decision-makers responsible for those myopic choices will likely have been promoted or moved to a new responsibility inside or outside the organization.

These problems can be exacerbated by senior decision-makers' frequent tendency to seek comfort in their status, experience and authority. These attributes are indeed often helpful in managing situations. There is a short step between this confidence and believing that problems will be managed just as any other *situation*, regardless of a flawed *process*. The irony is that while Metcalfe's Law provides a very elegant and effective way of summarizing relationships between computers, it also shows the limitations of humans in managing more than a certain number of relationships at a given point in time. Even internet messaging or video-conferencing can mitigate human limitations in managing multiple interconnected relationships only up to a point.

A dramatic example of neglect of such networks of interconnected cause–effect relationships comes from the 1986 disaster that occurred at the nuclear reactor of Chernobyl, in the Ukraine. This textbook case of risk management failure – regrettably with far more painful and irreparable consequences than in financial risk management disasters – is analysed in Chapter 11. For now, it is sufficient to say that these complex relationships were the pillars of the safety process and, eventually, their disregard made the reactor explode. In his insightful book *The Logic of Failure* (1996), Dietrich Dörner comments:

> This tendency to over-steer is characteristic of human interaction with dynamic systems. We let ourselves be guided not by development within the system, that is, by time differentials between sequential stages, but by the situation at each stage. We regulate the *situation*, not the *process*.

5.6 Symptoms of risk disorder syndrome (RDS)

Poor complexity management according to sequential processing often translates into poor preparation to face the unexpected problems that crop up according to the law of unintended consequences. A combination of the biases which have been discussed is likely to manifest in a variety of not terribly effective behaviours, which can be labelled as the 'risk disorder syndrome'. The characteristics of this syndrome come in a broad range of intensities and include:

■ *denial*, in which the importance of the sudden unexpected problem is partially or completely discounted.

■ *rationalization*, which means the development of more complex, conditional heuristics and exceptions for the rule, system, signal, or decision that has given unsatisfactory results. This process often goes under the elegant label of 'calibration' and is a dangerous sign that one's ego is taking over and generating ever more bizarre rules rather than accepting reality and rethinking the whole process. An example would be 'this rule applies only if so-and-so happens and only on odd days'. Technical analysis in trading is notorious for this tendency. Needless to say, the improvements in system accuracy obtained in this way may be dangerously misleading and due to randomness and survivorship bias rather than to the system's own merits. Would you rather have a system that works 60 per cent of the time on 1,000 observations or one that works 90 per cent of the time on 50? Ego will often tilt the choice towards the latter alternative despite its questionable statistical significance. Fischhoff & Slovic (1980) analysed this bias at length:

> The pseudo-power of our explanations can be illustrated by analogy with regression analysis. Given a set of events and a sufficiently large or rich set of explanatory factors, one can always derive postdictions or explanations to any desired degree of tightness. In regression terms, by expanding the set of independent variables one can always find a set of predictors with any desired correlation with the independent variable. The price one pays for over-fitting is, of course, shrinkage, failure of the derived rule to work on a new sample of cases. The frequency and vehemence of methodological warnings against over-fitting suggest that correlational overkill is a bias that is quite resistant to even extended professional training.

- *Fright,* as in a 'Rabbit frozen in the headlights' drama, in which people simply do not know what to do and are terrified to take any further action, fearing further unexpected consequences.

- *Blame anyone but me* or *conspiracy theories,* as in 'I/we have been set up to fail', whereby supposed schemes arranged by someone inside the organization (rival colleague(s) or groups, the relevant boss/management or, simply, 'they') are blamed for the poor results.

If you have suffered or are near those who suffer from any of these risk-defensive mechanisms, then you should contact your nearest local risk-doctor. Unfortunately, joking aside, there are no brand-X professionals to turn to. And the story with biases is far from over. As you interact with others most of the time, you also have to reckon with another set of biases affecting groups. You need to immunize yourself against these, too. If you would like to find out more, turn to the next chapter....

CHAPTER 6

We are not alone: group think, herding and game theory

If you see a snake, just kill it. Don't appoint a committee on snakes.

(Ross Perot, American entrepreneur)

Research indicates that markets are extremely efficient, effective and timely aggregators of dispersed and even hidden information.

(US Defense Department statement announcing a new $8 million online futures trading initiative, in which speculators will be able to bet on the likelihood of terrorist attacks, assassinations and coups. The Times, 30 July 2003 T2)

7±2:

- Conventional economics and finance assume decisions that are selfish and in isolation. But are they?
- Game theory
- Groupthink and group biases
- Game theory and higher-order beliefs in trading and risk management
- Other potholes in rational decision-making

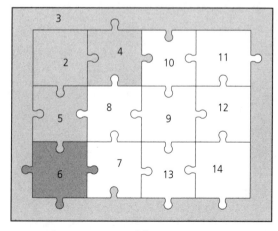

Abstract

The unbiased, selfish individual lies at the cold heart of conventional economics and financial economic theory. However, these theories do not account for the fact that the individuals are by no means alone and are normally influenced by others who are not always rational. While the previous chapters focused mostly on the individual, this chapter looks at the individual within the group context and what influences the group exerts. Today, business decisions and managerial actions are more akin to a team sport, and the existence of the autocrat who has complete power over his or her minions is unlikely in the extreme. Much more likely are individuals who are influenced by the opinions, beliefs, and the real and perceived power of others. Modern game theory and recent research on group decision-making help explain the apparent paradox between individual and group behaviour. A large body of evidence shows how the assumption of individual rationality has to bow to group pressures. To ignore or deny this breakdown and to insist that modern finance theory and its applications hold because of individual rationality is doctrinaire and smacks of priestcraft. It is tantamount to a case of selective attention bias.

Implications: Unless you are planning to live in a cave, there are very few professions today in which you can afford to ignore others' beliefs and biases. This is a major issue in risk management especially under those situations of market turmoil in which risk management discipline ought to become most useful.

6.1 Another challenge to conventional economics and finance

Conventional utility theory is at the heart of many assumptions on individual behaviour that were borrowed by modern finance theory. This chapter starts from a summary of some of the most important features of conventional utility theory. Modern game theory (GT) has provided alternative models of strategic interaction between individuals. Some of the most important are shown in 6.2, with examples being contained in Appendix C. That will prepare the ground for the discussion of group behaviours and biases. Later on, this chapter will turn to the significant body of studies that has applied these GT tools in practice.

6.1.1 Scope of present group discussion

Being a collection of individuals, the term 'group' lends itself to various definitions depending on the context in which the term is used. The purpose of this chapter is not to survey the range of definitions, nor to elaborate on all the possible characteristics. Characteristics of groups often mentioned include communication, interdependence, influence, cohesiveness, shared identity and a sense of belonging.

Our discussion of groups will be restricted to the business context. Formal committees and teams with official titles are by no means the only type of groups encountered in companies and banks. These official groups have their own procedures: what might be called 'rites and rituals'. Informal groups, formed by people who have similar interests, goals or views on a given set of issues, are also the subject of this study. Their relative influence on the decision-making process is great but because of their lack of precise definition, they are hard to deal with. To a considerable extent, this is because their objectives, means and borders will also tend to be difficult to identify.

6.1.2 Utility in theory and practice

Before setting out the framework and results of game theory, by way of contrast it is important to note that modern finance and risk management relies on rational utility as postulated by neo-classical economics theory. 'Utility' here means 'self-interested' – or, plainly, 'selfish motivation' from an individual's perspective. To illustrate this concept, during a meeting with the former chairman of one of the top banks in the world, the author found the conversation moving quite swiftly to the charming but slightly disarming rational – and familiar – question, 'Yes, yes, this is all very interesting. But what's in it for me?'

In practice, utility implies that an individual can independently decide on the most rational course of action that will maximize his own utility. The reality is that there are very few decisions that are made entirely and genuinely independently. Most decisions in business and finance are made by groups and teams rather than by individuals. Group influence aside, behavioural economics has also challenged the concept of rational utility as the essential attribute of individuals *per se* (Gintis, 2000):

▪ Rational decision theory is based on the concept of expected utility, whereby a rational agent (let us call him *homo economicus*) would choose an outcome that would maximize the expected utility of any payoff. In addition, the agent's preferences over a set of lotteries are consistent. This means the alternatives presented have both the property of transitivity (e.g., if A is greater than B and B is greater than C then A is greater than C) and independence of irrelevancies (e.g., where the alternatives are not silly or absurd).

▪ In reality, many choices are not reversible and thus are non-transitive. And an apparently irrational choice from a conventional point of view may not appear irrational simply because of its lack of reversibility. Prospect theory (see Chapter 4) provides many examples of situations where transitivity does not hold (Loomes, 1988; Sucden, 1993).

▪ *Homo economicus*, the term of comparison of rational decision-making, appears quite isolated from his brethren and sisters in reality. Real people appear to make biased probability assessments and suffer from a number of irrational decision preferences, such as representativeness in chosen heuristics, anchoring and loss aversion. (See the long list of studies by Kahneman and Tversky in Chapters 4 and 5.) Contrary to neo-classical claims, subsequent findings from neurological research experiments (Damasio, 1994) confirm that payoff evaluation in the human brain is not independent of the timeframe used. Specifically, long-term decision-making is located in the prefrontal lobes of the brain and is impaired when these areas are damaged. It is likely that our fundamental emotional nature is 'hard-wired' via evolution and is the way in which we respond to our environment.

■ The *homo economicus* model assumes exogenous preferences, that is, the agent's preferences are determined externally and are substantially unaffected by the structure of strategic interaction. In real life, preferences are partly endogenous, depending on the agent's personal history, the nature of the strategic interaction in which he is engaged and the type of frame that he chooses to employ in the interaction based on a set of subjective payoffs.

6.1.3 Other issues affecting group rationality in theory and practice

Major differences exist between group thinking processes and those adopted by individuals. Group conclusions may appear irrational to the individual and vice versa. This conundrum is captured many times in ancient history. Consider the story told by Gigerenzer & Selten (2001):

> Around 250 BC, King Ptolemy decided to translate some biblical writings into Greek. The king asked the high priest of Judea to help. The priest selected seventy scholars, sent them to Alexandria, put each in a separate room, and asked each to do his translation independently. When the job was done, a committee that examined the seventy translations found that they were identical. Word spread and everyone was astonished. But when an old Rabbi heard what happened, he said, 'Seventy scholars in separate rooms, and this you call a miracle? Put them in one room and get the same translation – *this* is a miracle.'

Groupthink, however, is not a miracle but very much a natural phenomenon. The term was coined to denote 'a strong concurrence-seeking tendency that interferes with effective group decision-making' (Forsyth, 1999). This term also means 'a mode of thinking that people engage in when they are deeply involved in a cohesive in-group and their strivings for unanimity override their motivation to realistically appraise alternative course of actions' (Janis, 1982).

This condition is supported by a number of case studies and empirical evidence (Forsyth, 1999). These have found a negative correlation between groupthink and the number of disagreements in a group. Leadership style in the group also plays a significant role in generating groupthink (Chen, Lawson, Gordon & McIntosh, 1996; Flowers, 1977; Hodson & Sorrentino, 1997; Moorhead, 1982). Other evidence, however, found that directive leaders could improve the effectiveness in their group decisions when they limited their control to the group decision-making processes instead of the decisions results (Peterson, 1997).

Compared with individual decision-making, groups usually have superior information and can process it in greater amounts. Their ability to curb the biases of their members is a very important function, too. In reaching their decisions, however, the group faces some major obstacles in matching the rationality that conventional economics would expect in a self-interested individual:

■ Unanimity is the exception rather than the rule in groups. If unanimity occurs too often, one should question whether the group (or some members thereof) is performing any genuinely useful function. Group decisions, almost by definition, require compromises.

- While group members may enjoy an informational advantage over individuals, they often have inaccurate and incomplete information *concerning each other*. They may not understand what kind of sanctions or reprisals the group may inflict on dissenting group members, or they may not know what ability an individual has to inflict these kinds of penalties.

- This interaction between members of a group is by no means stable and, as such, often affects the whole decision-making process and, consequently, the quality of the outcomes.

Studies in modern game theory focus on these issues of group conflict. Game theory also examines the strategic alternatives to decisions and the consequences on the behaviour of those members of the group who may influence the outcome. Group decisions will consist of individual biases. In addition, groups will also operate with a set of psychological values all their own.

6.2 Game theory and instability in strategic interaction

From Adam Smith to the more recent developments in the standard theory of economic behaviour of von Neumann & Morgenstern (1947), economics had been unanimous in assuming that everyone tended to maximize his or her own utility irrespective of the influence of others. Shortly after World War II, John Nash, a young mathematician at Princeton University, proposed an alternative explanation. According to the legend, summarized in the film *A Beautiful Mind*,[36] Nash had his intuition from observing the way in which several   colleagues were all courting the most attractive blonde girl. Then, one's utility would be maximized by taking these preferences of others into account. Accordingly, one would then look for another girl, probably the second most beautiful. The principle would then have universal application to many spheres of diplomacy[37] and economics. As will be shown later on in this chapter and in the discussion of risk disasters in Chapters 10 and 11, financial markets do not escape GT either.

Game theory has introduced a wealth of alternative models of strategic interaction. These are some of the most important amongst them:

- *the Nash equilibrium*, which shows the conditions under which a stalemate can occur in an interaction, without any of the players being able to alter the situation to his or her own advantage;

- *the prisoners' dilemma*, whereby two players have to decide whether or not to co-operate with each other;

- *the winners' curse*, which refers to bidders' tendency to overpay in an auction to get what they want.

---

[36] Incidentally, the film provides examples of other behavioural patterns, such as seeing trends where there are none. This is the case with the professor's illusion of a mysterious secret code created by a foreign superpower.
[37] The interaction between the nuclear arsenals of the USA and the USSR in the 1970s and early 1980s would be an application. MAD, or Mutually Assured Destruction, became the catchphrase to summarize each super-power's ability to destroy the other even after suffering a first strike by the other, making the final outcome of a nuclear war a largely moot point. Under such a terrifying scenario, the mutual fear of a nuclear holocaust would be sufficient to prevent a first nuclear strike and the resulting global conflict.

The detailed account of these and other models is beyond the objective of the present book but it is nevertheless very interesting. Appendix C gives a series of examples of these GT models.

6.3 Group risk biases and consequences

6.3.1 Major group biases

The unstable and occasional interaction that occurs amongst members is not the only challenge for groups. In addition to their individual biases (see Chapters 4 and 5), members of groups suffer from a number of collective psychological biases. A substantial body of academic literature and empirical evidence is available. Important studies include Janis (1972, 1982, 1983, 1985, 1989), Janis & Mann (1977), Longley & Pruitt (1980), Wheeler & Janis (1980). The key group biases include:

- *Interpersonal pressure* Groups are notorious for pushing their members to reach a consensus no matter what and bringing dissenting members into line (Forsyth, 1999). The means to align dissenters range from moral suasion to ridicule and, in more extreme cases, threats, intimidation and physical violence.

- *Self-censorship* This occurs when individual members curb their own opinions and express them too timidly (if at all) to impact the group decision in any meaningful way. This often generates apparent unanimity even though several members may not really support the group consensus. Group members who withhold opinions may be executing a deliberate strategy of political correctness to preserve their reputation (see Appendix C). The recollections of the decisions that ultimately led to the Bay of Pigs fiasco (Schlesinger, 1965; Janis, 1972) make an excellent case in point.

  > In the months after the Bay of Pigs, I bitterly reproached myself for having kept so silent during those crucial discussions in the Cabinet Room, though my feelings of guilt were tempered by the knowledge that a course of objection would have accomplished little save to gain me a name as a nuisance. I can only explain my failure to do more than raise a few timid questions by reporting that one's impulse to blow the whistle on this nonsense was simply undone by the circumstances of the discussion ... It was a curious atmosphere of assumed consensus ...

In the same case study, Janis (1972) added:

  > The group members played up areas of convergence in their thinking, at the expense of fully exploring divergences that might disrupt the apparent unity of the group. Apparently, the members felt that it would be better to share a pleasant, balmy group atmosphere than be battered in a storm.

- *Self-preservation bias* This is displayed in several behaviours which, to some extent, mask some form of overconfidence and include:

- *Group cognitive resonance*, whereby an opinion, incoming evidence or other pieces of information gain strength if they match the preconceived opinion that the group is forming sub-consciously. If, for instance, the group has a negative opinion of an individual, it will tend to weigh negative information about that person more heavily than positive information. Cognitive resonance is recurrent in groups forming the *status quo* bias.

- *Strength in numbers and herd behaviours*, whereby the conviction of group members strengthens as other members join that opinion. The size of the environment in which one finds him- or herself is often associated with safety and with the ability to avoid or resist some unfortunate event. This applies regardless of whether we are dealing with a large car, ship, plane or group.

- *'Can't happen here, not-me' bias:* the distinction between this and the previous one is that it focuses on 'Why me exactly?' when someone is surrounded by a group of peers. Being part of a group makes the odds of being hit look remote or very small. This situation leads to an over-optimistic assessment of the probability of one *avoiding* some adverse event – even though other group members will suffer. This is a variation of the lotto or small number bias described in Chapter 5, except that it is specifically triggered by the presence of a group. Consider the example of a trip in a large bus during the summer. With this bias, one might think: 'With all the cars and buses on the highway, why should an accident involve just my bus?' In the description of the previous bias, one might have thought: 'This bus is so large that it is virtually impossible to get hurt if an accident happened.' History provides us with many instances of this 'not-me' bias. For example:

  > During World War II, as part of the Invasion of Normandy, the Allies organized a major launch of paratroopers. 70 per cent of these thought they would not be amongst the casualties. Unfortunately, only 20 per cent of them actually survived.

- *Mutual reinforcement leading to delusions about the performance, competence and expertise of members.* A panel of 'experts' will more often praise and leverage the qualifications of its members than challenge them. Over-optimistic performance self-assessments are also called 'illusion of invulnerability' (Silver & Bufanio, 1996). One of these instances led to the Chernobyl nuclear disaster in 1986 in the Ukraine, one of the most spectacular risk disasters discussed in Chapter 11. In the words of Dietrich Dörner (1999):

  > The Ukrainian reactor operators were an experienced team of highly respected experts who had just won an award for keeping their reaction on the grid for long periods of uninterrupted service. The great self-confidence of this team was doubtless a contributing factor in the accident. They were no longer operating the reactor analytically but rather 'intuitively'. They

thought they knew what they were dealing with, and they probably also thought themselves beyond the 'ridiculous' safety rules devised for tyro reactor operators, not for a team of experienced professionals.

■ *Selective attention biases* Here, the subject of a group selects more or less consciously the information to be used. This is similar to cognitive resonance discussed above. A subset of these biases, labelled *mindguards* (Janis, 1982), involves the deliberate attempt to filter incoming information. In this subset, we would have so-called group vigilantes screening incoming information to 'protect' group members from the 'offensive' or 'incorrect' information. Groups that censor certain newspapers or information channels due to their differing ideological or political opinions are examples of this bias. Another excerpt from World War II, in the memoirs of German Field Marshal Erich von Manstein (1995), illustrates this tendency:

> The saying about bad news travelling fast seldom applies in the military sphere. Whenever things are going well, news usually finds its way back quickly enough. If, on the other hand, the attack gets stuck, a blanket of silence descends on the front, either because communications have been cut or because those concerned prefer to hang on till they have something more encouraging to report.

■ *Illusions of morality* This tendency shows a group explaining a given decision or action on some moral, justicial or patriotic grounds. The American decision to invade Cuba at the Bay of Pigs to end Castro's regime was justified with such arguments. Tetlock (1979) studied similar instances and found these explanations common amongst politicians, particularly those who fail. And of course groups that are normally procedurally conservative will be swayed by avowals of higher morality by authoritarians even when evidence of immediate threats is controversial. With hindsight, one can then reconstruct reality and use so-called 'moral reasons' to argue that there was no alternative to some failed choice.

■ *Biased perceptions of the environment* As a result of prejudices that may be more or less conscious, groups are prone to develop a distorted view of the situation. Again, during World War II, it is well known that ideological and other reasons led Germany to seriously – and repeatedly – underestimate the strength of the Soviet army.

These biases should not be viewed in isolation but taken together, considered in terms of their combined effect, which is self-reinforcing. For example, self-preservation biases often generate misleading impressions of the outside environment and are further reinforced by selective attention biases to filter out conflicting information. Disconfirming information from other group members is also rapidly discounted. You generally respect the opinion of your group peers and – especially in professional firms – believe that it is almost impossible that all these 'experts' can be wrong at the same time. The word 'almost', in turn, betrays a small number bias. A number of these biases that affect financial professionals are considered in the next section.

6.3.2 Risk consequences

If you are working in finance or trading, you probably see a number of parallels between the biases we have enumerated and your own experience. Indeed, group biases practically pop out at you everywhere in real life. Here are a few thumbnail sketches that you might recognize:

- *Hiring based on compliance with tribal instincts* This is the situation whereby job applicants are screened mainly for their expected compliance with the common wisdom of the group – including, of course, their would-be boss. Cognitive resonance and some self-preservation biases are in action here. The consequences may become particularly dangerous when candidates are hired in a trading team, as their compliant psychological set-up may lead them to assume the same position in response to a given event. These traders also become exposed to a herd behaviour trap when seeing their own opinions widely supported by their peers. The reasons they give to explain their positions become utterly irrelevant.

- *'Socialization' of risk* Risk committees are notoriously exposed to this type of risk. The risk is 'socialized' in the sense that some members of the group assume part or all of the risk on their own shoulders without doing anything objective about the risk itself. Contributing biases are cognitive resonance, some herd behaviour and some self-delusion about the competence of the committee. In general, the knowledge that other 'senior', 'competent' and 'experienced' committee members support a particular decision makes other members feel safer. This situation often occurs with decisions about fairly opaque risks and situations that require committing the bank's risk capital to some illiquid exposure for a long period of time. Credit and IT committees, or groups that decide the involvement in illiquid products for commercial reasons, are cases in point. If the decision results in a mistake, these attributes of committee members can be conveniently used as a justification. 'All of Messrs. X, Y and Z were fully behind that decision.' 'Software package X is the most widespread in the market, what would you have expected us to do?' Does this sound familiar?

- *Herd behaviour in risk and investment decisions* This is so remarkably frequent in financial markets that it has deserved the attention of a major body of academic literature and several empirical studies (see 6.4.3 and 6.4.4 below).

- *Selective attention biases* of various kinds, including:
  - Ask questions only after losses, rather than after gains. In trading as in war, reversals of fortune have repeatedly shown the dangers of the mindset: 'if it is not broke, don't fix it'. Readers who have worked in banks will probably find no shortage of such instances in their experience. Game theory provides ample evidence of this bias as well. For the sake of preserving political correctness, asking awkward questions in what otherwise appears to be favourable conditions can hurt one's reputation. Avoiding the question and the issue is then the path of least resistance.

- Group reframing This involves using one set of metrics to evaluate a decision and switching to another in 'mid-flight' to view it more favourably, especially after deterioration has occurred. Trades or credit evaluations carried out on a stand-alone basis are then followed by a re-frame into different performance metrics or criteria after they evolve unfavourably. The sentence 'but our competitors are losing even more than us' is one frequently heard in banks too for loans that have deteriorated after they were approved based on their stand-alone merits.

- Haphazard organizational setup to manage risk and safety issues All the manuals, books and training on risk management that are available may deceive one into believing that the surrounding organizational framework is fairly consistent across organizations. Far from it! Table 6.1 shows the decisive impact of culture in handling safety- and risk-related information. You can figure out the consequences by yourself.

TABLE 6.1 ■ How different organizational cultures handle safety information

	Pathological culture	Bureaucratic culture	Generative culture
Leaders…	don't want to know	may not find out	actively seek it
Messengers (whistleblowers) …	are 'shot'	are listened to if they arrive	are trained and rewarded
Responsibility is …	shirked	compartmentalized	shared
Failure …	is punished or concealed	leads to local repairs	leads to far-reaching reforms
New ideas…	are actively encouraged	present problems	are welcomed

6.4 Group and game theory experiments and empirical studies

Game theory and behaviour psychology have given us a more realistic view of how group behaviour operates in real life. Let's see how their ideas work in practice. The following show some concrete examples of how behavioural and game theoretic principles relate to our common accepted assumptions of the financial markets.

■ The assumption of independent decision-making that underpins modern risk management models holds only under normal orderly market conditions. Outside of these, however, the effect of human interactions and reciprocal expectations make these assumptions precarious. The next section illustrates this point with the example of the 1997 speculative attack against the Thai baht, an emerging-market currency.

■ Paired with the point above, herding behaviours, informational cascades and higher-order beliefs have played major roles in financial panics such as those witnessed in the second half of the 1990s.

■ Modern financial institutions suffer significant agency problems which are compounded by the tendency to justify decisions based on the 'winner's curse'. This tendency is most evident and has been uncovered in studies on lending decisions and auctions of Treasury securities.

■ No internal process for allocating capital and resources can match the efficiency of external capital markets. Power, influence and voting behaviour by internal group members all contribute to divergences from the efficiency espoused by modern financial theory. Many times the propaganda trotted out in the name of 'diversification' is merely a cognitive illusion, frequently quoted as the key advantage of multi-product or multi-divisional firms. The implication is that mechanisms that align internal performance metrics with outside ones, such as mark-to-market or benchmarking, should be pursued vigorously.

■ Last, the existence of behaviours consistent with game theory principles may be more hard-wired in our genes than the product of progress and education. That's the finding of an important body of research comparing pre-industrial and advanced societies discussed at the end of this chapter.

6.4.1 Risk management, game theory and higher-order beliefs

For the purposes of this book, a particularly rich seam of studies applying game theoretic methodologies to risk management and financial panics deserves special mention. The financial crises in question include the Asian crisis of 1997, the default of Russia and the debacle of long-term capital management in the summer of 1998 and the subsequent collapse of the dollar exchange rate against the yen during the following October. Morris & Shin (1997, 1998b, 1999) analyse these situations and the key assumptions used in risk management and regulatory actions which led to such adverse results. These studies[38] hold a few key conclusions:

6.4.1.1 The roulette view of modern risk management

Modern risk management systems and methodologies rely on a 'roulette wheel' view of market uncertainty as a basis for modelling market risk. According to this assumption, the actions of other market participants have no impact on the outcome, much like the behaviour of other gamblers has no effect on the spinning of the wheel. The uncertainty ruling price movements is assumed to be exogenous and independent of the actions of other decision-makers, because, as in conventional economics, the decision is assumed to be a single-person decision problem commonly referred to as a 'game against nature'. While reasonable in normal market conditions, these assumptions break down in turbulent situations. As short-term price changes depend on what others do, so do a trader's or an institution's decisions.

---

[38] The author would like to thank professors Stephen Morris (University of Pennsylvania) and Hyun Song Shin (London School of Economics) for the kind permission to draw on their thorough research on risk management with interdependence and higher-order beliefs.

This is a classic example of strategic uncertainty in the game theory sense. Staying with the gambling games analogy, one should view poker as a far more fitting metaphor, since one's decisions take into account the moves of other players at the table to a far greater extent. The instances of the demise of LTCM and their sometimes semi-incestuous interaction with major dealers and market-makers in the summer of 1998 is an excellent case in point. The disregard of game theoretic principles is further magnified in instances in which large leverage is employed by the portfolios of some participants. By the way, three key requirements of market efficiency are being simultaneously violated in these turbulent situations:

- the rationality of investors
- where they are not rational, their trades cancel themselves out, and
- the ability of rational arbitrageurs to correct mis-pricings.

6.4.1.2 Coupled illusions destroy liquidity

As a corollary of the previous point, many institutions entered the period of turbulence with very similar trading positions. This can occur if the prevailing conventional wisdom deems certain trades as being the most profitable and commonly available information supports this view. Cognitive assonance, previously discussed for individuals, and herd instinct, analysed in the following section, are all in action in these instances. The consequences of this thought process, however, manifested themselves when many institutions, in the process of unwinding their trades, encountered similar attempts by others. This, in turn, exacerbated price movements. Liquidity dried up even in the most widely traded instruments, such as the US dollar/Japanese yen spot foreign exchange market.

6.4.1.3 Total transparency beware

Transparency, while often invoked as a way to prevent or at least limit damages in the next instance of market turmoil, is not a panacea in and on its own and must be used wisely. Too much transparency at the wrong time can often do a lot of damage as too little too late. That's where smart regulation is required. A case in which this fair-but-not-total disclosure philosophy has recently been embraced is provided by risk management disclosure discussions at the IAFE, a hedge fund and institutional investor think-tank.

6.4.1.4 Noise 1, Information 0

The irony for market participants is that whilst they have access to a large mass of information concerning economic fundamentals, the disparities and differences in the information are relatively small between participants. Arguably, only some major dealers and market-makers are assumed to enjoy a marginal informational advantage over the domestic players, thanks to their supposedly superior information on global investor flows. To the extent that other major players also have this information and undertake virtually identical actions based on them, this advantage becomes minimal.

6.4.1.5 A convenient forgetfulness of history

Herd instinct and cognitive resonance were not the only biases displayed in these situations. As in other crises, they were joined by an utter disregard for recent history lessons. One was to neglect the strategic effects in risk management that occurred during the 1987 stock market crash. The Brady Commission Report (1988) attributed the magnitude and swiftness of the price decline to practices such as portfolio insurance and dynamic hedging techniques. As is common in option replication techniques, a dealer typically sells an asset when its price falls and buys it when the price rises. Best estimates at the time suggested that around $100 billion in funds were following formal portfolio insurance programmes, representing around 3 per cent of the pre-crash market value. However, this is almost certainly an underestimate of total selling pressure arising from informal hedging techniques such as stop-loss orders (Shiller, 1987).

An analysis of the most dramatic event of the Asian crisis, the removal of the Thai baht currency peg, also provides insights into the strategic interaction between speculators and monetary authorities. Ironically, many of the banks that suffered large losses in the turmoil of 1998 had profited handsomely on the baht a year earlier.

The costs of defending a currency peg are by now well known. They include depressing the domestic economy with a very restrictive monetary policy and high interest rates. This forces more bankruptcies, higher unemployment, social unrest and enhances the risks of classic bank runs by depositors. By increasing domestic interest rates, however, the monetary authority can inflict some pain on the speculators, too, since their costs of borrowing the domestic currency to sell it short against a strong currency – typically the US dollar – will also rise. The local monetary authority is confronted with various private actors, whose interests are affected by the actions of the other members of the group and by the monetary authority itself. The players are domestic corporations, banks and their depositors, foreign creditor banks and outright speculators, which are typically hedge funds or proprietary trading desks of investment banks. In the analysis of the various actions available, the study underscores two aspects of the interactions:

- Each actor faced a choice between actions which exacerbated the pain of maintaining the peg and actions which were more benign.

- The more frequent the actions which increased the pain of holding the peg, the greater the incentive for an individual actor to adopt the action which increased the pain. In other words, the actions which tended to undermine the currency peg were mutually reinforcing. The intuition was that, as the costs to the local economy become nearly unbearable, more actors are enticed to 'go for the jugular', and as they press harder, they see the rewards of their speculative actions apparently getting closer.

In the Thai baht case, domestic corporations with unhedged US dollar liabilities could either cover their positions or not. The step to achieve this – selling baht to buy US dollars in forward contracts – mirrors the mechanics of the trades undertaken by hedge funds and other players who were speculating against the baht. Domestic banks and finance houses which facilitated such dollar loans to domestic firms were faced with exactly the same decision as the other domestic companies, i.e. to hedge or not hedge. As more players decided to sell the Baht, the pain of maintaining the peg increased and the likelihood of its abandonment soared. This made speculation against the baht even more attractive. In game theory jargon, these actions – the speculation against the baht and the increased cost of maintaining the peg – are described as *mutually reinforcing*.

Other strategic effects were also occurring. Other domestic companies and banks – even without unhedged US dollar liabilities – were going to suffer from the recessionary pressures on the local economy caused by higher interest rates. Coupled with higher unemployment, this would soon take a toll on individual consumer and depositor confidence and runs to withdraw deposits from banks would soon follow. Both domestic and foreign banks also cut credit lines in response to the deteriorating situation. The following table summarises the series of actions that the various players would have been most likely to take.

TABLE 6.2 ■ The various actors' behaviours and the Thai baht peg

Actor	Action(s) undermining peg
Speculators	Short sell baht
Domestic firms	Sell baht for hedging purposes
Domestic banks	Sell baht for hedging purposes. Reduce credit to domestic firms
Foreign banks	Refuse to roll over debt
Depositors	Withdraw deposits

The most striking feature is that all these actions increase the cost of maintaining the currency peg regardless of the actors' various motives.

Mutually reinforcing interactions are sometimes called 'price cascades' – a lock-step interaction between traders' beliefs and the assumptions made by risk management. For example, traders' beliefs and the risk assumptions may agree that the returns on the products or securities that they trade follow a normal distribution. This was a key theme examined in a paper by Osler (2002). This empirical study used different samples of data between January 1996 and April 2000 to analyse the behaviour of foreign-exchange markets in response to dealers' stop-loss and take-profit orders. Consistent with the evidence from the 1987 stock market crash, its main conclusion is that stop-loss orders generate positive feedback trading and are likely to originate price discontinuities and price cascades. These cascades may play a major role in explaining the well-known 'fat-tails' in the distribution of exchange-rate returns. It adds that:

■ exchange rate trends are unusually rapid when rates reach levels near which stop-loss orders are likely to cluster, typically round numbers;

- the response to stop-loss orders is larger than the response to take-profit orders and more likely to cause feedback trading;

- the response to stop-loss orders lasts longer than the response to take-profit orders;

- most results are statistically significant for hours, although not for days.

For those concerned with systemic risk, there is a basic dilemma. Either markets rely crucially on a decentralized structure of players who are supposed to make critical investment decisions in isolation from each other, or the assumption of independence in their decisions collapses in the face of turmoil.

A considerable body of academic literature has explored various applications of higher-order beliefs. While their account is beyond the purposes of a risk management book, let me summarize a few important streams:

- *Information cascades leading to financial panics* Bikhchandani & Sharma (2000) and Chari & Kehoe (2000) provide a comprehensive review of the related literature. Conventional wisdom in financial markets holds that participants are concerned not just about fundamentals, but also about what others believe about fundamentals, what others believe about others' beliefs, and so on. One major weakness of the informational cascade argument is that it relies on data that is too coarse to reveal private information (see Lee, 1993).

- *Financial intermediation and bank runs by depositors* Diamond & Dybvig's (1983) model provides one example which illustrates how higher order beliefs about fundamentals determine outcomes.

- *Securities underwriting* Abel & Mailath (1994) examine the case of investors who underwrite securities while knowing that the overall return to all investors is negative.

- *Information tides driving market movements* Kraus & Smith (1989) describe a model where the arrival of information about others' information (not new information about fundamentals) drives the market. Kraus & Smith (1998) consider a model where multiple self-fulfilling equilibria arise because of uncertainty about other investors' beliefs.

- *IPO decisions* (Welch, 1992), which attempt to factor in other investors' information and decisions.

- *Other GT applications* to solve a variety of problems for which conventional MFT has not offered convincing explanations (Allen & Morris, 1998). Dividend policy and a variety of signalling behaviours by managers whose firm is a takeover target are points in case.

Herd behaviours and financial panics are often used as a convenient argument for recurrent calls for higher regulations and punitive tax treatments. Let's face it, the notion of 'speculator' is an easy target for cheap shots by politicians and the press. Wiser policymakers, however, know that the alignment of corporate incentives with other subsidies, such as taxes, stiffer regulatory charges or regulations, would be unlikely to lead to smoother functioning of these markets. Rather, such an alignment of corporate incentives would be far more likely to result in markets moving further away from efficiency by providing, ironically, additional arbitrage opportunities (Heaton & Lo, 1995). More permissive jurisdictions together with clever product structuring would provide the means to do so.

Contrary to what public opinion and politicians ask for, there is no easy 'pragmatic' solution here. The catch-all Holy Grail of timing a perfect exit from dangerous markets simply does not exist. Even if such tools existed, this section demonstrates how volatility would be exacerbated by the supposed speed with which several smart institutions would use these tools. The robustness in a financial institution's overall risk management process (such as who approves and who uses the limits, what questions are asked and what scenarios are made for these rare instances) is a necessary and desirable, but not sufficient, condition to avert disaster.

6.4.2 The winner's curse and game theory in lending and Treasury auctions

The winner's curse finds application in the banking industry, most notably in lending, where rejected loan applicants may apply and are welcomed by unwary banks. Contrary to the improvident intuitions of marketing or strategic planning departments, it is usually the case that bad news of losses and underperformance follows the good news of winning market share in a region or new market.

In the case of lending, if credit screening is not well synchronized across all banks, it is likely that poorer credit risks will be misidentified as good risks as the number of banks servicing a region, market or product segment increases. An adverse selection problem raises its ugly head. Credits that are good will soon do business with willing banks. Second-tier banks may be visited by an applicant pool that has already been skimmed of the best credits, so the average quality of the applicants will decrease. This problem is especially acute for new banks in a given region, community, or product segment, for they are most likely to vie most aggressively for market share. Broecker (1990) and Nakamura (1993) provide a detailed account of this theory.

An empirical study by Shaffer (1997) targeted adverse selection by banks and the performance of new entrants in the US during the period 1986–1995. Savings and loans (S&L) associations were not included in the study. Macroeconomic effects and economic growth resulting from lending policies and increased competition amongst banks in a given geographical area were also addressed.

The study confirmed the atypical distribution of loan losses during the first five years of existence of a new entrant in a given market. Such losses were found to be significantly below average during the first year and about average during the second. The average charge-off rate was then roughly double that of mature banks in years three to six and still about 40–50 per cent above mature banks in years seven to nine. The difference between losses of mature banks and those of new entrants became small only in the tenth year of the new entrants' activity. Broadly similar conclusions were reached for recovery rates, namely, that new entrants faced lower recoveries on their defaulting loans than mature banks.

As for the effects on the local economy, local economic growth is found to benefit from an unconcentrated local banking structure. This could, by implication, benefit from policies that discourage local structural consolidation.

Another empirical study by DeYoung & Hasan (1997) confirmed Shaffer's results, in particular the lower profitability (relative to mature peers) of new banks in their first nine years of operation.

International lending and adverse selection problems – specifically with respect to third-world countries and interaction between these and supranational lending institutions – have been another key area of the application of game theory principles in banking. The opacity of information on small- and medium-sized third-world companies is the very reason that makes domestic banking systems so important. In principle, a local domestic player should enjoy superior information about the state of a prospective borrower. Readers interested in issues of moral hazard and proposals for game theoretic applications to address informational asymmetries are referred to Bieta & Gelbhaar (1998).

The winner's curse also applies to Treasury bill auctions and, in general, to situations involving bidding behaviour. This theme is explored by a few studies in the US (Umlauf, 1990; Cammack, 1991; Bikhchandani & Huang, 1993; Simon, 1994) and in Sweden (Hedborg, 1997). These studies investigated whether the bidders were able to adjust their bids to the auction rules and conditions to avoid overbidding. Evidence against this thesis was found in the United States by Cammack (1991), as the mean auction price for the three-month Treasury bills studied over the 1973–84 period was on average *lower* than the post-auction secondary market price on auction day. These studies, however, did not incorporate the pre-auction market and as such were not able to analyse the adjustments in the participants' behaviours and their strategy before the auction. The conclusions, however, were broadly in line with other empirical evidence in the US. Conversely, evidence of some small inefficiency – and overbidding – was found in Sweden. In a study of six-month Treasury bills between 1991 and 1994, the auction price was found to be two basis points (or 0.02 per cent of the Treasury bill face value) above the post-auction secondary market price. This mark-up above the post-auction price was halved when the pre-auction price was used instead of the auction price. Some better-informed bidders – typically the professional dealers – were trading strategically to exploit the information advantage arising from their position.

6.4.3 Influence and inefficiency in internal capital markets

Game theory and group interactions have made a significant impact on the *homo economicus* model of the rational decision-maker. They have also had an important impact on how we view external and internal capital markets. The former is supposed to provide a well-functioning arbitrage activity to enforce its efficiency. Indeed, this is a major principle of modern finance and EMH. This book focuses on the internal risk capital allocation performed by risk management.

In the external capital markets, one often expects valuation by extern
a financial institution, examples of this process can be found in the mark[et] [count]erparts. For
ation of its portfolio of securities and derivative contracts. Ultimately, this[?] and valu-
the publicized value created by the agreement of many stock market invest leads to
holders. In practice, unfortunately, very few institutions can match such bond-
transparency and objectivity in their internal processes. In the following para[g]ree of
term 'internal capital markets' is used to describe the sequence of infor[ma]tion th[is], the
and the management decisions that are taken in the internal capital allocation process[?]

A very informative empirical study by Wulf (2000) used Compustat Segment™ da
assess the significance of divisional managers' influence activities in the behaviour of th
firms. The practices analysed in this sample are relevant and material to financial institutions, as the ultimate capital budgeting and allocation questions are the same: namely, how
much capital to allocate, what is its cost and what expected return is projected.

Not surprisingly, the survey results show that models of influence activities that lead to signal
and information distortion may have considerable value in predicting capital allocation decisions
of multi-divisional firms. Divisional managers are found to engage in costly influence activities to
distort private information about relative investment opportunities and skew capital budgets in
their favour. In response, corporate headquarters may offer *ex ante* investment contracts that
alter the sensitivity of investment to private signals (possibly distorted) and public signals (not
distorted, but noisy) relative to first-best. In other words, headquarters may offer rather vague
information which displaces or reduces blame on them for recommendations which turn sour.
They tend to issue information which gives them a way out, a formal sense of 'deniability'.

According to Wulf's paper, while headquarters place less weight on subjective, dis-
tortable information (e.g. managerial recommendations), the data used are objective but
noisy (e.g. historical accounting profits). Further, it adds that the relative importance of managerial recommendations versus accounting profits in the decision depends on the ability of
managers to distort information, the private cost of doing so, and the quality of the accounting measures. Finally, some preliminary evidence in the survey is consistent with influence
activities that lead to investment distortions in internal capital markets – i.e. a 'V-shaped' relationship is found to exist between investment sensitivity to profits in small divisions and the
firm characteristics representing the ability of managers to distort information.

These results suggest that while firms do not explicitly design investment contracts to
mitigate managerial incentives to engage in influence activities, they appear to allocate capital *ex post* based on distorted information leading to inefficient allocations across divisions.
Other substantial empirical evidence confirms Wulf's conclusions on the importance of
influence activities in the allocation of capital across divisions. Notable amongst these are
Scharfstein & Stein (1996), Shin & Stulz (1997) and Scharfstein (1998). With the benefit of
hindsight, several patterns found by the survey appear prescient when compared to the subsequent debates on the reliability of financial statements following the recent Enron and
Worldcom debacles in the US. Influence is – by definition – not an easily measurable activity
and is not the highest contributor to internal efficiency.

by Gillette, Noe & Rebello (2001) on the composition and voting behaviour of boards in the US have examined conflicts of interest between privately informed insiders. These are typically board members and owners. Their results show that trustworthy 'watchdog' outsiders would be able to implement institutionally uninformed outcomes more effectively than board insiders. Penalties are possibly the only preferred means of managing dissension among board members. Nevertheless, they show effect on the experimental outcomes. This is consistent with the experimental findings in Appendix C on the effectiveness of penalties as a means of enforcing cooperation.

In practice, this situation is sufficiently realistic, as independent outside directors are becoming increasingly important in corporate boards in the US (Report on US National Association of Corporate Directors on Director Professionalism 1996) and in the UK (Review of the Role and Effectiveness of non-executive directors, January 2003). Conversely, the empirical evidence on the correlation between return on equity and out-side directors' activity is mixed (Hermalin & Wiesbach, 1991; Yermack, 1996). In the experiment, outsiders do not know which projects are expected to be value-creating and which value-destroying. It is noteworthy, however, that outsiders are a necessary but not sufficient condition to implement shareholder-friendly outcomes. Insiders may indeed form coalitions to out-vote outsiders.

One may then wonder why multi-divisional firms should exist at all if investment inef-ficiencies are prevalent. Possible explanations that are often used come under the convenient labels of 'synergy' or 'diversification'. Indeed, you will see in the next chapter how piling up aggregate data provides the comfortable cognitive illusion of stability. Intuitively, if the performances of two divisions or product areas are negatively correlated with each other, combining their results should show stable figures.

This does not, however, agree with the empirical evidence. Buzzell, Gale & Sultan (1981) show that return on investment follows a V-shaped pattern across single- and multi-divi-sional firms. One interpretation is that single-product firms compete mainly on flexibility and product technology, whereas large multi-divisional companies compete as low-cost pro-ducers. Companies that find themselves stuck in the middle ground enjoy neither advantage. Buzzell (1983) also confirmed these broad conclusions with respect to the degree of vertical integration. Financial institutions are not exempt from the cognitive illu-sion of diversification. The next chapter will show examples of the psychological issues of perceived diversification arising from combination of activities.

In addition, consider how diversified conglomerates trade at a discount relative to a port-folio of comparable stand-alone firms (Berger & Ofek, 1995). This diversification discount is confirmed by Rajan, Servaes & Zingales (1998). Large firms also have difficulty in creating a desirable 'entrepreneurial climate' and are generally less successful than small firms in developing new products and businesses (Acs & Audretsch, 1988). These findings may help explain the tendency in the late 1990s for conglomerates to establish divisions in separate, self-sufficient subsidiaries or spin them out by listing them on the stock market or in a trade sell. Commercial and investment banks' recent bias towards spinning off and outsourcing certain activities (such as proprietary trading desks turning into separately capitalized hedge funds) are moves in the same direction.

6.4.4 Culture and strategic interactions

Problems with the *homo economicus* model are not just theoretical. Empirical evidence shows these issues appear consistently across the world. Possibly because mankind's genetic structure has not changed that much from our ancestors, it appears that game-theoretic principles can be found with remarkable consistency in both pre-industrial and advanced societies around the world. Simply put, do we have any clue at all about what, if any, is the genetic basis for the various forms of strategic interactions discussed above?

Researchers have tried to answer this question with experiments in both electronically advanced and non-industrial societies. At a very general level, we can say that culture has some impact on the experimental outcomes in various societies. But even more important, the results show that the canonical model of the self-interested, material payoff-maximizing actor is almost always proved wrong (that is, *homo economicus* is systematically violated, as exchanges appear to be strongly influenced by group beliefs, institutional and organizational constraints, habits, tradition, status and social hierarchy).

With respect to ultimatum games, Roth *et al* (1991) led experiments in four different countries (the US, Yugoslavia, Japan and Israel). Small differences emerged only in the level of offers, rather than in the probability of acceptance of a given offer, which was found to be fairly constant. The implication is that both proposers and respondents have a similar view of what is considered 'fair' in that particular society.

Experiments in 15 small non-industrial societies across five continents (Henrich *et al*, 2001b) showed a significantly larger dispersion in the level of offers, which ranged from 26 per cent to 58 per cent of the total amount to be shared in the ultimatum game. By comparison, the previous study by Roth had found a mean offer of around 44 per cent. Greater variability in the probability of acceptance was also found. Researchers found that the level of co-operation between proposers and respondents tends to increase as the degree of market integration in the society rises.

Preferences over economic choices are not exogenous, as the canonical model would have it, but rather are shaped by the social interactions of everyday life. This challenges the standard economics assumption of exogenous preferences, as these would disregard the different behavioural features that were found in response to changes in society. As the empirical evidence above shows, there would be a far higher likelihood of co-operating and negotiating with others as a society progresses and becomes more complex.

PART II

Practice

Let's cut the bulls**t. We are in this because we want to be filthy rich.
*(Sir James Goldsmith, former takeover raider, at a British TV roundtable
with other fellow billionaires who went into mental gymnastics to explain
why they did what they did for a living)*

CHAPTER 7

Risk framing and communication

Funny business, you know. You lure people in with that false sense of security and then totally f*** them.

(Infamous derivatives salesman's phone conversation, US Federal proceedings)

7±2:

- More information is better. Or is it?
- Context dependence and trading frames of risk
- Reporting frames
- Aversion to ambiguity and the law of unintended consequences in practice
- Complexity beware
- Risk communication

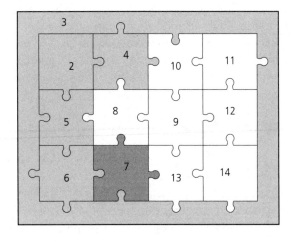

Abstract

It is an irony and a paradox that risk professionals with strong theoretical training in financial economics may be the only group of people who may seriously and severely object to the myriad psychological issues affecting risk decisions. Hopefully, the overwhelming evidence presented in the previous chapters has helped to bury whatever outstanding prejudice they might illicitly attempt to promote under the guise of authority or power. One must also be wary of simplifying metaphors turned to jargon which are used to justify senior consulting fees for risk management. With the sky-high stakes of today's trading rooms, the technology revolution that apparently dominates the scene is simply not the right analogy for how people can or should operate. Simply put, our brains are not, and have never been, designed to behave as digital computers.

This chapter focuses on the concepts of *context dependence* and *risk framing* and their relation to decision-making. First, this chapter presents a few irrefutable and surprising facts about cognitive perception and how deceptive it tends to be. That is the ideal starting point to proceed to dismantle, decompose and demolish a few popular myths which have become intransigently embedded as 'generally accepted truths' amongst financial institutions and their regulators. For instance, contrary to widely held belief, technology problems and information speed are *not* at the heart of information management and decision-making. Staying with the car analogy we used earlier, the important key is not in the electro-mechanical ignition but in the driver's head.

Finally, this chapter links these cognitive issues to the principles of risk communication, an area that has received little, but deserves more, attention.

Implications: No matter how stressed we may be with so little time left, we need to examine closely how risk problems are being framed. Regardless of how much faith we might have in fancy quantitative models, high-performance computers, and the specialists who run them, we need to be vigilant of the human weaknesses underlying them. There are no right or wrong standard performance metrics but, rather, correctly and appropriately applied or incorrectly and inappropriately applied metrics to suit the investor's specified needs.

7.1 The information fallacy

Few, if any, could have predicted the amazing results achieved by the information technology revolution over the last 20 years. Today's global trading would hardly be possible without it. Higher processing speed and information storage capability combined with a collapse in their costs have unquestionably enhanced the information standards in large organizations. The focus and resources devoted to the information revolution, however, have far surpassed the attention paid to information users. Let's face it, no car on its own can make up for a driver's flaws. The classic mis-management problem of information begetting more information is pervasive and entrenched. There are plenty of IT marketers and consultants feeding on and reinforcing this view. The following sections examine industry-wide themes where the sell-side metaphors of technology are themselves cause for concern.

Being risk-averse, people seek safety and comfort in a variety of ways. Insufficient information is a common argument used to delay decisions and actions. Craving larger amounts of information is one common expression of management's information quest. Frequency and timeliness of information is another. Nowhere do these needs express themselves more than in modern trading rooms.

Few amongst the IT departments and experts have much interest in discouraging this trend. Since the early 1990s it has become an institutionalized habit. As if on regular cue, many of these internal or external advisers are quick to use the example of some new fancy information technology being implemented by a few global trading banks as the critical proof and demonstration of a 'best industry practice' which should be replicated in-house at any cost. The 'best practice' argument makes a self-fulfilling prophecy of the transformation of nice-to-have features into must-haves. As a consequence, the *ways* of providing information become more important than the information itself, the uses or the users. By the way, this exemplifies *herd instinct*, a group bias that was discussed in the last chapter.

Without a doubt, complex trading books that contain a variety of instruments across different locations need cutting-edge technology to remain abreast of their positions. Fast-moving markets can viciously punish any hesitation caused by inaccurate and unreliable position information. This, however, does not imply that the entire organization requires real-time information processing as a pre-condition to good management.

But does quantity win over quality? Does more information equal better information? Is the amount of information available genuinely correlated with good decisions? The evidence gathered from studies in decision and information theory does not support this view. Recall from Chapter 2 that, according to the 7 ± 2 principle, there are objective constraints in the brain's processing abilities. No matter how fast one throws information at it, the human CPU is a constraint that cannot be eliminated. How do people cope with increasing quantity and complexity of information? They categorize. By doing so, they can indeed increase their information storage. This, however, opens the flank to representativeness, a bias described earlier, in Chapter 5. Besides, more information means more noise to weed out.

The empirical findings on the adverse effects of increased information availability should hardly surprise. This evidence supports the notion that increased information availability generally impairs subjects' processing efficiency to a considerable extent. The most important studies have been conducted by Beach & Mitchell (1978), Christensen-Szalanski (1978), Payne (1982), Wood (1986) and Handzic (1997, 2001). These findings are consistent with the theory of an inverted U-shaped relationship between performance and the amount of information (Schroder, Driver & Streufert, 1967; Wood, 1986; Dörner, 1999).

As discussed in Chapter 4, people are overconfident in their judgments. Accordingly, most studies find that the greater amount of information available to an individual increases the individual's confidence in his or her own assessments. This does not automatically translate into greater accuracy or better performance. The empirical record is by no means unequivocal. Better performance was indeed found in some contexts, such as basketball

(Peterson & Pitz, 1988) and lending (Casey, 1980), but not in others, such as clinical judgments (Oskamp, 1965), sport results predictions (Paese & Sniezek, 1991) and analysts' stock earnings forecasts (Davis, Lohse & Kottemann, 1994). This last study found forecast accuracy substantially diminished as a result of both redundant and non-redundant information. Similar unfavourable conclusions were reached by empirical research on the use of information in production scheduling tasks (Chervany & Dickson, 1974; Connolly & Thorn, 1987).

If anybody had any doubt about the effects of emotions and human processing in financial risk decisions, an excellent study by Lo & Repin (2001) confirmed their critical impact. The study tracked five physiological dimensions[39] and found statistically significant differences amongst traders during particular market events. A significant correlation was also found between traders' experience and these differences. While the limited sample size of ten traders studied makes the study findings preliminary, it is nevertheless a step in the right direction.

7.2 Frames in trading and portfolio decisions

7.2.1 Two examples in trading and risk management

No matter how efficient and rational one may believe oneself to be, the complex but not necessarily irrational ways in which we process information are at the heart of financial decisions. This section illustrates how the presentation of information in terms of granularity and frequency affects our judgement about the significance of information. Indeed, it does not take an Enron to understand the dangers arising from the complexity of large trading desks and organizations. While large trading desks have the ability to set up a significant number of portfolios, each pursuing a specific strategy, they also give unscrupulous management the chance to hide certain risks from scrutiny. You are not likely to be asked questions about that which you have purposely not presented and wilfully intended to de-emphasize. More to the point, you can hide behind a cloak of sophisticated numbers.

Consider the summary information for which the detailed source daily data is set out in Appendix D.[40] This assumes that the relevant firm uses – as is customary – the actual trading results to measure the *ex post* trading volatility of its business. Regardless of which method[41] the firm uses to estimate its VaR *ex ante*, this is standard practice to check its validity *ex post*. It shows what differences granularity – or lack thereof – may bring.

---

[39] They were: skin conductance, blood volume pulse, heart rate, electromyographical signals, respiration and body temperature.

[40] See Table A in Appendix D.

[41] Historical simulation, the method used here to check VaR *ex post*, can also be employed for *ex ante* estimates. Variance-Covariance (VCV) and Monte-Carlo simulation are the other two most widely used approaches to estimate VaR *ex ante*. The point of this example is not to analyse the pros and cons of each method but, rather, to illustrate how risk aggregation can be employed to disguise the actual volatility of a trading business.

TABLE 7.1 ▪ Five trading desks

	Desk 1	Desk 2	Desk 3	Desk 4	Desk 5	Aggregate
Bottom 5th Percentile P&L						(3,411,786)
Standard Deviation of losses						1,598,331
Number of Days	60	60	60	60	60	60
Number of Losing Days	35	30	25	16	24	22
Worst P&L	(8,367,185)	(7,071,708)	(7,547,660)	(1,155,824)	(2,129,553)	(6,351,504)
Best P&L	2,191,805	2,777,142	3,345,452	2,635,066	7,864,548	8,402,086
Absolute P&L Range	–6,175,380	–4,294,566	–4,202,208	1,479,242	5,734,995	2,050,582
Average Loss	–1,600,408	–1,430,953	–743,611	–250,957	–597,684	–2,005,432
Number of Days in which Loss exceeds Aggregate VaR	6	5	1	0	0	2

The 'Aggregate' column in the above table shows the outcome of all desks for one particular day rather than the sum of figures from the various desks; it also shows that the aggregation smoothes P&L considerably. As you look at the row indicating Number of Losing Days, only one desk (the fourth one) shows fewer losing days than the 'Aggregate' column. Each desk will experience the worst/best figures in different days, unless their activities are essentially in the same market(s) and strongly correlated.

7.2.1.1 Cognitive dissonance and hedonic framing

Consistent with cognitive dissonance principles, questions are far more frequent after losses than after gains. Also, recall from the hedonic framing theory discussed in Chapter 5 that accounting aggregations are more likely to appear when they allow the avoidance or delay of the recognition of losses. This application of mental accounting will probably result in less aggressive scrutiny and positive comments about the diversified earnings stream.

7.2.1.2 Limits and risk capital

Since historical profit and loss (P&L) is usually a critical input factor for limits and risk capital usage, a less volatile profit and loss usually translates into lower limit and capital usage. At a 95 per cent confidence interval, the VaR of this whole trading activity is only $3.41 million. This means that this amount tends to be exceeded in five instances out of 100, or one in 20. This is the case for the entire trading activity over the 60 days that are considered.

However, the detailed source data in Appendix D, Table A, show that two sub-desks (#1 and #2) experience, respectively, six and five such violations during just 60 days. Desk #1 has already exceeded its number of exceptions. In order to remain within VaR limits, Desk #2 should experience no losses exceeding the Aggregate figure for the Desk over the following 60 days. This implies that the VaRs of these sub-desks should be higher than the $3.41 million of VaR for the whole trading activity.

7.2.1.3 *Internal arbitrage*

The aggregation and smoothing in P&L may also facilitate internal arbitrages not only in the *amount* but also in the *cost* of risk capital. Specifically, some banks set different costs of capital hurdles across their various trading activities. Some of these, typically customer-oriented businesses, are likely to be deemed to have a more stable earnings stream than proprietary activities in which the bank trades its own risk capital. The smoothing in P&L volatility and the perception – or illusion – of stability in the earnings are also likely to affect the classification of a business as customer-facing or not, and so affect the cost of capital. This may then become too low relative to the substantial proprietary risk-taking content of some sub-desks. In the above example, one would be justified in questioning how the professed customer orientation is reconciled with the substantial volatility in P&L displayed by Desks #1 and #2. It is far more likely that we have a wolf in sheep's clothing. These desks should then attract a cost of capital above the lower figure used for the entire trading activity. Unfortunately, few trading heads are likely to show the intellectual integrity required without external scrutiny.

Consider another example. Figure 7.1 displays cumulative stock returns over time. Which of the two assets would you consider more stable? The answer is in the footnote below.[42]

This section demonstrates how the display of information is critical in pre-conditioning the human mind. 'It's not what you say, but how you say it' is really about optimizing the signal strength of a message. Indeed, having the appropriate level of information does not necessarily mean more abundant or more frequent data. Rather, it means having the correct level of detail based on the decision-maker's requirements. While useful in preventing surprises from dangerous positions buried in the aggregation process, detailed figures are not necessarily the right input for longer-term decisions.

---

[42] The correct answer is *neither*. The two charts refer to the same stock (specifically, CISCO Systems) in 1999 (provided by Bloomberg). The main difference is how the information was framed on a monthly and daily basis, respectively. If you answered otherwise, this example should illustrate the dangers of drawing conclusions based on a frequency that differs from the investor's proposed timeframe. The second chart looks much more zig-zagging (i.e., volatile) because it relies on more granular information. Conversely, daily volatility is smoothed in the monthly aggregation of data. In general terms, the second chart should concern only a trader with a daily or weekly proposed holding period. A long-term investor who uses different selection criteria (say, a fundamentals-orientated investor who plans to hold the stock for two years) would be well advised to use daily information only for execution purposes (for instance, of entry and exit points). Otherwise, the noise resulting from daily volatility may become another unintended screening criterion to hold the position or not. To avoid this bias, some investors deliberately limit their own exposure to short-term information.

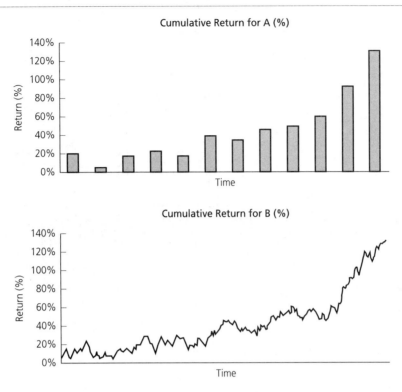

FIGURE 7.1 ■ Cumulative returns over time for Asset A and Asset B

For instance, in the trading desk spreadsheet example (see Appendix D, Table A), it would hardly make sense to use daily volatility figures for risk capital allocation decisions. The very availability of daily figures and the noise that they incorporate may introduce a bias in the decision-maker's mind. This will lead to an overstatement of the volatility of the business's revenue stream over the long term. The likely consequence will be a higher cost of capital hurdle for the business, causing a lower – and incorrect – allocation of risk capital. As a result, the business may be unfairly penalized.

It may be wise for the decision-maker to seal himself off from the detailed figures by delegating the analysis of the more granular figures to a junior colleague. By using only figures with a less granular frequency, the senior decision-maker will have a better chance of reducing his exposure to noise and concentrate on information that is more relevant for longer-term decisions. Appropriate calibration of data, where the size of data has a fitness for use, may explain the somewhat cloistered behaviour of some astute successful senior traders with long-time horizon who stay deliberately away from the daily noise of media, newspapers and screen-based news services.

7.2.2 Other frames in portfolio decisions

Let's suppose you own a portfolio, called Portfolio A, with monthly returns displayed as follows:

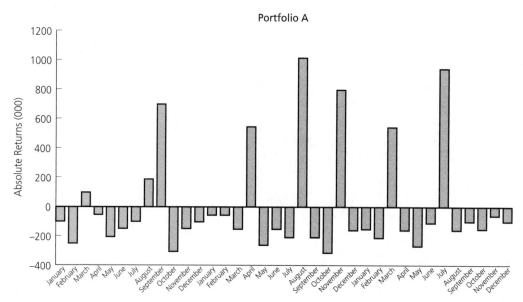

FIGURE 7.2 ■ Portfolio A

Your investment adviser offers you a switch into another portfolio, Portfolio B (see below). Would you accept it?

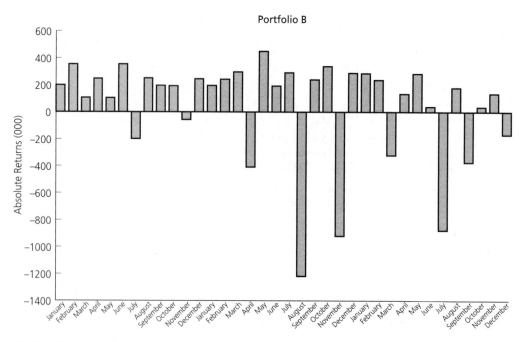

FIGURE 7.3 ■ Portfolio B

Some of you might balk at the track record of Portfolio B. Your investment adviser offers you another alternative. You can mix Portfolios A and/or B and, possibly, other securities, to form another portfolio, called Portfolio C. The next chart displays its track record. Which of the following would you prefer?

(a) Use the securities in Portfolio A that you already own to form C?, or

(b) Use the securities in Portfolio B to form C?

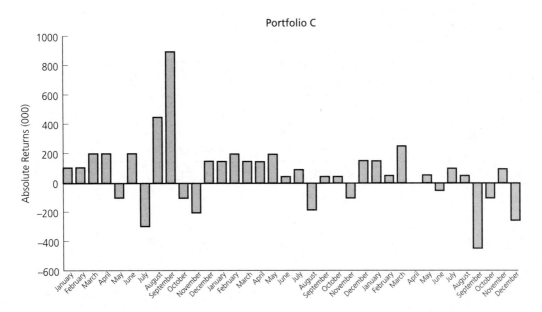

FIGURE 7.4 ■ Portfolio C

If you accepted the switch into Portfolio B offered in the first question, you likely felt the influence of the hedonic framing, a variety of mental accounting explained in Chapter 5. It is indeed natural for most people to prefer a series of positive cashflows with the risk of a major drawdown. Portfolio B compares favourably to the series of cashflows in Portfolio A, whereby the investor bears a series of losses and has the occasional winner. This exhibits another form of mental accounting, as the investor who selects Portfolio B obviously prefers adding something to his or her own wealth each month. The alternative of suffering a streak of losses is clearly unattractive.

Let us now consider the second question. If your answer to the second question is (b), then it is likely that you have incorporated the base information from the previous question, namely that Portfolio B is preferable to A most of the time.

However, the second question is a bit of a trick since Portfolio C is a 50–50 combination of Portfolios A and B! So, the answer to the second question should be *both* A and B. Simply put, Portfolio A looks far more acceptable when buried in the combined cashflows than on a stand-alone basis. Psychologically, it is far nicer to see a string of positive returns.

Recall the principle of hedonic framing wherein people tend to attribute a different value to combinations of events relative to individual parts. Under this principle, losses tend to be bundled together, to reduce the number of times one has to experience the associated negative feeling. This may explain why cashflows of some activities that provide insurance are lumped together with cashflows of other activities that are regarded as 'cash cow businesses'. Whilst there may be some diversification effect, the intention of the admixture is merely to deceive.

Let us move to another example. Consider the summary statistics for the following portfolios, for which the source daily data are given in Appendix D.[43]

TABLE 7.2 ■ Investment allocation to three portfolios

	Portfolio A	Portfolio B	Portfolio C
Std deviation mo ret	0.598151	0.551362	0.236177
Avg monthly return	−0.03871	0.2	0.080645
Negative months	25	7	8
Positive months	6	24	22
Avg mo ret/Std dev	−0.06472	0.362738	0.341461

Which portfolio would you choose in Table 7.2, A, B or C? If you select Portfolio B, congratulations! You display rationality. This portfolio has indeed outperformed the others not only in absolute but also in risk-adjusted terms. The ratio between the average of monthly returns and their standard deviation is the best of the three alternatives available. Winning months are over three times as frequent as losing months.

Let's move on and consider the situation a few months later, in the following January. The following grid shows the monthly returns and updated statistics.

---

[43] See Table B in Appendix D.

TABLE 7.3 ■ Portfolios A, B, C revised

	<==== Monthly Returns ====>			<= Portfolio Cumul Abs returns =>		
	Portfolio A	Portfolio B	Portfolio C	Portfolio A	Portfolio B	Portfolio C
August	4.1	–4.8	–0.35	2.803	1.237	2.163
September	–0.4	0.5	0.05	2.392	1.743	2.214
October	–0.6	0.7	0.05	1.778	2.455	2.265
November	3.2	–3.6	–0.2	5.035	–1.233	2.061
December	–0.3	0.6	0.15	4.719	–0.641	2.214
Std deviation mo. ret.	1.03923	1.16442	0.234859			
Average mo. return	0.133333	–0.01111	0.061111			
Negative months	28	9	10			
Positive months	8	27	25			
Avg mo. ret./Std dev.	0.1283	–0.0095	0.2602			

What would you choose now? (Tick the appropriate box)

☐ Portfolio A

☐ Portfolio B

☐ Portfolio C

Let's assume you've been honest. If you ticked Portfolio B, your choice makes sense only if you are expecting some form of mean reversion to positive returns in the future. Even after the negative streak, Portfolio B incurred losses only one-third of the time. This is mean-reversion bias and anchoring. Your decision is still anchored to the previous belief and is based on information that the portfolio will, on average, display positive returns about three months out of four. The new unfavourable information for Portfolio B is discounted based on your previous frame of risk and, as a result, does not carry much weight on your decision going forward. Of course, this choice also means that such outperformance is linked to an occasional major drawdown. This negative aspect threatens to spoil the party and is neglected or swept under the carpet.

If, on the other hand, the additional information of the returns of the last five months makes you switch portfolios into A and C, you may be displaying the biases of *recency* and *regret*. This example points out the dangers of confusing *frequency* and *probability* in risk decisions.

If your original choice was Portfolio B, you can state, with the benefit of hindsight, that you have been a victim of trend extrapolation bias. Indeed, your earlier decision relied on a high frequency of positive returns. You extrapolated from this information by expecting that frequent positive returns would continue in the future, too. Unfortunately, frequency is a poor predictor of future probability.

What is the right answer? *There is no strict right or wrong answer*.

The framing of the question in either–or terms might have led you to believe that there was indeed only one solution. If so, your choice reflects *aversion to ambiguity*, a bias discussed earlier in the book. Such yes–no, right–wrong frames of risk are natural and are, after all, at the root of teaching and examination methods since early schooling. However, what matters is not so much staying with the trend (as in Portfolio B) or betting against it (as in Portfolio A). It takes a lot of conviction – or, more likely, overconfidence – to think that:

- one can pick the winning portfolio, and
- that portfolio will also outlast the variety of phases that a market can generate.

The critical decision that an investor faces in structuring the portfolio is really one between *timing* and *time*, a topic that will be analysed in the next chapter. Regardless of the choice, the underlying trading view is what is really relevant. The above example shows the dangers of a mechanical approach to making choices based on past statistics alone. This is not just blinkered, it is as unreasonably dangerous as using only the rearview mirror to drive a car. Portfolios A and B will outperform depending on whether the trend is broken or not. Counter-trend trading views depend on timing to a critical extent. Longer-term views on a trend persisting over time will be exposed to market volatility over a longer period and should be sized appropriately.

The risk profile of Portfolios A and B can be compared to two companies who are, respectively, buying and selling insurance. The latter will experience a smooth series of positive returns from the premiums that it cashes in over time. It will also experience a sharp hit when a claim arises following the occurrence of the unlikely event covered. The former company will have the same return pattern but with opposite sign, paying a series of premiums and then recording a windfall.

Portfolio C, the third alternative, is more of an 'all-weather' portfolio that aims at smoothing volatility and preserving risk capital over the long term. Incidentally, for the purposes of this example, this is a 50–50 combination of A and B. This choice has a price, though, as this portfolio will underperform one of the others when trends continue or turn. The weaker one's conviction is in the trading view, the more the choice should veer towards the most neutral alternative, Portfolio C. However, there is no free lunch under this third alternative either. Mixing – or, more correctly, neglecting – the choice between timing and time is a dangerous sign of overconfidence that often results in long-term underperformance.

Many investors, particularly those with less market experience or formal education, suffer the consequences of staying in a trend too long and then overreacting by choosing exactly the opposite course of action when the trend is broken. The pain of regret can be very intense and often overrides any other rational consideration. For instance, many investors stayed in cash for 18 months after the stock market crash of 1987. Lending decisions often confirm the same sequence of events. The very banks that lent profusely during an earlier and more favourable phase of the economy are often the first to retrench most aggressively during a downturn. This has obvious macroeconomic implications, as the credit crunch that follows is hardly a good omen for macro-stability. *Procyclicality* is the term used to indicate banks' tendancy to magnify the effects of economic cycles by lending either too aggressively or too conservatively during expansions and downturns, respectively.

The issue of procyclicality attracted considerable attention after the publication of the revisions of Banks' Capital Adequacy standards (known as Basle-II, after the city where the Bank for International Settlement has its headquarters). Indeed, the agreement allows banks to adjust the capital reserve parameters and reduce provisions to reflect lower losses (or, equivalently, overfunded loan-loss reserves). Catarineau-Rabell, Jackson & Tsomocos (2002), Allen & Saunders (2002), Segoviano & Lowe (2002) and Altman, Resti & Sironi (2002) have published some of the most important papers on this topic. Some of these studies express concern that the latitude granted by the accord may drive less conservative provisioning policies, forcing banks to curtail their lending activities even more severely during the following economic downturns. This credit crunch would further exacerbate recessions. Over-reliance on public ratings is another frequent remark. While these problems are very important, their analysis is outside the scope of this book. Readers interested in this topic are referred to the papers mentioned above.

7.2.3 The arbitrage frame and fungibility

Few labels attract as much admiration and attention in trading rooms as the magic 'a' word. Strictly speaking, arbitrage is defined as the riskless profit arising from the simultaneous purchase and sale of a security. According to modern finance and the EMH, arbitrage on mispriced securities is very limited or non-existent, as investors are rational and arbitrageurs would eliminate it quickly. As such, arbitrageurs are known for their cunning in recognizing and exploiting these mispricings. As these trades present no risk, one can achieve a supposedly infinite return on risk capital while the arbitrage persists.

As markets have become increasingly competitive and the technology revolution has made information easily accessible, riskless arbitrage margins have indeed narrowed and the use of the word has become increasingly slanted. A variation known as 'risk arbitrage' has become more popular in trading rooms. This label is used as a connotation for trades that are not riskless but still offer a favourable risk–reward ratio, such as 4:1 or above. 'Relative value' is also often used to characterize these types of trades, which aim to exploit the price movement of one security relative to another.

This slant in the use of the word has originated abuses, too. As finding arbitrages makes one sound smart and makes it easier to obtain risk limits and capital, there is no shortage of ingenuity and salesmanship in portraying risky trades as arbitrages. This section presents some instances of such abuses and shows effective acid tests to unmask them.

Yield curve arbitrages are one example of such abuses. This term indicates positions whereby one simultaneously buys and sells short fixed-income securities in different segments of the yield curve to immunize against parallel shifts in interest rates. So, for instance, one may create such a trade in US Treasury notes by buying five-year securities and selling short 10-year securities. As the latter are more sensitive to changes in interest rates, one will reduce the size of the longer-dated security accordingly. Duration is indeed a measure devised in the late 1930s to measure such sensitivity. This will immunize the portfolio against parallel shifts in the yield curve. Figure 7.5 shows an example of a trade whereby one buys the 4 per cent T-Note maturing on 15 November 2012 and sells short the 5 per cent T-Note maturing on 15 August 2011. The fourth column from the left-hand side, entitled 'Market Value', shows that one will buy only $9.789m of the longer-dated security *vis-à-vis* $11.22m of the shorter one. The following four columns show how the combined position would be affected by a 10 basis point change in interest rates. As these two securities are not too far apart in terms of maturity and coupon, one can reasonably expect them to trade in a similar fashion. So far, no problem.

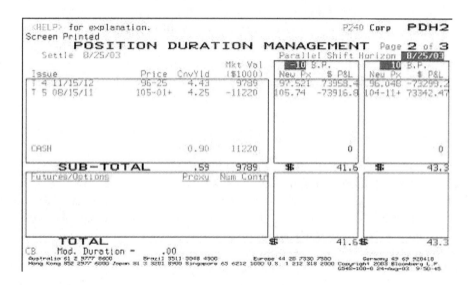

FIGURE 7.5 ■ A position duration hedge

Source: Bloomberg LP, *reprinted with permission*

The problems arise when the same computation mechanics is applied to compare securities that are far apart in final maturity or some other important feature. In his previous experience in trading rooms, the Author has come across more than one instance of sentences like: 'Oh, what a beautiful arbitrage we have set up between the three-month Euroyen Libor and the 10-year Japanese Government Bonds (JGB).'[44]

---

[44] Sentence uttered by the deputy global head of trading of a major trading house in London, 1992.

Computers will of course calculate hedge ratios for anything that you feed into them. The screen in Figure 7.5 can be used to immunize the trade described in this quote from parallel shifts in the yield curve. That cannot make up for the fact that supposed yield curve 'arbitrages' such as the latter are really two separate positions between completely different segments of the yield curve. Case or luck may have it that these segments might then experience similar interest rate moves. That is a far cry from calling this an 'arbitrage' or even a 'relative value' move!

This introduces the problem of *fungibility*, the main acid test to discover the extent to which a trade really offers an arbitrage. This refers to the investor's ability to exchange these two securities at a preset price at some future point in time or receive their equivalent cash value. Financial futures contract delivery dates are an example of fungibility, since the investor knows that at a future date he will receive an asset at a preset price[45] or get the difference from that price settled in cash.

It is easy to see that there is no fungibility between the two positions in the example above. There is no point in time when one can go to an exchange or counterpart and ask 'please take delivery of my three-month Euroyen Libor position and give me the 10-year JGB in return'. As the maturity of the two instruments is so far apart, very different factors drive their prices. While the longer-dated instrument can be expected to move mostly as a result of supply and demand, a three-month instrument is far more likely to be influenced by central bank monetary policy decisions. Last but not least, different investors may be operating in yield curve segments that are so far apart. Many investors may be prevented from investing in securities that have as long a maturity as the JGB's.

Many investors fall into the trap of seeing a trend or a spread between two securities when they watch charts comparing their price or yield difference. While the computer will obediently plot or compute anything you wish, the mathematical or graphical relationship does not imply at all that there is a trading relationship between these two securities. The *causal* link that your subconscious is making up is really a *casual* relationship. *Causality* requires a really strong economic reason validating the affinity between the two instruments, such as geographical, trade, maturity or some other striking similarity in features. Otherwise, the supposedly strong correlation that you claim to have found may be nothing but *casuality*.

So, next time someone approaches you touting the juicy credit spread of some exotic government bond over US Treasury Bonds, think again. Your computer screen may quote that credit spread at T+1035, or over 10 per cent over the yield of a Treasury Bond of comparable maturity. Nevertheless, what you have here are two fundamentally different securities and the comparison is not worth the paper that it is written on. For someone to offer you such a juicy spread, there must be higher risk associated with the exotic bond. In the case of Emerging-Market issuers, this yield premium is offered in return for the risk that the underlying sovereign country might default before the bond's maturity.

---

[45] This is used mostly to explain the main concept. There are complications with respect to contracts whereby one has to take physical delivery of the asset and different varieties of assets can be delivered. This is the case with bond futures and certain types of commodities and is referred to as *seller's option*, whereby the seller has the right to choose which grade of bonds or commodities will be delivered to the contract buyer. The broad concept of fungibility is not particularly affected by these important details.

As an aside, it is worth adding, for technical orthodoxy's sake, that a bond that offers such a hefty yield premium must trade at a very low price and, most likely, on a *price* rather than on a *yield* basis. This means that investors are evaluating the bond as if it was a piece of equity, that is, based on its expected cashflows. Such is the case with distressed fixed-income securities, since they involve a high likelihood of defaulting that investors attempt to discount in the price. In layman's terms, the 'spread' is as meaningful as adding up apples and oranges. Last, for the purists, it is worth reminding ourselves from basic security statistics that security prices are supposed to follow a log-normal pattern, whereas returns and yields tend to behave more in line with the normal distribution. So much for comparability!

Not convinced? Kenneth Froot & Emil Dabora (1998) led a study on the trading activity in stock pairs of related companies across different markets. These pairs, which they labelled 'siamese twin' stocks, were:

- Royal Dutch Petroleum and Shell Transport and Trading plc

- Unilever NV and Unilever plc

- SmithKline Beecham.

These pairs pool their cashflows and share profits and dividends according to corporate charter agreements. Therefore, the prices of their stocks in different markets should move in lockstep regardless of trading location. Of the three, the first is especially interesting, as it became the target of an 'arbitrage' trade by Long-Term Capital Management (LTCM), one of the unfortunate cases quoted in Chapter 10. According to the charter, the two companies split their joint cashflow on a 60/40 basis, the greater figure belonging to Royal Dutch. As a result, one should rationally expect the latter's stock to be worth 1.5 times the value of Shell's. What does the market think? Figure 7.6 plots the 1980–1995 period.

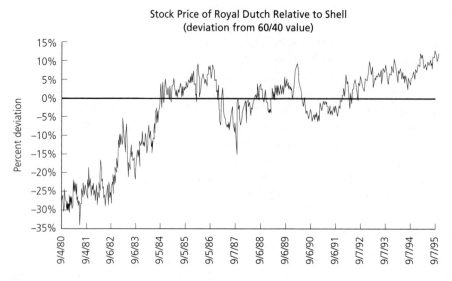

FIGURE 7.6 ■ Price ratio between Royal Dutch and Shell stocks[46]

According to the theory, the plot should not show significant deviations from zero. After all, this is the *same group of companies*. In practice, the lack of fungibility between one stock and the other leaves no osmosis between their prices, which trade as two separate stocks influenced by different domestic markets.

Unfortunately, LTCM did not heed the warnings of Froot & Dabora. As the premium at which Royal Dutch traded *vis-à-vis* Shell widened to 18 per cent, the fund created a large pairs trade. This involved selling the former short, buying the latter and levering up the trade. As rational as the expectation was for the premium to narrow, there was no fungibility to enforce it. Guess what, the premium actually *widened*!

The human tendency to see trends where there are none is another variety of the extrapolation bias that was described in Chapter 5. Indeed, it is often relied upon when one tries to project future trends, as it presupposes symmetry between causes and consequences. Writing in *The New Organon* in 1620, Sir Francis Bacon summarized it effectively: 'The human mind is prone to suppose the existence of more order and regularity in the world than it finds.'

7.3 Aversion to ambiguity meets risk management

The examples set out in the previous section have highlighted how 'aversion to ambiguity' is a powerful influence on trading and portfolio decisions. People are brought up on the doctrine and subsequently reinforce the mantra 'There is a single solution'. This belief becomes a source of certainty and comfort. Unfortunately, this belief beggars the mental discipline required to meet the ambiguity of the trading world.

Aversion to ambiguity implies that suspending one's disbeliefs and remaining in an uncommitted posture is a negative trait. This should come as no surprise, as you may recall that according to prospect theory, people are naturally risk-averse. Any ambiguity is seen as a threat to the certainty that one is craving for.

7.3.1 The main consequence: the one-market, one-approach myth

Unfortunately, this aversion carries even deeper consequences, some of which are not necessarily desirable for financial markets. For example, aversion to ambiguity also translates into a desire for standardization of rules and performance metrics. The next step to 'one-size-fits-all' measurement has perverse effects. To operate as a market with differences of opinions, financial markets need diversity of measurement and incentives, and a variety of segmentation. For example, diversity of incentives goes hand-in-hand with continuous liquidity, a highly desirable feature. Conversely, an increased similarity in performance metrics

---

[46] Reprinted from *Journal of Financial Economics*, 53(2), 1999, K. Froot and E. Dabora, 'How are stock prices affected by the location of trade?', pp. 189–216, copyright © 1999, with permission from Elsevier.

and incentives leads to more similar behaviours. This is a case in which a good objective, when applied to an extremely complex reality such as global financial markets, forces undesirable, if not unpalatable, revenge effects. It's also an example of the *law of unintended consequences* discussed in Chapter 5.

As modern risk management developed originally in the trading rooms, it is no surprise that the metrics reflect mostly traders' standards. Comparability and transparency in metrics is one thing. Sameness is another. Recall that greater information frequency translates into more noise and a greater perception of volatility. Relying on daily figures to calculate VaR may make perfect sense for a trading room. However, for a longer-term investor, it may become dangerous. Insurance companies, for instance, have as their main line of business the selling of insurance coverage. This requires a set of disciplines and time horizons distinct from the daily trading of US Treasuries. This does not mean the insurance company should ignore dramatic changes in Treasury prices during a month. But focus on daily movements for the insurer could lead to overtrading and inappropriate short-term trading activity.

Where does all this leave us? Using the same risk management metrics and standards for every player means greater comparability not only in the figures but also in the return on capital. For a given level of risk, a rational investor would rather invest in a financial institution with a higher return on capital. VaR ultimately relies on daily figures, hardly the best metric for a long-term investor. Nevertheless, the use of VaR for everybody puts an institution with a different risk-return profile in competition with trading desks that are supposedly the most efficient users of risk capital.

While few may have the responsibility to decide which type of risk measures to use, if the metrics and standards for risk are applied homogenously across all areas of business, then serious consequences are likely to result. The main fault in this risk-homogenizing exercise is that the process neglects the importance of longer-term capital, or so-called 'patient capital'. Aligning target return on capital with that of the trading rooms, hardly the cheapest source of capital, is not a move in the right direction. Consider the increased volatility resulting from the behaviours of the patient investor who suddenly loses patience. This inflection point increases the trading room's volatility, which is a direct result of the homogenized risk policy. Such volatility, though disturbing, is not where the main problem lies. After all, one should expect that where the same metrics are being used, the incentives and results will be similar to those obtained by short-term traders. Rather, the inappropriate standardization of metrics is the key issue.

7.3.2 Credit derivatives and procyclicality

The issues of procyclicality discussed in the previous section offer one example of how distorted incentives result in undesirable behaviours. The recent engagement of European insurance companies in credit derivatives is another.

Credit derivatives, an innovation of the early 1990s, allow two counterparts to transfer the credit risk of the underlying debt of a specified issuer. For practical purposes, they represent a type of insurance contract wherein one party (the investor or insurance seller) offers a protection or cover to another (the hedger or insurance buyer). If the underlying debt issuer, say a company or sovereign country, defaults or experiences an adverse credit event, the investor writes a cheque to the hedger.

In return, until the adverse event occurs, the hedger pays periodically a pre-agreed premium to the investor. The classic example of this product is called a credit default swap or, simply, CDS. Let's consider an example in which Investor A receives an annual premium in return for offering insurance to the counterparty, Hedger B. Say the annual premium is equal to 1 per cent of a reference amount of $10 million, or $100,000 per annum. If the chosen reference name, say Company C, defaults on their debt during the life of the CDS, A will pay a certain amount to B. This amount is usually equal to the depreciation of a reference bond issued by C. If the bond issued by C is worth 100 at the CDS inception date and drops to 60 after the default of C is announced, A will have to make B whole for the difference. Based on the $10m reference amount of the swap, A will have to pay $(100 − 60)/100 \times 10m = \$4m$.

Economically, the exposure of Investor A is similar to what could be achieved by buying the bond issued by C at the swap inception date. This is exactly why Hedger B will have to entice A by offering some extra benefit on top of what could be achieved by investing directly in C's bond. Typically, this will be some additional yield relative to the reference bond. Leaving aside this economic incentive, market capacity constraints create other incentives for A. The cash market in corporate bonds is not always large enough to accommodate the large investment size that a major institutional investor wishes to trade. Being an agreement between two private parties, credit derivatives trades are free from such constraints. The diagram in Figure 7.7 summarizes the cashflows involved in this type of transaction.

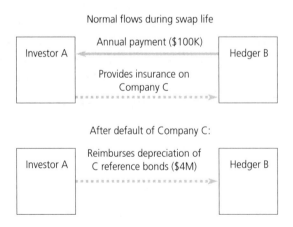

FIGURE 7.7 ■ Credit default swap (CDS)

Over the life of a trade like the one described above, counterparts will have to periodically reassess the value of their position. Such process is called mark-to-market. As seen before, the more frequent this periodic reassessment, the more impact and significance short-term noise will have, and the more volatile the position will appear. Academics aside, 'noise' does not enjoy the same status as 'volatility' in technical jargon, yet the distinction is crucial. Investor A may have entered the trade based on a positive view of the long-term fundamentals of Company C. Hedger B, on the other hand, may have engaged in the trade because it believes that the yield on C bonds is too low. From A's standpoint, the short-term vagaries of the market are just noise. From B's perspective, they translate into volatility from which to profit. The same market behaviour may be framed very differently depending on the respective points of view. Such diversity of opinion is at the very heart of maintaining market liquidity.

If, however, both counterparts mark their position to market, this diversity of opinions and, more importantly, *diversity of use* will vanish. Regardless of how sound their respective original analyses and motivations were, these now become far less critical to Investor A's future behaviour than the short-term incentives and punishments of a mark-to-market regime. Price-sensitive limits will be set up in the same way as is standard practice in any trading room. Positions will be entered and exited far more often than what may be consistent with the objectives of the investor's long-term mandates and strategic asset allocation. Unfortunately, the current trend towards uniformity of risk measurements is encouraging this unconsciously perverse behaviour.

Lest I be accused of purporting an implausible Armageddon theory, it is worth noting that since 1998, several large European insurers have been amongst the most consistent providers of protection through credit derivatives. Their counterparts are financial institutions headquartered mostly in the US. The major drop in government bond yields is at the root of these asset allocation choices. It is not unreasonable to assume that these insurers have to take more risk to achieve yields that are comparable to those that were the norm ten years ago. Credit risk is one of the alternatives. What about the consequences? Despite a less significant slowdown in the economy than in the US in 2002, European equity markets have been affected at least as severely.[47] The following charts compare the performance and volatility of the S&P500 Index in the US with the German DAX Index.

---

[47] The author would like to thank Professor Avinash Persaud for permission to draw from his lucid analysis of this phenomenon at the November 2002 Gresham College Lecture on 'Where have all the risks gone?' in London.

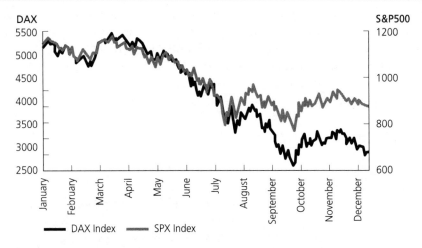

FIGURE 7.8 ■ DAX German Stock Index vs US S&P500 in 2002

Source: Bloomberg LP, *reprinted with permission*

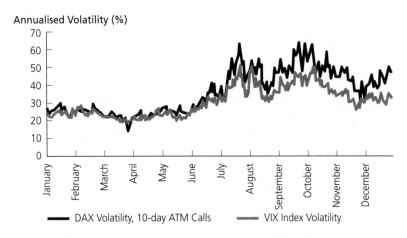

FIGURE 7.9 ■ Volatility of DAX German Stock Index vs US S&P500 in 2002

Source: Bloomberg LP, *reprinted with permission*

These charts almost speak for themselves and are a particularly good demonstration of the dangers of changing the rationale and measurement metrics of a trade in mid-flight. There is nothing wrong with mark-to-market and using a trading mindset while managing a position, as long as the same approach is also used to evaluate the trade *before* entering it. Rather, it is the *mixture* between metrics for a long- and short-term horizon that drives investors into trouble. For example, some long-term investors approach the trade by evaluating its fundamental merits as they should and then sell in panic after seeing a large mark-to-market loss for positions that are fundamentally sound.

Likewise, some traders enter a position with some trading view or technical reason in mind and then switch to a long-term fundamental view once the trade goes underwater. All this, of course, does not mean that a stop-loss should not be set for a position, regardless of its intended holding horizon. The point is just that the position sizing and the way in which a stop is set should be clearly agreed upon *before* a trade is entered into. Chapter 8 is specifically dedicated to traders and discusses the dangers of changing trade metrics in mid-flight.

7.3.3 Complexity and the risk transfer process

The issues of credit derivatives and procyclicality are only the iceberg tip of a broader issue in global financial markets.

For all the benefits, sophistication and scale of modern financial markets, advances in financial technology have increased complexity and created a false sense of security. Large organizations and the supposedly ever smarter regulators, analysts and other external constituencies who surround them should, in principle, create a screen against the consequences of human biases. The attention has shifted to this shield and away from individual biases.

In any market, there is always a risk buyer (who will be labelled insurance seller) and a risk seller (who will be denominated insurance buyer). As risk aversion is a basic individual self-preservation bias, people's natural display of this attitude should come as no surprise, and indeed the next chapter will show some of the consequences. There is never any shortage of insurance buyers. The question is, how conscious is the process of insurance selling on the other side? The question is hardly academic.

More efficient and smoother risk transfer has been one of the promises of the derivatives revolution of the last 20 years. On paper, it would look like that promise was fulfilled. After the 1987 stock market crash in the US, for instance, modern Western markets have never witnessed another one-day shock of equal magnitude. But does that mean that they are any safer and more volatile?

The record is mixed at best. Globalization of trading markets may well have succeeded – to date – in preventing another cataclysmic crash of equal proportions, but that has involved a price. Markets are far more interlinked than ever before and the chain between cause and effect is more extended. Shocks may be less deep in any particular market but the ripple effects spread globally at unprecedented speed. Events such as the Asian currency crisis of 1997 and the LTCM debacle a year later would hardly induce one to think that the financial world is any safer. The former started from the collapse of the currency peg between the Thai baht, the currency of Thailand, and the US dollar. It set off a domino effect that brought down virtually all stock and currency markets in South-East Asia. The demise of LTCM, in the words of US Federal Reserve Chairman Alan Greenspan, brought the financial world to the brink of collapse.

These accidents of financial globalization of capital markets are just some examples of the perverse effects of complexity. These instances meant that at least two categories of investors became unwitting risk insurance sellers:

- those who sought safety in global markets and relied on their supposedly greater diversification; and

- those who maintained their regional allocation unchanged but thought that their home market was made safer by the increasing interconnectivity with global markets.

These and other financial war stories will be dealt with later in the book. The instances above should be a stern reminder that greater complexity and less transparent risk transfers are harbingers for trouble. Figure 7.10 will provide you with some examples – albeit a bit extreme – of increasing complexity in risk transfer from financial markets and real life:

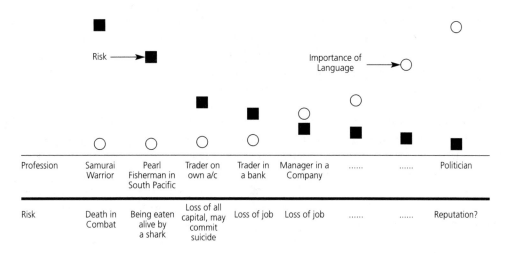

FIGURE 7.10 ■ Complexity, language and risk transfers

That is exactly one of the key points of this book: individual biases are pervasive and people attempt to fight them by creating ever more complex organizations, processes and counter-measures. That does not cure the underlying problem. As a result, complexity makes the transfer of risks less transparent and results in some unwitting selling of insurance at some point of the risk transfer chain.

7.3.4 Solutions

What is the solution? First of all, strict suitability standards should be adopted and enforced to prevent the involvement of certain types of investors in some unsuitable products. Products that are particularly volatile, leveraged or complex are best managed in the trading room rather than outside it. Secondly, this book is not seriously advocating a return to accrual accounting as a means of hiding losses. Rather, it is proposed that longer-term investors adopt *different* mark-to-market standards based on their relevant time horizon. An investor with a three-year time horizon could probably live with monthly mark-to-market at best and have to disclose only if losses within any given year reached a preset threshold.

Limits could then be published internally ensuring compliance with such a threshold. Risk capital consumption, in turn, would depend mostly on *monthly* P&L volatility figures and benefit from the smoothing effect that time has on the investor's portfolio. This would create a significant competitive advantage for the investor, who could in turn translate this regime into a lower cost of capital. Other explicit provisions could be made to prevent abuses and limit excessive regulatory arbitrages that this mechanism might inadvertently introduce.

From a systemic point of view, arguing that credit derivatives are 'financial weapons of mass destruction' (Buffett, 2003) strikes a familiar chord in favour of increasing regulation of these instruments. It does not, however, address the fundamental crux of the matter, how many pockets of complexity and illiquidity the system can afford. Historically, the track record of financial-market regulation has been mixed at best. Hurting liquidity and creating a non-level playing field are ever-present dangers that policymakers should always bear in mind. Nothing, however, is as effective as hitting the P&L to shape behaviours. Accordingly, increasing capital requirements for some complex products could be one way to discourage less sophisticated players from engaging in products that are too complex for them to manage.

Some readers may perceive these two statements – creating different incentives for different categories of investors and avoiding an uneven playing field – as contradictory. Pursuing a broadly level playing field does not mean sameness in metrics! It is exactly this dogmatic pursuit of standardization at all costs that has penalized patient capital. Patient capital requires some extra incentives exactly because it is committed over a longer time horizon!

This reckless pursuit of standardization and comparability at any cost is just a variety of the herd behaviours with which the investment banking industry is rife. The next section is about some of the most common.

7.4 Other trading frames

Mark-to-market versus accrual accounting and the impact of observation frequency on the perception of noise are only two examples of frames. Many statements commonly found in the investment banking and trading industry are the result of other frames of risk.

7.4.1 Client business is more stable. Or is it?

According to a common banking adage, 'client revenues are less volatile than trading activities'. On the face of it, the statement seems indisputable. After all, very few stock and rating analysts like banks that rely heavily on proprietary trading revenues. When compared to the steadily rising upward-sloping curve of client revenues or net interest margin[48] from loans, the traders' large swings in P&L hardly qualify for a beauty contest. The hectic atmosphere of the trading room is seldom associated with the gentrified relationships with important clients.

---

[48] Net Interest Margin (NIM) is the difference between the total interest rate that banks charge to their borrowers and the rate at which banks fund those loans.

Yet, the real difference is mostly a matter of frames of risk. This section demonstrates how the theory of hedonic framing – discussed earlier in Chapter 5 – is at the root of this portrait of businesses as 'stable' or not. This theory postulates that people's preferences are skewed towards lumping losses together and savouring gains one by one. Recall that according to mental accounting theory, people tend to prefer lumping losses together and showing gains one by one. The odd large loss hurts less than a series of smaller losses.

In a similar fashion, client activities and loans have a tendency to display a few isolated large losses, whereas trading activities show several small or medium losses. Indeed, loans suffer from defaults only occasionally. A large salesforce, research team and relationship network means high fixed costs and a higher operating leverage.[49] These can become particularly painful when client revenues drop. Conversely, aside from ever more expensive workstations, proprietary trading involves fewer people and a lower fixed-cost base.

Hindsight bias in portfolio decisions was discussed earlier in this chapter. The statements about how one business outperforms another are all examples of hindsight bias depending on the most recent phase of the economic cycle. They are also examples of recency bias (see Chapter 5). Regardless of whether the business involves widgets or financial services, a firm with a higher operating leverage will probably outperform when the cycle is favourable. This is the model adopted by most dealers with large salesforce and research operations. Conversely, lower-cost proprietary trading operations will tend to fare better under less favourable economic conditions – that is, they are counter-cyclical. Rather than categorizing businesses as 'good' or 'bad', the real issue is rather *how a given activity is positioned for a particular view on the economy* (and, by reflex, financial markets). Once again, the view is what really matters. The paradox of buying the customer stability frame of risk at face value is that it will actually become risk-additive when taken to the extreme. This complies with the old adage according to which 'taking no risk is one's largest risk'. While politically correct, eliminating proprietary trading means getting rid of a counter-cyclical activity that can offset slumps in client-related revenue during recessionary phases of the economy. In short, this is as wise as taking away the brakes from a car.

Even without loan losses, another factor contributes to reinforce this illusion of stability. Taken on its own and without consideration of the overhead line, the upward-sloping revenue line of a customer operation will inevitably look more stable and appealing than the zig-zagging line of a trading desk. The cost line – far less transparent than the revenue line and less visible to outsiders – will generally portray a very different picture. More often than not, the greater accessibility of revenue figures will influence the biases of outside analysts and tilt their views towards stability.

With the benefit of hindsight, it is obvious that the strong economy and financial markets of the late 1990s favoured more client-centric businesses. This supposed stability of such

---

[49] Higher operating leverage means that a firm, say Company A, has a higher percentage of fixed costs over total costs relative to another Company B. As a result, Company A requires higher sales volumes to achieve its break-even point between revenues and costs. Company A's results are also more sensitive to sales volumes. Therefore, their profits beyond the break-even point will grow faster than Company B's with high sales levels but also drop faster in response to sales reductions.

client-focused activities, however, failed to stop a major drop in revenue and downsizing in the investment banking industry after the tide turned in 2000. So much for strong clients! The *tactical* benefit of averting short-term revenue volatility resulted in the foolhardy *strategic* positioning of most banks as high-cost producers.

This proves beyond doubt how the point about some businesses being more stable than others is all relative to the phase of the economic cycle. Few amongst the big egos that characterize investment banking, however, will have the honesty to admit that their earlier success in the 1990s was based on a correct bullish view on the economy. Self-attribution bias, anyone? Unsurprisingly, most banks prepared for the first decade of the new century by extrapolating from their previous success. As a result, most of them were caught off guard by the sudden drop in customer flows resulting from the 2001–2002 recession.

Exceptions obviously exist, and some customer-focused banks outperform others even in bad times thanks to particularly established clients who will continue doing business with them no matter what. Likewise, some more cautious proprietary trading desks will do well in good times but underperform more aggressive competitors during unfavourable times.

7.4.2 Reporting tools

Other frames and applications of biases in the risk and trading world loom large. In the context of large organizations, reporting tools proliferate. Some of these are indeed very useful in keeping top management abreast of the latest developments and methodologies both inside and outside their organization. Some problems that nouveau reporting tools can generate are as follows:

7.4.2.1 Inappropriate use

The tools might be used in a completely inappropriate way relative to the purpose for which they were originally designed. For instance, in some markets, such as the one in which corporate loans are traded, portfolio management processes were originally designed more for *reporting* than for *trading* purposes. At the same time, a new market in credit derivatives blossomed. These two approaches were destined to create conflicts. Even worse, some less sophisticated institutions made trading decisions in their portfolio based on the indications of their portfolio reporting system. As discussed previously, the point is not about extending the trading methodology to the portfolio but about making sure that the execution is consistent with the purpose. Using credit derivatives pricing for long-term positions such as those that a normal loan portfolio would expect is incorrect. Using portfolio models for individual trading decisions is equally wrong.

Watch out for VaR ('Very Approximate Risk')

For all its merits as a reporting tool, VaR can be seriously misinterpreted and is apt to generate a dangerous false sense of security. Let's leave aside the frequent – but often forgotten – 'health warning' that VaR must be treated with caution as it relies on historical data. Given a confidence interval of, say, 95 per cent, VaR is almost always explained as 'a loss that is 95 per cent of the times within a certain value'. One could also state as correctly that it is 'a loss that is five per cent of the times beyond a certain value'.

This, however, is seldom heard. Why? Recall from the discussion of lotto bias in Chapter 5 how people simplify their thought processes by framing decisions on a binary 0 or 1 basis. In this case, those five instances look very remote and tend to be disregarded. The more remotely the event is framed, the higher the likelihood that it will be discarded. This is similar to the phenomena examined later in Chapters 10 and 11, which will show more than one instance of high-profile announcements forswearing the possibility of failure being ignored prior to a catastrophe.

Also, VaR does not give us any information on the severity of those five occurrences beyond its value. Are those events 1 per cent larger than the 95 per cent c.i. VaR figure or six times as large? Once again, this shows how dangerous it is to confuse frequency and outcomes.

Last but not least, VaR says nothing about the behaviour of the other 1001 institutions that are using it at the same time as an important driver of their trading and portfolio decisions. This latter higher-order belief problem was analysed in the previous chapter. Later on, there will be an opportunity to see more than one risk disaster resulting from the neglect of higher-order beliefs. Needless to say, using VaR without a deep understanding of all these implications and consequences is another symptom of overconfidence. Forcing trading behaviours to avoid breaches in a reporting tool may please board members but is as wise as using the steering wheel to slow down a car!

Hopefully, these examples will have given you an inkling of the range of frames and nuances available in presenting risk information and how decisive their effect can be to the organization.

7.5 Risk communication

The common assumption of rationality and objectivity that most practitioners associate with risk management includes not only the way in which risk is defined and calculated but also the process that is used to communicate it. For the purpose of this book, understanding the frames inherent in the process of risk communications – in other words, how one frames the risk information that is transmitted and received – is of critical importance. Few assumptions could be more dangerous.

7.5.1 Definition and objectives of risk communication

Risk communication is a process that takes into account the agenda of both the communicator and the recipients and attempts to package it in the most efficient way to persuade the relevant decision-makers to adopt a given course of action.

The objectives of risk communication can be summarized as follows:

7.5.1.1 Advice and answers

In the depths of our subconscious, one is often looking for someone to suggest an answer and to tell us what to do. It takes more time and mental energy to develop an independent answer that is not just an amalgam of impractical noise. Generally, it is a wise strategy to simplify the decision-making process. In an increasingly complex world, it is foolhardy to claim superior knowledge of anything. Our positivist stance is that we will use what works, so it is therefore tempting to outsource the quest of solutions to others who are deemed more competent. This is a double-edged sword though. On one side, another adviser may offer fresh insights and a different perspective on a given problem. Conversely, however, relying on such an expert means that his agenda may interfere with the objectivity of his analysis and recommendations.

7.5.1.2 Numbers

In another variation, people want to make the choices themselves but outsource the search for the relevant information parameters to plug into their own decision-making models. Here, decision-makers are looking for quantitative summaries of expert knowledge.

7.5.1.3 Processes and intelligence

Sometimes, notably in very complex situations, people are looking for more than just numbers. They want to understand how a risk develops and what the context is. Here, the objective is to develop a more informed view on a particular subject.

7.5.2 Context-dependent meaning of reality and facts

It is rather apparent that the use of the words 'reality' and 'facts' in normal communications do not automatically engender an objective scientific approach. Far from it! Rather, we use the definitions that come from the audience's model of experience where 'reality' and 'facts' are used as labels and slogans. In this respect, these labels matter more in relative rather than in absolute terms. The 'reality' and 'facts' are insidiously playing the same role as the mental filters discussed in Chapter 5. To turn the tables, so to speak, effective risk communication is about leveraging and exploiting the biases that we know exist. The 'real' meaning does not exist in the message or in the signal but in *the people who receive it*. The context and the feelings of those involved are what really matter in any form of risk communication. The popular saying that 'perception becomes reality' captures the nub of the matter.[50]

Strong relationships exist between the risk communication, the psychological profile (as shown by the psychometric measurement model) and the cognitive modes (see Chapter 2). Let's consider the position of the communicator, that is, the one who initiates and transmits a message. The importance of his or her psychological set-up increases in direct proportion to their vested interest in a decision to which they has contributed information. This is hardly surprising, as it results from sunk cost and recency biases.

The recipients' psychological set-up makes the means of communication almost as important as the message content. As stated in Chapter 2, recipients have preferred sensory representation systems and preferred modes of convincer strategies. We can view the message in the process of communication articulating itself along the following major dimensions:

---

[50] For the Aristotle fans: 'You become what you perceive'.

7.5.2.1 Motivational themes

Communication may appeal to *fear* or *greed* and *hope*. These are obviously the most common features of risk communications in finance. Examples that evoke the need for safety may be the funding of one's retirement expenses or a product that is targeted at pension funds. A statement that is intended to convince an audience of the seriousness of a particular risk may emphasize it in very vivid terms, thereby trying to exploit their availability biases. Instances that are more associated with greed include the aggressive marketing of products and strategies touting the virtues of investing in the recent internet and new-economy stocks. More subtle themes are also present. With respect to the matcher-versus-mismatcher distinction discussed in Chapter 2, some messages provide evidence and information to reinforce the common wisdom whereas others provide the opposite. Other messages aim to exploit other biases discussed previously in this book, such as confirmation bias, lotto bias. The latter is evoked with reassuring messages that state, for instance, that a given adverse event can happen only once in, say, 1,000 years.

7.5.2.2 Main cognitive modes underpinning the message

It is obvious that risk information will get through to the recipients only inasmuch as it matches their sensory representation preference. Someone with a strong visual orientation will likely overweigh graphs and discount other types of information such as the auditory (e.g. 'I hate telephone calls') and kinesthetic (e.g. 'My feelings don't count'). Such a person is unlikely to give the same weight, for example, to information that is provided during a telephone conference call.

7.5.2.3 Level of detail

Information that is very detailed will make little impression on a big-picture strategic decision-maker. Likewise, an introverted and detail-orientated person will hardly believe information that is excessively concise even though it is precisely illuminating to the big-picture person.

7.5.3 Elements of a fair risk communication

With the subtleties that underpin it, risk communication can become very much a double-edged sword. While it can advance positive change in a large organization, it can also result in superficial decisions that are unlikely to add value in the long term. Taking into account the experience and sophistication of the audience is obviously key to an effective communication. Explaining risks in accessible terms does not mean making the message too simple.

The following is a useful checklist for good risk communication:

- What is the subject of the risk communication? How does one define the context and what is specifically generating the communication?

- How does one generally measure the risk in question? If different metrics provide contradictory results, what are they? No more than three or four alternative measures should be provided. Indeed, recall from Section 5.4.2 that the brain can utilize only a handful of items at any one time.

- What are the alternatives for managing or reducing the exposure and their costs?

- What are the cash and non-cash effects of the current status quo? For instance, are there any particular costs that, despite being beyond the current financial year, may arise at some point in the future?

- What are the other major participants in the industry doing or not doing to manage and reduce that risk?

- If something has worked out well in the past, is that a result of randomness or can it be traced to specific factors and decisions that were made in the past? Could things have turned out otherwise? If so, what would be their consequences?

- What are the potential reputational and regulatory implications of the current decisions?

- What information can be provided to help the audience in the evaluation of the risk?

7.5.4 Implications and dangers of risk communication

Risk management is more about asking the right questions than providing fast answers or, worse, pretending to provide the new slick solution. In that respect, the frequent association of risk management with systems is dangerous at best, since it fosters the belief in risk management's clients that providing answers and reports is the main task. In the words of the legendary Spanish painter Pablo Picasso: 'Computers are stupid. They can provide only answers.'

Chapter 8 discusses some of the major differences between risk management and risk reporting. The dark side of risk communication is that it can be used to obtain those answers that people expect to get. These are confirmation biases and aversion to cognitive dissonance at their best. As seen in Chapter 5, both these tendencies have been documented empirically. Most procedures for risk communication will be skewed towards helping get decisions approved. Few will ask questions about the substance of the decisions. Avoiding nasty surprises after rosy numbers is very much what a good organization should be about. A critical part that should be embedded in risk communications is the *process* of vetting decisions rather than the *number* of decisions being approved. A slick risk communication system may, left on its own, cause decisions to get through without the appropriate attention to their quality.

Where is this supposed to leave the reader? Next time some major risk decision needs to be made, consider the mindset of decision-makers first. What constitutes 'rational' and 'objective' information is mostly relative to *them* rather than to some abstract, absolute external benchmark. If the top decision-makers do not put their hearts behind a given risk decision or requirement, they will simply oppose it or dismiss it as some regulatory or bureaucratic hassle. Communication will simply provide the conscious means of expressing what their subconscious has already decided.

If you run a large desk or organization, you should then ask yourself why you receive certain kinds of risk information. More often than not, you will realize that the information reflects your beliefs of what is and is not important. If you receive other pieces of information, think twice before dismissing it as irrelevant. Such information reflects a different view of your risk and your organization and it may actually be more useful than you think. It is just that your mental screens normally filter out such information.

An even more relevant point looms large. How unbiased are certain questions that are being asked about risk? Normally, you would likely be pleased with prompt answers. If these happen frequently, however, chances of biases in the questions are good. In this case, your process may be good for corporate entertainment but add little value for risk purposes.

CHAPTER 8

Riding the tiger: the trader

The market can remain irrational much longer than you can stay solvent.

(*John Maynard Keynes*)

7±2:

- Empirical evidence on why trading psychology matters
- Proper human resources management vs HR accounting
- Psychology of the pros and cons of futures speculators
- Psychology of other risk-takers
- The seven cardinal sins of trading
- Gambler's fallacy, position sizing and timing or time

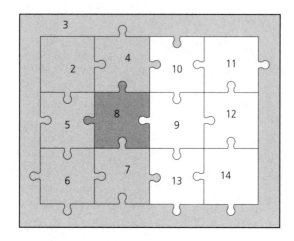

Abstract

OK, you have heard this before, traders are not known as the most gentrified members of today's society. The standard stereotype of a trader is someone who has ego and greed in spades, is probably overpaid, prone to bullying others and is not known for good manners or healthy eating and drinking habits.

For all their issues, traders are ultimately responsible for making liquid markets possible. Their role as the actor who ultimately pulls the trigger may be poorly understood and not particularly glamorous but is nonetheless very important for society. Their ability to withstand tremendous psychological pressure and handle large trading positions means that there is always someone who is willing to take the other side in executing apparently unattractive trades. Across the hundreds of thousands of trades executed each day, this translates to enhanced market depth and liquidity and increased efficient execution for customers, be they corporate clients or investors. They alone – and no computer or artificial intelligence machine – can manage markets' complex and perennial transmission chain between fear and greed.

While there is no such thing as a 'standard trader' (the author has yet to meet one), certain personality traits are fairly common. A large body of literature, including empirical surveys, has analysed how the biases described in previous chapters apply to traders in their working environments, be they trading rooms or futures' trading pits. My key message boils down to this: the modern risk manager would be well advised to understand a trader's brain before they analyse his trading book.

This chapter provides a bird's-eye view of some of the outstanding studies in this area, with practical demonstrations of how these findings apply to traders and their game keepers.

Implications: Many risk managers view traders as the key potential sources of danger for the organization and attempt to corral and box them in using controls, mathematical models and watchdog-type controllers. No matter what one thinks about them, traders are one of the most important sources of revenue, the lifeblood of the organization. As such, they need to be not only cautiously and warily watched, but also, and most importantly, helped and supported. They must not be overly eulogized or grotesquely demonized. After all, first and foremost they are human beings and require the help of others to spot their biases and other psychological weaknesses. Most humans crave some attention and traders are no exception. Through genuine care and attention, you will probably discover that the other person is more reasonable than you would have expected, but equally, you will always find some loose cannon somewhere that needs serious curbing. As usual, the wild card should not be confused with the pack.

8.1 Psychology in the trading room: a diamond buried in the sand

'People are our most important asset' is an oft-heard statement by top business leaders, both within and outside the financial services industry. But are they? Judging from the data on the way most human resources departments in the City manage this 'most important asset', certain questions and doubts naturally arise. For instance, if staff really were crucial, one would reasonably expect banks to monitor and manage the psychological state of their staff on an on-going, if not continuous, basis. Unfortunately, the opposite is true.

While some banks require prospective recruits to take some fairly general psychometric tests, there is no evidence of anything remotely resembling a psychometric standard for staff who work in the City. Even those banks that require psychometric tests generally do not follow them up and manage this important dimension over time. This means that psychological tests are essentially used as general screening devices, as one might use references from previous employers or maths proficiency tests, rather than as the first step of an active human resources management process. Once someone is hired, the key dimensions that are managed are: the employee's cost, how much revenue he or she produces (if he or she works in a profit centre) and the tenure and title at the company. That's more or less about it.

As basic management practice tells, one cannot manage what is not measured. And even more precisely, what is not measured may be believed to be non-existent, which in the case of traders' psychology is exactly the dark side of management. Because they do not measure or observe the trader's mind, management may pay attention to other details which are simply irrelevant to the central issue at hand. Particularly in the case of traders, where the psychological state plays a critical role in driving performance, some questions are then in order:

- What is the 'psychometric portfolio' in a given organization or trading desk?
- What key personality traits are over- and under-represented in this portfolio?
- What are the key dimensions of the leaders' personality and how much diversity exists in the groups that they manage?
- How would different personalities fare under a variety of market conditions?

These questions are hardly theoretical. Recall that cognitive resonance and tribal instincts are likely to skew hiring decisions towards mirroring and extending the existing psychological profile of a group. Consequently, most if not all the members of a team are likely to respond to a given situation *in broadly the same way* and assume the same trading position. The position was caused by the portfolio of unconscious and unintended psychological profiles!

The fact that each team member may then offer a conscious explanation of the position with different arguments becomes utterly irrelevant. In the same fashion, the organization has created an illusion of diversification, since it is commonly thought that having five people trading a certain risk is preferable to one alone. That misses the point that, if all of them broadly think alike, their response to situations will not differ much.

It is evident that the term 'managing of human resources' in the world of investment banking refers mostly to the *effects* of an employee's productivity rather than to its *sources*. No doubt, one should know how many employees there are in the various areas, how much they cost and what they produce. However, reducing the process of managing staff resources to just this set of analyses becomes little more than a pure accounting exercise. Group learning exercises captured in latest catchphrases such as the 'corporate culture' or 'leadership seminars' provide very little guidance on what lies behind successful individuals. As the organizational environment strongly interacts with the performance of the individual, let me try to articulate the question of how to manage human resources into something more specific:

- What frames of risk are adopted in various areas of the organization?

- Do the frames of risk support or hinder the performance of the groups in question?

By answering these basic questions, one can then look to establishing optimal frames of risk, to those where performance is linked to psychological profiles.

8.1.1 People management today = bond portfolio management *circa* 1970s

One can compare the current state of people management in banking to the way in which bond portfolios used to be 'managed' until the late 1970s, prior to the derivatives revolution. At the time, marking a portfolio to market was probably the most advanced and enlightened method for measuring exposures. It is worth noting that some key conceptual advances, such as the basic fixed-income concepts of duration and modified duration, dated back to the late 1930s. However, most would look to a static picture of their bonds, whereby their face values would be just added up. In some countries with less stringent rules and regulations on accounting disclosure than in Anglo-Saxon jurisdictions, accrual accounting has remained the dominant valuation metric for very large bond portfolios even after derivatives appeared on the scene. Many countries in continental Europe are cases in point.

Fuelled by a massive increase in computing power, the derivatives revolution brought a dramatic improvement in the quality and granularity of information used to manage portfolios. All varieties of sensitivities, be they related to changes in interest rates, currency rates or even changes to the sensitivities themselves, suddenly appeared. Other than for accounting purposes, the face value became rather irrelevant to portfolio management. That is the quality leap that banks have to make with respect to their human resources management.

8.1.2 Measuring the sensitivity of performance to psychological attributes

While there is no shortage of human resources analysts who look at performance, relatively few look at the *sensitivity* of performance to one's psychological attributes. This is the major 'call to arms' of this book. Throughout this chapter, a detailed set of studies demonstrates the existence of psychological biases both in investment banking professionals and amongst amateur traders. As the importance of psychology in trading is well known, continuing to manage an institution's psychometric portfolio in a purely passive fashion – if that has anything to do with management – is probably as useful as arranging deckchairs on the *Titanic*.

8.2 The London Business School studies[51]

The Centre for Organizational Research (COR) at the London Business School (LBS) has been spearheading a major research effort into the behaviour of traders and managers concerning financial decisions involving risk (Fenton-O'Creevy *et al*, 2004). The research starts from the premise that modern financial theory attempts to explain the aggregate behaviour of markets but has not specified in great detail what traders actually do and how they behave in practice. This 'failure at the margin' of modern financial theory does not matter much in the context of the aggregate behaviour of markets as a whole, but becomes relevant when dealing with individual trader behaviour. Their research articulates a few key themes:

- *Illusion of control.* Traders want to believe that they enjoy a certain degree of control over the circumstances that surround them. They will use a variety of arguments – some may say fetishes – to explain their ability to be in control.

- *Risk propensity, psychological traits and behavioural biases.* Prominent amongst these are attribution and selection bias, first and foremost with respect to so-called contrarian views against the market's prevailing belief. Contrarian views are seldom discussed openly prior to the occurrence of a given event. Conversely, these views receive high attention and status after the fact if they are proven correct.

- *Management behaviour, loss aversion and contextual influences on traders' behaviour.* The LBS research underscores how management's style is tight with respect to losses but laissez-faire with upside risk. This draws on prospect theory principles to elaborate on people's asymmetrical sensitivity to profits and losses.

The next few sections examine each of these themes in turn.

8.2.1 Illusion of control[52]

Illusion of control comprises three elements – dispositions, learning and environmental factors (Langer & Roth, 1975).

Illusion of control is relevant to the trading context because it influences individual reactions to situations and decision-making processes. Research suggests that the illusion of control is very common and that there are circumstances in which it is more likely to arise. A number of these are inherent in the trading situation. These include: skill-related cues, stress, a focus on goals to the exclusion of reflection on process, and early successes.

Several authors have investigated these peculiar circumstances and how they can result in illusion of control. Langer (1975) has studied skill-related cues and demonstrated how

---

[51] Thanks to Prof. Nigel Nicholson of the London Business School and Prof. Mark Fenton-O'Creevy of Open University Business School for their permission to draw upon the research and their invaluable suggestions.
[52] The parts of the original article were used here with special permission of EBSCO Publishing and Prof. Fenton-O'Creevy.

individuals can attribute to themselves a certain degree of control in situations that are essentially ruled by chance. By 'skill', Langer denotes the properties of the situation such as involvement in the decisions, competition and familiarity with the stimulus and the situation itself. Kahn & Cooper (1993) targeted stress in the trading room with a study of 600 dealers. Of the 225 who replied to their questionnaire, over two-thirds feared 'misreading the market' (73.8 per cent) and having too much work (70 per cent). Sixty-two per cent complained of the challenge of learning new techniques for handling information, as opposed to only 41 per cent who complained of information overload. So much for the propaganda that technology makes one's life easier!

Stress is also shown by Friedland *et al* (1992) to contribute to a heightened illusion of control. As far as excessive goal focus is concerned, Gollwitzer & Kinney (1989) also show that illusory beliefs about control are not conducive to sound decision-making. According to these authors, insensitivity to feedback, difficulty in remaining open-minded and a predisposition towards greater risk taking are some of the adverse side-effects that stem from an illusion of control.

One hundred and seven traders across four investment banks in the City formed the sample set that was used to measure the illusion of control. More specifically, the study sought to validate the hypothesis that performance deteriorates as illusion of control increases. A number of factors were taken into account in the definition of performance, including the traders' self-ratings, total annual earnings and assessments by senior trader-managers. Under-performance was also articulated in terms of some of its key attributes, such as risk management, ability to analyse the market, lower contribution to firm's profits, poor interpersonal skills and lower remuneration relative to peers. The sample was well diversified according to a broad set of criteria:

- Education: half of the participants held a higher degree and over three-fourths at least had a degree.

- Responsibility: 52 of the 107 participants were traders. Of the others, 40 were trader-managers and 15 were senior managers.

- Remuneration: over 30 per cent of the participants earned over £500,000 per annum. The remainder was evenly split between the £300,000–£500,000 and £100,000–£300,000 per annum ranges.

- Age and trading tenure: participants were aged between 24 and 48 with a mean of 32.5. Trading experience ranged between six months and 27 years, with an average of five years.

Two key theses on the adverse effects of illusion of control were tested:

- *High illusion of control leads to underperformance.* Specifically, the performances of traders with a high illusion of control were compared with those of their peers with low or moderate illusion of control. This bias would indeed cause the former traders to be less effective in their assessment of market movements.

■ *High illusion of control leads to lower risk awareness and, in broader terms, sloppier risk management.* A high illusion of control may drive traders to persist in their attempts to control the environment (so-called *primary control behaviour*, such as maintaining or even increasing a losing position) rather than adopting the more appropriate behaviour of adapting to the environment (so-called *secondary control behaviour*, such as complying with stop-losses and exiting losing positions).

After a set of interviews in which subjects were asked for a self-assessment of their ability *vis-à-vis* their peers, a computer game followed. The mechanics of the test, carried out with a computer game simulation tool, are proprietary. For confidentiality reasons, these will not be revealed, so as not to jeopardize their application in future tests. Senior managers were then asked to rate the traders' performance. These assessments showed a lower dispersion than the traders' self-assessments. At the same time, traders' profit performance exhibited a significant correlation with the managers' views of profit performance, risk management and analytical skills. This means that, in the eyes of the managers, only interpersonal skills were not affected by a trader's profit performance.

The regressions in the study supported the key hypotheses of the study. Total earnings and performance contribution are positively correlated with analytical ability and risk management skills. These attributes present a *significant negative correlation* with illusion of control. In other words, the greater the illusion of control, the less analytical ability, risk management skills, total earnings and performance contribution – a dire set of circumstances. This confirms the intuition according to which master traders – those who are most likely to display risk management skills – are those who are less likely to fall prey to illusion of control. The apparent irony is that those with the best risk management skills are most likely to be aware of their limitations in managing the vagaries of the outside environment. Of the key traits studied, only interpersonal skills did not present any meaningful relationship.

The findings from other experimental studies are consistent with these conclusions. Biais *et al* (2000) led a study of 67 subjects at the University of Toulouse. They devised a psychological questionnaire to measure a variety of psychological dimensions in their subjects, such as their degree of overconfidence, impulsiveness and self-monitoring. Their availability, representativeness and confirmation biases were also tracked. Thereafter, the subjects participated in an experimental financial market. Impulsive subjects tended to place more orders but did not incur larger losses. Overconfident subjects showed a greater tendency to place unprofitable orders. Finally, confirmation and representativeness biases were found to create major obstacles for the subjects' learning processes.

8.2.2 Risk propensity

Sitkin & Pablo (1992) first advanced the definition of *risk propensity* as 'the tendency of the decision maker either to take or to avoid risks'. In their model, propensity is presented as the outcome of several factors, including habits and previous risk experiences. This is different from risk *perception*, which is a function of a variety of environmental and psychological elements. According to these authors, perception itself is an effect of risk propensity. To prepare the study, the LBS researchers chose to attribute a stronger causal role to risk perception. Scarce data availability, difficulties in defining conceptual boundaries and the oft-inconsistent use of the term 'risk behaviour' in several studies are just some of the obstacles that prevent a more straightforward definition. These issues make it difficult to define, let alone measure, the contribution of environmental factors and individual risk preferences to risk decisions and behaviours.

Risk perception and propensity are by no means constant over time even for the same individual. The perceived riskiness of the environment and beliefs about one's own capabilities have a major impact on one's risk perception (Slovic *et al*, 1980; Bandura, 1982). Accordingly, the LBS team classified risk-takers in the following categories:

TABLE 8.1 ■ Self-control versus environmental risk matrix

	Perceive high environmental risk	Perceive low environmental risk
Perceive high self-control of risk consequences	**Daredevil** = Calculated risk-taker (*deluded*)	**Strategist** = Confident risk-taker (*blinkered*)
Perceive low self-control of risk consequences	**Gambler** = Hopeful risk-taker (*fantasizing*)	**Drifter** = Oblivious risk-taker (*fatalistic*)

Seasoned managers may, by virtue of the confidence engendered by their own experience, engage in high-risk behaviours when they believe they can reverse or cope with negative consequences (Shapira, 1995). Some traders may assume major positions in very volatile markets by believing that their analytical skills or, simply, their 'luck' (Thompson *et al*, 1993) immunize them from trouble. Anecdotally, despite the growing level of education and experience amongst traders, more or less every trading room features traders with some degree of superstition.

The study, spearheaded by Fenton-O'Creevy *et al* (2003), identified some key aspects in decision-makers:

8.2.2.1 Dispositions

This summarizes traits and motivational propensities that drive people to take risks. Sensation seeking is the trait that surfaces most often in a broad review of the literature (Zuckerman, 1979, 1983; Zuckerman, Ball & Black, 1990; Bartram *et al*, 1997; see also the empirical findings on futures traders' motives in section 8.3).

8.2.2.2 Causal beliefs

This refers to guidelines that risk-takers believe they have to comply with to be successful. This may have to do with the mental imagery and attitude that is considered necessary or with desirable position-management principles. These may include, for instance, the established recommendation to 'cut your losses quickly and let your profits run'. Another principle that some traders follow involves setting up some positions that aim to generate a regular stream of income within their portfolio. This way, they hope to have more time and less psychological pressure to generate profits on other positions that require more time to work out. A trader may have a position in which he is riding a positively sloped yield curve, thereby generating some positive carry if bond prices do not drop. Alongside it, he may have another position with a strong directional content that requires a month to produce the expected outcome.

8.2.2.3 *Salience*

This explains how individuals differ in their utilities for loss and gain as a function of past experience (MacCrimmon & Wehrung, 1986). In the case of traders and their managers, salience refers to how and when they encountered losses in the past. Readers will recall that salience is a feature of availability bias. It affects risk perceptions by increasing or reducing the decision-maker's estimation of control possibilities and the perceived riskiness of the environment.

8.2.2.4 *Ability*

This refers to the individual's capability to manage risk. This concept encompasses both the set of skills and abilities that are relevant to the specific risk at hand and general coping skills such as intelligence, flexibility and organizational ability. It affects his perception about the ability to manage risks and recover from negative outcomes. For instance, a trader may believe that his trading book requires someone with a painstaking attention to detail, which he has. In addition, he considers himself to be an outgoing entrepreneurial person who can manage himself self-sufficiently without a lot of supervision. The trader may deduce that he has plenty of ability to manage risks.

The above study concentrated on the trader as an individual. The influence of the environment – while recognized as an important factor – was not within the ambit of the questionnaires. It was indeed important to simplify the decision-making process being studied. These influences on the decision-maker can express themselves in three ways:

- Other people may influence and reinforce the decision-maker's beliefs and orient him or her to assume more or less risk.
- Various social forces are at play in the risk environment, including people acting as suppliers of information about outcomes and causes.
- Other people may reinforce the decision-maker's judgments of situational riskiness and control capabilities.

A sample of 800 managers, business professionals and students was created. Based on the literature and pilot interviews, subjects were asked with what frequency they engaged in a variety of high-risk activities. All these activities involved choice by the subject and, as such, excluded involuntary risks. They fell into three groups:

- Livelihood: e.g., how risky would one's career and financial moves be?

- Recreational: e.g., would one be involved in risky sports?

- Personal: e.g., would one engage in intense drinking or gambling?

These questions aimed to identify correlations between past and current risk behaviour and consistent patterns across these domains. They also attempted to detect significant differences in individuals' portfolios of different risk situations (e.g., would risk-seeking in one's financial and career choices be positively correlated with pursuit of high-risk sports?). The answers were used to run regressions against a variety of demographic variables, that is, age, gender, job level, organization size, tenure at the organization, number of employees in career and number of major career changes in one's track record.

The results not only supported the notion of the existence of consistent patterns in one's propensity scale across a variety of domains but also showed a strong correlation (0.7) between past and current behaviours. Further, the study showed significant correlations – ranging between 0.327 and 0.528 – between risk propensity in the three domains and the demographic patterns. For instance, a negative correlation was found between risk-taking and age, meaning that younger people take higher risks. The sex differences in risk appetite, with men scoring higher, were also consistent with other empirical and experimental evidence from other studies (Powell & Ansic, 1997; Byrne *et al*, 1999; Odean & Barber, 2001a).

8.2.3 Management behaviour, loss aversion and risk knowledge

Another important stage of the research project looked at how traders are managed and what biases may be inadvertently fostered by them. In particular, the study examined how some of the dilemmas described by prospect theory may apply to the trading room. Following some of the 1990s' most notorious trading debacles, such as Barings, Sumitomo and Daiwa, the study also sought to investigate how managers monitor their trading subordinates to avert such disasters.

The survey used a sample of 100 professionals from the London offices of three investment banks. Of these, 44 were traders, 46 were trader-managers and ten belonged to senior management. In this last category, seven people did not trade directly. Both equities and fixed-income traders were covered. No foreign-exchange dealers were involved.

The study relied mostly on questionnaires that were classified as belonging to a set of standardized categories. Heuristics such as illusion of control and changing risk propensity were confirmed but were hardly the only ones. A widespread belief in several other desirable traits for an ideal trader also emerged and was labelled as 'work the world' theories. These *ex ante* traits have little or no representation in modern finance theory and as such may be deemed as irrational aberrations. In the hustle and bustle of the trading room, they are nevertheless important and feature:

- *flair and intuition*, which reflects the general belief that strong technical knowledge of markets is simply not enough. Sometimes, gut feeling is an oft-heard expression for these traits;

- *reflexivity*, according to which a trader has to blend his quantitative skills with an understanding of how other people react. Indeed, this point has already been underscored in the discussion on game theory (see Chapter 6);

- *contrarianism*, which involves trading against the market's prevailing common wisdom. The researchers, however, acknowledged that this trait was plagued to some extent by survivorship bias. Contrarian trades that were mentioned during the interviews were the most successful ones.

The study also underscored how the managers' behaviour, incentives and intervention points diverge from conventional utility theory. Figure 8.1 shows this pattern:

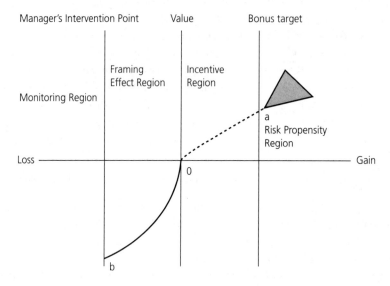

FIGURE 8.1 ■ Prospect theory and trading managers' behaviour

This graph is consistent with prospect theory. It shows that if you begin with the reference point at the centre (0,0), which is your starting position for profit or loss, the curve is asymmetric where the curve is steeper in the loss region than in the profit region. Contrary to conventional utility theory, the risk preference is far from constant.

Comparing this picture with the prospect theory graph in Chapter 4, you see the behaviour in the profitable regions is plotted as a straight line, rather than as a flattening curve as normal prospect theory would dictate. In practice, other framing effects coming into play over time may help explain the flattening effects in the profit region. For instance, accounting deadlines, most critically near year-end, generally encourage trading managers to reduce their trading inventory if they have already met the annual profitability target to which their bonus is tied.

8.3 Behaviour of speculators in commodity and futures markets

The studies above refer mainly to individuals in the trading rooms of large investment banks. Belonging to a large professional organization involves observing certain rules of behaviour which are particular to that corporate culture. It is inevitable that these rules influence one's behaviour to a considerable extent. A significant body of literature and empirical evidence also exists on the behaviour of individual professional traders, for the most part in futures markets. One should distinguish these independent professional and retail traders from their brethren at major investment banks in that the former rely more greatly than the latter on self-discipline in managing their own positions and risk attitudes. In surveying the literature in this area, two key themes are particularly relevant:

- the impact of noise trading, and

- the psychological issues and constructs of traders.

8.3.1 Noise and the positive feedback trader

With respect to the former, Black (1986) defined 'noise' as non-information, such as technical charts, unproven investment selection methods that suddenly become fashionable, investing fads and others. In other words, 'noise trading' is the activity of traders who rely on these methods as if they generated real information. Sanders (1996) and Sanders, Irwin & Leuthold (1997) studied the impact of demand by so-called noise traders in futures markets. These are divided into positive and negative feedback traders. These definitions refer to traders who buy ('positive') and sell ('negative') after price increases. Feedback traders may exhibit short- or long-term memory, depending on the horizon of returns that they use as a basis for their decisions. Using a large cross-section of market returns and popular sentiment indicators, such as the Consensus' Index of Bullish Market Opinion and Market Vane's Bullish Consensus Index, these authors find long-term positive feedback to be a common behaviour of futures traders. Other studies (Cutler *et al*, 1989) had previously found positive feedback to be a dominant trait of traders, albeit over a shorter time horizon. A few key aspects surface and these are broadly consistent with the results of the LBS research shown earlier.

8.3.1.1 The hopeful trader

Feedback trading is another variety of hope, a common and dangerous trait that often inter-feres with rational risk decision-making. Hope does not bode well for future expected returns. Indeed, futures markets do not show any evidence of predictable market returns using noise trader sentiment indicators. These are the conclusions of a follow-up empirical study by Sanders, Irwin & Leuthold (1997). Their investigation demonstrated that noise trader sentiment does not generally create a systematic bias in futures prices. Some scant evidence was found only in isolated markets and in very peculiar circumstances. These findings on positive feedback trading are consistent with other empirical evidence (Sentana & Wadhwani, 1992; Antoniou *et al*, 1999).

Another body of empirical evidence confirms that these not-so-rational heuristics are fairly widespread. Smidt (1965) conducted a survey of 349 amateur futures speculators to classify their trading styles and decision-making criteria. Over half of them relied exclusively or moderately on price charts to render trading decisions. Only 4 per cent of those surveyed considered themselves information specialists who obtain and use information before it is widely available to other traders. Finally, most amateur speculators surveyed preferred to trade commodities about which they had personal knowledge or advice.

8.3.1.2 *Trading for excitement*

Other surveys confirm that small speculators do not behave in an entirely rational manner (Brennan, 1995; Nagy & Obenberger, 1994; Draper, 1985). According to these surveys, the average futures trader is highly educated and trades for leverage and the excitement. Furthermore, their important sources of information include: articles and publications, broker and newsletter recommendations, advisory services, and their own analysis. In line with these findings, Canoles (1994) carried out a survey of 115 retail futures traders in Alabama. He found that speculators enjoy the drama and suspense of carrying open positions. Professional trading advisory services and general financial publications emerged as their favourite sources of information. Collectively, these results suggest that retail speculators generally do not bring new information to bear on the markets, and gather much of their information from targeted media sources.

Moving on to the psychological issues of traders, a few other studies emphasize the existence of other cognitive biases. Speculation can be viewed as a form of insurance that is offered to clients as a way to obtain gains. From this point of view, a particular type of speculator known as the scalper may also be viewed as a type of a rational trader who engages in very short-run trading for gain. By scalper, one refers to those who trade positions hoping to achieve a series of small, very short-term gains, without carrying large overnight positions, if any at all. Indeed, Silber (1984) describes these speculators as having a horizon between one and three minutes, where at least nominally they appear to be expecting gains in return for the liquidity that they provide. Other empirical evidence on futures traders confirms that locals generally do not carry overnight positions (Kuserk & Locke, 1993; Manaster & Mann, 1996).

8.3.1.3 *The scalper*

The *scalper* is a sub-set of a category of professional traders in the pits known as the *locals*. *Locals* usually operate in the pit in which a particular product is traded. Locke & Mann (1999) examines trades by a sample of locals for behavioural patterns described by prospect theory and other behavioural finance literature. Based on previous performance, floor traders were divided into four quartiles. 330 locals trading four contracts (Deutsche mark, Swiss franc, live cattle and pork bellies) were studied with minute-by-minute data from the Chicago

Mercantile Exchange (CME) for the first six months of 1995. On average, the most successful traders (first quartile) were shown to hold winning and losing positions for less than half the time needed by their less successful colleagues in the fourth quartile. These findings provide some support for the existence of prospect theory's *loss realization aversion* amongst professional futures traders. In the context of finance, this is called *disposition effect* (Shefrin & Statman, 1985), where there is a tendency to sell assets that have increased in value and to hold on to assets that have lost value (Weber & Camerer, 1998). At the same time, these effects on asset pricing were not found to have a significant impact on most disciplined traders. Other empirical studies on disposition effect performed in the Chicago pits (Heisler, 1994) and Sydney futures markets (Frino *et al*, 2002) reach similar conclusions.

End-users of futures markets are by no means exempt from these biases. Pennings & Leuthold (2000) surveyed 440 farmers to investigate the factors affecting their decisions on the futures markets. Specifically, the study sought to understand why a farmer may accept or reject the use of a futures contract as a hedging device and how his risk attitudes are shaped. Product understanding handsomely beat the farmer's risk exposure and risk attitude as the main driving factor for his decision. The sample was further decomposed based on the subjects' professed product understanding. Those who appeared less knowledgeable decided on the basis of their financial wherewithal, and in particular their debt/equity ratio. The most knowledgeable farmers, on the other hand, wanted mainly to keep in touch with markets to achieve more advantageous prices for their goods. This segment mentioned that using futures helped increase their freedom for business action, so the farmers' perceptions and their psychological constructs played a major role in shaping their risk attitudes.

A follow-up survey of 373 Dutch hog farmers by Pennings & Garcia (2001) found their risk attitude to depend to a considerable extent on whether the farmers would use or reject futures markets as a hedging device. Risk attitude, it was concluded, was a higher-order and too complex a piece of information to be summarized in a single measure. Intriguingly, the farmers displayed increasing risk aversion that was fully consistent with the S-shaped utility curve postulated by prospect theory. Specifically, they were presented with decision alternatives that were framed as lotteries. Lotteries with relatively low utility saw almost two-thirds of the farmers become risk-seeking. Conversely, lotteries with high utility saw 39.6 per cent of the participants display risk-averse behaviour.

This was not the only prospect theory principle to find confirmation amongst futures traders. In a later survey of 450 Dutch hog farmers performed by Pennings (2002), the reference price emerged as a key factor influencing the farmers' decisions to initiate a futures position or not. 'Pulling the trigger' was indeed how this researcher defined this decision. By reference price, one means a level that was set previously to enter a position. Less experienced and more emotional traders are indeed prone to choking when their reference price is touched. Rather than 'pulling the trigger', they can simply freeze like scared rabbits caught in the light. While prospect theory discusses people's preferences relative to their initial reference price, here the reference price matters only as an execution level. Full rationality would require the trader to execute immediately after the level is touched.

8.4 Additional behavioural research on other types of risk-takers

Other studies have targeted specific areas and classes of investors. While their detailed account is outside the primary scope of this book, the serious issues they raise should not be underestimated for institutional investors. Indeed, some financial institutions attempt to address and exploit these issues in their marketing and product design efforts. It is important to note that the findings across a broad class of investors consistently confirm a large number of behavioural biases.

8.4.1 Retail investors

Major studies focusing on retail investors have been conducted by Odean (1998a, 1998b, 1999; Odean & Barber 1999, 2000a, 2000b, 2001a, 2001b, 2002a, 2002b; Odean & Gervais 2001). These studies confirm the existence of host biases amongst retail investors, including the disposition effect, over-trading and gender differences. In addition, the apparent ease of online trading influences their perceptions of risk and their own abilities. Their detailed account is beyond the scope of the present book. Readers who are interested can explore these topics further in the bibliography.

Studies have also focused on the portfolio management strategies of retail investors and the advice that they receive from mutual fund companies. In behavioural portfolio theory (Shefrin & Statman, 1999), it is hypothesized that investors structure their portfolio as a pyramid based on their safety needs. This means there is a broad, 'protect the nest egg' base and a narrow, very risky 'get-rich-quickly' top. Principal-protected financial products are designed exactly to meet both capital protection and capital growth needs with only one package.

Ravi Dhar & Alok Kumar (2001) analysed the impact of price trends on the trading decisions of more than 40,000 households with accounts at a major discount brokerage house and found that buying and selling decisions of investors in their sample were influenced by price trends of up to three months. They show systematic variations in the response of these investor segments to reference points such as recent high and low prices. Furthermore, consistent with differences in expectations, the disposition effect varies across the investor segments.

An important research project led by Zurstrassen & DeBondt (2000) investigated behavioural differences among European retail investors. The survey featured 237 questions and had a sample of over 3,000 individual investors in the five largest European countries (France, Germany, Italy, Spain and the UK) plus Belgium. Despite all the rationality that is supposed to underpin financial decisions, 43 per cent of the Germans stated that 'investing is fun'. Most investors who resided in the other countries disagreed. Most Germans answered the 'Are you a leader?' question affirmatively. It is not surprising that they also were the least worried about risk and that they supported taking calculated risks as the key means of achieving capital growth. Some basic tenets of prospect theory with respect to one's price reference point were confirmed. Indeed, all supported the statement that it is imprudent to increase a position in a stock after it has doubled or tripled in price. Showing little regard for mean-variance optimization principles, most would put one-third of their portfolio into real estate, bonds and stocks.

8.4.2 Corporate hedging and Treasury decisions

In tandem with the much publicized trading disasters in corporate treasury departments in the mid-1990s to the present day (Procter & Gamble, Gibson Greetings, Metallgesellschaft just to mention a few), a significant body of research has focused on the rationale for corporate hedging and, more generally, on financial risk management outside the financial services industry. The blow-ups in corporate hedging also led to an increased awareness inside these firms. In a 1995 survey of US industrial firms, Smithson (1996) found that almost two-thirds, or 63 per cent, had conducted or planned to implement an internal audit of their derivatives practices. Some of these risk disasters are analysed in greater detail in Chapter 10. This section sets out the main findings in this research area.

Recent finance literature identifies several factors behind corporate hedging decisions, particularly with respect to using futures and other derivatives. These include:

- financial distress costs;
- the firm's risk exposure (Tufano, 1996);
- managerial risk aversion (Smith & Stulz, 1985; Stulz, 1984, 1990, 1996);
- growth opportunities;
- access to financing sources, including capital markets (Froot, Scharfstein & Stein, 1993);
- tax liabilities and incentives (Graham & Smith, 1997).

Nance, Smith & Smithson (1993) surveyed 535 firms, based on the union of the Fortune 500 and the S&P 400. One hundred and ninety-four firms completed the questionnaires, with 169 of these being usable responses. Almost two-thirds of the respondents (104 firms) had used hedging instruments during the fiscal year 1986. These hedging instruments included futures, swaps and options.

According to this questionnaire, the firms that hedge display the following features. They all:

- face rising tax brackets;
- have less coverage of fixed claims;
- are larger in size;
- enjoy more growth options in their investment opportunities;
- employ fewer hedging substitutes.

After the large corporate debacles on derivatives of the mid-1990s, there was a surge of empirical research on corporate users of derivative products and risk management. Tufano (1998) argues that the adoption of risk management may limit the scrutiny of external capital markets. This applies especially to those instances in which managers may want to fund some pet project that has a negative expected Net Present Value but still offers them some private benefit. This argument corroborates the point made earlier about the influence of the group and inefficiency in the internal capital markets of corporations (see Chapter 6).

Other important surveys on the usage of derivatives by corporations have been led by Bodnar *et al* (1996) in the US. On the international side, other similar studies have been performed in the UK (Grant & Marshall, 1997), Germany (Bodnar & Gebhardt, 1999), Finland (Hakkarainen *et al*, 1997) and Portugal (Mota, 2001). Section 8.3 has already demonstrated Pennings's conclusions with respect to the use of futures markets by small Dutch farmers.

8.4.3 Other professionals' biases: FX dealers and institutional investors

Other studies look at the behaviour of a specific category of risk takers without going into the same degree of detail on their psychology as in the LBS studies.

Foreign exchange (FX) dealers have been the subject of a few studies. These dealers undergo an inordinate amount of stress and as such provide an interesting sample on how rational people can behave when placed under significant stress.

Cheung, Chinn & Marsh (1999) looked at UK traders' beliefs with respect to three important areas:

- the microeconomic operation of the FX market;

- the importance of macroeconomic fundamental factors in affecting exchange rates;

- microstructure factors in FX.

Over a sample of 110 responses, they found that most traders believe fundamentals to affect prices over an horizon of about six months, as opposed to the 36 estimated by the academic community (Meese & Rogoff, 1983). Fundamentals were utterly discounted within a six-month horizon. In addition, and perhaps surprisingly, the survey showed very little difference of opinion between fundamental- and chart-orientated traders. Purchasing Power Parity was deemed virtually irrelevant amongst the fundamental factors exerting an influence over the previously mentioned six-month horizon. The study also found market 'norms' and behavioural phenomena to exert a strong influence on the way bid-offer spreads are set in the FX market.

Another more recent study by Bjonnes & Rime (2001) examined the impact of electronic dealing systems on FX traders' behaviour. These systems have grown in importance, rising to about 50 per cent of interbank trading in 1998 (Cheung & Chinn 1999, Cheung *et al*, 2000). According to these authors, direction is more important than size for any given trade in electronic trading systems. Evidence of wider bid-offer spreads was found only after series of cumulative orders all going in the same direction. This survey looked at four FX dealers during one week in March 1998. The findings confirmed the conclusion of a previous similar study (Lyons, 1995) based on 1992 data. According to these studies, market-makers display both information and inventory effects in their pricing behaviour. These effects manifest him- or herself in the market-maker's widening of spreads to protect him- or himself against the effect of private information and then adjusting the midpoint in the spread (so-called quote shading) to induce trade in a preferred direction to adjust the risk inventory.

Other empirical research is about the behaviour of institutional investors. Barber & Odean (2001) examined the impact of attention in the decisions of individual and institutional investors. These authors looked at how momentum and contrarian investors respectively follow stocks that are often in the news or are not, and how the buying and selling decisions may be affected by different psychological factors. They applied this to all investors. They also compared buying decision mechanics of individual and institutional investors. While individual investors comply with the thesis being tested during high- and low-volume days, value money managers stand out amongst institutional investors as the players most willing to take the other side of the trade in those days. Consistent with their previous studies discussed in the section on the behaviour of individual investors, Barber & Odean find that this active momentum trading activity results in underperformance *vis-à-vis* the major stock market indices. A similar study on the behaviour of institutional investors exists outside the US, too. Ersoy-Bozcuk & Lasfer (2001) test for the existence of timing patterns and their impact on returns in the 1993–1998 period. Market timing is indeed anathema for the prophets of market efficiency, who would discourage it due to its higher-than-necessary transaction costs and inability to pick securities that will beat the market. While market timing with a value bias – that is, looking to buy and sell underpriced and overpriced securities respectively – is shown to be widespread, no return benefit seems to accrue to those who practise it.

Major differences in behaviour also emerge across different categories of institutional investors, with pension funds attempting to time the market more with a momentum approach than with a value bias. Ersoy-Bozcuk & Lasfer tend to attribute these differences in behaviour to the differences in incentives and outside pressure between pension funds and other institutional investors. This question is examined in greater detail by other studies of the UK market for pension funds. Two studies by Blake, Lehman & Timmermann (2000) and Blake & Timmermann (2001) studied the impact of performance benchmarking on the behaviour of pension funds. Over the 1986–1994 period, these studies found a significant clustering in the performance of a large cross-section of UK pension funds. According to these authors, the incentive fee structure in the UK pension funds industry does not justify the considerable risks of deviating from market benchmark indices. In addition, the UK pension fund industry is shown to be far more concentrated than its US equivalent.[53]

---

[53] As of 1998, the top five fund management houses accounted for 80% of total assets under management, as opposed to only 14% in the US.

Consistent with game-theoretic behaviour, the long-term survival of managers is found to depend more on performance relative to this small reference group than on absolute performance. This finding is even more striking as mandates are found to leave more freedom to managers in moving away from indexing in the UK than in other markets.

8.5 The seven cardinal sins of trading

The previous chapters and the empirical evidence presented in this chapter should confirm how critical one's psychological make-up is for performance. The human subconscious is a powerful but largely unknown double-edged sword. It is important to summarize some of the most frequent mental traps that traders often succumb to:

- *Denial* The trader finds himself in an unfavourable situation but just pulls down the shutters on reality, pretends the problem does not exist or is not his. He finds solace in a sort of fantasy world ('It is just a technical aberration, these prices on the screen do not make any sense, it is crazy to sell at these prices').

- *Reframing* In the fast-moving world of trading, this is pervasive and can assume a variety of forms:

  - *Changing the rationale of the trade or its performance measurement metrics in flight*, even worse if one is underwater ('I was long in these treasury futures contracts but now have changed this position to a relative-value spread against the European market by selling Euro-denominated treasury futures contracts'. 'It was a volatility trade but I have now changed to a directional one').

  - *'The trade is underwater but we will book it in the investment account'*, or, 'My normal position timeframe is one week but we'll keep it for one month', 'The mark-to market on this emerging markets bond is underwater but we are earning this wonderful positive daily carry. It would be a crime to exit', or even 'Stop-losses are for chickens'.

  - *Turning a trading play into a credit view* 'This country is not going to default' (favourite statement of underwater emerging markets traders when their positions approach their stops).

  - *Invoking not better identified 'fundamentals' as a rationale to remain in the trade* These may eventually assert themselves over a few weeks or months but will one still be in business to profit from them? Also, if the trade involves a fundamental play, position sizing should be dramatically tighter. Why weren't they mentioned when it was time to size up the trade at the beginning? ('Ultimately, economics will prevail'.)

- *Conditional benchmarking* ('I am losing less money than my peer street competitors.') This is also recurrent amongst salespeople when justifying proposed trades with an unattractive return on risk capital.

- *Self-attribution bias* Something or someone else has to be blamed for trouble. This could be limits, an incompetent boss who forced cuts in a losing position before it recovered, unreasonably tight limits and so on. By magic, positions that move in the trader's favour have a knack for making all these problems disappear.

- *Hindsight bias*

- *Gambler's fallacy or law of small numbers* Here one is disregarding the staying power of his or her own risk capital. The case of LTCM in Chapter 10 will show an example of one of their famous Nobel Prize winners dismissing prescient calls for caution the year before the fund collapsed. Traders often like quoting probabilities reverting to the mean. As the sum of collective human behaviours, however, markets do have a memory that the fair coin of probabilities does not have. Based on their supposedly more informed view of a company's fortunes, credit officers are also prone to fall for gambler's fallacy. How many times does one need to hear the common statement 'If we give the company more time, they will be fine'? Does anybody worry about the real magnitude of mark-to-market hits that the institution will have to suffer in the meantime?

- *Averaging down losing positions*, or the ultimate price anchoring example ('Look at what a great value we are getting, we are increasing the position on more attractive terms'). What matters is price direction and probability, rather than absolute level. Any trader worth his salt knows that positions should be increased only as they move in the trader's favour, since his rising equity gives him or her more ammunition to be leveraged. On balance, even the best traders have no more than 10–15 per cent of their trades generate 80 per cent or more of their profits. This can work out in an attractive return on risk capital to the extent that those winning trades have a proper – and generally higher – size relative to the losers. As a variation on the mis-application of position-sizing rules, mediocre traders often reduce size as positions move in their favour. As a result, they often find themselves with large losers and small winners.

8.5.1 Gambler's fallacy and position sizing: trading for timing or for time?

At this point in the book, it is important to underscore one more aspect of the gambler's fallacy and position sizing that is behind the undoing of many traders – even the most experienced. The issue is strictly related to the reframing tendency in which traders often seek refuge when they find themselves in a losing trade. One could summarize it by simply asserting the following:

You can trade for time or timing, but not for both.

What do *'time'* and *'timing'* mean in this context?

8.5.1.1 Trading for time

This occurs when a trader needs time to have the price of his position come back in line with some fundamental and/or theoretical value. For instance, a stock may be trading very cheap relative to the intrinsic value of the company that it represents. Or, a bond may trade cheap or expensive relative to another bond with similar features, coupon and maturity. In these instances, the security is said to be mis-priced. The trader, of course, does not know how long it will take for the market to correct that. Also, he does not know how long it will take for other traders to get in and put in place the same trade that he has got, so it may take weeks or months for the security to get to a fair price. Arbitrageurs make their living by attempting to outsmart the market in correcting these mis-pricings. This activity was the mainstay of Long-Term Capital Management (LTCM), the hedge fund created by John Meriwether, the premier arbitrage operation of the second half of the 1990s. Mean-reverting trades are an important subset of this category.

8.5.1.2 Trading for timing

This, on the other hand, is a shorter-term activity that aims to exploit sudden and relatively unpredictable market moves, regardless of how closely those moves reflect the underlying fundamentals of the security. Nobody embodies this figure better than the online day-traders and their frantic activity of swapping 'rumours' in internet chat rooms and bulletin boards at the height of the New Economy Bubble. These players are mostly out to get part of the action in securities with fast-moving prices, which are said to enjoy substantial momentum. This is why these are often referred to as *momentum traders*. As these often lack or simply neglect longer-term fundamental information, they are also called *noise traders*.

While being targeted by several empirical studies shown earlier in this chapter, noise trading has never been a highly regarded activity for either the popular psyche or in academia. Let's face it, becoming a day-trader has lost a lot of appeal after the apparently unstoppable rise in internet stocks came to an abrupt end. Nevertheless, short-term trading is by no means a less important or 'worse' activity than longer-term fundamental trading or arbitrage.

What matters is which of these two one consciously chooses. Over a longer time period, a security will be exposed to a more prolonged series of uncertainties and therefore greater price volatility. This means that, *ceteris paribus*, if the investor wishes to maintain a certain target of price volatility for his portfolio, the size of its positions will have to depend on their intended holding period. A security that one intends to hold for a longer period will need to have a considerably smaller size than one that one will probably get rid of in the next two days.

How will the size need to be gauged? One crude but effective way is simply to weigh the portfolio holding by the level of volatility to which the security will be exposed. Option practitioners relate short- and long-term volatility by means of *scaling*, whereby

$$\sigma_T = \sigma_t \sqrt{(T/t)},$$

where:

σ_T = volatility between time 0 and time T

σ_t = volatility between time 0 and time t

So, for instance, if the 10-day volatility was 12 per cent, and one wanted to find the equivalent 250-day volatility:

$t = 10$

$T = 250$

$\sigma_T = 10\% \times \sqrt{(250/10)} = 10\% \times \sqrt{25} = 50\%$

Accordingly, one may relate the size S_t and S_T of two trades for holding periods t and T, respectively, according to the following:

$S_t \times \sigma_t = S_T \times \sigma_T$

This simply equates the volatility-adjusted size of two trades in the same underlying securities for different holding periods. In our example, if $S_t = 10$ million, one can solve the equation for S_T and obtain:

$S_T \times 50\% = 10$ million $\times 10\%$, or $S_T = 10$ million $\times 10\%/50\% = 2$ million

This is a crude method which relies on a variety of assumptions, first and foremost on the behaviour of short- and long-term volatility and on the path that it will assume. For instance, the long-term volatility estimate based on the short-term figure does not guarantee that volatility will not rise beyond the short-term period (after 10 days in our example). In addition, the cautionary remarks discussed with the square root rule earlier in Chapter 5 apply. It is nevertheless a healthy sizing discipline that is easier to set before becoming emotionally involved in an active trade.

Flipping between the short and long term leads many traders into trouble. Once a position is underwater, new reasons will crop up to justify the trade and why it is worth staying in it, even as the intended holding period elapses. Much like a magician pulls a rabbit out of the hat after some time, 'fundamentals' and 'good value for the money' will often be cited at this point. All this is hardly surprising, after all. Recall from the earlier discussion of mental accounting in Chapter 5 that people will go out of their way to avoid taking losses. This includes repeated choices to delay it rather than crystallize it immediately. Why wasn't the position set up as a fundamental trade at inception then? Because this different rationale and higher holding period would have resulted in a smaller size than the trader desired! – another demonstration of gambling instincts in action.

Having a smaller size, by the way, offers also more trading flexibility to add a short-term trading position to the longer-term one if favourable opportunities crop up. Conversely, loading the boat completely means that one will have no risk capital to spare to take advantage of such future possibilities.

If, as a result of the reframe, the trade remains on the books, however, the size of the trade is what does *not* usually change. As a result, the trade is several times beyond its proper size *and* for a different reason from the original one! 'Value' is also used to increase the size even further, leading to an even greater escalation of financial and emotional commitment. Needless to add, the latter is a trader's single worst enemy. It does not take a genius to figure out that the path from here to the classic gambler's ruin is a short one.

What can be done to avert gambler's fallacy? First of all, the rationale for the trade and its take-profit and stop-loss targets should be written in advance. You cannot cheat with your own writing! Secondly, a *time stop* equal to the trade's intended holding period should also be paired to the monetary stop-loss and, of course, be in writing. If you are a day-trader, your holding period should not become overnight. If you are a weekly trader, you should shut down all positions before the weekend.

Choosing the right time frame is important for long-term traders, too. Some of these fall into the trap of getting into a trade for time and fundamentals, keeping the size adequately small and then panicking to get out by applying short-term trading stops! While stop-losses are imperative for any trade, it is evident that long-term trades require looser guidelines than short-term positions. Achieving this greater flexibility is exactly the purpose of smaller position sizing.

These concepts are summarized in Figure 8.2:

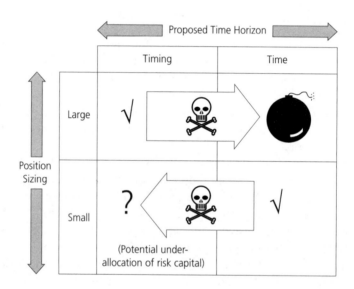

FIGURE 8.2 ■ Time horizon and position sizing

The diagram shows the importance of choosing one's time frame well and how dangerous it is to switch it in flight:

■ for the short-term trader, it is lethal to extend one's time horizon as a position goes against him;

■ for the long-term trader, it is almost as bad to curtail the capital and staying power of a long-term position by applying short-term stops and metrics.

You have already encountered some of these patterns earlier in this book. Chapter 5 illustrated the disposition effect, the investor's tendency to dispose of winners quickly and hang on to losers. Chapter 7 illustrated some of the issues that supposedly long-term investors face when applying short-term metrics. Ideally, a trader should keep the following graph in mind when setting the size and time horizon of a prospective trade:

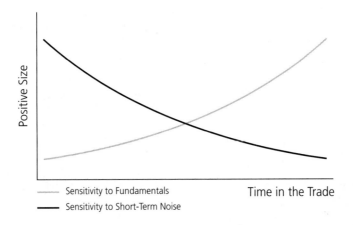

FIGURE 8.3 ■ How size and time decide the position drivers

This chart shows how the combination of size and time decides which factors will drive a prospective position. As the intended holding period increases, one is trading more information and less noise. In return, however, the position will be exposed to market volatility over a longer period. Therefore, an adjustment in its size will be necessary to limit potential losses.

While unsophisticated, some of the principles illustrated in this section should be sufficient to take active, conscious control of size *and* time, the two key ingredients of basic money management.

8.6 Future indications for research

If anyone has any doubt about the importance of psychology in trading, the evidence presented in this chapter should be a stern reminder against dismissing it. One should then wonder whether human resources are properly 'managed' in investment banks. With this background, it is hardly surprising to notice the paucity of time and resources that the trading industry earmarks to study this highly specialized territory across trading, organizational behaviour and psychology. Nor does the situation look any better in other major financial centres.

Tight cost control and an aversion towards research in a largely unknown territory is one, but by no means the only, reason. For instance, the LBS study found institutions very reluctant to provide any information to outsiders even when anonymity was guaranteed. Despite these assurances, only one participant firm provided data on how well individual traders' performance matched their psychological scores. Needless to say, the subsequent actual trading results achieved by their traders in the sample displayed a strong correlation with their psychometric profile.

In light of this short-sighted attitude, City firms should only blame themselves for the paucity of information on this important area. Sadly, some regulatory moral suasion rather than management enlightenment may be the only means of obtaining more information to move forward in this area.

Denis J Hilton (1998), a British researcher, summarizes research developments in four categories:

- personality and decision styles;

- links between information and overconfidence;

- how trading bosses manage their junior colleagues and what impact this has on decisions in a trading room;

- financial product design.

Of these, the first one is possibly the most challenging but also the one that offers the most exciting applications inside a financial institution. There is no shortage of ears for any project that can increase trading profits! This area also presents exciting side applications in the field of risk management:

- Risk capital should be diversified by psychometric profile so that undesirable concentration is curbed or made costlier.

- Risk capital should also be managed so that traders who are likely to underperform under certain market conditions are prevented from jeopardizing the financial standing of their desk or trading unit, let alone the whole bank.

- Traders whose personality is more skewed towards patience should have lower limits but more flexibility to ask for capital in a few instances during the year. Traders who are more impulsive may need more capital on average but less at the peaks.

- Particular attention should be paid to those firms who do not have an explicit policy and training programme to track traders' and managers' personality characteristics. As Chapters 10 and 11 will show, there are already plenty of disasters both in finance and outside to leave this important understanding of one's decision-making process unmanaged. Simply put, this is the ultimate source of operational risk. As such, this negligence should be penalized with higher risk capital.

CHAPTER 9

Risk management, financial alchemy and illusion of control

(Our decisions) to do something positive ... can only be taken as a result of animal spirits ... and not as the outcome of a weighted average of quantitative benefits multiplied by quantitative probabilities.

(John M. Keynes, A General Theory of Employment, Interest and Money (1936), p. 131)

7±2:

- Two words, many meanings
- The ideal role of risk management
- Frames in risk management
- Key internal clients and their delusions
- External constituencies and their motivations

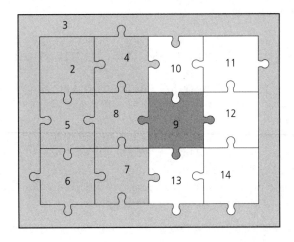

Abstract

Since the early 1980s, the rapid growth in trading and the derivatives markets has engendered a call for ever greater controls. No one captures the spirit of enhanced controls better than modern risk management teams, whose behaviour is dictated not only by senior management but also by the compulsion of regulatory regimes. Senior management relies on the risk management team for their experience, skills and resourcefulness. This can often degenerate in the misplaced belief that the risk management function can box in and vivisect risk in ever more minute and manageable components. In reality, today's modern risk manager is mainly a communication broker between risk takers and senior management. For risk management to achieve world-class quality, a deep and yet delicate balance must be struck between both constituencies, where each enjoys the same client status and fair treatment.

For all its sophistication, risk management can often be trapped by its own aura of alchemy. This is where the big egos of both management and clients take over. Here the illusion of control appears an endemic and pervasive problem. The growing list of trading disasters and risk management breakdowns is a stern reminder of how strong controls are the point where good management begins rather than ends.

Implications: Beware of the claims of financial alchemy and the actions of overly-smart people. Regardless of education and experience, no risk manager can plausibly be cleverer than the market. If you are in top management, demand that risk management units report to you with as much objectivity and impartiality as possible. There is always a potential risk for risk managers to drift too far from their role as information brokers between the traders–deal-makers and the rest of the organization. If that applies to your organization, they are straying from their job and exposing the organization to increased risk. There are already too many assistants and analysts for traders and top managers anyway! Rather than reports, ask them to offer you different trading perspectives to counterbalance the common trading wisdom in your organization.

9.1 Risk management: two words, many meanings

What else but a magical power can explain how money and gold can make people abandon their sense of proportion and override otherwise rational behaviours? While modern technology has made geographical boundaries disappear and transaction time almost instantaneous, it has also made the allure of becoming rich quickly more palpably intense, if not more real. In the terminology of biases, let me suggest that this wealth is more *available* than ever before. Many an illustrious personality in science, economics and philosophy has commented on the power gold has over people. Niccolò Machiavelli expressed the problem with pristine clarity in the sixteenth century:

> *Men always crave what they do not own more than they protect what they own.*

It is important to note that fraud may be a species of the same type of risk bias. What may motivate the conservative trader and the fraudulent are different degrees of impossible to fulfil desires – namely, greed. And the borderland between outright fraud and dishonest behaviour appears to be shifting, too. Some high-profile trading disasters over the last few years have made society and its legislators seek punishment. For example, the classic questionable behaviour of hiding losses that used to harm only one's professional reputation is now putting its perpetrators in jail.

Strictly speaking, while modern risk management developed mostly out of the need to manage large risk concentrations responsibly, product control grew out of accounting operations to catch and prevent both borderline and outright fraudulent behaviours. This book focuses on the former and leaves the lawyers and securities regulators to squabble about the latter.

The distinction between genuine risk management on the one hand and control and reporting activities on the other hand is critical. As organizational complexity has escalated over the years, risk management has become a buzzword with very different meanings across organizations. The word *management* implies human-to-human interaction. In communications systems, we would call this the human-to-human interface. Indeed, no measurement or information production activity can make up for its absence. If the risk management unit of your organization is mostly about producing reports or catching people out, your risk management exists only as a label rather than as a function. Without more, your risk management unit would serve as an extension or as another more or less sophisticated product control function.

Yet someone, whether in top management, amongst senior traders or both, ultimately has to evaluate how the whole organization is managing their risk capital and make some judgments on how much is too much. Trade-offs between risk and return and between commercial needs and a fair return on the firm's risk capital for shareholders exist in any organization. If they are not managed consciously, the market will do it on the firm's behalf. This signal is often a harbinger of trouble. This decision-making process, and nothing else, is the truest form of risk management. In fact, the strict meaning of the word *management* involves a decision. Of course, decisions require information. However, the *provision* and the *use* of information should not be confused.

The following sections illustrate various types of roles which different organizations label as risk management. Section 9.2 outlines what risk management actually is. Being not exempt from all human frailties described earlier in this book, the author does not claim to escape all the routine biases.

9.1.1 Once upon a time: the watchdog

With the explosive combination of financial and IT technology and deregulation of markets on a global basis since the late 1980s, trading operations reached an unprecedented degree of expansion and complexity. Product innovation, most apparent in derivative technology and in global geographical coverage, meant that several people or groups could effectively assume the same view simultaneously, regardless of whether that was intended or not.

A handful of large US money centre banks realized that the growth in front office had far outstripped the organization's ability to control their activities. No matter how skilfully veteran trading heads were keeping an eye on their junior colleagues, the organization could not rely on them alone to prevent trouble. Top management needed smart independent eyes and ears to keep on top of what was happening.

9.1.2 The risk reporter

The unprecedented growth in volume and product variety and sophistication that global trading rooms experienced in the 1990s brought with it a substantial increase in organizational complexity. The simple spreadsheets that had formed the backbone of basic risk management in the 1980s could no longer cope with trading books featuring thousands of positions and ever more ingenious customized products. The evolution and industrialization of reporting processes was the natural response to these challenges. The world of risk management would not escape the challenge of consolidating figures across products, businesses and geographical locations.

Some side-effects would long be felt, though. Despite the immense improvements in IT, computers' processing speed and lower cost of information storage, trade-offs between process efficiency and flexibility were inevitable. In line with an old adage of industrial management, the greater efficiency pursued by industrializing processes meant lower flexibility and a higher fixed cost base. The trading industry was no exception.

The human decision-making process became increasingly dependent on these information production activities. As the resources devoted to the latter generally dwarfed the former, many organizations did not pay sufficient attention to the critical importance of the *art* of risk decision-making. More information does not necessarily equate to better information. More often than not, it will mean mostly more noise. The human brain has a limited capacity to process information, creating a bottleneck in information processing due to its lower bandwidth relative to what our eyes and ears can input.

How flexibly and sensibly information would be aggregated would also become increasingly relevant in the following years. This aggregation process which itself is biased might be used to disguise a unit's activity and lead to internal arbitrages.

In and of its own, *reporting* information is a necessary but not sufficient condition for appropriate decision-making. Nor does it mean that top management, even when presented with sufficient information, would know how to use it properly. This is another example of the knowledge-equal-solution fallacy. This fallacy, which the ancients might have called hubris, is one of the contributing factors to major risk disasters.

9.1.3 The capital optimizer

As competition in financial markets intensifies, so does the internal pressure escalate for everyone inside an organization to improve their service and performance. Using a modern soccer analogy, defenders are no longer expected just to wait and protect their goalkeeper from the opponent's strikers. They have to be able to set up the action and occasionally even strike at the other team's goal as well.

In the same fashion, preventing trouble remains key among a risk management unit's responsibilities but is no longer enough. Risk capital optimization has become a standard risk management practice that is at the heart of decision-making by risk managers, traders and management in general. In short, the organization now has to ask itself not just 'how large a loss can we afford on this trade?' but also, crucially, 'what profit will this risk capital attain?' 'Yes, but' has replaced 'no' as an acceptable answer. For a moment, let's leave aside the complexity of an organization's risk portfolio and its correlations and diversification parameters. If one views a trading activity as a series of bets, the following figure illustrates the risk manager and capital optimizer's key challenge:

FIGURE 9.1 ■ The risk capital optimization process

Whether for a trader, a risk manager, or an entire desk, division or organization, the key decision remains, first and foremost, how to maintain a balance between these two extremes. Let's examine the issues arising from drifting away from this equilibrium:

■ If the decision over-emphasizes profitability and over-allocates risk capital, this may jeopardize the unit's survival if the bet goes wrong. The trader may be fired, the desk shut down, the division absorbed into others, the entire organization go bankrupt or be taken over by financially sound competitors.

■ The decision, on the other hand, may veer towards 'playing safe' and result in excessive risk aversion. In this case, too much risk capital may be allocated to other supposedly safe businesses at the expense of others that may offer a more attractive expected return on risk capital. Ironically, not taking enough risk may actually turn out to be the biggest risk. Eventually, this will result in sub-standard return on risk capital, not a welcomed proposition for shareholders and talented staff. Over time, this will result in underperformance of the organization's stock relative to peer competitors. This will make the organization more vulnerable to a takeover. And, at the micro level, an excessively cautious trader will see his risk capital reduced and reallocated to other more aggressive colleagues.

We discussed the position-sizing problem earlier in relation to the gambler's fallacy and the St Petersburgh game. However, despite the simplicity of these principles, more trading risk disasters continue to happen. This suggests that people responsible for such decisions, regardless of their experience or education, are either ignoring or failing to implement the sizing lesson. Remember, sizing errors are not just a trader's problem. A gambling trader who moves up the managerial ladder of an organization is psychologically inclined to overextend his bets – albeit on a magnified scale – when making such decisions for a desk or division.

Leaving portfolio diversification aside, there are other variables that make the decision more complex. The impact of time is very important, since a position that is kept open for a longer period is obviously exposed to more uncertainty and requires more risk capital than a shorter-term trade. One way to accommodate a very large position is by setting very strict time limits, that is, the horizon by which the position ought to be completely liquidated.

9.1.4 The reassurer: helping people see what they want to see

The main principles of human aversion to cognitive dissonance, confirmation bias, and illusion of control were discussed earlier. Taken together with the scientific and statistical foundations of risk management, these cognitive biases can become dangerously potent. This is especially true in instances where marketing requirements are involved. Generic catch-phrases and nominalizations such as 'commercial instinct', 'adding value' or 'team player' are often heard to reward or punish those risk managers who use more or less accommodating assumptions in assessing the risk capital associated with existing or prospective trades. The analysis of the Space Shuttle *Challenger* disaster later on in this book will show the disastrous consequences of mixing marketing and PR with risk and safety considerations.

As almost everybody craves security and dreads risk – including anything that threatens one's reputation – the pressure to 'square the circle' by tweaking risk parameters is very real. How many times have practitioners heard sentences such as: 'What numbers would make the deal work?' and 'What would obtain a certain rating or achieve a given return-on-capital or profitability threshold to get a deal approved?'

It does not take a genius to understand that working backward from desired results to the input parameters defeats the whole purpose of an objective and orthodox risk analysis! The fault does not begin in practice *per se*, but in academic circles which teach finance in a 'practical way'. This is used to denote situations in which students are taught to adjust numbers so that they are more plausibly aligned to market conditions and may be deemed 'acceptable' to a hypothetical senior management. If schools teach this way of thinking as being hard-nosed and practical, then any formal rationality is subverted by confirmation bias. In real practice, setting excessively aggressive parameters and assumptions appears to be culturally required and is at best a charming lie, or at worst an unconscious, fallible tendency. These behaviours remind us of children who, feeling helpless and wanting to please, look for parental reassurance after experiencing the early disappointments and fears in their lives. This sort of dependency will only occlude good risk judgment.

Pushing assumptions to make a prospective trade look more appealing is, of course, the path of least resistance. Once the adverse consequences are experienced, however, the blame-shifting game and the digging into the supposed reasonableness of the *ex ante* assumptions begin. From the shareholder's point of view, there is no need to add any other comments on how productive this condescending setup and subsequent not-me behaviour really are for the organization.

9.2 What proper risk management really is

9.2.1 The world of soccer

The previous section on the capital optimizer's role should leave no doubts on the author's thoughts on risk management as a purely defensive function. At this point, let me take a digression from finance and wander into the world of soccer. This can provide us with a role model for how the risk manager could add most value to his organization.

The name of Franz Beckenbauer is far better known in the world of soccer than in finance. A key icon in German football nicknamed *der Kaiser*,[54] Beckenbauer won the World Cup in 1974 as team skipper and then repeated the feat 16 years later as team coach. Beckenbauer achieved legend status by revolutionizing the role of the sweeper, the last defender protecting a team's goalkeeper from the opponent's attacks. Previously, a sweeper would just be another defender who would have no responsibility for covering either a particular opponent's striker or a pre-set zone of his defence. The sweeper would just have to double up and cover any potential threats to his team's goal when an opponent would get a break and have a chance to strike. Beckenbauer reinterpreted the role and added to it a more active support of his team's midfielders in creating offensive opportunities.

Much like Beckenbauer in the world of soccer, the modern risk manager is called to a more active support of his financial institution. Averting catastrophe is still required but no longer enough.

This analogy will hopefully help achieve clarity about what the role entails and become a starting point for what any organization should demand of their risk manager.

My starting point was the definition of the capital optimizer's role. Life and business are about results and an active, responsible management of capital and limits can become very important in steering an organization towards better performance. Forcing dealmakers and senior management into serious discussions based on risk facts and aligning risk perceptions and realities are some of the most productive contributions of a modern risk manager. Let me offer the following principles based on our observations of the marketplace:

9.2.1.1 The healing force of risk regret

Managing the balance between risk and return is a well-known aspect of the modern risk manager's responsibilities. Another aspect, though often neglected, is managing the balance between risk and regret. Leaving political correctness aside for a moment, this is unfortunate

---

[54] The Emperor.

because risk and regret are equally important and differ only in that they involve a forward and a backward view, respectively. Neglecting the importance of regret is a childish avoidance of responsibility and leaves the organization exposed to useless after-the-fact witch-hunts. Within the limits of an organization's financial and managerial resources, one could indeed argue that no risk is too large if disclosed and suitably approved in advance. But, of course, it is only when risk bombs detonate that the various ranks of the organization are forced into a frank dialogue about what went wrong.

9.2.1.2 Improve the dealer's risk consciousness

Dealmakers have to realize that overly aggressive deals jeopardize an organization's future flexibility and theirs as well. For those who are genuinely thinking of staying in a firm for a while, a financially stretched firm in the future means foregone opportunities and the inability to service clients, hardly a good marketing policy. It is not worth worrying about those who ignore such future adverse consequences of their deals. Such disregard betrays their intention to switch jobs anyway.

9.2.1.3 Lead from the front

Top management, at the same time, has to realize that their commitment to certain activities is best demonstrated with facts, specifically by backing them with risk capital amongst the other resources. The loyalty that an organization can engender in its traders and dealmakers is directly proportional to senior management's ability to withstand the possibility of significant losses in the future as the price to pay for doing business today. What is the added value of top management's endorsement only under fair-weather conditions anyway? Withdrawing risk capital too quickly from underperforming businesses speaks volumes about an organization's commitment.

No one is better positioned than the risk manager in brokering this relationship between management and dealmakers while safeguarding the shareholders' entitlements to their property.

In the context of bloated egos for which modern investment banking is notorious, this distinction between *owning* and *renting* a property is critical. The distinction under the law is that ownership implies a full set of ownership rights over property in perpetuity, while renting means that you have merely a contractual right to use a particular property under well-defined terms and conditions. In management parlance, 'empowerment' has become a buzzword in recent years and few would question the value of moving decision-making down an organization's hierarchy. Yet, on the negative side the word empowerment is often used to justify a more extreme sentiment, heard in phrases such as 'I *own* this business.' This is, of course, incorrect.

When this is applied too extensively, the organization finds itself walking down the primrose path. It is not only a helpful distinction, but one that is embodied in the facts of commercial life: *only shareholders own the business*. Everyone else in the organization, including its top management and board of directors, are employees with rights protected by employment contracts, and therefore serving in a status similar to tenants. To draw this analogy more firmly, the employee is in an economic sense renting an organization's reputation and managerial and financial resources to make a profit. The shareholder/landlord is obviously interested in the maximization of the value of his property, which means achieving a competitive return on risk capital. Again, this is where world-class risk management has the best opportunity of proving itself.

But, to accomplish these goals, the risk manager must be suitably – ah, again! – empowered by the business and plugged into the information flows. Top management needs to delegate and balance its sense of ownership with the risk manager. It is this implementation of a risk manager's role that has a decisive bearing on how well an organization will be managed. This will be the topic of the next section.

9.3 Frames in risk management

Whilst we have discussed some of the problems modern risk managers face, many of the most interesting frames of risk are those found in the way in which their role is viewed and in some common practices and tools in the financial services industry. Ever since Harry Markowitz's breakthrough in statistical finance in 1952, finance theorists have tried to refine their calculations of risk and return. A quick reflection of our argument so far shows there are many challenges to the standard assumptions in economics and modern finance. When these assumptions are treated as presumptions of human nature then we are in for real trouble. Ignoring the consequences and flaws of some of these assumptions can become very costly. This is especially true for modern risk managers and their responsibility over a firm's risk-adjusted return on capital.

9.3.1 The independence mantra

The independence of a risk manager in his operations in an organization is probably the most uncontroversial of all risk management principles. At first blush, this makes sense since the earlier varieties of risk managers were chosen from the watchdogs described earlier in this chapter. The principle of independence and the related segregation of duties, however, has been transformed into the top marketing message of the financial risk management consulting arms of major audit firms. So, the broad support that this principle receives is by no means surprising. This apparent unanimity is symptomatic of two biases we already discussed, namely aversion to ambiguity, and group cognitive resonance. A *better* principle, of *interdependence*, is needed.

There is no question that someone has to assess risk and figures independently and keep an organization's top management abreast of what is going on. This control requirement, however, is best met by a strong product control function. Modern risk management is most significantly about being at the forefront of the information flow and, from this angle, interdependence would be the more correct principle. What is the point of having an independent risk management function if that independence jeopardizes the trust of people who do business in the organization and their vital information flows? Who would willingly provide information to another group in the organization if this intelligence can be used against its providers? Interdependent risk management does not mean, however, *subservient* risk management. Risk managers must be granted some right of appeal to higher courts of authority within the organization if the business, as is likely, tries to demean its enhanced influence. Anything short of these requirements means that risk management becomes akin to corporate entertainment.

So, independence on its own is a necessary but insufficient ingredient for top-flight risk management in an organization. If the thought of risk management being completely independent from traders and top business managers frightens you, then perhaps it's time to re-examine the background and context to your own thinking. Let me be so bold as to suggest that the biases and frames of risk are so indiscriminately rampant that one's own pivotal assumption of independence may just be another sign and symptom of the disease.

9.3.2 The PV syndrome and the quant race: valuing the unquantifiable

Since the 1980s, the consequences of the unprecedented explosion in the trading and derivatives industry have been deeper and more liquid secondary markets, and a closer integration between primary and secondary markets. By primary markets, one means the markets in which securities like bonds and stocks are initially placed with investors. Thereafter, securities are traded on the secondary market.

While the growth of the markets drove traders to work more closely with the bankers, this development brought a new problem. Previously, an investment bank would arrange a deal and pocket an upfront fee. The bank would act as a pure intermediary between investors and issuers and use its balance sheet for a limited period of time, if any at all. Under the new market regime, banks would manufacture and manage cashflows and stand in between two or more counterparts for years, maybe even for the entire life of a deal. How would one value that deal at inception and over its life? The answer would have a direct bearing on a related question that is constantly close to the hearts of the new wave of aggressive financial engineers: How would their compensation be calculated?

The solution would be found in a massive application of the concept of present value, an old principle of basic finance that most practitioners simply abbreviate as 'PV'. At the heart of PV lies the simple concept that one unit of money today is worth more than the same unit of money tomorrow. To defer consumption, the holder of that unit of money wants to obtain some compensation in the form of interest. This acts as compensation for the many forms of uncertainty that he is facing between today and tomorrow, including:

- default risk of the counterpart to whom he is lending money;

- adverse changes in the purchasing power of that unit of money due to inflation;

- delaying the gratification of consuming that unit of money until tomorrow.

This principle assumes that the PV of the quantity that is being evaluated can rely on a snapshot picture of the relationship between risk and return over a given timeframe. This is a reasonable assumption over short periods of time, since a small incremental change in risk (or return) would have a proportionally small impact on return (or risk). This is because those effects would be measured over a limited period of time only.

Figure 9.2 illustrates the basic dilemma which the present value (PV) methodology attempts to resolve. Over a given time horizon, the return for the assumed risk changes, the snapshot that one uses to calculate the PV falls behind very quickly. Simply put, the amount of time over which funds have to be invested to earn a given return is a moving target. If I earn a given return over a one-year period and the expected return of that asset changes, my holding period will also increase or drop depending on whether the return offered by the investment after the change has decreased or increased.

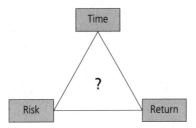

FIGURE 9.2 ▪ The unstable relationship between risk and return

Let's consider, for instance, the situation whereby the PVs are calculated for two positions A and B, based on zero coupon yields of, say, 11 per cent and 9 per cent for ten and one years, respectively. For simplicity's sake, let's assume there are no cashflows before maturity. Three months after that PV calculation, interest rates increase by 1 per cent. While A should be valued at 12 per cent for $10\frac{3}{4}$ years, B should be valued at 10 per cent for only nine months. In fixed-income terminology, A is considered *more sensitive* to interest rate changes than B.

Unfortunately, the relationship between risk, return and time is by no means stable. In the example above, PV is calculated at year-end. It drives many other important events, including the evaluation of performances, promotions and, most importantly, the payment of dividends and bonuses. As is customary in investment banking, some staff will defect to competitors after receiving their bonus. While these 'hunter-gatherers' may have already departed with rich pickings, the risks they assumed to get their deals done are left buried like time bombs. Some of these may indeed tie a bank's balance sheet and credit lines for years. As an aside, even real hunter-gatherers are not capable of such feats. Studies (Hawken, 1993) have shown that they tend to leave the grounds in qualitatively better condition than when they first came upon them. Anthropologists theorize that it is probably because they know they must return to these grounds to survive.

Vast amounts of talent and other resources have been thrown at this daunting problem of quantifying this inherently unstable relationship. Coupled with growing product complexity and supported by a dramatic improvement in computing cost and power, this quest has been one of the major forces behind the rise of 'quants'. This is used to refer to staff with strong quantitative talent to summarize complex phenomena through mathematical and statistical relationships.

While culturally fascinating for bringing together people from a broad variety of backgrounds, this trend towards hiring quants brings with it a dark side. Some major issues are as follows:

9.3.2.1 Analytical solutions do not translate into liquidity

No matter how conceptually elegant and sophisticated they are, analytical solutions do not necessarily bring liquidity to markets. In the context of default risk, for instance, the author contributed to the development of a mathematical relationship bringing together equity and default pricing as early as 1995. As of this book's release date, nine years later, an actively traded market has yet to develop in this area of risk arbitrage. The development of new risk technologies can engender a very dangerous false sense of security. Some may indeed confuse the ability to mark-to-model with the existence of a market to manage a risk position. The capability to *quantify* and *report* a position is a very different thing from the ability to actually *trade* it.

9.3.2.2 Complexity begets complexity

As analytical solutions are found – or so it is presumed – to old problems, new, fancier, problems arise. This does not necessarily mean, however, that the rest of the organization and its infrastructure are keeping up with these advances. Quite the contrary – there is a genuine risk that the quant commandos are leaving the rest of the organization even further behind and potentially stranded! Remember, a basic law of risk management states that you cannot segregate value without segregating liquidity. Accordingly, a more complex product created to extract some value will always be less liquid than the original basic products from which it was derived. This process will give birth to at least one product that is less liquid than the previous generation. Alternatively, you can picture the process of new product development as taking often simple products and decomposing them into sub-components. Unfortunately, neither of these components will get close to the liquidity of the original simple product. In brutal terms, if you cut a person into two pieces, you are likely to get two zombies that will be more difficult to deal with than the original.

9.3.2.3 What's available is not always best

For example, the establishment of statistical credit matrices is prone to generate availability bias by retrieval (see below for discussion). More specifically, in instances where market pricing is opaque, the first tool that becomes *available* is susceptible to being tweaked and distorted for improper uses.

There is no easy way out of this dilemma. A more conservative pricing and evaluation of products and their risks means stashing aside more reserves for the future. More reserves means more capital on the wrong side of the return-on-capital ratio, the denominator. That's not the maximization of short-term figures and bonuses that shareholders and employees are clamouring for. These short-term pressures are real.

What happens in the real world? A more aggressive PV regime may be attractive in the short term but means leaving an organization's flank more exposed to the inevitable return to reality and lower flexibility during downturns in the cycle.

It is natural to look for an all-weather solution. After all, seeking such a fix betrays an aversion to ambiguity bias. Unfortunately, there is no such panacea, there are only measures that can suit a particular phase in the business cycle. Remember the aggressive use of pro-forma earnings figures instead of GAAP accounting in the US at the height of the late 1990s raging bull market in equities? How often would one hear the argument that financial GAAP-based financial statements would not reflect an organization's growth potential?

Among the empirical studies on the impact of pro-forma versus GAAP accounting rules, Bradshaw, Moberg & Sloan (2000) present evidence of a growing disparity between earnings under GAAP and earnings followed by Wall Street analysts and investors. As a result, the study argues that calculated earnings growth rates differ significantly under the alternative definitions of earnings. Likewise, the more recent years of the study display strong earnings growth under the street definition, but more moderate growth under GAAP. The article illustrates how investor reaction to the modified version of earnings reported by the analyst tracking services is greater than the reaction to earnings under GAAP. The study documents how the growing disparity between the two definitions can be attributed to three sources:

- firms and analysts have been overlooking large amounts of expenses required under GAAP;

- a marked increase in the exclusion of significant expenses from the earnings reported by analyst tracking services;

- a corresponding increase in firms specifically identifying large portions of their expenses as non-recurring.

Compare this with the outrage against aggressive accounting that followed the Enron and WorldCom bankruptcies. Is it by mere chance that the tightening in directors' responsibilities over the fairness of their organizations' financial statements in the US coincided with a serious recession? The regulatory trend would suggest otherwise. At the time of writing, the Financial Services Authority (FSA), the British financial services regulator, is also considering similar stricter rules.

It is difficult not to agree with the spirit behind these clearer responsibilities. One has to caution, however, that no one should expect these regulations to eliminate the problem once and for all. Looking at return on capital through rose-tinted glasses and faking accounting numbers is unsavoury and, in the end, unsound business practice that is as old as business itself. There is no reason to expect a world devoid of unscrupulous people in the future. One can, however, stiffen the price by imposing criminal penalties. The personal risk then becomes, at once, a powerful deterrent and an acid test by exposing the extent to which people are willing to share in the dire consequences of their decisions. Simply put, what bonus value would a manager require to risk a ruined career and, possibly, a jail term? One or two years? How about up to 20 years and $5 million per violation under the US Sarbanes-Oxley Act 2002?

9.3.3 Credit risk management: the kingdom of frames

Prospect theory and mental accounting teach us that investors seek early gratification and delay the recognition of losses in their portfolio. Chapter 5 shows that empirical studies show the tendency of hanging on to losing positions considerably longer and magnifying losses relative to profits. From the investor's point of view, this resembles the payoff of an option. Indeed, the investor's maximum upside is the amount of premium that is received when the option is sold. The investor's downside is very large and sometimes – such as in the case of a call option sold – can even be unlimited.

Lending provides a fertile application of option theory and mirrors the pattern of an option being sold by the bank-lender to the counterpart-borrower. Net of funding cost, the lender's payoff is capped by the amount of interest that is received from the borrower. Leaving reputation aside, the latter has the option to declare bankruptcy, thereby exposing the lender to a potentially large loss. Lenders sell insurance, although they may not call it that. As earlier discussions of the gambler's fallacy and the law of large numbers have shown, selling insurance requires a lot of risk capital. Let me examine the art and science employed in the management of options.

9.3.3.1 *The faith in cashflow models*

Lending, according to written historical records, has been around for at least seven millennia, as King Hammurabi is known to have issued rules for loans in ancient Babylon as early as 5000 BC. According to these rules, the borrower could postpone his repayment of a loan if the harvest was poor. After foreign exchange, interest rates, equities and commodities, credit was the latest major exposure to benefit from the application of modern risk management technology. Despite these impressive advances, credit remains an art and as such cannot eliminate the element of human judgment. And by now you have hopefully developed an appreciation of the multitude of factors influencing your own judgment.

As it is arguably the oldest banking practice, credit has always been associated with client relationships. These supposedly intimate relationships give banks the confidence – and often the *over*confidence – to assume that they enjoy privileged knowledge of a company's affairs and can therefore make a more informed credit assessment. Multi-billion loan loss reserves should be a stern reminder of how far-fetched that competence claim is. For all their supposed competence, bankers have negligently or intentionally ignored learning the lesson. For instance, a single default in 2001, by Enron, cost major banks billions of dollars in write-offs. This deserves particular attention, since some of these banks had arguably been at the forefront in adapting market risk techniques to credit risk management in the 1990s.

Cashflow models involving a company's financial projections are one of the most established tools in assessing a company's creditworthiness. They involve pro-forma financial statements over a period of at least two years and magical 'what-if?' sensitivity analyses. Loan originators have a vested interest in getting their deal proposals approved by their bank's credit officers. These will perform the most important screening of a company's prospects and determine what kind of financial deterioration it may be able to withstand before facing bankruptcy and jeopardizing the lenders' interests.

As these cashflow models and their inputs rely on parameters that are applied to historical information, it is obvious that their users are all more or less subject to extrapolation bias, the tendency to project past information into the future to form expectations. Recall that this involves projecting an existing image or a situation into the future and balancing conflicting tendencies:

- Excessive reliance on base rate information will lead to anchoring and, likely, recency bias, a variant of availability bias by retrieval. In practice, the projection of base rate information in the future may smooth the intensity with which a given situation may unfold. Recency bias may cause the user to assume that recent parameters will remain broadly unchanged, thereby making projections resemble a straight line.

- Excessive extrapolation, on the other hand, will under-weight base rate information and cause overly aggressive projections about the way in which a given trend may unfold.

Cashflows and 'what-if?' analyses are, at present, the best toolkit available and a clearly superior alternative has yet to be found. Again, the issue lies more with the way in which they are adopted than in cashflows in and of themselves.

9.3.3.2 Squaring the circle: uses and misuses of statistical credit matrices

A bank's excessive reliance on its insights into a company's prospects is an important source of overconfidence. The application of statistical techniques to loan portfolios reinforces this false sense of security even further.

As credit risk management technology improved dramatically in the 1990s thanks to innovations such as credit derivatives, collateral management and margining, the need to establish some homogeneous standards for less sophisticated clients increased. This created a fertile ground for the rating agencies, consultants and even banks to offer various models. The best known among these are:

- Creditmetrics™, the rating migration matrix developed by JP Morgan;

- CreditRisk+™, the portfolio management model created by Credit Suisse Financial Products (CSFP);

- CreditPortfolioView™, the so-called Wilson model, after its author;

- KMV Portfolio Manager™, the credit portfolio model originally developed by consultants KMV (who have recently become part of the Moody's credit rating agency).

As banks have increased their reliance on these models and ratings both for their own capital allocation processes and to meet increased regulatory requirements (as part of the Basle II International Capital Accord for Banks), the importance of these methodologies has increased rapidly. Accordingly, a substantial body of empirical studies and academic literature has analysed these models and their assumptions, strengths and weaknesses. The misuses of these models are the main area of interest here, as they appear to reflect exactly the types human biases that are the subject of this book. Unfortunately, an in-depth analysis is beyond the scope of this book, and we will review only major themes developed in the literature.

Among the most significant studies are those of Kolyluoglu & Hickman (1998) and Kolyluoglu, Bangia & Garside (1999), who found that most differences in the results between some of these portfolio models (such as CreditMetrics™, CreditRisk+™ and CreditPortfolioManager™) are explained more by parameters than by model construction *per se*.

Credit models based on macroeconomic variables (of which Wilson's CreditPortfolioView™ model was the first) rely to a considerable extent on the stability and predictability in the correlations between these variables and default rates (not to mention recovery rates). The evidence in this respect is mixed at best. Using data from the US bond market, Altman, Resti & Sironi (2002) show that, within a low-growth environment (defined as an annual GDP growth rate of below 1.5 per cent), the year-on-year change in GDP explains only about 16–17 per cent of the annual change in recovery rates. A higher-growth GDP figure yields even less promising results. Negligible correlations are also found with other variables, such as the annual change in the Standard & Poor's 500 Index.

There are other important methodological issues with models of credit risk exposure that incorporate macroeconomic and systematic risk effects. A survey by Linda Allen & Anthony Saunders (2002) analysed both academic and proprietary models. According to the study, many models consider the correlation between the probability of default (PD) and cyclical factors. Few models, however, adjust loss rates (loss given default, or LGD) to reflect cyclical effects. The possibility of systematic correlation between PD and LGD is also neglected in currently available models.

Following the Basle II Capital Adequacy Accord, external credit ratings are assuming a prominent role in driving bank risk capital allocation. This has led many to raise the question of how consistent ratings are across rating agencies, geographical borders and sectors.

A robust set of studies has extensively documented differences in the meaning of ratings across rating agencies. Noteworthy amongst these are Beattie & Searle (1992), Cantor & Packer (1994), Jewell & Livingston (1999) and the Basle Committee on Banking Supervision (2000). These findings are hardly surprising since each rating agency employs a different set of descriptions for their respective ratings. Competitive factors drive these differences, too.

Other studies have examined differences between the performances across sectors. With respect to Moody's bank and non-bank ratings, in particular, Nickell, Perraudin & Varotto (2000) note that, between 1970 and 1997, Moody's bank ratings were more volatile than Moody's industrial ratings, yet no evidence of significant differences in the default rate experiences of these two sectors was found. Other authors (Ammer & Packer, 2000) found that

Moody's ratings on speculative-grade banks were associated with significantly higher default rates than similarly rated US industrials during the 1983–1998 period. These authors attributed these differences in default experiences to the fact that the US thrift industries had abnormally high default rates between 1989 and 1991.

Other studies investigated potential geographical inconsistencies and, in particular, the existence of a so-called 'home-country' bias among local rating agencies. Beattie & Searle (1992) found evidence of this behaviour. With respect to international banks, however, Cantor & Packer (1994) attributed most differences in ratings to discrepancies in the rating scales applied by individual rating agencies, rather than to a home-country bias.

Ammer & Packer (2000) analysed this theme further using the historical database that Moody's has made publicly available. With respect to the 1983–1988 period, they found no statistically significant differences in the average one-year default rate for speculative-grade issuers in the US and outside.

What about the *uses* of these tools? Almost by definition, credit risk involves the lack of exchangeability for positions when compared to more liquid markets, such as foreign exchange or fixed-income. What does this mean? The liquidity and variety of tools that exist in foreign exchange or fixed-income makes it straightforward to convert a position that is denominated in British pounds into US dollars or to swap a position in two-year Treasury Notes into 30-year Treasury Bonds or exit the market altogether. In credit, the risk of counterpart X going into default is unique and can only be managed by means of an offsetting position in bonds or products of counterpart X. In this sense, the normalization that the rating matrices have brought about was long overdue to measure performance.

There is a dark side, though: tools that were originally developed to *report* credit portfolios can be tweaked to generate the risk capital figures associated with a particular credit position. Sometimes these tools may even be used to *price and trade* credit portfolios. For instance, by using the amount of risk capital generated above and working backwards, we can obtain the price that would meet a given return-on-capital threshold. This is exactly opposite to what normally happens in any trading room: there, one would take prices and their volatility first and use those as inputs to compute risk capital. Any trader worth his salt would hardly believe in a process that derives prices from risk capital and volatility rather than the other way around.

This is by no means a theoretical issue. Rather, it is standard practice in the banking industry to have originators demand that loans to outside clients be held in their institutions' loan portfolios. Portfolio models and mechanisms such as those described earlier are often employed as the standard to calculate a price regardless of a bank's ability to sell a loan or to cover the exposure through other means, such as taking collateral or hedging via credit derivatives.

The main argument behind the use of portfolio models in pricing credit risk is that there are some diversification benefits which should be taken into account when making a price to the originator of that loan. This, however, implies that the diversification benefit should accrue to the originator, rather than to the risk book and the trader who is responsible for it. Conversely, with most market risks the responsible trader prices each existing and prospective position on a stand-alone basis. Any diversification benefits the risk book. In addition, some key credit pricing parameters, such as default correlations, default probability and the severity of losses in default (LGD) are neither easy to quantify nor stable over time. Contrary to standard banking practice, this should further encourage more conservative pricing of each position on a stand-alone basis.

It goes without saying that this industry standard creates internal pricing discrepancies. The use of different pricing tools can mean that a loan to a company gets approved and risk capital is allocated despite the far lower return-on-capital relative to bonds or loans to that company that are available on the secondary market. This is an excellent example of influence and inefficiency in internal capital markets (see Chapter 6). The statistical foundations of the rating matrices are then often used as an alternative pricing tool instead of the most orthodox valuation metric: the market price.

The different preferences of pricing mechanisms between a trader on one side and an originator or credit officer on the other are the tip of the iceberg of two fundamentally different frames of risk:

- Traders would like their risk book to be long, short or flat and, as important, want to retain flexibility to shift that risk profile. For any trader, a loss on a credit-risky bond or loan is a loss, full stop. The existence of other business between his institution and the loan borrower – or bond issuer – has limited or no bearing on the trader's perspective on that loss. That loss tends to be viewed on its own.

- Conversely, loan originators and credit officers – many of whom are former loan originators themselves – like to speak of 'commitment' to clients. The 'commitment' word alone involves some emotional attachment, something that any good trader dreads with a passion. Losses are portrayed as a 'cost of doing business'. This is because they assume that a bank's duty is to be always a buyer (i.e., 'long') of loans and credit risk and they believe that the loss will be more than offset by revenue from ancillary business with that client. Accordingly, bankers and credit officers will be interested in statistical assumptions of 'expected' and 'unexpected' loss, something that their trading colleagues will likely dismiss as utterly irrelevant.

This is frames of risk at their best. The same class of risk – and often the same product – is viewed from two completely different perspectives by two types of actors in a bank. Both will, of course, consider theirs as the 'rational' view and dismiss the other. Based on the above, do you still believe that there is only one 'truth'?

The conflict between fair mark-to-market of credit portfolios and maintaining loan pricing as reasonably competitive may appear unsolvable. What is the solution? Create a P&L reserve equal to the difference between the price of hedging or selling loans (which we will label as the marginal price) and the actual terms of the loans to borrowers. Over time, if the actual default record is lower than the marginal price would imply, loan originators can then recoup this difference. If the portfolio manager wishes to hedge or sell the loan, he will be able to draw from the reserve to do so. This way, the reserve works as an insurance premium pool from which a bank can draw to ensure risk mobility. Of course, loan originators and marketers would rather have no reserve charged up-front. Avoiding the reserve means higher immediate profits and bonuses. However, having the financial soundness of a credit portfolio being held hostage by marketing or ego trips is nothing short of irresponsible.

9.3.3.3 Calibration, calibration ...

For all their merits in setting the standards, quantitative tools generally provide average measures (for a sector or region or rating cluster). The challenge for banks – other than maybe those who created the tools in the first place – is how to tailor them to their own loss and default experience. After all, the ability of these tools to match an institution's loss record is considered to be one of the best demonstrations of a model's value.

That rearview mirror perspective is also a potential source of problems down the line. The fact that a model's parameters can be tweaked and adjusted – or calibrated, using the technical vernacular – is a poor predictor of a model's ability to calculate the risk of positions *in the future* correctly. Those successful calibrations tell us only that the chosen model can, by applying those parameters, replicate the loss record of given portfolios *in the past*. Once again, as in many other examples in this book, we see an application of hindsight bias, confirmation bias and extrapolation bias at their best.

9.4 Key internal clients and their delusions

Chapter 8 discussed at length the trader, one of the key internal counterparts that risk managers are supposed to *look after*. This verb has been chosen deliberately: it implies both the traditional watchdog role and, more important, the critical help and support role that modern risk managers can and should embody.

Being one of the key revenue producers, the trader is one of the most important internal clients but by no means the only one. Senior management and salesmen are also key internal players whose frames of risk are by no means exempt from human biases. Especially in the case of senior management, a longer track record in the industry and in the organization does not mean outgrowing one's judgmental weaknesses. Rather, one's advancement in the organization may actually reinforce them, first and foremost by fostering overconfidence.

9.4.1 Top management

Within a financial institution, top management (both at board and executive board level) are the ultimate risk decision-makers. For all the smart assistance that a risk manager can offer, this is the place with the ultimate responsibility for pulling the trigger. Admiration, flattery and myths are frequent in the upper echelons of management and are part of the aura that the industry tries to project and maintain. Visibility and attention-grabbing are a vital part of service sectors, after all. While many top managers would like to be portrayed as superhuman, they are nonetheless still subject to the tendencies and biases described earlier in this book.

The irony is that promotions and upper management titles can act as a giant magnifying glass of one's personality traits, thereby making some feel potentially more exposed and vulnerable. Successes in earlier stages of one's career foster confidence – and often overconfidence. Over time, judgmental flaws eventually come back with a vengeance. Individuals often suffer from self-attribution bias when assessing successes and failures (see Chapter 5). Few industries display it as consistently as the ego-bloated world of high finance. In short, luck may have played a far more significant role in someone's past successes than he or she is willing to acknowledge. Remember, responsibilities and authority may change and increase but basic personality traits are fairly stable over time. The same applies for problem-solving approaches and biases, regardless of the higher scale and complexity of the decisions at hand. In short, you cannot hide from your biases.

Noteworthy amongst top management's most consistent frames of risk are the following:

9.4.1.1 Action/inaction imbalance

Moving around and wheeling and dealing are part of the script that top management are expected to play out on behalf of the organization. Delaying action to gather more information on how a department, division or firm behaves on its own for a while is out of character if not out of the question. Analysing more information is taken for lack of decisiveness and confidence. At the opposite extreme stand those who ask for more information to delay the pain of taking action, rather than because it is really necessary. Those who suffer from either extreme would do better to take a few small, calculated risks with a series of small incremental decisions. These are very unlikely to compromise the organization and the decision-maker's future and can even yield additional valuable intelligence.

9.4.1.2 Mixing risk with hope

As discussed previously in the gambler's fallacy section in Chapter 5, humans tend to simplify decisions by framing them in mostly binary 0/1 terms. Then, information that states that a certain loss threshold will be exceeded 1 per cent of the time will be generally disregarded. In risk management, VaR is the most eminent example of such information. Indeed, human primordial survival instincts make one *hope* that such catastrophic loss will be irrelevant. That frame of risk and its associated false sense of security are destroyed when that occasional, particularly adverse event does happen. The shock that such an event causes can be compared to awakening from hypnosis. Unfortunately, financial markets can make such errors very costly.

9.4.1.3 Illusion of control

Managing several people and vast resources is apt to create the impression of 'strength from numbers' and a sense that any risk can be easily mastered. Unfortunately, the opposite is normally the case. As the organization grows, the risk that critical information will not find its way to the top can only increase. Size, complexity and poor transparency often reinforce each other.

9.4.1.4 Knowledge equal solution fallacy

Receiving information does not necessarily mean that it is the *right* information (in quality and level of detail). Nor does it mean that the user will definitely act on it. This means that receiving information is a necessary but not sufficient condition for knowledgeable, informed action by those at the top. Consider, for instance, a board member of a European bank who is in his late fifties. His early working years, often amongst the most formative in one's career, predated the derivatives revolution. He puts a credit and accounting tilt on his views of situations. Yet, he is on the distribution list of some fairly complex reports that include sensitivity to credit spreads and option greeks. He has little use for them and would much rather get some summary updates on credit trends in the bank's key counterparts based on their financial statements. At the opposite extreme, consider a successful derivatives trader who has just left a competitor to join the same board. He is naturally cautious and asks several hard-hitting questions which cannot be answered by the lengthy reports that he receives. Both men receive a lot of information that is, for different reasons, mostly irrelevant.

9.4.2 Management decision theory

There is a rich body of academic literature on management decision theory, particularly with respect to uncertainty and risk. While most of the literature focuses on traditional industrial companies, these studies have major implications for the way in which bosses view their peers and subordinates. For all its glamour, bosses and their subordinates in the world of high finance face substantially the same issues as their colleagues in other industries. The implications of these views are crucial to the way people behave, their risk preferences and risk-adjusted utility curves. The frequency of management problems in financial services firms should remind us of the folly of ignoring or making light of serious people issues.

Theory X and Theory Y, conceived by Douglas McGregor (1960) at MIT, marked the first attempts to summarize the set of assumptions that managers make about workers. Theory X involved mostly negative assumptions. The average human being, it was said, has an inherent dislike of work, prefers to be directed, has little ambition, wishes to avoid responsibility and values security above all else. Theory Y argued that human beings enjoy and actively seek work, self-direction, responsibility and the opportunity to utilize their imagination.

There is no conclusive empirical evidence showing a strong correlation between Theory X and Theory Y and management behaviour and performance. More recent research (Wood & Bandura, 1989; Dweck, 1999) and empirical studies have found significant correlations between other sets of assumptions and management behaviour and performance. One of our recommendations is simply that we ask managers in banks and trading rooms to adopt a more proactive approach to managing human resources based on their multi-dimensional psychological makeup, rather than simply a single dimensional number – i.e., the difference between revenue and cost. The mental model which managers use to determine the flexibility of human characteristics is important. The two extreme views, entity theory and incremental theory, are discussed below.

9.4.2.1 Entity theory and incremental theory

Entity theory derives its name from a person's assumption or belief that human characteristics are fixed entities that do not change much, if at all. People are viewed as either smart or dumb and there is little interaction or movement between these two categories. However, if mental ability is fixed then a person who has that basic aptitude should be able to demonstrate it at will, in any situation. Entity theorists construe a person's failure at a task as evidence of a lack of ability. Tasks that are novel, involve evaluations by others or require experimentation all pose a threat to the entity theorist because they carry a higher risk.

Conversely, incremental theory views human characteristics as malleable and subject to change with experience. As such, these features can be further developed. In any situation that requires mental ability, they tend to think of performance in terms of skills, effort and strategies, which can vary from one situation or one problem to the next. These performance characteristics are also easier to change and develop than basic aptitudes. For incremental theorists, experimentation, public accountability and novelty all pose less of a threat because they believe that you can always try something different when you encounter setbacks or failures.

Entity theorists are more likely to adopt a defensive or avoidance frame while incremental theorists adopt an approach frame and attack the task more directly. These two mindsets may be summarized by the following different questions that may be asked when dealing with a new task or challenge:

- An entity theorist may wonder: 'How do I make sure that I do not make any mistakes or avoid looking ridiculous?'

- An incremental theorist will likely ask himself: 'What approach or strategy will give the best presentation?'

Where does this lead us? Someone who has an entity view is likely to be more risk-averse and have a harder time in distancing herself emotionally from a negative result than one who holds an incremental view. A loss is a loss, she may argue, regardless of the potential gain that it may offer. Control, or illusion thereof, will be the main tool to which this person will resort. Avoiding excessive risk aversion is the main challenge.

Supporters of the incremental theory tend to analyse, or overanalyse, the situation. In their quest for an attractive risk-adjusted return, their philosophy will rely on calculated risk-taking. Their faith in statistics and measurements may make them fall prey to the gambler's fallacy. Also, the numbers may lead them to see patterns that do not exist and base their decisions on them.

How would one face these two different personalities when they are involved in risk decisions such as, for instance, a deal approval?

- 'Even in our worst-case scenario, we cannot lose more than X' may be the most adequate pitch to a decision-maker who subscribes to an entity view of the world.

■ 'We'll make a profit nine times out of ten', or 'Our 95 per cent confidence interval loss is X' will be the approaches that will be more attuned to the mindset of a decision-maker who supports the incremental view.

How we approach these two different personalities will make a big difference to how they are motivated and, in the end, to how we may be able to derive better performance from each.

9.4.3 The salesman/structurer/dealmaker: the instant gratification providers

Few things can be classified as a purer commodity than money itself. From this viewpoint, the prominence of the salesman on the sell-side of financial services firms and investment banks should come as no surprise. Other than for exceptional trading performances, abnormal profits from product differentiation are a key source of revenue for major financial services firms. No professional investor or market counterpart would pay more than a fair price for a product that can be easily obtained elsewhere. But if financial products are made of various combinations of cashflows, how does one differentiate a commodity?

The driven Wall Street salesman has become a well-recognized archetype character in pulp bestsellers. *Liar's Poker*, *F.I.A.S.C.O.* and *Riding the Bull* are a few titles that come to mind. Aside from these popular images, we might wonder what are the mental challenges that salesmen face in their risk decision-making?

First of all, to uncover the salesmen's frames of risk, one has to understand that their timeframe perspective presents major differences from the rest of the organization. Weeks, days or just minutes of interaction may be necessary for a salesman to complete a transaction with an outside client. Conversely, an organization will pursue financial and risk capital viability over months or years. This timeframe differential can have major repercussions for the subsequent decision-making process. Indeed, a tug-of-war often follows between the salesman's wish to win the next deal and others in the organization who want to ensure that the organization remains sound and profitable in the long term.

These problems are further reinforced and compounded by differences in salary mechanisms between salesmen and those who have to approve their deals, such as credit or other risk officers. While the former can command large bonuses at year-end based on the commission that they have generated, the latter are often evaluated based on less straightforward criteria, such as the perceptions that they have generated in the business. This asymmetry is further exaggerated since the latter are most exposed to the blame if old deals blow up.

As the organization's fortunes change, so does the time perspective affecting these decisions. In tough times, the survival objective becomes more important and results in a tighter evaluation screen on prospective trading and investment decisions. This tends to shorten the time focus of many senior decision-makers and make shorter deals preferable. In good times, the organization is often awash with risk capital and the tide will favour the salesman. These behaviours are not that straightforward. However, we find almost no exception to prospect theory. When the organization is facing the most difficulties and is losing money, the search for revenue can border on desperation. This encourages more aggressive decisions exactly when risk capital is the scarcest resource and its preservation should top the priority list. This is yet another demonstration of the inherent tendency to 'gamble the ranch' when the situation gets tough.

9.5 The external constituencies and their motivations

A large number of stakeholders in a financial institution have vested interests to protect. These are highlighted whenever we consider the risks to the institution. Among the most important stakeholders are shareholders, regulators, analysts, the media and the general public. It goes without saying that each external constituency is exposed to the same biases and judgmental errors that plague inside players.

The trading drama unfolds in tragedy when financial losses manifest. The hunt for the culprits vents moral indignation. Interestingly, whatever the bogeyman is in fashion – be it derivatives, hedge funds or other products or players – the debates and attacks often focus on the *tools* rather than on *who* uses them, *how* and *why*.

There is of course little point in blaming the tools for their misuse. Screwdrivers have befitting and misbegotten uses. If they injure, this is not sufficient cause to ban their use. Rather, the user is personally responsible for how the screwdriver is used. Applying the same principle to finance, we should look to the user who misuses rather than just the misuse itself. Perhaps because of the way in which the popular psyche nominalizes and demonizes money, the same principle of personal responsibility is often disregarded in finance.

9.5.1 The shareholders

What can be more pervasively strident than today's shareholder demand for results, or, more bluntly put, money? Increasingly militant shareholders are pressing top managers to squeeze greater profits out of a firm's resources, which leads directly to thinning risk capital. Compare the following sentences and think about which one is most likely to be included as part of the Chairman's statement in the Annual Report:

(a) 'In a year of tough trading conditions, this firm has maintained its performance in line with previous years thanks to the strong increase in trading profits achieved by doubling the risks taken'; or

(b) 'In a year of tough trading conditions, this firm has maintained return on capital in line with previous years thanks to a strong trading performance and an aggressive cost-cutting programme'.

Both statements can be true, as actual VaR is only disclosed in the notes to financial statements. Under (b), the more prudent statement, shareholders can find out by digging deeper. What is interesting is how more carefully hedged statements can become in response to the higher degree of formality that accompanies the firm's top management and their relationship with shareholders. This is another frame of risk. Thereafter, the organization must live with the consequences of its artful approach. When sudden crises eventually shatter the frame of risk, the hunt for the culprits begins.

Analogous to absentee landlords, shareholders entrust the handling of their property to professional managers. The clarity in their communication to the managers and the alignment between the respective objectives of shareholders and managers have a crucial interlocking bearing on the future results.

9.5.2 The regulators

Regulators, like soccer referees, have a tough job. Seldom loved by those whom they regulate, they are viewed as the ultimate guarantor of fair rules and fair play on the field by several important constituencies. The government, the media and the general public have large stakes in market outcomes. At the same time, regulators are expected to get the job done while being pathetically under-resourced and under-funded. When asked to decide on some important controversial issues, they may often have no second line of defence or opportunity to change their opinion later. No one can make up for the regulator's own mistakes. To top it off, they have the unenviable position of being held responsible and are often criticized by those who have the benefit of hindsight for the way in which they failed to prevent financial crimes and mis-managed market crises. They are, however, seldom praised when the regulatory regimes work well.

The perceived risks of social cohesion are magnified further in finance, where technological progress and globalization of markets enable an ever more rapid dissemination of information and the transfer of vast sums of money. As the protection of savers and investors plays a decisive role in managing public psychology, it is no wonder that the spotlight is often on financial regulators.

Regulators, however, are all too human and oblige biases by virtue of their role. As referees, they cannot afford someone questioning their independence. The leads to a more general definition of fairness, which is defined *vis-à-vis* a group opinion or authoritative benchmark. We see the development of 'important committees' and lobbies forming think tanks that drive existing and prospective regulations. A vast number of public voices are grouped under heading 'public opinion'. It is far more difficult to see through this label. This public voice becomes the ultimate judge.

This conformity and methodical application of the rules help keep regulators on safe ground. They can also become a source of major biases, since blind adherence to procedures may increase precision and meaningfulness of taxonomies but stray farther and farther away from the objectives tested in reality. Precision is not accuracy. The Shuttle *Challenger* disaster of January 1986 is an example of how procedural theology led to a disconnection with reality. The decision to launch relied more on the application of well-rooted rules and behaviours than on an honest assessment of the danger of the peculiar situation. The decision on the fatal o-rings relied to a considerable extent on the previous flawless track record of the space programme and ignored the technicians' warnings.

To be fair, financial services regulators have, in spite of all their human weaknesses, achieved significant milestones over the last 20 years. The management of the Latin American debt crisis in the 1980s, the handling of several instances of market turmoil in the 1990s, the introduction of capital adequacy standards for banks and the avoidance of any cataclysmic meltdown in derivatives markets are only a few examples that deserve praise.

The point of this section, however, is that regulators must be urged to retain what might be called 'a healthy sense of paranoia'. It is well known amongst practitioners that banks are notorious for having often overstated the prowess of their risk departments to lull regulators into a false sense of security. In spite of the innate needs for comfort and security, regulators should not fall into the trap. Crises will continue to happen, despite the growing cadre of able risk departments in banks. Humans will continue to steer processes, whether in the production or use of information, and in the very act of steering, will betray their Achilles' heel. At the same time, the continuing existence of crises does not negate the need for risk management. Rather, this is exactly what should prompt a quest for better risk management.

Regulators may be aware that biases take root and flourish in the unexciting arid soil of micro-management – and micro-regulation – of financial markets. Micro-regulation leads to companies faced with escalating costs of the bureaucratic paper multiplier effect, which leads to regulatory arbitrage and forum shopping. Complex systems are best managed by leaving them alone and by making some small incremental changes occasionally over time. At the same time, there must be no doubt that risk management is one of top management's responsibilities.

It is encouraging to see that some modern regulators are implementing more enlightened principles. The Financial Services Authority (FSA), the recently established UK financial services regulator, is pursuing exactly this route. Under the System and Controls (SYSC) principles, risk management is made an explicit part of the proper organization and setup of any firm conducting regulated business in the UK. Failure to comply with this principle can lead to the FSA revoking the firm's authorization. Needless to add, very serious career consequences can follow for senior management of the non-compliant firm. Other regulators would be well advised to follow the FSA's lead in this field.

9.5.3 The outside analysts

Analysts are another set of external players with whom financial firms often interact. While not actively involved in top management's decisions, these actors can have a significant influence on them. Stock market and rating analysts can affect investors' decisions on a firm's stocks and bonds, thereby making equity and debt financing more or less attractive.

We are most interested in the set of frames of risk that analysts adopt when they interact with financial institutions, purportedly assessing their risks. For the purposes of analysis, we aggregate this lot, taking account of the commonalities of their function and incentives.

The topic is not easy to define, as analysts' performance assessments, compensation and promotions have historically been tied more to their ability to bring business to their employers than to the objectivity of their recommendations. This is particularly true with respect to risk hidden within an organization, which has minimal disclosure in the financial statements. Aside from relatively specious VaR figures at the end of the relevant reporting period and some information on derivative losses where mark-to-market is adopted, there is not really that much that firms need to report in their financial statements.

Following the end of the internet stock market bubble and the toughest investment-banking market in years, analysts and the role of research in sell-side firms have often been in the limelight. This section will not dwell on stock analysts' conflicts of interests and biases, which have already been targeted by a robust body of empirical evidence.

A study by Michaely & Womack (1999) underscored how underwriter analysts issue 50 per cent more 'buy' recommendations than non-affiliated analysts after Initial Public Offerings (IPO's). After IPO date, the recommendations of non-affiliated analysts were also found to outperform. Hansen & Sarin (1998) confirmed an optimistic bias in analysts' earnings expectations by analyzing seasoned equity offerings over the 1980–1991 period. Pointing to the earnings game between analysts and companies, Degeorge, Patel & Zeckhauser (1999) argue that earnings announcements by company executives rely on specific decision-making thresholds. Shefrin (2000) presents a comprehensive analysis of these patterns, including anchoring and adjustment. Others have targeted the impact of new regulations on earnings announcements, such as the so-called Reg FD by the SEC in October 2000. Reg FD prohibits companies from disclosing earnings or other material business information to some analysts or large investors before announcing it publicly. Using forecasts for a large set of public companies for three quarters following FD, Agrawal & Chadha (2002) show a significant deterioration in earnings forecasts for both individual analysts and consensus estimates. They also present empirical evidence of increased dispersion in earnings estimates following FD.

In very general terms, a significant 'disconnect' exists between the risk and the accounting world. Simply put, external risk disclosure is scant and buried in an ocean of accounting data and language in modern financial statements. This is by no means the complete basis of information on which outside analysts rely. It should come as no surprise that accounting, rather than risk in the strict sense, pervades the evaluation frame of risk for financial services firms. This accounting view of the world ascribes a premium to stability, which suits people's natural risk aversion. Banks will duly comply by emphasizing those risks in their portfolio which are most associated with stability and clients and curbing those most prone to generate questions, such as trading. As Chapter 7 showed, taking little or no trading risk may paradoxically be the biggest risk, as it may increase a bank's exposure to the economic cycle. Do not assume that politically correct risks are necessarily the best over the long term.

9.5.4 Consultants and expert judgment

Turning to consultants, few figures can match them in providing arguments, conceptual models and figures that comply with their clients' unconscious frames. Cognitive resonance with the client, whether an individual or a group, is one of the key biases that they have to guard themselves from. To be fair, there are often commercial realities. The odds of retaining a client for the next mandate increase if you do not disagree with them too often. Ethical concerns aside, these very same realities often defeat the purpose of having an outsider bring an unbiased point of view into an organization. Consultants can prepare studies and evidence that may be used to steer top management's decisions – and are indeed sometimes hired precisely to present confirming evidence of what a firm's top management is already orientated towards (confirmation bias, anyone?). While consultants do not escape human biases, they can mitigate and highlight some of their client's decision-making biases.

9.5.5 The media and the public

The *attention economy* (Davenport & Beck, 2001) is one of the various labels that have been proposed to highlight the visibility obsession that is often witnessed in today's society. Within this context, the line between the economy and the provision and perception of information thereon has progressively disappeared. The impressive advances in virtual reality and the internet bubble have shown how dramatically the perception of value established by the media can define value itself.

Vast amounts of funds invested in mutual funds and global media have been among the leading forces making the fancy reality of global financial markets more accessible to ordinary people. By fostering a greater understanding and education in retail investors, this phenomenon has been, on balance, positive for financial markets. Large financial institutions have actively encouraged it and profited handsomely from it.

All these positives notwithstanding, this trend has brought with it some unwelcome side effects, too. The media thrive on providing ready-to-consume versions of fairly complicated products and risks. This simplification process sometimes results in important details being completely snowed under the inordinate amount of information that is generated every day. After all, this is another frame of risk that is created in the audience's minds. Compare, for instance, the straight, decisive message of TV or newspapers when providing news of some scientific or medical discovery with the long series of disclaimers that infest scientific and academic papers referring to that discovery. In the case of finance, those very details often come back to haunt traders and investors with a vengeance when unexpected reversals destroy that frame of risk.

Unlike science, the world of finance is susceptible to major simplifications, first and foremost in its basic risk-return tradeoff. The ability to show a more intelligent process to model that tradeoff is what these frames of risk are all about and what media are especially fond of. That may be achieved, for instance, with some 'magic' formula, trading system or computer-generated artificial intelligence system. Who in the general public is not interested in some way in earning a superior risk-adjusted return for their money?

This is also what gives birth to more or less self-appointed 'gurus' – the attention-getter and the headline-grabber that the media and the public are craving for. The process bears striking resemblances to the popular fascination for movie stars. The hunt for the 'hero', of course, generally obfuscates the hard work and the competence of all those who are working around him or her. As the hero tries to put some distance between him- or herself and common mortals, the popular interest in anything that makes his or her reality more accessible grows.

It Ain't Necessarily So (Murray, Schwartz & Lichter, 2001) is an excellent book that documents in detail how the media can and often do distort the supposedly scientific view of reality. It is worth mentioning some of the biases that it underscores, as they pervade financial information, too.

- The dramatic rise in human data mining capabilities that has mirrored increased computing power has also increased mankind's *association* capabilities (the ability to relate certain factors to others). This is often confused with *correlation* and, worse, *causation*. Humans dread uncertainty and are often looking for causes and explanations to control a particular trend, phenomenon or behaviour. After all, this suits the human illusion of control. Once a supposedly intriguing cause–effect relationship is found, the rationalization begins. Seldom is enough time or attention spent on considering that the link may result from pure coincidence. One example of this illusory link was mentioned during the derivatives training programme that the author attended in New York at the beginning of his trading career. That instance pointed to the strong correlation (without any causal link) between the years in which a major US baseball team won the World Series and the years of strong positive performance in the S&P stock market index.[55] The more terrifying and fearsome the effects are, the more credible the argument gets. This is another example of availability bias by retrieval based on an image's vividness.

- 'The news isn't the truth and the truth isn't the news'[56] was a saying in the dying days of the former Soviet Union. The news is the result of a choice, of an information extraction process that is inevitably influenced by values and frames.

- Media display a preference for bad news (Wattenberg, 1984), as this is more exciting for the audience. In addition, the willingness to assume an adversarial and generally sceptical stance against big businesses is the trademark of a good journalist. This, it is assumed, will lead to better regulations, safety and consumer protection.

- The audience presents different and often inconsistent risk tolerances. Fischhoff *et al* (1978) show that these are divided between more and less tolerable. The former category includes those that can be avoided or are familiar, such as skiing or smoking, or those that have been known for a long time, such as fireworks. The latter category includes those that are involuntary, such as exposure to nuclear waste, those that have long-delayed effects, such as pesticides, and the unknown ones, like genetic engineering. Flynn, Slovic & Mertz (1994) also show statistically significant differences in risk preferences across race and gender.

The last few years have provided major examples of how important the interaction between media and finance has become, most interestingly with respect to derivative products. Consistent with Wattenberg's and Fischhoff's findings, these examples illustrate both

---

[55] Ken Garbade, the then Head of Research made the example, during a derivative training program at Bankers Trust in the summer of 1988.

[56] '*Isvestia nye Pravda, y Pravda nye Isvesti*'. In Russian, Pravda and Isvestia mean 'truth' and 'news', respectively.

media bias towards shocking bad news and the general public's aversion towards something as mysterious and unknown as derivatives.

A recent paper by Huang, Krawiec & Partnoy (2001) provides a thorough analysis of the mixture of derivatives, media and public. One of these three authors, Frank Partnoy, has previous direct experience on the topic, having sold derivatives at two major Wall Street firms earlier. The study reviews the format of the TV coverage of two major derivative debacles that will be discussed in greater detail in the next chapter, Orange County and LTCM. These authors reject the widespread view of derivatives and television as complex and simple, respectively. As the average person's knowledge of derivatives is more likely acquired through television and popular media than through formal training, the paper argues that the depiction of derivatives on television is extremely important. Accordingly, a juror's exposure to television may bias decisions in subsequent derivative-related lawsuits. He or she may indeed be led to believe that derivatives cause large losses but provide little benefit. Several congressional debates are also added in which quotations from the media are proposed in support of the prospective introduction of tighter regulation and legislation.

Few instances have shown a more dramatic impact of media and public opinion on the derivative industry than the notorious Bankers Trust–Procter & Gamble incident of the mid-1990s. Major global business magazines such as *Business Week* provided extensive and very detailed coverage of the incident. This even featured transcripts of the taped telephone conversation between the derivative salesman involved in the affair and other BT colleagues. Major off-the-record sarcastic remarks made the headlines. Not surprisingly, the reputation of Bankers Trust was irreparably damaged, contributing to its demise and eventual takeover by Deutsche Bank in 1999. Oddly enough, few in the media, if anybody at all, ever mentioned that several corporate treasurers had made significant profits on the very same structured trades when markets had turned in their favour. Evidently, the frame of risk of the greedy Wall Street firm taking unfair advantage of an unsuspecting client was far more interesting for the public. After all, this is just another display of cognitive resonance.

CHAPTER 10

Frames in action: financial risk disasters and panics

I can calculate the motion of heavenly bodies but not the madness of crowds.

(Isaac Newton, after losing a significant portion of his wealth in speculative investments in the South Seas Company)

7±2:

- Consequences of flawed decision and risk rationality assumptions

- Finance disasters

- Financial manias and panics

- Today's risk models persist in ignoring heavy evidence against rationality assumptions

- How prepared are decision-makers to use information from their risk processes?

- How does the framing of information affect their decisions?

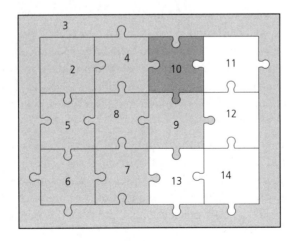

Abstract

It is now time to see what framing and flawed human decisions are capable of. This chapter illustrates some stories that made the headlines in finance. Financial professionals who are involved in risk decisions, be they risk managers, traders or senior managers, are hardly alone in making mistakes. The next chapter will show the striking similarity of patterns between them and their counterparts outside finance.

Implications: Regardless of how much you believe in fancy quantitative models, high-performance computers and the glamour of the people who run them, never underestimate the human weaknesses underlying them. Run periodic fire drills to push people outside of their comfort zones and vaccinate them with some stress before they experience it in the next crisis.

10.1 New accidents, old mis-management

By now, you should have understood how people are affected by many limitations and biases in processing information, especially with respect to probabilities and decisions involving risk. Later on, this chapter will show how these biases are at the heart of many risk disasters, both in finance and in the real world. After the fact, it is common to see 'aberrations', 'anomalies', 'exceptional events' or even the adverse forces of nature blamed for them. This should come as no surprise, as it is one of the key facets of self-attribution bias, a tendency that was already encountered in Chapter 5. In practice, nature or markets just expose the dire consequences of flawed decisions or behaviours that occurred earlier. Some key lessons emerge:

- Decisions about benefits and costs ought to happen simultaneously before a commitment to the new venture is made. Also, cut-loss points and milestones in the future should be set out clearly and in advance. These decisions will probably become far less objective while the venture is underway and after a significant amount of time and resources have been spent on it. Under these circumstances, sunk cost biases, framing and groupthink are prone to exert a significant influence on the future course of action. Cutting corners on safety and skimping on infrastructure and support costs over time are examples of this attitude.

- The seed of self-destruction is often planted well before the risky endeavour begins. More often than not, people fall prey to the fascination of the opportunities created by the new product, market or technology without realizing completely the consequences and costs that it involves. Often, the initial enthusiasm results in these 'details' being dismissed or overlooked to start quickly. One could label this behaviour as the dark side of the 'just do it' approach.

▪ More often than not, complexity is a harbinger for trouble. This problem manifests itself in two ways:

– in the technical sphere, greater efficiency is often correlated with a more rigid process in which the various stages become increasingly dependent on each other. This heightened dependency is called *coupling*. Tighter coupling means that failure in one stage is likely to affect others and possibly compromise the whole process;

– in the organisational realm, a more complex process leads to several specialized stages and divided responsibilities. This also involves a potentially dangerous extension of the whole accountability chain. This means that a decision that may be optimal for one particular stage may have unintended – and not necessarily positive – consequences for the others and for the whole process, especially when responsibilities are split for decisions that involve risk and cost trade-offs. In these instances, the praise for cutting costs should also be accompanied by the responsibility for the increased operational risk that cost-cutting decisions generate.

▪ 'Impossible' and 'unrealistic' events do happen. Next time you hear the 'it will never happen' tune, consider how ill-equipped humans are to make probability assessments. You may recall from Chapter 5 that people tend to round the probability of rare events to zero to simplify their decision-making process. The same may also happen if the memory of the event is not very recent or vivid. It was also shown how people often tend to confuse frequency and probability. As a by-product of availability bias, the fear of these consequences is so vivid that it also triggers a defensive psychological mechanism of denial. Let's face it, it is far more comfortable and quick to just shut one's eyes, dismiss the event as impossible and shift thoughts to something else.

10.2 The dangerous mix of leverage and overconfidence

In the ego-bloated world of finance and investment banking, there is no shortage of colourful expressions that feature a mixture of mystery, magic and admiration. The popular press and the media actively contribute to reinforce these forms of labelling (see section 9.5.5). After all, they generate interest for laymen and that, in turn, drives sales up. Derivatives and the trading industry are no exception to the rule. Phrases like 'money masters', 'masters of the universe', 'rocket scientists', 'whiz kids' and others are heard often. If popularity and visibility translate into the ability to command a higher salary next time a job switch is in sight, so much the better. Some readers may have already detected a selective attention or survivorship bias that is built into these glamorous labels. Indeed, those who have been successful enough to make the news or the front page of some popular magazine are very few in comparison with the thousands of good souls who have suffered some losses or just led a more normal existence.

Much like the ancient gods who sometimes fell back to Earth, even these 'geniuses' are not infallible. Modern financial technology allows the use of leverage to an unprecedented extent. Compared to the past, this means that a relatively small amount of equity can allow an institution to finance a very large position inventory. Relative to that small equity base, it also means that the impact of gains and losses is magnified. Let us consider an example.

Bank XYZ wishes to buy US Treasury bonds worth $100 million. It can finance this investment in one of two ways. It can:

- use spare cash and short-term liquidity that it owns, for instance, by liquidating a deposit that it has with another institution;

- fund the position with a particular type of loan called a *repurchase* agreement or simply *repo*.[57] Under this arrangement, a counterpart funds a given percentage of the market value of the bond that Bank XYZ intends to invest in, let us assume, for instance, 90 per cent. The bond is then pledged as collateral for the loan. If Bank XYZ were to go bankrupt during the life of this loan, the counterpart could take possession of the bond and sell it in the market to get the loan repaid. The difference between the bond's market value and the amount lent by the counterpart maintains a safety cushion to offset fluctuations in the bond's market value while the loan is outstanding.

Under these alternatives, bank XYZ is tying up equity for, respectively, 100 and 10 (=100 less 0.9 × 100 borrowed under the repo). If the bond price rose by, say, 2 per cent, it would achieve a return or equity of 2 per cent (=2/100) and 20 per cent (=2/10), respectively. Leverage works both ways, though. If the bond's price were to drop by 5 per cent, half of the bank's equity under the second alternative (minus 5 divided by 10 = minus 50 per cent) would be wiped out.

Futures contracts traded on organized exchanges and forward contracts traded over-the-counter with a counterpart present the same opportunity to use financial leverage. In the case of futures, the existence of a daily mark-to-market and settlement mechanism allows exchanges to offer very substantial leverage opportunities to their participants. It also means that one's equity can be burned very quickly.

This chapter shows how overconfidence is the first standard ingredient of trouble, both in finance and outside. Financial leverage, the second element behind all financial risk disasters in individual companies or in market crashes, is at least as dangerous. By allowing a quick multiplication of results, the effects, it acts as a giant magnifying glass of human judgment errors.

As the human mind goes, the mirage of getting rich quickly is simply too alluring to resist, and definitely worth the 'negligible' risk of going bankrupt. Under pressure from competition and ever more militant shareholders, banks are in the business of maximizing their return on capital. Table 10.1 features the Who's Who of trading and risk disasters.

---

[57] The bank can achieve the same result by selling the bonds spot to the counterpart and committing to buy them back at a pre-specified price at a given future date. The difference between the spot and the forward price reflects the coupon paid on the bond and the funding rate that the counterpart is willing to grant.

Notably absent from this list are several other horror stories, ranging from failed loans to the disaster that struck the California power generation companies in 2001. Other major bankruptcies that are not featured but should never be forgotten include Worldcom Inc. Also missing are a few major hedge funds that went out of business, such as Victor Niederhoffer's Askin Capital Management and Julian H. Robertson's Tiger Capital Management. These were forced to shut down after suffering catastrophic losses. In all those unfortunate instances, as in the list in the table, human overconfidence is the one single recurrent theme.

At the time of writing, other major mishaps in late 2003 and early 2004 at Parmalat, the Italian food giant, and National Australia Bank are being investigated. Based on some preliminary reports, one should reasonably expect them to become two additional instances in the long story on internal control failures. The lesson is that a process is only as good as the people who run it. 'Smart' people will always try to cut some corners and circumvent others. That is an inescapable fact of life. Rationalizing it after the fact with arguments such as cost-cutting, meeting emergencies, 'we thought that ...', 'adapting the rules to the specificities of the situation' does not change reality.

Finance presents plenty of instances of people *hoping* that the problem will go away, whether in a poor trade or in some management problem. This verb is used purposefully, because that is what is really happening. According to prospect theory, problem situations induce people into risk-seeking behaviours (see Chapter 4). In addition, it was shown that there is a widespread belief in the existence of *hot hands*, whether in basketball or in business. Whether self-appointed or not, these gurus are in plentiful supply in the trading rooms of Wall Street and the City. Then, the presence of some hot-hand money-maker in some part of the operation encourages rolling the dice. Sometimes, most often when trouble has already appeared, the mere *hope* that this person will get out of an unlucky streak is sufficient. Unfortunately, the passage of time alone is not a cure for all diseases.

Errare humanum est, perseverare diabolicum, as ancient Latins would put it. In at least three major instances, Barings, Daiwa and Allfirst, internal audits had underscored the risks associated with a lack of separation of duties between front- and back-office. Enron, too, witnessed several instances of prescient internal alarm calls that were quashed and resulted in reprisals against their bearers.

In some of these instances, things continued as if nothing had happened. Consistent with prospect theory, management just 'kept going'. That's the path of least resistance and one that will be shown again in the account of real-world disasters in the next chapter. Finance shows just another series of high-risk instances that management consistently chose to face by putting up a strong *personality* in a difficult situation rather than by *sorting out a flawed process*. Do you see a pattern here?

Unlike several other excellent analyses of these disaster case studies, the use of technical details is limited to the bare minimum to understand the developments. Readers who want to gain a more thorough understanding of these situations can find excellent sources in the bibliography. Rather, the spotlight will be on the behavioural profile of these instances, which is the particular focus of the present book.

TABLE 10.1 ■ A hit parade of mishaps

Company	Year	Amount Lost (US$)	Loss Nature	Behavioural Issues					Person involved and consequences
				Overconfidence	Ability to understand	Gambler's fallacy Doubling-up/ Get-even itis	Hot-hands effect	Under-estimation of game theory	
Enron	2001	60 bn bankruptcy	Aggressive accounting over unconsolidated subsidiaries' losses in private equity and high-tech companies.	Internal controls that were largely made irrelevant by internal politics.	Involvement in a hodgepodge of opaque and complex businesses.	N/A			Jeff Skilling, Chairman and CEO (under investigation). Andrew Fastow, CFO (charged with fraud, money laundering and conspiracy, awaiting trial).
Long-Term Capital Management	1998	2.5 bn	Liquidity crisis affecting several highly leveraged relative-value trades.	In VaR, theoretical quantitative models and partners' academic credentials.		Staying power of risk capital to support arbitrages.		X	John Meriwether. While nothing ilegal occurred, the stability of global financial markets was under question for a few weeks.
Sumitomo Corp. (Japan)	1996	2.6bn	Copper trades.	Internal controls.					Yasuo Hamanaka, trader (convicted).
Orange County, California	1994	1.7 bn	Interest rate derivatives.	Internal controls.	Risk of leveraged trades.	Large position increases in the face of rising trading losses.	Strong per-formance due more to secular drop in rates than to Treasurer's ability.		Robert Citron, Treasurer (convicted).
MGRM, US trading subsidary of Metall-gesellschaft AG (Germany)	1994	1.5 bn.	Oil futures.	Internal controls.		Staying power of risk capital.		Excessive visibility of MGRM trading positions on NYMEX exchange.	

TABLE 10.1 ■ A hit parade of mishaps (continued)

Company	Year	Amount Lost (US$)	Loss Nature	Behavioural Issues					Person involved and consequences
				Overconfidence	Ability to understand	Gambler's fallacy Doubling-up/ Get-even itis	Hot-hands effect	Under-estimation of game theory	
Barings plc (UK)	1995	1.4 bn	Japanese equity index futures.	Internal controls.	Top management unable to figure out setup in Singapore.	Position repeatedly increased betting on the odds of market trend reversal.	Mistaken belief in Leeson's outstanding trading skill.		Nick Leeson, trader (convicted).
Daiwa Bank (Japan)	1995	1.1 bn	US T-bonds.	Internal controls.	Disregard of several adverse audit reports.				Toshihide Iguchi, trader (convicted).
Showa shell sekiyu (Japanese subsidiary of Royal Dutch/Shell)	1993	1.1 bn	Foreign exchange.	Internal controls.					Yukihusa Fujita, General Manager of Finance Department.
Allfirst (US subsidiary of Allied Irish Bank, Ireland)	2002	691 million	Foreign exchange options and exotics.	Internal controls.	Selective attention bias against adverse internal audit reports.	Positions repeatedly increased despite soaring losses.			John Rusnak, FX option trader (under investigation). Allfirst sold to M&T Bank.
Merrill Lynch (US)	1987	377 million	Mortgage-backed securities.	Internal controls.		X			Howard S. Rubin, mortgage trader (denied charges).
Salomon Brothers (US)	1991	291 million	US T-bonds auctions.	Internal controls.					Paul Mozer, bond trader (plea bargained).
Kidder, Peabody (GE Group) (US)	1994	210 million	Allegedly unauthorized 'phantom profit'	Internal controls.					Joseph Jett, Head Gov. bond trader, denied charges.
Codelco (Chile state-owned copper company)	1996	170 million	Fraudulent trades.	Internal controls.					Juan Pablo Davila, futures trader.
ABN-AMRO Bank (The Netherlands)	1993	70 million	FX options.	Internal controls.					James Martignoni (convicted).
Chemical Bank	1996	70 million	Mexican pesos.	Internal controls.					Victor Gomez, Vice President.
Bankers Trust – Procter & Gamble (US)	1995	70 million	Exotic interest-rate and cross-currency derivatives.	Internal controls (of P&G's Treasury and BT sales practices).	Risk and suitability of leveraged trades.	P&G increasing exposure to exotics when in loss.			P&G sued Bankers Trust alleging poor disclosure of trade risks. Settled out of court in 1996. Reputational damage eventually cost BT its independence.

Source: adapted from table 3.1 ('A Dozen Rogues'), from *Outsmarting the smart money*, p. 50, Lawrence A. Cunningham, © McGraw-Hill, reprinted with permission.

10.3 Houston, we have a problem:[58] Enron

Among all the stories of finance 'wizards' falling back to Earth, few will ever manage to match the scale of the drama that took place in the Houston-based energy trading power-house. Fraud aside, the largest US corporate bankruptcy to date shows the spectacular results of an explosive mix of greed, overconfidence and other important behavioural traits. Readers may wonder why this is analysed, as it is not a market or credit risk debacle. Their absence is precisely what makes this case so interesting. There are no wrong models, 10-standard deviation moves or some major country default to blame here. Rather, this instance shows pure overconfidence and human risk at their best (or worst).

Chronology	
1990	Kenneth Lay, Chairman & CEO of Enron, hires Jeffrey Skilling from McKinsey as CEO of Enron Gas Services (to become Enron Capital & Trade Resources, or ECT). Skilling hires Andrew Fastow as Account Director.
1991	Andrew Fastow forms the first of many off-balance-sheet partnerships. Over time, these will be used to hide losses on Enron's investments.
1993	Enron begins trading over-the-counter energy derivative products, mostly energy swaps. CalPERS, the California Public Employees' Retirement System, teams up with Enron in the Joint Energy Development Investments (JEDI) partnership. Meanwhile, the US power deregulation intensifies. International expansion in Britain.
1996	Construction of the $2 billion power plant in Dabhol, India, begins. Kenneth Lay, Chaiman and CEO since 1986, appoints Jeffrey Skilling President and Chief Operating Officer.
1997	Energy trading activity is extended to other commodity markets such as weather derivatives. A new partnership, Chewco, is created to buy out CalPERS's stake in JEDI.
1998	First internet investment by Enron ($10 million in Rhythms NetConnection, a privately held Internet Service Provider). Shortly thereafter, Rhythms is listed at $21 per share. Its price will more than treble in the first trading day.
1999	Azurix, Enron water services subsidiary, goes public. The Board of Directors appoints Andrew Fastow CFO of two LJM partnerships. A series of hedging transactions between Enron and LJM begins.
2000	In April, Enron creates first Raptor partnership. In August, Rebecca Marks resigns from her position as Azurix's CEO. Enron's stock price peaks at $90. Raptor II and III partnerships created. Derivative transactions exceeding $1.5 billion in notional follow between Enron and the three Raptor partnerships. They will generate a questionable $500 million profit. This will account for over three-fourths of the $650 million profit that Enron will declare for the second half of the year.

[58] Apollo 13 astronauts' call to NASA flight centre after one oxygen tank exploded while circling the Moon. A mixture of ingenuity, skill and luck brought all the crew back to Earth safely. In this instance, Houston flight controllers left more initiative to the capsule's crew than under normal circumstances. The case is often mentioned as an example of the amazing results that can be achieved when emergency and time pressure force people to go back to basics and ban complexity in their decisions.

2001 (first half)	In February, Skilling is appointed CEO. He is expected to succeed Kenneth Lay, the Chairman, within a year or two. Despite apparently brilliant first-quarter results, the company shows a deteriorating cash position in the mid-May SEC filings. Enron's poor disclosure of the individual divisions' questionable results starts attracting scrutiny during difficult quarterly results conference calls with analysts and investors.
2001 (third quarter)	10-Q form filed with the SEC on 14 August 2001 with respect to first-half results shows $1.3 billion drop in cash position despite a $823 million profit. Quoting unspecified 'personal reasons', Skilling resigns. Kenneth Lay is re-appointed as CEO to restore confidence. A day later, he receives an anonymous memo from Sherron Watkins, an accountant in Enron's finance division, who warns of a potential accounting scandal. In September, Arthur Andersen, Enron's audit firm, asks to reverse the company's aggressive accounting treatment of partnerships, wiping out $1.2 billion of equity.
2001 (fourth quarter)	On 16 October, the SEC initiates investigation of Enron's off-balance-sheet partnerships. Nine days later, Enron draws its $1 billion credit line with banks to avert a liquidity crisis. An internal investigation committee is appointed. They will produce the so-called Powers report in February 2002. On 8 November, an additional $1.2 billion write-down is necessary to restate the earnings at Chewco between 1997 and 2002. Enron attempted merger with energy industry rival Dynegy fails due to Enron's credit downgrade to sub-investment grade ('junk') status and other internal accounting problems. Enron files for Chapter 11 bankruptcy protection on 2 December.
2002	In January, the Justice Department confirms that it is conducting a criminal investigation of the Enron case. The energy trading business is sold to UBS Warburg. Cliff Baxter, Enron former Vice Chairman, is found dead in his car. In February, Skilling, Lay and Watkins testify before Congress. Skilling, Lay and Fastow plead the Fifth Amendment. In April, Andersen lays off 7,000 workers as clients leave in droves. Andersen will be eventually shut down.

In the aftermath, many blamed the failure of internal and external checks-and-balances for this disaster. But people have always been trying to circumvent processes. Rather, the problem is in the very overconfident belief that processes *per se* will prevent troubles. If one ever needed a proof that a process is always a bet on the people who implement it, there is hardly a better one. For investors, Enron became a rude wake-up call after being duped for years on the value of 'strategic' synergies and deals. Better go back to basic accounting.

Enron's aggressive deal-at-any-cost culture was by no means a novelty for outsiders. The company's international expansion strategy had already resulted in a few expensive missteps that should have underscored how financial prudence hardly figured atop decision-making criteria at Enron. Amongst them:

- a questionable two-stage power project in Dabhol, India, which eventually defaulted in 2001;

- pioneering trading in bandwidth, the use of broadband cable for a specified period of time. This had been a major attention-getter at the peak of the internet mania but also a very costly expansion with doubtful profitability prospects;

- the acquisition of British water utility Wessex Water for $1.9 billion;

- an over-aggressive $438.6 million bid for a 30-year water concession in Argentina's Buenos Aires province.

The situation at Azurix, Enron's water subsidiary, had started unravelling as early as November 1999, when the company announced the layoff of one-third of its workforce to cut costs. Rebecca Marks, Azurix's CEO, eventually resigned in August 2000.

Nevertheless, Enron's stock price kept climbing, peaking at $90 in August 2000. This appeared even more remarkable, since the internet boom had peaked in March of that year. Jeffrey Skilling was made CEO in February 2001. Few – if any – questions were asked. Given the favourable trend, this should come as no surprise. Outsiders – no doubt based on the 'informed' advice of most stock analysts and plenty of praise from several top consultants and business school professors – had formed a sharp picture in their mind – a frame of risk. Simply put, they were anchored to the view of Enron as a remarkably brilliant company with visionary management. And what did the media think? Well, that's easy. In February 2000, the respected *Fortune* magazine had named Enron 'the most innovative company in America' for the fifth year in a row. That explains some under-reactions to unfavourable news well before the fateful summer of 2001.

From that point onward, the wake-up call came when the company drew on its revolving lines of credit to avert a liquidity crisis. The market's view of Enron as an astute and financially strong company was completely shattered. The stock, which had already fallen to $50 in the summer, dropped to $11 in late October and $1 a month later, shortly before Enron filed for Chapter 11. There are two very different frames of risk at play here: 'strategic vision' and the 'basic actual net worth'. As the crisis worsened, the reframing from one to the other became increasingly painful.

10.3.1 The lessons to be learned from Enron

■ When something just looks too perfect, it probably is. Despite Enron's practising aggressive accounting for years, the heightened scrutiny began only late in the second quarter of 2001. It does not take a genius to figure out that zooming stock price in the previous years had hardly encouraged anybody to take a closer look. Many top managers and traders keep falling into exactly the same trap during favourable periods. During good times, the self-attribution bias that ascribes success to one's ability jails the intellectual honesty and curiosity needed to understand the relative contribution of skill and luck. In the case of Enron, the unwillingness to understand the real economics of a hodgepodge of activities was further compounded by internal political pressure and an intimidating internal performance ranking system named 'rank and yank'. No wonder internal processes did not stop the problem earlier!

■ Processes are based on people. No flowchart can sort out problems without someone implementing it properly. A satisfactory answer to the 'what' question cannot do without an understanding of the 'who' aspect.

■ For investors, the poor disclosure of the separate results of Enron's disparate businesses is also a stark reminder of the information framing problem and illusion of diversification outlined earlier in Chapters 5 and 7. Recall the 'you cannot ask questions on what you cannot see' principle. When one does not know for sure whether a company's operating activities are extremely concentrated in a particular sector, scepticism is imperative. This applies especially to conglomerates and multi-business firms that hide information behind 'synergy' and 'strategic value'. The degree of vagueness in these catchphrases is equal to their allure. Firms that lack or are unwilling to provide more details on the value and profitability of the separate pieces involve greater uncertainty and risk for the investor, full stop. As such, they should simply be punished with a higher cost of capital. In the case of a company's equity, this means a lower stock price.

10.4 Overconfidence in processes

The trading industry's tendency to neglect the balance between front-office on one side and middle-/back-office and related infrastructure on the other is as old as the industry itself. Several factors are behind this problem. Key amongst them:

- Increased competition and squeezed revenue margins have forced banks to cut costs wherever they can. It is obvious that revenue-generating areas in front-office have the first claim on budgets and resources. The other areas have a lower priority but are nonetheless extremely important. In the world of finance, this is a subset of a broad area named operational risk. The industry's profit-linked incentive compensation is a further reason for trying to increase the revenue base and keep the other costs down. Aware of these tendencies, the FSA, the UK's financial services regulator, has made senior management explicitly responsible for risk management and proper controls. Non-compliance can have extremely serious consequences for managers and firms.

- Generating the lion's share of profits and bonuses, front-office is the most prestigious area to work in. Consequently, it has first claim on the industry's best managers and brightest minds. The other functions are not viewed as the fastest track to the top.

- Most top managers in major financial institutions have grown in a deal culture in both the trading room and the corporate finance departments. Once a deal or a trade is completed, they will try to move to the next as soon as they can and worry little about what happens in the prosaic functions beyond front-office. This lack of responsibility is not necessarily the best background to understand the importance of processes. Eventually, poor processes generate problems in the form of higher processing costs, losses or both. Only then are others finally forced to pay attention.

The cases described in this section will show the impressively regular patterns that brought more than one bank down the primrose path. The sequence can be summarized as follows:

- Initially, there is an expansion into a new product or market in which management wants to keep the initial costs down. As all the cases in this section will show, the new entrant's lack of any competitive advantage in the chosen area is a factor that encourages this approach. Most often the choice of *what* risks to run overshadows the critical decision of *how* to run them. Often, the belief that the operation is supposed to offer some marketing or brokerage service with little or no market risk is prone to fool headquarters into a false sense of security. The cases of Barings and Metallgesellschaft are illustrious examples of this pattern.

■ A 'champion' is chosen to run the activity in the local market or chosen product. To keep costs down, this individual is granted responsibility for the whole operation, that is for front- and back-office. That authority may not necessarily require a formal title. The champion may, for example, be allowed to bully and intimidate the persons and departments that are supposed to check his performance. This will weaken the controls' effectiveness in enforcing the headquarters' mandate.

■ Initially, the new local operation thrives or at least survives in the chosen area. As the firm is often an underdog in that market, even more responsibility, compensation and authority follows. Calls for internal segregation of duties by staff or, more formally, by internal audit are dismissed.

■ Some adverse event takes place. As the champion holds sway over the back-office, he will develop some scheme to disguise his losses.

■ At the same time, the champion will probably increase his position to try to recover losses when the market turns. He will justify this more aggressive stance by arguing that the current situation presents some 'special value' on fundamental, statistical or technical grounds. The law of large numbers is often invoked at this stage to provide some semblance of objectivity to the decision. Ironically, after the whole scandal has been exposed and his position cut, he may sometimes even be proved right. That will offer him one last platonic ego boost against his institution's supposedly stupid management who 'did not understand the trade'.

■ As losses mount, the cover-up becomes more extreme and so does the trader's psychological position, which will induce him to further increase his exposure.

■ In the final stage, losses and positions grow out of proportion and eventually attract some external scrutiny. At last the scheme is exposed. A witch-hunt usually follows.

10.4.1 Barings

If one person has the right to claim the questionable title of rogue trader, that is likely to be Nick Leeson. *Rogue Trader* was indeed the title of a book and a movie inspired by the crisis. Bankrupcty may not be considered feasible or relevant within the world of theoretical finance,[59] but it sure has a seat in the real world! The availability of risk capital is certainly more constrained in the real world than in financial theory.

---

[59] Quote about economist Franco Modigliani, from *Beyond Greed and Fear*, Chapter 1, p. 9.

At first, some analysts deemed this a market risk problem and, sure enough, the standard tabloid articles on the perils of derivatives showed up. Only later, after more detailed investigations and a comprehensive Bank of England report, was the real nature of the case as an operational risk failure confirmed. For all his weaknesses, Nick Leeson was not the only person responsible.

Chronology

1990–91	Nicholas Leeson joins the futures settlement division of Barings, a British merchant bank founded in 1776. He solves several nagging back-office problems and works in Singapore and Jakarta.
March 1992	Leeson is offered the opportunity to run Barings' futures trading operation on the Singapore International Monetary Exchange (SIMEX). While he is soon appointed as General Manager and Head Trader, there is much confusion in London over what that title involves. He oversees both trading and back-office. Leeson mostly executes trades on behalf of clients. He also runs the Singapore leg of a low-risk Nikkei index arbitrage activity with Barings' Osaka office.[60]
1992	A wrong order to sell (instead of buy) by a junior staff member in Barings' operation creates a short position of 40 contracts. As the Nikkei index rose during that day, that would create a loss of £20,000. Leeson hides the loss by sweeping the trades into the newly created '88888' error. The account numbers are based on Chinese mythology, which deems 8 to be a lucky number. A week later, the index has increased further and so have the losses. More than 30 of these will make the 88888 account by the end of the year. Instructed by Leeson, an outside computer consultant excludes the account from the daily trading, position and price reporting to London. The ghost account will be discovered by the London office only three days before the bankruptcy.
1993	Practising the customary mistaken understanding of the law of large numbers, Leeson begins doubling his losing positions to recover previous losses. Halfway through the year, he has accumulated £6 million of losses. Then, in July, he makes back all the previous losses by gambling correctly on an increase in the index and becomes convinced of the merits of doubling up. Later on, however, he loses again. At year-end, he is underwater by £23 million. By hiding the losses, he shows a profit of £10 million for the year. Inexplicably, an internal audit investigation is stopped.
1994	As of July, Leeson has piled up losses of £50 million. He keeps asking London for more margins to post with the exchange, justifying them with the huge size of the supposedly hedged positions. In the summer, another doubling-up and an additional £30 million of losses follow. Following a major fraud of $350 million at Kidder, Peabody in New York, Barings' management decides to send an Internal Audit Team to the Singapore office in July and August. The team expresses concern at the lack of separation of duties between front- and back-office. At the same time, the internal auditors attribute the large declared profits of £28 million to Leeson's supposedly exceptional (…) abilities. As a matter of fact, his hidden losses are a staggering £170 million. External auditors Coopers & Lybrand give 'unqualified clearance' for the year-end reporting, too.
18 January 1995	A devastating earthquake hits Kobe, Japan. The Nikkei falls by 300 points and Leeson loses another £50 million and, once again, doubles up. Indeed, he considers the drop a buying opportunity. The index loses another 800 points thereafter, adding further enormous losses.

▶

---

[60] The Nikkei is the most actively followed benchmark index for the Japanese stock market. As the contracts traded on the SIMEX and Osaka exchange have the same underlying asset – the value of the Nikkei stock market index at a given date – their values must eventually match at contract maturity. During their lives, however, the two contracts may present tiny price differences for a few seconds. Barings' arbitrage activity involved buying the cheap contract and selling short the expensive one.

23 January 1995	Leeson's last day in the office. He is long 61,039 Nikkei futures contracts and 26,000 Japanese Government Bond (JGB) futures and has sold a straddle that is losing profusely. He leaves Singapore with his wife, officially to take a vacation. He is actually trying to get back to England before the Singapore authorities catch him.
27 January 1995	Leeson's £600 million losses make the headlines in all the newspapers in the world. After a brief manhunt, he is arrested at Frankfurt airport.
26 February 1995	The High Court in London appoints joint administrators to manage the affairs of Barings plc, the Barings Group parent company.
1 March 1995	Leeson's £660 million loss, over two times Barings' £300 million equity, has wiped out the 223-year-old bank. ING, the Dutch insurance giant, acquires Barings for a notional £1.
22 November 1995	After spending a few months in a German prison, Leeson is extradited to Singapore. The following week, he is sentenced to $6\frac{1}{2}$ years in prison.

As he was in charge of both trading and back-office, Leeson successfully concealed the magnitude of the loss. But is such an elephant sneaking under the carpet conceivable for an institution that was far from the largest in the global trading arena? Consistently with cognitive resonance, the odds are that few people asked questions as long as profits were rolling in. After all, derivatives were the fast-growing profit centre within Barings. Unsurprisingly, a potentially dangerous investigation from internal audit was stopped.

It is legitimate to question Leeson's objectivity in his autobiographical *Rogue Trader* book. The following interesting statements in the book and elsewhere, however, should dispel any doubt about the atmosphere of self-complacency and overconfidence that reigned in the upper echelons of management before and during the crisis. Listen to the following:

'Derivatives need to be well controlled and understood, but we believe we do that here.'[61] (Peter Barings, Chairman of Baring Brothers, October 1993)

'The recovery in profitability has been amazing …. leading Barings to conclude that it was not actually terribly difficult to make money in the securities business.'[62] (Peter Barings, Chairman of Barings Brothers, to Brian Quinn, of the Bank of England Division in charge of Supervision, 13 Sept 1993)

'It's just a non-transaction. It's an error. It's a back-office glitch. Don't worry about it.'[63] (James Bax, Regional Manager of Barings South Asia to Ron Baker, Head of Financial Products Group, 3 February 1995)

---

[61] Quote from *The Economist*, 4–10 March 1995, p. 19.
[62] Quote from DerivaQuote http://www.bus.lsu.edu/academics/finance/faculty_/dchance/MiscProf/DerivaQuote/Qt23.htm).
[63] Quote from *Rogue Trader*.

Jokes and anecdotes were in no shortage after the problem exploded. Listen to the comment of a British merchant banker:

> 'Even Colombian drug barons don't throw that sort of money around without a few signatures.'

Leeson's own thoughts on his responsibilities after the fact are also an interesting spin on regret management:

> 'I don't think of myself as a criminal. I was trying to correct a situation. And however naïve and stupid this might sound, I was always working in the best interests of the bank.'

What are the lessons to be learned from Barings?

- Beware big flashy numbers from 'hot hands' and superstar traders. Putting them in the most favourable position and giving them support and resources does not mean *eliminating* controls. Besides, how will you find out whether their performance is for real?

- Understand the economics of one's trading performance in good times *before* hard times strike.

- Think hard about expanding into new products or markets. The revenue-versus-direct cost picture offered by front-office is only one part of the story. There are substantial costs and decisions to make about the support functions, too. Cutting corners by skimping on the infrastructure may work for a few weeks at best but creates a shaky foundation for the business going forward.

- Position sizing and avoidance of gambler's fallacy are the best insurance against markets' vagaries. Leeson's doubling-up strategy shows how adverse streaks can easily outlast one's expectations and risk capital. For all their street smarts and guts, even the most successful traders cannot predict markets, let alone exceptional events. Earthquakes, defaults or terrorist acts are rare but happen from time to time. In these situations, excessively large positions mean extinction.

10.4.2 Daiwa

Barings was not alone in having an inappropriate setup between front- and back-office. Toshihide Iguchi had worked his way up the hierarchy starting from book-keeping and accounting. While maintaining these responsibilities, he was promoted to bond trader in 1984.

The New York operation of Japan's giant Daiwa Bank, at the time the thirteenth largest in the world by assets, discovered a huge $1.1 billion loss in the summer of 1995. About two-thirds of these were in Daiwa's own trading capital. The rest came from the unauthorized sale of customers' securities. In order to provide some perspective, the losses had been going on for some *eleven years*!

This case shows that major mishaps do not necessarily require complex products or exotic markets. Daiwa's loss occurred in the simplest high-quality financial instruments: US Treasury bills and bonds. As in the case of Barings, auditors had criticized the lack of separation of duties between front- and back-office as early as 1993. This time, the audit was from the branch regulators. Daiwa's promise to fix things was of course left unfulfilled.

To make matters worse, management took two weeks to notify the Japanese Ministry of Finance and another four to inform US regulators. This was the last straw for the US authorities. On 2 October 1995, the bank was ordered to pay a $340 million fine and shut down all its US operations in 90 days. Daiwa sold all its US branches to Sumitomo Bank.

Iguchi paid a stiff price. He was sentenced to four years in prison and a $2.6 million fine. Masahiro Tsuda, his boss, was sentenced to two months in prison and a $100,000 penalty. An additional $775 million of fines were imposed on the bank in Japan in 2000.

10.4.3 Metallgesellschaft

The $1.5 billion loss suffered by MG Refining & Marketing (MGRM) in 1994 was the first and worst major derivative-related loss suffered by a German corporate group. The latter, Metallgesellschaft AG (MGAG), was in good company, as several other non-financial firms took big hits from their forays into derivatives in the mid-1990s.[64] An intense corporate governance and product suitability debate ensued to address, amongst other things, the question of where the line is that divides hedging from speculation. As we will show, marketing-versus-trading frames of risk played a pivotal role in this case.

	Chronology
1989	MG acquires 49 per cent of Castle Refining in the US. It renames it MGRM and aims to serve independent and unintegrated gasoline oil dealers all over the US by offering them the ability to secure long-term fuel supplies at a pre-agreed price. The tenor of such contracts could extend as far as 10 years. The absence of long-dated exchange-traded energy futures contracts created a void that the German group intended to target. Indeed, unlike large, integrated competitors, many of these small independent oil dealers did not have the financial strength to weather price volatility in their fuel supplies. By subscribing to MGRM's programme, the independent dealers were able to lock in their profit margins.
1990–1993 August	MGRM implements the strategy by selling the long-dated supply to the oil dealers and hedging against price increases by buying short-dated crude oil futures on the NYMEX exchange. In doing so, it performs what is called a 'stack-and-roll strategy', whereby MGRM buys short-dated futures to cover the amounts of crude oil that it is obligated to deliver under long-term obligations. At each future maturity date, the excess number of contracts is sold and an equal amount of excess is bought in the next delivery month. It also exploits the downward-sloping shape of the oil price curve, which is in *backwardation*,[65] that is, contracts with longer maturities trade at a lower price than short-dated futures. Under those conditions, MGRM's traders expect to achieve a profit at most futures roll-over dates, as the price of the longer-dated oil futures contract that they own should experience an upward bias as time elapses. Despite their official maturity of 45 days, the agreements between MGRM and the independent oil dealers offer the latter the ability to defer delivery by as long as 5 to 10 years. According to a report to the CFTC filed by MG in 1995, no one will ever take delivery at the official 45-day maturity date.

[64] Procter & Gamble (discussed later on in this chapter), Gibson Greetings and Air Products & Chemical Inc. were other casualties of the 1994 bear market in bonds.

September 1993	MGRM's huge long position in NYMEX energy futures contracts is no secret. At the end of the month, it accounts for 16 per cent of all the open interest in the NYMEX. That, of course, makes it an easy target for other traders to play the other side of the market. The structure of the US crude oil futures curve flips unexpectedly from *backwardation* to *contango*, the opposite situation in which short-dated futures trade below longer-dated contracts. MGRM starts losing on each futures roll-over. Later assessments that relied on the company's large position estimated that MGRM could lose almost $600 million from these rolls.
December 1993	The market remains in contango, and MGRM's large position is amongst the decisive factors maintaining that situation. MGRM's own large hedging requirements mean downward pressure on the front-month contract and upward pressure on longer-dates futures. Other NYMEX traders, guessing the flow of MGRM's roll-overs, position themselves short, driving prices even lower. Alarmed by the increasing futures margin requirements, MG's management decide to stop MGRM's trading operations. MGRM's positions are so large that it will take three years for NYMEX to reach 1993's open-interest peaks in the crude oil and gasoline contracts.
6 January 1994	An unspecified large loss is announced and the trading in MG stock is suspended in Frankfurt.
November 1994	The large loss, in excess of $1.5 billion, wipes out MG equity and requires an infusion of fresh funds.
January 1995	MG's external auditors release a report that accuses MG management of inadequate supervision.
Summer 1995	MG settles a complaint brought against it by the Commodities and Futures Trading Commission (CFTC), the regulator of US futures markets.

An intense corporate governance debate followed MG headquarters' decision to shut down their US subsidiary's oil trading activities. Christopher Culp and Nobel Prize winner Merton Miller (1999) vigorously defended MGRM by attributing the responsibility for the case to the hasty shutdown decided by the German parent at the end of 1993. These authors claimed that MGRM was offering an innovative hedging product to fill a void in the market and its hedging rationale broadly made sense. According to this view, the contango profile of the oil futures prices in late 1993 and early 1994 was an exception and the market could be reasonably expected to revert to its normal backwardation shape. MGRM's large open-interest positions required margins to be posted with the NYMEX futures exchange, resulting in significant cashflow requirements. By cutting off the financing of this require-ment, the parent forced MGRM into a fire-sale wind-down of positions. Culp & Miller believed that it made sense for MGRM to offer this service to clients in the quest for a su-perior risk-adjusted return on capital.

Other important essays on this case (Mello & Parsons, 1994) argued that MGRM had breached its mandate by disguising speculation as hedging. According to this view, the German headquarters had authorized a marketing activity that was supposed to take as little

---

[65] The opposite shape of the oil price curve, in which short-dated maturities trade at a lower price than longer-dated maturities, goes under the name of *contango*.

risk as possible, if any at all. Rigorous adherence to the mandate would have required MGRM to seek long-term hedges in over-the-counter agreements with the major derivative dealers and keep only a smaller margin. Conversely, the US subsidiary opted to manage the risk in-house.

In principle, the former view looks appealing. However, as is often the case in finance theory, the argument of weathering an unfavourable period in which markets display an abnormal behaviour holds only to the extent that one's risk capital can outlast such adverse periods. By extending its bets, MGRM fell prey to gambler's fallacy and its equity was wiped out. This is a fact rather than just an opinion. Therefore, it is questionable that bankruptcy is a price worth paying for overreaching in activities that look attractive from a marketing and strategic point of view.

Interesting lessons emerge from this case:

- Regardless of how one views the debate above on MGRM's appropriate risk profile, clearer boundaries – and controls to enforce them – should have been set in the mandate from the German headquarters. While hindsight bias looms large over this remark, MGRM was able to maintain very large risks for over three-and-a-half years and probably took advantage of some grey areas in the mandate that it received, specifically on the kinds of risks that it was allowed to carry.

- This case is second only to LTCM as one of the best examples of game theory in trading, particularly when other traders can easily guess the risk position of a large player in a given market. Under these particular circumstances, the standard economic – and risk – assumption of every player deciding independently of the others collapses.

- Often, a large structural risk is hidden behind the reassuring façade of a marketing and distribution operation. There are no shortages of distant headquarters' managers who are told only what they want to hear and shown only what they want to see. This management shortsightedness makes this a case of textbook cognitive resonance. As a board or top management member, one has the duty to see beyond such reassuring thoughts.

- No matter how strategically attractive an activity looks, limits should always be set in advance. Short of these, one will soon find himself enslaved by capital markets and their willingness to extend credit. Bankruptcy is the most extreme of these negative consequences.

10.4.4 Allfirst

Barings' and Daiwa's lessons have yet to be fully learned in the upper echelons of management. Headquartered in Ireland, Allied Irish Bank (AIB) had a small operation named Allfirst, based outside Baltimore, Maryland. On 4 February 2002, John Rusnak, a Foreign Exchange (FX) option trader, announced a $695 million loss on his trading activity. This was the largest incurred by the US offices of a foreign bank since Daiwa.

Chronology

1989	AIB acquires the majority of First Maryland Bancorp and turns it into a wholly-owned subsidiary through a cash-out merger. The new subsidiary is renamed Allfirst and granted substantial autonomy from the Dublin headquarters. David Cronin, a highly respected AIB officer with Treasury and FX experience, is appointed as Treasurer in the Allfirst senior management team. Cronin reports both to the AIB Group Treasurer and to Alllfirst's Chief Executive.
1993	John Rusnak is hired from Chemical Bank. He gets the job based on his FX option expertise. Initially, he reports to a trading manager who, in turn, reports to the Head of Treasury Fund Management, Mr Bob Ray. Ray is one of David Cronin's direct reports. Another one is the Senior Vice President in charge of Asset & Liability Management and Risk Control. While bullying of the control functions by Ray is well known, not much gets done about it.[66]
1995	The audit of the OCC,[67] one of America's key banking regulators, is concerned about a weakness in Allfirst's back- and middle-office. These areas in fact do not obtain FX rates independently from traders. While this suggestion is quickly incorporated into Allfirst's Funds' Management Policy, nothing gets done in practice.
1997	Rusnak starts accumulating serious losses from wrong bets on the $/Yen exchange rate. At about the same time, he starts booking fictitious currency options that make his position appear hedged. Most trades have mysterious counterparts in the Far East, mostly Tokyo and Singapore, and involve supposedly offsetting option positions. Of these, the deep-in-the-money option bought by Allfirst remains on the bank's books and hides the actual losses. This scheme exploits the fact that back-office does not require trade confirmation from the counterparts.
1998	Internal audit reports how the weaknesses in independent price verification by the control functions remain unsolved. In return, a feed from one of Rusnak's spreadsheets is created. Of course, after the crisis, manipulation in the spreadsheet is found. This shortcut is devised because management did not authorize the $10,000 cost of a Reuters direct price feed to back-office.[68]
1999	Following his trading manager's departure, John Rusnak reports directly to Mr Ray. In the meantime, his losses keep mounting. So-called 'prime brokerage' accounts at other major money-centre banks provide him with another source of financing for his losses. Due to the back-office's inability to keep up with them, Treasury suspends these activities, only to restart them a month later. Despite Rusnak's consistent bullying of back-office staff, no concrete steps are taken.
2001	By now, John Rusnak has devised new creative ways of funding his losses, such as fictitious repurchases of the original deep-in-the-money options by the usual mysterious counterparts. Inquiries by other banks on $1 billion balances in the prime brokerage accounts do not lead to any substantial scrutiny of John Rusnak's activities. In addition, he has severely undermined VaR, the key measure of the bank's risks. He uses both his bogus options and so-called 'holdover' positions, trades that are entered late in the day. According to later tests after the scheme is discovered, he will use the false holdover positions as many as 52 days out of the 58 sampled over a three-month period. His activities, however, are using a growing portion of Allfirst's balance sheet and the Treasurer is getting concerned. He orders Rusnak to reduce his balance sheet usage to less than $150 million by year-end. In the meantime, one of the back-office supervisors discovers unconfirmed trade tickets.

[66] Ludwig Report.
[67] OCC stands for Office of the Comptroller of the Currency. This US body charters, regulates and supervises national banks to ensure a sound, competitive banking system.
[68] Ludwig Report.

January 2002	Rusnak's use of the balance sheet is back to $250 million. The Treasurer also discovered that the foreign-exchange turnover in December was $25 billion. This prompted a request to close all of Rusnak's positions by 1 February. As more unconfirmed trade tickets emerge, back-office finally calls the Asian counterparts for confirmation. These counterparts are found not to trade FX options at all.
1–4 February 2002	Rusnak attempts to forge the confirmations but his ploy is discovered. He does not show up at work on 4 February. In the meantime, the back-office is unable to get his trades confirmed. The subsequent investigation reveals that $89 million of losses had been incurred before 2000, another $210 million in 2000 and the rest in 2001.

The embarrassing setback crippled AIB's ambition to stay solo in the US. On 26 September 2002, AIB agreed to merge Allfirst into M&T Bank. The Irish group received a 22.5 per cent stake in M&T and $886 million in cash.

The major holes in Allfirst's internal controls that were evidenced at various points in time will probably provide excellent material for many case studies. In particular, they show beyond doubt the costly consequences of neglecting supposedly unglamorous back- and middle-office functions in banks. The behavioural lessons of this story are by no means less interesting:

- Overconfidence and the 'not-me, not here' biases described in Chapters 5 and 6 often mean that banks and their management never learn the previous disasters' lessons on practical matters, let alone their behavioural aspects. Some seven years after the previous Barings and Daiwa cases, one person controlled both front- and back-office. Worse, the overconfidence in one supposed 'star' trader prevented hard questions from being asked.

- Top management's disregard for prosaic back-office and portfolio valuation functions also bears an eerie resemblance to the previous Daiwa and Barings situations. In this instance, significant losses went undiscovered for some *five years*. The ease with which the ploy was eventually discovered should leave no doubt as to how much complacency surrounded Rusnak's operation. Adverse internal audit reports and frequent back-office issues provided several opportunities to discover the disaster without management taking any serious steps.

- As in many other sad trading stories in this chapter, Rusnak kept upping the ante as his losses mounted – another example of prospect theory in action.

10.4.5 Trouble always strikes from an unexpected angle: Bankers Trust v P&G

The corporate debacle that pitted a consumer giant against one of the most aggressive derivative dealers is by no means the largest derivative loss to date. Yet, a few key themes that it involved make it one of the most interesting cases. In particular:

- Much like the instance of MGRM earlier, where is the line between hedging and speculation for a corporate treasurer?

- If trading is deemed acceptable for a treasurer, what kind of risk-taking and trading execution, first and foremost with losses, is to be expected of him?

- How are the dealer's fiduciary responsibilities toward their clients defined? These issues apply especially with respect to product suitability.

■ To what extent are the media and the public supposed to have a stake in a private, tailor-made financial transaction between two large corporations?

This case underscores the major difference between the clear-cut acceptance of risk responsibility in a trading room and clients' frequent self-attribution bias in blaming their dealers only for the losses.

At the time, the author worked for Bankers Trust – albeit in the completely separate area of proprietary trading. This account relies completely on information gathered from public sources. Readers who are interested in an even more detailed and colourful discussion of the case should consult Frank Partnoy's excellent *Infectious Greed* (2003).

To discuss this instance, it is important to provide some background on the activities of both companies, as they had a major effect on their widely different corporate cultures. Founded in 1837, Procter & Gamble is one of the ultimate consumer and marketing icons. Serving households worldwide, the company stakes its performance mostly on its operating activities. The highly regarded Treasury Department is mostly a service centre to fund the company's operating activities, invest the excess cash as efficiently as possible and manage the company's foreign-exchange exposures all over the globe. Nevertheless, the company has established the Treasury Department as a profit centre and set an aggressive funding target of CP[69] minus 40 basis points.

Trading and arbitrage were at the very heart of Bankers Trust's activities. Founded in 1903, the bank realized at the end of the 1970s that it had no competitive edge in retail banking and sold its branches. At the same time, it did not have the kind of high-profile relationships with blue-chip clients that formed the backbone of the activity of large investment banks and of its major commercial banking competitors. Last but not least, the Glass-Steagall Act of 1933 prevented the bank from underwriting securities, the main activity of major investment banks. BT, as it was nicknamed on Wall Street, was nevertheless developing an interesting franchise in trading, particularly in foreign exchanges. At the helm of the bank was Charles S. Sanford, an unassuming but visionary former manager of traders. Sanford and BT top management decided to stake the bank's success on risk-taking, product technology and a growing presence outside the US to avoid the Glass-Steagall limitations. The traditional lending activity to blue-chip clients did not offer any interesting competitive advantage to BT and was limited to those instances in which it could help selling more profitable products.

During the 1980s and early 1990s, BT became synonymous with trading and derivative innovation. Derivative products developed to manage traditional interest-rate and foreign-exchange risks were adapted and extended to new classes of risk, such as equity, commodity and even credit. As competition tried to catch up, BT always seemed somewhat ahead of the pack.

BT was also at the forefront of a risk capital system called RAROC[70] to make its various businesses comparable and decide proactively how much capital to allocate to them. With its asset-light balance sheet and an after-tax risk-adjusted return of capital in excess of 20 per cent, BT found itself in a far better position than most competitors when the global

---

[69] Commercial Paper Index.
[70] Risk-Adjusted Return On Capital.

economic recession of 1990–92 struck. Lacking the research and underwriting infrastructure of major investment banks and the large lending operations of the other major money-centre banks, BT had a break-even point far below its competitors. At the same time, new end-users for derivative markets, its stronghold, meant larger sales commissions from these activities. BT's net income peaked just above $1 billion in 1993.

BT's somewhat maverick culture seemed successful and presented some points in common with another earlier nemesis of the US establishment, Drexel Burnham Lambert. Indeed, most US blue-chip companies had hated Drexel for its role in financing hostile takeovers in the 1980s. While BT relied on trading and derivatives, Drexel had introduced another financing technique, so-called high-yield or 'junk' bonds.[71] In both cases, success bred some arrogance. This meant that overconfidence and its unwelcome consequences were just around the corner.

In 1994, the worst bear market in bonds in 60 years meant trouble for BT and many of the highly leveraged, sophisticated products that it had sold to customers over the previous years. In many instances, these were essentially leveraged bets that interest rates would remain low or drop further or that the spread between US and foreign rates would remain below a pre-specified threshold. Leverage, of course, works both ways, magnifying the client's results in terms of both gains and losses. In a leveraged derivative trade, what matters is not so much the notional amount of the trade but, rather, the multiplication factor behind the bet. So, for instance, let us suppose that there is a $100 million notional trade that can normally earn or lose $1 million for the client if interest rates change by a certain number of basis points. A leverage factor of 3 times, when applied to the same trade, makes it as many times as risky. One or both parties may make or lose 3 times as much for the same interest rate move. BT would of course hedge its bets wisely by taking offsetting positions in Treasury bonds, swaps or other derivatives.

One of the key attractions of leveraged products was that they often helped trustees and treasurers circumvent their organizations' internal limits. These limits would generally not match the limit sophistication at major Wall Street firms. For instance, clients' limits may be expressed in terms of a swap's notional amount, rather than with respect to its sensitivity to an interest-rate move. Or, the client's guidelines may dictate that only an investment in AAA-rated notes, those with the lowest probability of default, would be allowed. BT and other major Wall Street derivative dealers would then creatively get around the obstacle by linking the capital repayment on the note to some risky and often obscure market, say the exchange rate between the US dollar and the Thai baht or the Mexican peso. So, while AAA rating made the product appear of the highest quality from a *credit* risk point of view, the repayment was still tied to some *market* index or exchange rate of variable quality. In layman's terms, you had a wolf in sheep's clothing. By offering an above-average return, these risky exposures would be quickly snapped up by otherwise very conservative clients. These would construct limits under the assumption that their main activity would not be in trading and that they would engage only in relatively simple products with moderate risks. Or did they?

---

[71] These bonds are issued by companies that have a sub-investment grade credit rating (BBB- and Baa1 according to the agencies Standard & Poor's and Moody's, respectively). Before Drexel, only investment-grade issuers could place bonds. Lower-rated companies could rely only on their banks for financing. This created less competition for the banks and more onerous terms for the borrowers.

Chronology

2 November 1993	BT and P&G enter a 5-year leveraged swap in which P&G receives 5.30% fixed and pays the 30-day daily Commercial Paper (CP) Average Rate minus 75 basis points plus a spread.[72] In essence, these 75 basis points of saving represent a premium that BT has paid to purchase from P&G an out-of-the-money option. P&G has unlimited downside potential in return for the 75 basis points that it receives. At the same time, P&G has a six-month option to lock the below-CP funding spread at any time. Under the critical assumption of volatility and correlations remaining constant, P&G would have saved already 20 basis points relative to their funding target.
4 February 1994	The Federal Reserve increases interest rates by 25 basis points.
14 February 1994	Despite the first swap being heavily underwater,[73] P&G enters another $93 million notional leveraged swap with Bankers Trust. This $4\frac{3}{4}$ year trade offers a very favourable rate to P&G in the first year and an additional $940,000 savings over the residual life if the German interest rate swap rate remains within a certain band until 14 April 1995. The rate, 5.35% at the time, was to remain above 4.05% and below 6.10%. Otherwise, P&G would pay a large spread[74] over the residual $3\frac{3}{4}$ years of the swap.
Early March 1994	The second leveraged swap touches the upper side of the band. Between 10 and 29 March, P&G closes out the original swap at an average level of CP+1269, or $106.5 million in Present Value (PV). As the original trade was an option, BT uses its proprietary option pricing models – and all the related volatility and correlation parameters and assumptions – to set the price of the unwinds.
11 April 1994	P&G locks in the second swap paying 16.4% above the base rate set under the swap, about $89 million in PV. Once again, the price of the unwinds is set using BT's option pricing models.
27 October 1994	P&G files a complaint against BT claiming a loss of $195 million due to the bank's alleged fraud and misrepresentation of the risks. Specifically, P&G complains that it was totally unaware of the trade's optional nature and volatility assumptions when the trades began.
December 1994	BT signs consent decrees with Federal Securities regulators and pays a $10 million fine for the allegations that it wilfully gave Gibson Greetings, another client, inaccurate valuations for their derivatives portfolio.
1995	The legal and Public Relations battle intensifies, with the media and banking regulators becoming increasingly involved in the case. Remarks of BT personnel recorded over the taped phone lines make the headlines of *Business Week* magazine. In the same month, the US District Judge allows P&G to add civil racketeering charges, which enable the company to ask for treble damages.
10 May	BT and P&G settle in court. P&G agrees to pay only $35 million of the $195 million that it 1996 owes to BT and forgo between $5 and 14 million of gains arising from another contract.

[72] The spread was to be set on 4 May 1994 according to the following formula:

$$\text{Max}(0, \frac{98.5 x (5yr\ CMT\ Rate)\ /\ 5.78\% - 30yr\ Treasury\ Pr.}{100}), \text{ where}$$

5yr CMT = 5-year constant-maturity Treasury note yield that the Federal Reserve publishes regularly. 30-year Treasury (TSY) Pr = midpoint of the bid and offer prices on the 6.25% T-bond maturing in August 2023, excluding accrued interest. That bond was the benchmark most actively traded long-maturity.

[73] At this time, P&G would be obligated to pay the equivalent of CP+400, or about $35 million. Later on, at a meeting between Edwin Artzt, Erik Nelson and Raymond Mains (P&G's CEO, CFO and Treasurer, respectively) and BT officials, it became apparent that Artzt was informed neither of P&G's opportunity of existing at a loss in February nor of the second swap in March.

[74] The spread would be (difference between the actual swap rate and 4.5%) multiplied by a factor of 10.

No clear winner emerged from the battle. According to the court, BT did not owe P&G fiduciary duty. At the same time, the obligation to deal fairly and in good faith translated into a duty to disclose material information about the transaction, which weakened BT's position.

The damage to BT's reputation, however, was beyond repair. Between 1994 and 1995, three other US corporate clients (Federal Paper Board, Air Products & Chemical and Gibson Greetings) sued the bank over its derivative sales practices. Frank Newman, formerly with the US Treasury Department, replaced Sanford at the helm of the bank with the mandate of fixing it and making it more customer-friendly. This featured the acquisition of two advisory boutiques, Alex Brown and Wolfensohn & Co, a most aggressive return to relationship lending and de-emphasizing trading and derivative activities. The summer of 1998 caused the bank major losses, which were blamed on Russian bonds and other emerging markets. Few will ever know the relative contribution of the Russian default and the bank's more aggressive stance in loan underwriting. However, the market decided quickly. BT stock sank even below the levels reached during the darkest days of the P&G controversy. Deutsche Bank, eager to buy itself a foothold in the US, took over the ailing bank in 1999. Newman could content himself with a hefty golden parachute.

Several interesting lessons arise from this controversial case:

- Overconfidence, yet again, was fundamental in creating this lethal embarrassment to BT. No matter how brilliant an organization and its controls are, trouble has a knack for striking always at the weakest spot. In the case of BT, it was precisely its well-honed risk processes and strong controls in the trading room that created overconfidence in management and prevented tighter controls in its sales and marketing practices. BT did not experience the 'doubling-up' or concealment of losing trades that were shown earlier. Nevertheless the ways in which volatility and correlation parameters were manipulated inside the bank further reinforced outsiders' suspicions.[75]

- Complacency was also displayed in both organizations by not asking enough hard questions as long as bond markets were rallying and the trades were profitable. BT was happy with the large commissions that these trades were generating and P&G was achieving its aggressive funding targets. In hindsight, it would not have taken a genius to realize that the complexity of the spread formulae was well beyond the understanding of an industrial company's treasurer or CEO. Once again, as in so many other cases, no questions are asked as long as the tail wind helps.

- As a major author (Bernstein, 1996) remarked, P&G's behaviour in assuming risky positions and then 'doubling up' with the second leveraged trade between US and German rates was textbook prospect theory.

- The case illustrates beyond doubt the lethal nature of mixing accounting and trading frames. Specifically, an option premium and its huge underlying risk were disguised as a hefty saving on funding rates.

---

[75] See Frank Partnoy's *Infectious Greed*, p. 59.

■ Regulators and policymakers should not underestimate the dangerous side effects of having the media involved in dealer–client controversies. As the media have to adapt themselves to their audience's taste, their opinions are by no means unbiased. As members of the judicial system do not always have the means to form an unbiased view of the merits of a derivative controversy, the media have a major responsibility to avoid steering such views based on what the public wants to hear. Attributing good or poor performance to 'smart' treasury management or to unfair dealers, respectively, may suit the public psyche but is pure self-attribution bias. The real question is what kind of risk management mandate a client receives from his top management. Dealers have to check who signs off and clients have to enforce it internally. Significant opinion-leaders, and first and foremost the media, should not be allowed to create any confusion between these different responsibilities.

10.5 Markets beat overconfidence in quantitative models: LTCM

Few would probably disagree that the instance that brought the world's financial markets to the brink of disaster (as described by the Federal Reserve's chairman, Alan Greenspan, in September 1998) will remain amongst the top case studies in risk management failure for a long time. Risk management flaws, however, are by no means the most interesting lesson to be learned from the crisis. At the heart of this matter is the behavioural framework surrounding the case, and in particular the neglect of the interrelationship between risk management, modern finance theory and human overconfidence. Having said this, no one disputes the issues of over-reliance on liquidity and model assumptions that have been extensively analysed after the fact.

In light of LTCM founders' impressive academic and professional credentials, overconfidence comes as no surprise. After all, Robert Merton and Myron Scholes, the Fund's most prominent academics, had laid the foundations of option pricing theory with the model that became known as the Black-Scholes model, which has become a standard piece in the repertoire of young, technically savvy dealers. In performing that feat, they had created a bridge between modern finance theory and real markets that had paved the way to the explosive derivative technology revolution in the 1980s. The very pride in all these outstanding achievements degenerated into the arrogant belief that models can rule markets rather than the other way around. The LTCM 'dream team' included John Meriwether, himself a trading and arbitrage icon, and David Mullins, the former Vice-Chairman of the Federal Reserve.

As an old trading adage of Jewish origin reminds us:

Markets are fickle, better being lucky than being smart, so pray often.

Any good trader knows how important it is to remain humble. The LTCM elite fell into the trap of believing they knew best. Roger Lowenstein's excellent book *When Genius Failed* (2001) quotes an earlier concern expressed by Professor Robert Shiller. According to Shiller, markets were too volatile to fit the model of perfect markets. Shiller was speaking with some experience on the topic, having led the comprehensive report on investor psychology and the factors that contributed to the 1987 stock market crash. Key amongst these was the controversial portfolio insurance strategy for which Merton had claimed credit later.

Lowenstein also included Merton's response: 'We need hardly mention the significance of such a conclusion. If Shiller's rejection of market efficiency is sustained, then serious doubt is cast on the validity of this cornerstone of modern financial economic theory.' Later on, borrowing a famous sentence of Alan Greenspan's, Shiller would return to the issue of investors' questionable rationality in his book *Irrational Exuberance* (2001).

Lowenstein also mentions a prescient article by Andrei Shleifer & Robert Vishny (1997), who warned that an arbitrage firm such as LTCM could be overwhelmed by 'noise traders'[76] if these pushed prices away from their true value. Under such circumstances, arbitrageurs would experience 'adverse price shocks' and be forced to liquidate at market lows. Lowenstein points out that, at a subsequent conference of scholars in Cambridge, Merton 'pooh-poohed the notion that market-savvy arbitrageurs could ever be overwhelmed'.

	Chronology
1980	John Meriwether forms a quantitative bond trading team at Salomon Brothers, a major Wall Street investment bank. The desk aims to exploit mis-pricings in a generally inefficient market dominated by traditional traders who rely mostly on their guts. A handful of bright finance professors form the backbone of the operation. The team generally bets on price discrepancies between similar securities rather than on outright market direction as traditionalists do.[77]
1991	Paul Mozer, a trader running the government bond operations, tries to corner the US Treasury auction market. To placate the fury of US Treasury and Federal Reserve officials, John Gutfreund resigns from his CEO position at Salomon Brothers. Despite being deemed not responsible, Meriweather is also asked to leave.
1993	Meriwether attracts the cream of Salomon's quant trading team to prepare the launch of a hedge fund. Two Nobel Prize winners, Robert Merton and Myron Scholes, and David Mullins, the Federal Reserve Vice Chairman, are also enlisted to boost the fund's credibility.
March 1994	LTCM commences trading with $1.25 billion in capital. In the worst bear market in bonds in over half a century, LTCM will generate a 20% return to investors after large fees.
1995	LTCM earn their investors a spectacular 43% after fees. Another $1 billion is raised.
1996	With funds from new investors and reinvested profits, LTCM has a $3.6 billion war chest. It uses it to borrow $98 billion, thereby achieving a 28:1 leverage ratio. The fund repeats the previous year's stellar performance with an annual return above 40% after fees.

[76] Uninformed speculators.

[77] In these bets, often known as *spreads* or *relative-value* trades, what matters is the change in price of one security versus another, rather than the price direction of either security. So, if at time 0 one buys bond A at $99 and sells short a similar bond B at $100, the bet will profit as long as the price difference between these securities narrows, regardless of the absolute price of the two securities. As these securities' features are similar, one would reasonably expect broad-based market moves to have about the same effect on both bonds.

1997	In June, UBS becomes the single biggest investor in LTCM. Under the deal a group of the partners pay $289 million to UBS and in return receive what an investor with $800 million worth of LTCM would make over the next seven years. In addition, the bank has the option to invest an additional $266 million in the fund. As a result of the deal, LTCM partners leverage themselves to keep invested in the highly leveraged fund. In addition, they defer significant gains for tax purposes. In October, Merton and Scholes are awarded the Nobel Prize in Economic Science. Despite a very good return (25%), the fund underperforms the S&P500 Index. LTCM starts looking for mis-pricings in other markets, mostly equities and emerging markets. At year-end, the fund returns $2.7 billion to investors against their wishes. The leverage ratio zooms back to 28:1 from the previous 18:1. The portfolio, comprising billions of largely illiquid positions, remains unchanged.
First quarter 1998	LTCM starts the year with $4.8 billion in capital. Large short equity volatility positions – whereby the fund bet on a drop to lower and supposedly more normal levels – earn LTCM the 'Bank of Volatility' nickname in the Street. Soon, LTCM will have $40 million at risk for every percentage point change in equity volatility. Other positions range from a variety of emerging markets to junk bonds and outright bets on equities. Leverage has continues unabetted, so that the notional value of LTCM derivative contracts has grown to over *$1 trillion*.
Second quarter 1998	Worried about potential credit problems, large dealers start reducing their inventories of less liquid securities, the mainstay of LTCM's portfolio. Widening risk premiums on less liquid securities in developed and emerging markets start hurting the fund's returns. May and June are the fund's two worst months in a row. The fund's minus 16% return in the first half cuts capital to $4 billion at the beginning of July. Its leverage soars to 30:1. Daily VaR limit is cut from 45 to 34 million.[78] According to the fund's risk figures, a 10 standard deviation event such that the fund may lose half of its capital could happen only once every 10^{24} days. To put things into perspective, 10^{12} means some *three billion years*! Of course, these figures rely on historical volatility data.
July– August 1998	Russia imposes exchange controls on the ruble and then announces a debt moratorium on 13 and 17 August respectively. Swap and credit spreads over Treasury bonds explode. Emerging market bonds are crushed. On 21 August, the fund suffers a daily loss of $535 million. This is over 15 times the 35 million figure calculated by the fund's VaR model. Equity capital has dropped to $2.9 billion since April, a one-third drop from the start-of-the-year figure. As every risky market in the world is dropping fast, LTCM is stuck with enormous illiquid positions for which there is no market. By month-end, the equity volatility in which the fund is short has risen to 30%. Monthly losses of $1.9 billion have cut equity to $2.28 billion. Its portfolio is still at $128 billion.
September 1998	The LTCM partners hold several talks with America's top investors and banks to raise fresh funds. A proposal by fund tycoon George Soros collapses due to the fund's inability to raise sufficient funds elsewhere. Thereafter, a tentative agreement is reached with Goldman Sachs. Finally, on 28 September, a $3.625 billion bail-out consortium is organized by the President of the New York Fed. It includes 16 banks and is led by Merrill Lynch, Goldman Sachs, Morgan and UBS. The fund continues haemorrhaging in September, and equity drops to just $0.6 billion at month-end.
1999	By October, LTCM has repaid $2.6 billion of capital owed to the consortium. The portfolio will close at the end of 2000. In the meantime, Meriwether and six of the other partners form a new fund, called JWM Partners. By 2003, it will grow to over $1 billion in assets.

Selective attention bias and the very human tendency towards sequential processing of information often result in a substantial neglect of the interrelationships between variables (see Chapter 5). This often has adverse unknown effects, according to the law of unintended consequences. Accordingly, LTCM shows an unmatched example of how painfully inadequate human information processing ability becomes when dealing with complexity.

---

[78] This was based on a 95% confidence interval, that is, this figure would be exceeded no more than one day in twenty.

The interrelationship between LTCM trading positions and the behaviour of its other major derivative counterparts in September 1998 is just one example of such complexity.

Consistent with the theory, the case also proves beyond doubt the paramount importance of one's risk capital adequacy. That means it takes time and financial staying power for mean reversion to display its effects and correct statistical anomalies. At that point, and only then, can one profit from such anomalies. Ironically, Scholes had vehemently opposed the re-leveraging of the fund at the beginning of 1998.

LTCM's fascinating story offers many lessons:

- People, rather than models, make markets. Neglecting irrationality and the extremes to which it can lead is arrogant and overconfident at best.

- For all their extreme sophistication, LTCM's eggheads and professors neglected the basic position-sizing rules under duress that any trader worth his salt should practise religiously. This is, once again, gambler's fallacy. LTCM simply bet that their capital would outlast the markets' extremes. Markets, unlike the fair coin of statistics, have emotions and memory. Availability of risk capital in the markets is not as unlimited as modern financial theory assumes.

- As a by-product of the previous point, over-reliance on trading and position-sizing decisions on the well-known VaR models was also heavily criticized after the crisis. Unfortunately, it is the very demise of this giant that has magnified the importance of portfolio stress-testing portfolio for extreme events.

- Often neglected in modern economics and standard finance theory, game theory struck back with a vengeance. The standard assumption that everyone maximizes his own utility independent of other actors' behaviours may hold under normal conditions whereby one's position is small and fairly invisible in a large and liquid market. The fast-moving markets of late summer 1998 showed that major market players' trading and risk management decisions do take others' expected behaviour into account. Ignoring higher-order beliefs becomes far less reasonable for a player as large as LTCM, which had about a dozen major dealers as shareholders, credit counterparts or both. When a dealer fears that a swap counterpart might fail, he worries that such a party may not honour the derivative obligations arising from contracts that are hedging the dealer's book. When the default is announced, the dealer will have to replace that counterpart's obligations with another party so that his market exposure remains as before. If the default looks imminent, as seemed the case with LTCM in September 1998, the dealer will start looking for replacement positions or options thereon *before* the counterpart announces its default. In addition, several dealers pre-positioned their derivative books to prepare for the massive unwind of LTCM's gargantuan positions, no doubt exacerbating the Fund's losses further. The dealers had a common cut-exposure-at-any-cost reaction to the similar signals from their VaR models. This was yet another example of higher-order beliefs in action. By the time the positions were reduced, the market had moved further against those who wanted to shed their risk.

■ Started as a bond trading elite, LTCM eventually ventured into increasingly exotic markets and strategies in which it could hardly boast any competitive edge. At the end, LTCM's repertoire ranged from markets as diverse as Russian bonds, equity pairs and merger arbitrage trades. The less mainstream a market is, the less tenable many of the models' statistical assumptions are. If your mainstream market does not offer as profitable opportunities as in the past, it is wiser to downscale the fund and wait for better times. For investors, the lesson is a stern reminder of how strategy drift can annihilate even the most prestigious and experienced manager.

■ *Fungibility* between the two products that are used in an arbitrage trade is the ultimate acid test of how real the arbitrage is and a basic one that often escapes computer models and their watchers. As mentioned earlier, in Chapter 7, a large pair trade between Shell and Royal Dutch went against LTCM's leveraged position betting on a convergence to fair value. Unlike individuals or institutions, the market is accountable to no one and owes no explanations. That may be one of the reasons for its supposedly 'irrational' behaviour in certain circumstances.

10.6 'Hot hand' and overconfidence in trading skill: Orange County

The instances of Enron and Daiwa discussed earlier demonstrate that complex derivatives are not always to blame for their users' mishaps. Rather, financial leverage is prone to magnify their mistakes (see 10.2). Orange County's $1.7 loss earned the questionable record of being the largest bankruptcy by a municipality at the time. This is another demonstration of how users and their biases cause the trouble, not the tools that they employ.

To put things into perspective, it is useful to review the set of priorities – in decreasing order of importance – which a municipality Treasurer ought to have:

■ invest the excess cash of the municipality in safe instruments;

■ manage liquidity, so that exactly the right amount of funds are available at the right time to fund the municipality's projects and initiatives;

■ subject to the above requirements, enhance investment returns.

Robert Citron had been managing the municipality's investment portfolio since 1973. To understand Citron's supposedly strong performance track record, it is also useful to provide some market background. Orange County's leveraged portfolios benefited from the major downward trend in US interest rates that unfolded in the 1980s and the first part of the 1990s. As inflation expectations receded, interest rates were adjusted accordingly. The 1987 and 1990 pauses in this prolonged bull market in bonds were relatively brief.

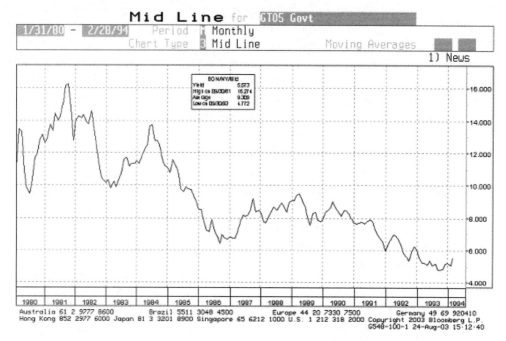

FIGURE 10.1 ■ The long-term decline in interest rates, 1980–1993

Source: Bloomberg LP, *reprinted with permission*

An investor such as Orange County who owns fixed-income securities benefits from falling interest rates and sees his bond prices soar. The existence of leverage means that, for a given amount of own equity, the investor is allowed to own more bonds, so that his returns are magnified. As long as the trend is favourable, leverage works in the investor's favour. It also means that the investor will outperform more prudent managers who use less or no leverage at all. Table 10.2 shows the effects of leverage in the case of Orange County:

TABLE 10.2 ■ Effect of leverage from reverse repos on portfolio return when interest rates increase 2.75% during the year

	No Leverage (Lev. Ratio = 1)	Some Leverage (Lev. Ratio = 1.8)	Orange County Leverage (Lev. Ratio = 2.6)
Interest rates increase by 2.75%			
Decrease in value of bonds owned ($ billions)	$ –0.84	$–1.50	$–2.17
Portfolio return from capital loss	–11%	–19.8%	–28.6%

How did Citron describe his strategy? Hersh Shefrin's book *Beyond Greed and Fear* (2000) offers a thorough analysis of the case and of Citron's own biases. The case study features the following excerpt from a 1988 interview:

Q: So, your money managing decisions revolve around the kinds of notes or bonds you're willing to buy?

A: Yes. I have around $900 million in US government securities, from two to five years in maturity.

Q: Do you actively trade based on fluctuations in interest rates?

A: I'm not a trader ... I buy and hold, and I do matched reverse repurchase agreements ... It is not trading, because the spread is always locked in.

Chronology	
1973	Robert Citron is appointed to the Treasurer office of Orange County, California. He immediately starts a massive technology upgrade of the office and consolidates his financial power in the region.
1980	Citron lobbies the State Legislature successfully to relax investment restrictions on the nature and risk of instruments in his portfolio.
1980s–early 1990s	His positions turbocharged by leverage, Citron takes advantage of a long-term decline in interest rates to earn an extra $755 million for the County. At the end he will have amassed $7.6 billion in equity. Repos allow him to leverage his portfolio to $20 billion.
1991	County auditor's report recommends stronger oversight of Citron's activities, in particular those involving unusual and risky investments. Recommendations are not implemented.
1992–1993	Mark Robles of AG Edwards writes on behalf of municipal investors in the Orange Country pool and asks for disclosure of unusual risk in the portfolio. Citron writes a furious reply to the Chairman of AG Edwards. Merrill Lynch, Citron's clearer, repeatedly warns him of the risk in his portfolio and offers to buy his interest-rate sensitive positions. Nothing happens.
February 1994	As the US economy's growth consolidates, the Federal Reserve shifts from neutral to tightening bias to ward off potential inflation. The Fed Funds rate is increased by 25 basis points to 3.25%.
Spring 1994	John Moorlach vies with Citron in the local elections to Treasurer's Office. He strongly criticizes how the portfolio priorities between safety and yield enhancement are actually flipped. Citron dismisses the criticism and wins thanks to his apparently strong investment track record. Time is running short, though. Following the sharp increase in rates since February and the steepening yield curve between 2- and 5-year Treasuries, the Orange County pool receives 'collateral calls' for $215 million. The Federal Reserve increases rates again during that month.
August 1994	The Federal Reserve increases rates again. Leverage in Citron's fund has soared to nearly 3:1 from 2.4:1.
September 1994	In his last annual report, Citron notes concern over 'paper losses' due to rising interest rates. He adds that the County did not plan to record any losses and did not plan to sell its securities.
November 1994	Last increase in the Fed Funds rate by the Federal Reserve.
December 1994	Citron announces a $1.5 billion paper loss. He resigns on 4 December. The County files for bankruptcy under Chapter 9 two days later. Market movements during the liquidation of the fund's portfolio increase the loss to $2 billion.
April 1995	Citron pleads guilty to six felony counts. He and Assistant Treasurer Matthew Raabe are sentenced to one and three years in jail, respectively. They are also ordered to pay $100,000 and $10,000 in fines, respectively. Raabe's conviction and fine are subsequently overturned by an appeals court in 2001.

Several behavioural phenomena surface in this sequence of events and statements. First of all, Citron's claim that the 'spread is locked in' applies only based on the professed buy-and-hold-to-maturity investment philosophy that is confirmed in his last annual report. This is nothing but an accounting frame of risk folded around a concrete market risk.

Indeed, Citron's 5-versus-2-year Treasury spread would have worked in his favour only if rates had remained constant or had dropped. In the latter case the strategy would have shown a mark-to-market profit well before maturity. This is because the 5-year Treasury note which he purchased is more sensitive to interest rate changes than the 2-year rate at which he leveraged himself. The presence of leverage means that, in the case of an adverse move in interest rates, creditors may force the portfolio into a fire-sale based on current market values. This is exactly what happened. As a result, the spread is by no means 'locked in'. This would apply only to the extent that the portfolio was not leveraged and completely funded by equity alone. Under those conditions, the Treasurer would actually be able to hold the position until maturity, regardless of the spread or the actual level of interest rates.

Further, Citron's earlier statement that 'he is not a trader' is a marketing and politically correct frame of risk that masks the actual risk in his activity. Let's face it, 'investor' is generally regarded as a more politically correct and respectable label than 'trader'.

In addition, the County actually *increased* its risk and leverage in the summer of 1994 despite (or as a result of?) the large paper losses on which it was sitting. This is textbook prospect theory. Indeed, recall from Chapter 4 that situations of distress are prone to induce more aggressive risk-taking. In these instances, there is a high probability that one might end up below his reference point.

Last, this is yet another case in which past success has probably resulted in overconfidence. A long winning streak of the leveraged strategy in the previous 15 years meant strong psychological reinforcements for Citron.

The lessons from this case are:

- Understand the sources of profits in trading strategies *before* the wind turns against them. In this specific instance, no one asked probing questions for a remarkably long period, probably because profits were rolling in.

- Watch carefully for the investments' suitability. The presence of leverage itself makes it evident how the policy and limit guidelines were simply too loose for the supposedly risk-averse portfolio of a municipality.

- As in several cases earlier in this chapter, gambler's fallacy strikes again. Define tight position-sizing rules and stick with them.

- Beware strong egos, even more so during a favourable period. The County portfolio's earlier strong performance had to be attributed to a major bullish interest rate bet, rather than to particular skill. Again, no questions were asked. This underscores the disastrous consequences of extrapolating one's skills from past track record alone, in line with the 'hot-hand' effect described in Chapter 5.

10.7 Herds and financial panics

These mishaps involving one organization may have attracted most publicity. But human overconfidence and leverage are rife behind events that led to major financial panics. The South Sea Bubble, mentioned in the opening quote of this chapter, the tulip mania in 1634 in the Netherlands and the 1929 Wall Street Crash are well known. The problem situations of the last quarter-century alone, however, have plenty of lessons to offer. When you look at the following table, it should not be difficult to spot some repetitive patterns:

TABLE 10.3 ■ A selection of panics, 1980–2001

Crisis	Year	Overconfidence in ...	Consequences
S&L Crisis (US)	1980	Yield curve risk management	Thrifts and S&Ls decimated
LDC Debt Crisis	1980s	'Countries do not go bankrupt'	International lending crisis, 1980s recession in Latin America, major US banks on the brink of bankruptcy.
Stock Market Crash	1987	Effectiveness of portfolio insurance as a mitigant of major stock market moves	1987 stock market crash, billions of savings and pensions wiped out.
Japanese Nikkei stock market crash	1990	'Over here, stocks are valued on their long-term story rather than based on myopic quarterly data'	Major depression, lending and real estate crisis in Japan, still continuing as of late 2003.
ERM Crisis (Europe)	1992	Ability of central banks to maintain currency pegs against speculation	Collapse of system in late 1992/early 1993, European integration threatened.
Tequila Effect	1994/5	Ability of central banks to maintain currency pegs against speculation	Setback for economic progress in Latin America.
Asian Crisis	1997	Ability of central banks to maintain currency pegs against speculation	End of 'Asian tigers' miracle, recession in SE Asia.
Russian Default	1998	'Too big to fail'	Collapses in world's major stock markets, worldwide recession threatened.
Internet/New Economy Bubble	2000/1	'New Paradigm'	End of New Economy boom, over $1 trillion in paper wealth destroyed.
Argentina Default	2001	'Too big to fail'	New threat to stability in Emerging Markets.

Common patterns emerge in these stories, too:

■ Financial markets have never been short of marketing ingenuity in inducing prospective investors to believe that the proposed investment opportunity will create some revolutionary and phenomenally profitable breakthrough. Remember, investors have two mental compartments, respectively a 'play safe' and a 'get rich quick' account. They want to hear something that triggers the 'get rich quick' frame of risk. In addition, you have learned in Chapter 8 that investors are often looking for something to arouse sensation and excitement. The relative merits of the opportunity are generally viewed under an optimistic light. No comment is necessary on people's remarkably poor risk-probability assessment.

- Investors have to build some resemblance of objectivity into their valuation process. Accordingly, the opportunity drives its own metrics. Old metrics are discarded as inadequate owing to some unique peculiarity of the prospective investment. The memory of the internet bubble metrics[79] is still fresh in too many investors' minds to see this pattern in practice.

- Financial leverage is readily available to help investors put their dream into practice. The vague assessments of the previous steps cause people to view leverage's result-magnification power in a lop-sided fashion. This means that people see the rewards of fabulous returns becoming even larger, but not its dangers. Needless to say, this is selective-attention bias.

- When reality finally strikes, the cautious 'play safe' frame of risk takes over and regret over the previous risky decision follows shortly thereafter. As values come back to earth and leverage ravages investors' portfolios, the witch-hunt begins to find someone – and, most interestingly, 'someone else' – to blame for the losses.

Several excellent and ageless books have been written on the remarkably similar lessons on the patterns that investors experience during and after a bubble. Charles Mackay's *Extraordinary Popular Delusions and the Madness of Crowds* (1841) is a classic reference book on the topic. Amongst all, the following anonymous sentence should stand out for investors to remember:

> *Men, it has been well said, think in herds; it will be seen that they go*
> *mad in herds, while they only recover their senses slowly and one by one.*

A poem, written by British poet Alexander Pope on the South Sea Bubble, should strike a familiar chord on how people get sucked into financial manias:

> *'All this is madness', cries a sober sage:*
> *But who, my friend, has reason in this rage?*
> *'The ruling passion, be it what it will,*
> *The ruling passion conquers reason still'*

---

[79] Examples thereof were companies for which the prices were evaluated based on multiple of sales, as opposed to the customary cashflow or earnings figures used by traditional security analysts. 'Clicks', meaning mouse clicks by users, were also devised as a proxy measure of the expected revenue of websites.

10.7.1 The 1987 portfolio insurance fiasco

Few stories, if any, will ever be able to match the explosive combination of marketing ingenuity and superficiality, financial product technology and market reality displayed by portfolio insurance in the US in the 1980s. Beyond the technicalities, this story has many lessons for anybody involved in risk management and trading, many of which have still to be fully learned.

Briefly, portfolio insurance consists of a set of strategies designed to secure a floor under the value of a portfolio when stock prices fall without imposing a ceiling when stock prices rise. In essence, the investor would like to protect his downside in adverse market phases and retain most of the upside in favourable ones. Any investor will find this strategy behaviourally appealing, as this is attractive for both their 'play safe' and 'get rich quick' mentalities. These different states are triggered depending on the phase of the market cycle.

Portfolio insurance can be implemented in a variety of ways:

- by stop-loss and buy-stop triggers (sell securities when a preset floor or a higher threshold is reached, respectively);

- by the purchase of 'put' options (which are exercised if the security price drops below the strike price);

- by a combination of investing in risk-free assets – typically Treasury bills or short-term money market instruments – and purchase of 'call' options to retain upside potential;

- by the creation of artificial 'put' options with a combination of short positions in shares and 'call' options;

- by the creation of synthetic 'put' options with short positions in stock-index futures.

Of these, the last one is the most interesting and the one commonly associated with portfolio insurance. According to option pricing theory and its most popular mathematical expression, the Black-Scholes model, an investor can replicate an option payoff dynamically by buying or selling securities as the underlying security price changes. For instance, an investor who wanted to replicate a 'put' option should create a position to profit from drops in share prices. He will borrow shares and sell them short in increasing quantities as the share price drops. If the share prices soar, he will need to reduce his short position by buying back shares at higher prices.

The development of the Black-Scholes model in the early 1970s, however, borrowed heavily from continuous-time mathematics and physics, including even models used in rocket technology. They included two oft-forgotten but critical assumptions:

- the path of stock prices is smooth; and

- the investor can continue executing his strategies at any point in time. In layman's terms, this can be defined as continuous liquidity of the market. A perfectly liquid market offers the investor the ability to buy or sell in any size that he wishes without any significant transaction costs, if any at all.

These assumptions also mean that, should market liquidity decrease or become non-existent, the investor's transaction costs will inevitably rise. Under extreme market duress, the investor may not be able to execute his intended trade at all. After all, there must always be someone to take the other side of the trade.

Firms such as LOR,[80] who spearheaded the product aggressively in the US, saw their mandates with prestigious institutional investors skyrocket. As tens of billions of dollars were funnelled into portfolio insurance programmes in the 1980s, the most popular version of portfolio insurance involved mixing a proportion of stocks and risk-free instruments depending on stock-index price levels. As prices rose, investors would increase their portfolio allocation to stocks. Shares falls would trigger stock sales and purchase of Treasury bills or other risk-free money-market instruments.

The notion of buying shares at higher prices and selling them at lower levels may sound counterintuitive and it is indeed true that it results in transaction costs for the investor. Nevertheless, the attractiveness of protecting the downside sounded just irresistible. These strategies were built into mass-execution automated computer programs. Programme trading was born.

An activity which was closely related to portfolio insurance was stock-index-arbitrage between cash stock portfolios and stock-index futures. Strictly speaking, this arbitrage activity involves buying stocks and selling stock-index futures or vice versa depending on which of the two looks more expensive. Thanks to their superior liquidity and lower transaction costs relative to the cash market, stock-index futures also allow investors to execute portfolio switches amongst asset classes more quickly and efficiently. An investor would then simply buy or sell stock-index futures and then decide whether or not to maintain his underlying stock portfolio. As his stock holdings drop, he has the ability to re-establish his portfolio allocation to stocks quickly by simply buying back stock-index futures.

Until the stock market crash of 1987, there was no reason to question the fundamental assumption of the ability to execute trades. After all, the New York Stock Exchange (NYSE) had always been amongst the most deep and liquid markets on the planet.

For all its merits, portfolio insurance had one critical bottleneck that would prove fatal. As in many other stories in this chapter, regardless of how good the technology at hand is, the human link of the chain is very often the weak point. No matter how automated a market is, the two extreme and opposite emotions of greed and fear are always present. Technology can, at most, make the transmission of information, prices and execution between these two extremes more efficient. It cannot remove or change the extremes. In spite of the sophisticated automation of programme trading activities, order execution depended on an important human step called the *specialist*. In 1987, this professional figure was ultimately responsible for ensuring efficient execution and continuous markets on the NYSE. This profession remains very important at the time of writing, although there are plans to reform the system to account for the increased importance of electronic trading *vis-à-vis* open-outcry over the last few years.

---

[78] After Leland, O'Brien, Rubinstein, its founding partners. Of these, Rubinstein is the best regarded in finance academia and well known amongst practitioners for his landmark *Options Markets* textbook.

This chapter has already demonstrated how trouble has a knack for striking at the weakest spot. Following a wave of increases in Treasury bond yields in the previous six months, the stock market had already appeared nervous the week before, losing over 10 per cent during the three days ending on 16 October 1987. The following Monday, 19 October, a series of massive sell orders hit the NYSE. Program trading orders to sell were set off in massive size. After a while, many specialists simply stopped answering the phones. How about that for efficient markets?

The next best avenue for execution was in the stock-index futures pits at the Chicago Mercantile Exchange. Huge and unprecedented sell volume struck. At this point, the futures prices dropped below their fair value relative to the cash market in New York. Index arbitrage would have called for arbitrageurs to buy the cheap stock-index futures and sell short the stocks in the New York cash market. That is how the futures' markets price stabilization is brought about. The latter leg, however, could not be executed. As a result, for almost the whole day, the stock-index futures continued to trade cheaply relative to their cash counterparts and kept falling without respite. The cash market was dragged down accordingly. The Dow Jones Industrial Average, NYSE's bellwether, closed down 508 points that day, or minus 22.61 per cent from the previous close.

Most portfolios that had relied on portfolio insurance to protect their downside were devastated. In the aftermath of the crash, futures were widely blamed for exacerbating volatility. While popular as a scapegoat, futures indeed offered an alternative market that had prevented a complete meltdown. Of course, as is customary under these circumstances, instruments are easier to blame than incompetent users, as only the latter can argue back.

More usefully, several studies revisited the fundamental assumptions of the Black-Scholes model, concluding that investors had been blindsided by an 'illusion of liquidity'.[81] This term is especially appropriate and one that you'd better remember next time you meet someone pitching some fancy product offering special value or an alluring return.

Stretching for yield involves, almost always, sacrificing some liquidity. Indeed, it is a general law of finance and of derivative markets that segregating value generally involves segregating liquidity. A bespoke product tailored specifically to one investor's needs may meet his market view but will likely depend on a very restricted number of dealers to quote him a price to exit if he so decides.

Bruce Jacobs's brilliant book *Capital Ideas and Market Realities* (1999) provides one of the most comprehensive analyses of portfolio insurance and its myths. It will benefit those readers who are interested in understanding the topic in greater detail.

Once again, people have been slow to learn the illusion of liquidity lesson. The case of LTCM, 11 years after the Crash, shows how slick marketing, dogmatic application of financial theory and limited market capacity mix like benzene and fire. As greed is as old as mankind, it is reasonable to expect the lesson to be forgotten again in the future.

---

[81] Statement by Robert Glauber, Director of the Brady Commission that investigated the causes of the 1987 stock market crash.

CHAPTER 11

Other masterpieces outside finance

The word 'impossible' exists only in the dictionary of fools.

(Napoleon Bonaparte)

7±2:

- Flawed decisions and rationality assumptions, one pattern, many applications
- Mankind's troubles with unproven and risky new technology
- Space disasters
- Nuclear mishaps
- Pollution accidents
- Ship losses

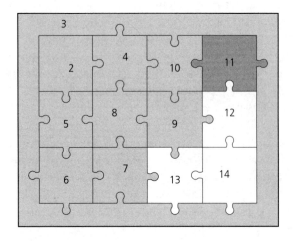

Abstract

Engineers and managers outside finance keep good company with their counterparts involved in risk and trading decisions. This account of a few notorious instances should dispel any doubt about the similarity of thought patterns.

Implications: The quote at the beginning of this chapter sums it up beautifully. Either safety is your top priority or it is not. When in doubt, do not let statistics obstruct the investigation of possible escape routes and damage limitation devices.

11.1 Human issues in new technology management

Human mishaps are by no means confined only to business and finance. Behavioural issues have produced far more catastrophic consequences in the real world, particularly when high-risk technologies are involved. As discussed in Chapter 6, groupthink and politics are hardly conducive to good decisions even in the private sector. Poor performers cannot always be fired as easily in the public sector. A common pattern underlies these unfortunate instances:

- The new technology makes the achievement of some highly visible important objective possible. Few statements have ever sounded as captivating for public imagination as US President John F. Kennedy's ambitious objective of getting man to the moon by the end of the 1960s. Nuclear power offers an alternative and inexpensive energy source to oil and makes industrialization and its benefits more available. Airplanes and transatlantic liners brought the world together for both businessmen and humble people looking for better opportunities abroad.

- The effects and consequences of the new technology are not completely known, manageable or reversible. Failure in space and flight leads to virtually certain death. Nuclear accidents mean highly likely loss of life, whether immediately or as a result of diseases originated by nuclear fall-out and contamination.

- An elaborate set of safety measures is devised to mitigate and pre-empt accidents and their fearsome consequences. These measures involve a combination of the following:

  - design, in which the projects for the new ship, space vehicle, nuclear reactor and so on are drafted. For instance, one may design a nuclear reactor so that more than one alternative exists to support the functioning of the critical reactor cooling process;

  - process, which involves the way in which the process is supposed to work on an ongoing basis;

  - maintenance has to do with the periodic check-ups of various component parts of the process, so that preventive remedial action can be taken. Faulty parts, for instance, may be fixed or replaced;

  - emergency procedures are also set forth to manage high-risk instances if all else fails. Many offices, for instance, practise routine fire alarm drills to train employees to deal with such emergencies.

■ Of course, all of these measures carry a cost. Thaler (1995, 1999) reminds us that the cost of a safety device or saving thereon is an out-of-pocket cost that looms large over the decision. This is the stage in which accounting and budget constraints show up and, with them, the familiar temptation to cut some corners that we have already encountered in finance. This happens regardless of the potentially more devastating consequences of failure. The latter has some remote probability that is often difficult to assess due to the nature of the process. People are poorly equipped to associate probabilities with the necessity to reach yes–no, proceed–reject decisions (see Chapter 5). Such decisions require a binary 0/1 probability assessment. They will have a bias to round off the probability of some accident to zero until it happens. Calls for caution are dismissed as 'unrealistic' or 'unreasonable'. Such dismissal does not stem from mathematical rounding-off of probabilities alone. The human mind will also do its utmost to avoid thinking about the consequences of failure, which most likely mean loss of human life. This is fear of vividness triggered by availability bias. How best to escape from such fear than assessing the risk of failure as zero?

■ In addition, the new technology generally involves complex processes and additional cost overruns over time. Once substantial sums, years of research and a lot of political capital and prestige have been invested in the new development over the years, cutting losses and getting out of the project becomes increasingly harder. Political, media and public opinion's pressure make it even more difficult. Sunk cost biases cloud the picture further and sometimes the project continues due more to its political or PR significance than based on its actual merits. Simply put, bearing an additional set of annual costs equal to 100 is more palatable than taking the big outright loss of writing off the 1,000 invested in the project to date.

■ As time goes by, many of the important features of the safety process get forgotten or disregarded as 'details'. As such, responsibility for them moves down the organization to levels of relatively low authority. This means that these lower-ranking officials will have relatively scant opportunity of opposing changes in priority, budget cuts and so forth imposed from the top. Cost cuts and budget constraints are then used to cut down on safety and maintenance. Worse, the cuts may already be in action during the design phase, with the engineers being held hostage by accountants and funding constraints. Requests for increased investments on safety devices will face an uphill battle for resources. After all, it is not with brakes or escape devices that spaceships lift off and amuse people watching TV! This bears some resemblance to the familiar question that cost-cutters pose when asked to fund better controls that may even be critical: 'How will that help us make more money?' At this point, unfortunately, the flaw in the design and funding of controls has been put in place long ago and people are likely to have got dangerously used to it. All the ingredients of complacency are in place.

■ In the following stage, there is some forewarning of the impending disaster. Cognitive resonance will drive decision-makers to seek confirming, rather than disconfirming, information. In light of the 'extreme' importance of achieving the pre-set important objective, the decision is taken to ignore the alarm calls and proceed. The consequences of failure fall completely off the radar screen. Politics, PR and other visibility objectives compound the pressure further. These constituencies have little incentive to stop anyway.

The prospect of landing on the moon is a far more attractive TV show than an aborted launch anyway. This underscores the dramatic difference between managing *situations* and *processes*. The decision to proceed and disable the safety device at Chernobyl and the choice to go ahead with the *Challenger* launch despite very clear signals of impending trouble are cases in point. You may recall from Chapter 5 that these decisions are often made in spite of a superficial understanding of the overall process and its interdependencies.

■ In the final stage, as the accident unfolds, all the weaknesses in the technology design implementation of the emergency procedures are finally exposed. Impromptu, ad hoc decisions are taken to limit damage. In these instances, the individuals involved reveal their tendency of managing these complex technologies as *situations*, that is by improvising, rather than as *processes* with their own imperatives. These accidents unfold with their own timeframe and interdependencies and the odds are good that the people involved understand neither.

■ The accident's post-mortem will see the media zooming in on its fearsome consequences. As the new technology is largely unknown to laymen, a massive potential for availability bias exists. The shifting tide of public opinion leaves no option for the involved government or regulator but to intervene. Usually, this will be accomplished by an investigation report drawn up by an appointed commission of experts.

For those readers who want to delve deeper into the subject of managing technological progress, let me recommend Edward Tenner's international best-seller *Why Things Bite Back* (1996) and Charles Perrow's *Normal Accidents* (1990). The latter's title is telling, because it underscores how a culture of tolerance of 'acceptable' faults soon becomes the norm, particularly in large organizations. The dire consequences are just around the corner. As in Chapter 10, technical details will be kept to the bare minimum for clarity's sake.

11.2 The Space Shuttle

The impressive TV and media coverage that has always accompanied the US space programme and the Space Shuttle, its latest offspring, turned into a high-profile boomerang on the twenty-fifth mission. On 28 January 1986, the *Challenger*, Mission 51-L, exploded 73 seconds after launch, killing all seven astronauts on board. The case has become a classic in decision-making for the mixture of overconfidence, groupthink, persistent neglect of adverse information and technical complexity that it featured.

After achieving the spectacular Moon landing in 1969, NASA, the US space agency, had not escaped budgetary cuts. Under the previous *Apollo* programme, only 5 per cent of the original ship would return to Earth. Safety was the top priority, as the capsule would find itself three days from Earth. As a result, virtually every component was duplicated. Conversely, the rationale for the Shuttle was to design a largely recyclable vehicle that could be used for several missions. Rotating around the Earth's orbit was deemed far less risky than going to the Moon. You will not have to wait long to see the consequences of this misleading assumption. Cost containment had loomed large over the design of the vehicle, influencing critical design decisions. For instance, no provision had been made to provide astronauts with an escape hatch. Budget constraints also tilted the design towards highly flammable solid-fuel rockets instead of the safer, but more expensive, liquid fuel alternative.

A chain of events triggered by the failure of inexpensive rubber O-rings caused the explosion. Nearly 146 in. (3.7 m) in diameter, 38 ft (11.6 m) in circumference and $\frac{1}{4}$ in. (6.4 mm) thick, O-rings are rubber cylinders that seal the space between separate sections of each of the two solid-fuel rocket boosters (SRBs). These, in turn, are the two missile-shaped boosters that flank the external tank, which contains two separate chambers that store liquid hydrogen and liquid oxygen, respectively.

As the Space Shuttle is a remarkably sophisticated and complex machine, this case will keep technical details to a minimum to facilitate the understanding of what went wrong. Due to their length (126 ft, or about 38 m), the SRBs are transported to the launch site in separate sections and assembled there.[82] If the O-ring fails to seal, gas may leak out of the SRB, a process known as blow-by. This criticality prompted engineers to equip each SRB with two sets of O-rings, known as the primary and secondary sets.

A spectator's view of the Shuttle at launch would be as follows:

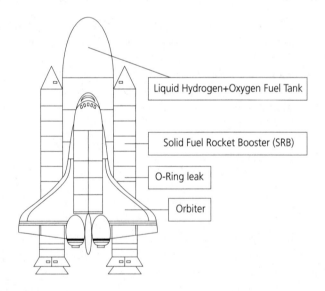

Liquid Hydrogen+Oxygen Fuel Tank

Solid Fuel Rocket Booster (SRB)

O-Ring leak

Orbiter

FIGURE 11.1 ▪ The Space Shuttle

---

[82] The gas pressure formed by combustion inside the SRB helps the O-ring to seal the space between the two different sections of the SRB. This process of sealing is called *Pressure Actuation Of O-Ring Seal*. As the gas goes toward the O-ring, gas meets one side of the O-ring and pushes the O-ring from all the sides possible into the gap, helping to seal the joint. The pressure is needed in the very early stages of SRB ignition.

During the 24 launches in the previous five years, O-rings had already displayed problems. Failure to seal owing to O-rings becoming stiff at low temperatures was the most consistent of them. This was first observed in developmental flight STS-2 in November 1981, some *four years* before the fateful *Challenger* mission. Another mission – the shuttle *Discovery* – also launched under low temperatures on 24 January 1985 had been a near-miss. On that occasion, the primary O-rings failed but the secondary ones saved the day. The same situation had repeated itself in the previous *Challenger* mission, 51-B, launched on 29 April 1985. Being aware of the problem, NASA asked Morton-Thiolkiol to fix it. While an apposite task force was assembled at the SRB supplier, the problem was studied but not fixed. Echoing other concerns[83] about the adequacy of the task force's political weight and resources, the Rogers Commission added the following comments in their post-accident investigation report:

> The Space Shuttle's Solid Rocket Booster problem began with the faulty design of its joint and increased as both NASA and contractor management first failed to recognize it as a problem, then failed to fix it and finally treated it as an acceptable flight risk. ... However, as tests and then flights confirmed damage to the sealing rings, the reaction by both NASA and Thiolkiol was to increase the amount of damage considered 'acceptable'.[84]

Ominously, data kept by engineers at Morton-Thiolkiol showed a failure rate well above average already at 53°F (about 11.5°C). To work on the Shuttle SRBs, the O-ring was supposed to seal in the first three-tenths of a second. While no data existed for lower temperatures, earlier tests at 50°F (9°C) showed that *ten minutes* would not suffice. As a result, when record low temperatures below 30°F covered the *Challenger's* launchpad with icicles on 27 January 1986, Morton-Thiolkiol's engineers were unanimous in recommending NASA to stop the launch. This was the only such recommendation in some *twelve years*. At that point, the *Challenger* launch had already been called off twice due to strong winds and technical problems, respectively. Feeling under strong pressure, NASA asked Morton-Thiolkiol to reconsider the decision. The reply from NASA's Level III Manager left no doubt on the Space Agency's spirit and expectations: 'My God, Thiolkiol, when do you want me to launch, next April?'

Over the next half-hour, Morton-Thiolkiol was the stage of an intense discussion. The engineers stood by their earlier decision. This put top management in a dilemma, as their colleagues' legitimate arguments meant disappointing NASA, their largest and most prestigious client. At the end, 'a management decision[85]' to proceed with the launch overruled the lower-rank engineers, exactly those who were most familiar with the O-rings issues. In their tightly hedged reply to NASA, the contractor's top management stated that the evidence was 'not sufficiently conclusive' to argue that the O-rings would fail to seal properly. Launch could proceed.

---

[83] Morton Thiolkiol Internal Memo to R. Lund, Vice President of Engineering written by S.R. Stein, Space Project Engineer, 1 October 1985.

[84] Presidential Commission, *Report* 1:120.

[85] As reported by A.W. Macbeth in a March 1986 interview. Macbeth was a manager in charge of so-called 'case projects'.

You are likely to come across 'management decisions' or, equivalently, 'strategic decisions' often in your career. When you do, be prepared to expect seniority or title to override more rational and objective arguments. In layman's terms, one may just translate such types of decisions with 'we cannot say no'. These 'just do it'-style approaches speak volumes about management's supposed rationality when assessing information and evaluating alternatives.

Other interesting opportunities to avert disaster were missed on launch day, too. These show the dangers of split responsibilities in complex processes when people down the chain of command but closer to the problem do not have a chance to ring the alarm bell. The temperature forecasts were 26°F (−3°C) at launch time and as low as 18°F (−6°C) during the night. The Ice Inspection Team that NASA dispatched to evaluate the conditions on Launch Pad 39-B, where the *Challenger* was docked, was shocked to discover the launch pad covered with ice. One of the team members appropriately described the situation as 'something out of Dr Zhivago'.[86] The head of the ice team radioed H.L. Lamberth, the Director of Engineering at the Kennedy Space Center, and told him, 'The only choice you've got today is not to go.' The temperature at the SRB joint, where the O-ring was located, was measured to be 8°F (−11°C). Since no specific launch constraint existed for ambient temperature on the boosters, it was not reported.

Rockwell, another key supplier of the Space Shuttle programme, reported that the day was deemed 'unsafe to fly', the first time such an announcement was ever made. Again, no reaction followed from NASA.

The sequel is history: 59 seconds after ignition, when the Shuttle was already six miles in the air, a flicker of flame emerged from the leaky joint of the right SRB. As the flame engulfed the main tank, this ruptured and then exploded.

In the definitive book on the case, *The Challenger Launch Decision* (1989), Diane Vaughan attributed the mis-management of the O-rings to a long-established culture of 'normalized deviance' inside NASA. In her lucid analysis, she describes how the 'culture of production' – that is, going ahead based on a set of institutionalized beliefs and in spite of mounting adverse information – was at the root of cutting corners on quality on an ongoing basis. While acceptable in the short term, this strategy is the first step towards trouble. These short-term pressures for results and the same temptation for 'smart' cost savings are common in the investment banking and trading industry, too. These decisions are then often paid with compound interest when adverse probabilities reassert themselves at some point in time and problems occur.

Other more recent research work (Murnighan & Mowen, 2002) on the go-ahead decision has emphasized the preference for action that top decision-makers often display under stressful conditions and time pressure. These authors point out that waiting or no-go behaviours resulting from technical concerns – as in this case – do not conform to the stereotype of the decisive, effective role that most managers would like to be known for. While managers are trained to present findings and recommendations with confidence, the quest for confidence may influence their objectivity and drive in obtaining critical information.

---

[86] U.S. Congress, House, *Investigation: Report*, 238. The chilling Russian winter was the setting of the famous movie from which the analogy was drawn.

The case shows beyond doubt the negative impact of PR and groupthink and the extent to which humans will go in making subjective probability assessments in highly uncertain situations. More often than not, these guesstimates will emphasize how remote the risk is and provide a false sense of security to people who are not so close to the case and the general public. You will see other examples of such far-fetched statements in the Chernobyl and *Titanic* cases later on.

Before *Challenger*, NASA's official launch risk estimate was one catastrophic failure every 100,000 launches (Feynman, 1988, as quoted in Plous, 1993). As failure meant almost certain loss of crew, the incident would simply be deemed impossible. In short, the probability assessment would depend on the fear of adverse consequences rather than aim to prevent them! This makes the case a second-to-none application of *denial*, a defensive mechanism discussed in Chapter 5. People often resort to this self-preservation bias when faced with particularly unfavourable information. As shown earlier, this denial had persisted for years.[87] Testifying at the meeting of the Rogers Commission, Noble Prize winner physicist Richard Feynman argued that, based on the scant information available, the probability of failure could range from the original 1 in 100,000 to a figure as low as 1 in 100! In his own words:

> For the next flight, we can lower our standards a little bit because we got away with it last time. ... It is a kind of Russian roulette. You got away with it, and it was a risk.[88]

Unfortunately, even the low end of that range proved aggressive as a risk estimate. While NASA revised failure probabilities *ex post* towards Feynman's estimate, changes in behaviours did not follow through in the controversial programme. After several improvements, the Shuttle programme resumed in 1989. Fast-forward to 1996, when NASA decided to privatize the programme operations by handing over day-to-day management to a consortium of US aerospace companies. This consortium was named the United Space Alliance. Additional reductions by one-third in the budget of the Space Shuttle programme followed until 2000. In August 2000, a report published by General Accounting Office, the investigative arm of the US Congress, raised concerns over the safety implications of these budget cuts. The Aerospace Safety Advisory Panel (ASAP) also expressed similar fears in its March 2002 report.

In February 2003, *Columbia*, Mission STS-107 and the one hundred and thirteenth of the programme, disintegrated at re-entry into the atmosphere. In the event, a piece of foam insulation broke away 82 seconds after launch and damaged the tiles underneath the left wing. These tiles protect the shuttle from the intense heat (over 3000° F, or 1600°C) during re-entry phase in the atmosphere. During the re-entry phase, superheated air was allowed to penetrate the wing's aluminium frame and melt it. Bearing an eerie resemblance to the

---

[87] This was hardly the lone instance in which people become accustomed with a problem and end up neglecting it until disaster strikes. Nakina, located in Ontario, Canada, was the stage of another extreme case of protracted complacency. In the event, no action was taken to correct a 1916 railway design failure. This was allowed under the construction standards of that period. The fault resulted in a train derailment in 1992. Two people were killed and the train driver was seriously injured. (Reason, 1997).

[88] Presidential Commission, *Report* 1:148; 5:1446.

communication breakdown before the *Challenger* launch, memos written by NASA engineers that expressed concerns about the damage after launch never reached top-level staff. The same fate occurred to as many as *twelve*[89] of their requests for pictures on the damaged portion of the wing while *Columbia* was in orbit. Once again, the decision was, by default, to continue the normal re-entry procedure as if nothing had happened and hope (...) for the best. One should seriously question whether the lesson has been learned.

Investigating the accident, the Gehman Commission moved major criticisms to NASA's practices and culture in their report:

> The accident was probably not an anomalous, random event, but rather likely rooted to some degree in NASA's history ... The Board's conviction regarding the importance of these factors strengthened as the investigation progressed, with the result that this report, in its findings, conclusions and recommendations, places as much weight on these causal factors as on the more easily understood and corrected physical cause of the accident.

One might argue that the original failure estimates covered mostly launches, the most dangerous phase, rather than the entire mission. Nevertheless, discriminating failure based on its source is a semantic nuance that is largely irrelevant for the final outcome. Indeed, none of the unfortunate astronauts survived either mission. Having budgets drive safety rather than the other way around is ultimately a choice that puts an implicit price on the value of human life. Doesn't a 2:113 loss ratio strike as being quite high a figure for what is supposed to be a rare catastrophic event?

11.3 Nuclear disasters

Few developments in modern technology have aroused as much controversy and debate as the civilian use of nuclear energy. Nuclear incidents have potential consequences that are either unknown or too horrible even to consider. No less an authority than Albert Einstein stated: 'The splitting of the atom has changed everything except our way of thinking and thus we drift towards unparalleled catastrophe.' Nevertheless, at the time of writing, nuclear energy is still the only commercially viable mass-production alternative to crude oil.

Despite several small near-misses, mankind has yet to learn completely the lesson of the full responsibilities that nuclear energy involves. A few reasonably serious nuclear power mishaps, labelled, with dangerous complacency, 'normal accidents', had already happened in the US and elsewhere before the cases that will be shown later:

- 1952 (12 December), Chalk River (near Ottawa), Canada: partial meltdown of a reactor's fuel core due to the accidental removal of control rods. Millions of gallons of radioactive water accumulate inside the reactor. No casualties.

- 1957, Windscale Pile Nr. 1, near Liverpool, England: fire in a graphite-cooled reactor. Radiation contaminates a 200-mile area.

---

[89] As reported by the *New York Times* on 26 September 2003.

- 1957, South Ural Mountains, Soviet Union: explosion of radioactive waste at Soviet nuclear weapons factory located 12 miles from city of Kyshtym. Over 10,000 are evacuated from the contaminated area.

- 1976, near Greifswald, Germany: radioactive core of reactor in the Lubmin nuclear power plant nearly melted down due to the failure of safety systems during a fire.

Nothing, however, comes close to the instances showed in the next sections.

11.3.1 Three Mile Island (TMI)

The worst nuclear accident in the US occurred near Harrisburg, Pennsylvania, on 28 March 1979. It is yet another story in which cost containment was achieved, for a change, by increasing operational risk. The series of mishaps that occurred at TMI has been studied in several cases. It shows that the culprit was not nuclear power, but the way it was mismanaged.

Few operations match a nuclear power plant in complexity. (This account will keep technical details to a bare minimum required to understand the developments.) Two cooling systems exist in a plant such as TMI:

- The primary cooling system contains water under high pressure that circulates at high temperature through the core where the nuclear reaction is taking place.

- The secondary cooling system is a set of tubes that receive circulating water from the primary cooling system. This water is also under high pressure until it is called upon to turn into steam.

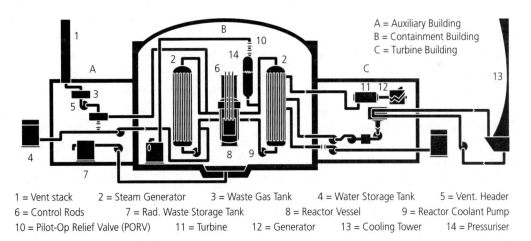

1 = Vent stack   2 = Steam Generator   3 = Waste Gas Tank   4 = Water Storage Tank   5 = Vent. Header
6 = Control Rods   7 = Rad. Waste Storage Tank   8 = Reactor Vessel   9 = Reactor Coolant Pump
10 = Pilot-Op Relief Valve (PORV)   11 = Turbine   12 = Generator   13 = Cooling Tower   14 = Pressuriser

FIGURE 11.2 ■ Three Mile Island, Unit 2

Source: Kemeny John et al, 'Report of the President Commission on the Accident at Three Mile Island'. Washington D.C.: Government Printing Office, 1979. Available in the public domain at http://stellar-one.com/nuclear/report_to_the_president.htm

The passage of water from the primary to the secondary cooling system prevents the plant from overheating. The heat is used to turn water into steam with a steam generator. This, in turn, moves the turbines that generate power.

Unlike the water in the primary system, the water in the secondary system is not radioactive. It must be very pure because the steam that it generates moves the relatively delicate turbine blades. This clean-up task is performed by the condensate polisher system, which removes particles from the water.

The polisher had already failed three times in the few months of activity at TMI. At 4am on 28 March 1979, the turbine stopped again after about eleven hours of activity. As this stops the whole water-cooling process, an alternative process starts to remove the heat from the core. Emergency pumps draw water from a tank and run it through the cooling system to compensate for the increasing temperature of the water in the system. Such increase is due to the lack of circulation of the water.

Unfortunately, a series of other inconveniences were looming:

- The emergency pumps were activated but could not feed the water due to one of their valves being left closed after maintenance two days earlier.

- The valve indicators in the plant's huge control panel were covered by a repair tag.

It took the operators about eight minutes to work out that something was wrong at the plant. All the stages described above occur in the main building of the plant, called the containment building. The operators assumed that the source of the problem could be in a pipe break somewhere. In an incredibly complex operation such as a nuclear power plant, locating a faulty pipe is similar to looking for a needle in a haystack. Only later did they realize that radioactive water was travelling to a different – and wrong – tank in the auxiliary building. Two minutes later, the High-Pressure Injection (HPI) emergency device went off and started forcing water into the core at a high rate. The operators still ignored why this had happened, as they incorrectly assumed that the secondary cooling process was still active thanks to the emergency pumps. One of the main risks of the HPI's activity is that it may flood a tank called the pressurizer, which is designed to hold both water and steam. The pressure on the steam controls the pressure of the water that cools the core. If the pressurizer is flooded and no room remains for steam, this may cause coolant pipes to burst.[90] With no coolant, a meltdown could occur.

Important conflicting signals on two key dials further compounded confusion amongst the plant's operators. One dial indicated that the water pressure in the reactor was still falling. The other indicated that the pressure in the pressurizer was well above safety levels and still rising. Fearing the consequences of the latter failure, the plant operators cut back on HPI after two minutes. A few minutes later, the reactor coolant pumps started thumping and shaking and several alarm bells and radiation indicators went off. Two hours and twenty minutes after the start of the accident, a new shift came on. The new shift supervisor decided to check the PORV[91], the core's relief valve. Immediately, he decided to shut off the flow of coolant to the PORV.

---

[90] This is called a Loss Of Coolant Accident, or LOCA.
[91] PORV stands for Pilot Operated Relief Valve.

Testifying at the Kemeny Presidential Commission that investigated the accident later, the operator described this decision as 'more an act of desperation than an act of understanding'. By sheer luck, a complete meltdown had been averted. Nevertheless, a substantial part of the core had melted. The trouble was not yet over. Thirty-three hours into the accident, at 1pm Wednesday, a soft but distinct bang was heard in the control room. Hydrogen, freed by the chemical process of the fuel rods becoming too hot, had been the source of the explosion. Bubbles of hydrogen can be ignited if they meet oxygen and a spark. Luckily, the hydrogen found no other opportunities to explode. If it had, the whole containment building could have been threatened. Even without explosions, hydrogen can impede the regular flow of coolant in the plant.

The Kemeny Commission concluded that the operators were 'oblivious' to the danger and that two readings from the gauges should have alerted them to the loss of coolant. According to the investigation's conclusion, the plant had been no more than *one hour* away from a complete meltdown. In more general terms, this case illustrates how complexity, time pressure and incomplete understanding of the workings of a process cause people to improvise and expose themselves to the law of unintended consequences later.

11.3.2 Chernobyl

TMI and the many 'normal accidents' that had preceded it would not remain on record as the worst-ever nuclear power accident for long. Seven years after TMI, Ukraine's largest nuclear power plant at Chernobyl[92] was the scene of a far more catastrophic chain of events.

Western experts and even the mighty KGB had already questioned Chernobyl's design and safety practices. As early as 1979, a letter from the KGB informed the Soviet Union's Party Central Committee of several flaws in the plant. As lack of follow-up knows no ideological boundaries, no corrective measures were taken. In addition, the reactor was key in supplying the Ukraine's power grid. The line between local pride in the plant and the related safety probability assessments was quite blurred. For one, listen to the following statement by Vitali Skylarov, Minister of Power and Electrification in the Ukraine, in February 1986:

The odds of a meltdown are one in 10,000 years.

On 25 April 1986, a test was scheduled to take advantage of Reactor Four's shutdown for routine maintenance. The test consisted of ensuring that, in the event of a shutdown, enough back-up power would be available to operate the emergency equipment and core cooling pumps until the diesel power became available. Unbelievably, the principal testers were electrical engineers from Moscow. According to a Russian report (Reason, 1990), 'their head was not a specialist in reactor plants'.

In the course of the shutdown, when the reactor operated at approximately half power, the electric grid controller refused to allow further reductions. As part of the test the emergency core cooling system was switched off and the reactor carried on at half power. At about 11pm on 25 April the grid controller agreed to a further reduction in power.

---

[92] Located 80 miles north of Kiev.

According to the test plan, the reactor power was to be set at 1,000MW prior to shutdown. By 1986 standards, the safety operating level was about 700MW. An operational error made the power fall to only about 30MW as of 0:28am on 26 April. At such low level, the positive void coefficient[93] became a problem. The operators tried to raise the power by freeing all the control rods manually and at 1am the reactor stabilized at 200MW. Note that, under normal circumstances, the plant would need at least 26 control rods to operate. The minimum safety requirement called for at least 15 control rods to be inserted in the reactor at all times.

Between 1:03am and 1:07am, the operators continued the test by activating two additional pumps to increase the water flow to the core, thereby removing heat more quickly. In the following minutes, an increase in coolant flow and a drop in steam pressure occurred requiring the operators to withdraw nearly all the rods at 1:19am. Two minutes later, the feed water flow was reduced, decreasing heat removal from the core. At 1:22am the spontaneous generation of steam in the core began. While abnormal, the gauges seemed to indicate that the reactor was stable. A minute later, the automatic control rods were withdrawn from the core.

With neither the control rods nor adequate water flow cooling the core, the reactor's positive void coefficient and increased steam generation led to a rapid increase in power. At 1:23am, this escalated uncontrollably to about 100 times the design value. The activation of the emergency button by the operator a few seconds later could not prevent fuel channels from rupturing and two major explosions occuring at 1:24am. The explosions were from steam and fuel vapour, respectively. The explosion destroyed the reaction core shortly thereafter. Some 8 of the 140 tonnes of fuel, containing plutonium and other radioactive materials, were ejected from the reactor, along with a portion of the graphite moderator. Caesium and iodine vapours were also released. An estimated 5,000 died, most of them being clean-up workers. The people of Chernobyl were exposed to radiation 90 times greater than from the Hiroshima bomb. A United Nations 1995 Report estimated that over nine million people were directly or indirectly affected by the accident. Over 400,000 had to be evacuated. As an effect of the Chernobyl accident, 125,000 km^2 of land in Belarus, Ukraine and Russia was exposed to radiation, with radioactive levels sometimes greater than 37 kBq/m^2. Among the land affected was 73,000 km^2 of forest, water bodies, and urban centres.

During the years following the accident, several reports underscored the design flaws in the RBMK reactor, first and foremost in its instability at low power levels. The mis-management lessons that surface from this drama are by no means less important and are in fact impressively similar to the other cases illustrated in this chapter.

- ■ Overconfidence in the handling of the plant safety flaws before the accident and in the flagrant violation of basic safety procedures. By now, you should be familiar with the arch-remote failure probability assessment such as the one uttered before the accident. During the accident, the control rods were removed and the emergency cooling system disabled. In his insightful book *The Logic of Failure*, Dietrich Dörner said:

---

[93] A positive void coefficient means that the loss of coolant leads to an increase in the reaction rate. Short of any other countermeasure, this can result in runaway heating of the reactor core.

Another likely reason for this violation of the safety rules was that operators had frequently violated them before. But, as learning theory tells us, breaking safety rules is usually reinforced, which is to say, it pays off.

- Sequential processing bias described earlier in Chapter 5. Here, the plant operators showed a poor understanding of an overall complex process and managed it as just another situation, regardless of the potentially catastrophic unintended consequences.

- Communications breakdown. The test was carried out without a proper exchange of information between the team in charge of the test and the personnel responsible for the operation of the nuclear reactor.

11.3.3 Tokaimura

The Ukraine will suffer from the disastrous consequences of Chernobyl for a long time. Earlier on, this chapter showed how lessons from past disasters are never learnt well enough and people need reminders. Generally, Mother Nature sends these reminders in the form of new disasters and the cycle continues. Nuclear power is no exception.

Despite the lessons from TMI and Chernobyl, Tokaimura,[94] Japan, was the place of another accident on 30 September 1999. Tokaimura is not strictly a power plant but, rather, a nuclear fuel reprocessing operation that prepares the raw material for use in nuclear power plants. Nevertheless, the nature of the raw material and the consequences require just as many precautions as at a nuclear power plant. The accident occurred in the conversion building (auxiliary plant) at the uranium conversion facility of JCO Company Limited. A solution of enriched uranium (18.8 per cent $235U$ by mass) in an amount reportedly several times more than the specified mass limit poured directly into a precipitation tank, bypassing a dissolution tank and buffer column intended to avoid criticality. In a December 1999 report, the Japanese Nuclear Safety Commission attributed the direct cause of the accident to workers putting uranyl nitrate solution containing about 16.6 kg of uranium, which exceeded the pre-specified critical mass of 2.4 kg, into the precipitation tank. This tank was not designed to dissolve this type of solution and was not configured to prevent eventual criticality.

While the Japanese authorities classified this instance as Level 4[95] on the International Atomic Energy Agency (IAEA) International Nuclear Event Scale (INES), the event resulted in three JCO workers suffering acute radiation syndrome and a number of workers and members of the public receiving radiation doses. Some 161 people were evacuated from within about 350 metres of the facility, and some 310,000 people were advised to stay indoors for about 18 hours as a precautionary measure.

---

[94] Located in the Ibaraki Prefecture, 120 km north-east of Tokyo.

[95] This scale ranges from 1 to 7. 4 means an event without significant off-site risk. By comparison, Chernobyl received a 7 rating.

The accident resulted in an increase ranging between six and 80 times in the gamma dose[96] within a radius of 7km of the facility.

The IAEA also led an investigation shortly after the accident. According to a preliminary report, issued in November 1999, this action was reported to have been in contravention of the legally approved criticality control measures. The accident seems to have resulted primarily from human error and serious breaches of safety principles. Key amongst these:

- No specific arrangements for an event such as the one that occurred at JCO, which was considered to be an 'unrealistic' scenario. So much for scenario and contingency planning for unusual and highly unlikely events! In Japan, a national plan drawn up by the Central Disaster Prevention Council sets out measures to deal with nuclear emergencies that could have off-site effects.

- The critical dissolution process for uranium oxide (U_3O_8) powder in a dissolution tank was modified in November 1996, without permission for the modification having been granted by the regulatory authorities. Under the revised process the dissolution would be performed in stainless steel buckets.

- Last but not least, the steel buckets did not have the geometric shape to prevent criticalities such as the one that occurred.

11.4 Bhopal

The mirage of industrialization and its opportunities has been an irresistible magnet for many emerging economies ever since the end of World War Two. India has been a favourite location for several multinational firms seeking cheap but skilled labour and potentially large domestic markets. This story shows how naively a large American corporation and the Indian government embarked on an industrial adventure that would indelibly mark the lives of a large community.

The pride and ego of the Indian government during the late 1960s was a key catalyst for the chain of events that brought pesticides into the country thanks to one of its major multinational guests, Union Carbide. In the pursuit of food self-sufficiency, the Indian government needed to boost farm crops. This included increasing the use of chemical pesticides. MIC, or *methyl isocyanate*, is one of them and amongst the most dangerous chemicals. A little lighter than water but twice as heavy as air, it has the ability to react with many substances such as water, acids and metals.

The Indian subsidiary of Union Carbide imported MIC from its US parent until 1979, when local production began. Rather lax environmental standards are just one of the attractions that emerging economies offer to international companies. Accordingly, the Indian plant had a few problems to sort out when a safety task force from US headquarters was dispatched to India in May 1982, two-and-a-half years before the crisis. In a prescient warning,

---

[96] The normal background level for the gamma dose is 0.04 μGy/h. In the two hours following the incident, the gamma dose was as high as 3.1 μGy/h 1.5km south of the JCO plant and 0.24 μGy/h 7 km from the plant.

the report pointed to 'a serious potential for sizeable releases of toxic materials in the MIC unit either due to equipment failure, operating problems, or maintenance problems thus requiring various changes to reduce the danger of the plant'. Surprise surprise, there is no evidence the recommendations were ever implemented (Weir, 1987).

On the night of 23 December 1984, a dangerous chemical reaction occurred in the Union Carbide factory when a large amount of water got mixed with MIC in storage tank # 610. The leak was first detected by workers about 11:30 p.m. when their eyes began to tear and burn. Their supervisor, despite being informed, failed to take action until it was too late. By then about 40 tons of MIC had poured out of the tank for nearly two hours and spread into the air. This deadly cloud extended for eight kilometres, reaching a nearby city of nearly 900,000. Death estimates ranged as high as 4,000 people. Hundreds of thousands remained injured or affected, in many cases permanently.

The effects of MIC are extensive and not completely known to this day. They include, amongst others, eye, lung and gastrointestinal problems and a variety of neurological and musculo-skeletal disorders. Last but not least, few local doctors are sufficiently skilled to treat MIC victims.

The immediate cause of the chemical reaction was the seepage of water (500 litres) into the MIC storage tank. The results of this reaction were exacerbated by the failure of containment and safety measures and by a complete absence of community information and emergency procedures. The long-term effects were made worse by the absence of systems to care for and compensate the victims.

Divergent explanations were offered for the initial stages of the incident, prior to the lethal chemical reaction. A subsequent investigation led by consultants A.D. Little demonstrated that only a deliberate action by a disgruntled employee could have possibly caused the water inflow. It is less clear, however, how a tank containing such dangerous substances could be left without adequate surveillance to allow such internal sabotage. Indeed, according to the alternative explanation, a lone individual would have poured a large amount of water into the tank by means of a simple water hose. According to Perrow (1990), the plant had already experienced several layoffs and workers were not told about safety conditions. Internal sabotage was not completely absent amongst the risks to manage at Bhopal.

Perrow (1990) summarized how some safety and emergency management basics at the plant left much to be desired:

- there was no training on how to face such a massive emergency;
- no alarm went off when the first contamination of water was discovered;
- a large number of people were living – relatively speaking – in barracks and shanties just outside the plant without any emergency vehicles to carry out a mass evacuation;
- the authorities were not notified after the release of the deadly chemical started;
- there were inadequate safety devices to manage large-scale incidents.

The disaster, arguably the worst industrial catastrophe in history, resulted in a massive lawsuit and a $470 million out-of-court settlement by Union Carbide on 14 February 1989.

11.5 The *Titanic*

One cannot blame modern technology for loss of human life at sea. Rather, the dangers come from the promises and false sense of security that modern technology often engenders. All the human drama notwithstanding, the set of behaviours that led to this catastrophe is the prime area of attention. As unsuitable behaviours led to many other disasters during the twentieth century, serious doubts are legitimate over mankind's ability to learn from their own mistakes. This is yet another story created by human overconfidence rather than adverse forces of nature. Modern mass transportation, one of the most visible signs of technological progress of the new century, suffered a devastating blow as the supposedly unsinkable[97] *Titanic* sank in the North Atlantic after colliding with an iceberg during the night of 14 April 1912. Arguably, the ship was the safest means of intercontinental transportation of her age.

Headed for America, the *Titanic* had left Southampton on her maiden voyage on 10 April with 2,200 passengers and a crew of 892. As in most other real-life risk disasters, this was to become yet another case in which risk arose in the design of the machine, well before it went into operation. The reality was that intense competition amongst liners' operators over the previous half-century had resulted in a steady deterioration of safety standards. In modern risk terminology, one would say that the ship operators traded immediate cost savings against increased operational risk. Simply put, safety standards were subordinated to budget constraints rather than the other way around. Sound familiar? This pattern was most evident in two critical aspects:

- The construction of the ship around the waterline.[98] The *Titanic* had an illustrious predecessor in the *Great Eastern*, the first major transatlantic liner, which had been built in 1858, or *over half a century earlier*. The *Great Eastern* had a double hull, one inside the other. 15 transversal bulkheads and a longitudinal one further subdivided the inner hull. All these compartments had watertight lower decks. By comparison, the *Titanic* had only transversal bulkheads, no longitudinal bulkhead and no inner hull. The ship could remain afloat with as many as 4 of its 15 bulkhead compartments flooded. Yet again, as with many disasters waiting to happen, it was felt to be 'impossible' that anything worse might occur.[99] The difference would prove fatal. As a result, the *Great Eastern* had been able to survive a collision with a large iceberg comparable to the one

---

[97] This was the version popularized by the press, not by the builders or by the ship operator, the White Star Line. The *Titanic* was not the only 'unsinkable' ship to sink. In yet another demonstration of people's inability to learn from previous disasters caused by their far-fetched claims, three huge 'unsinkable' warships of the Imperial Japanese Navy were sunk by the US Navy between 1944 and 1945, thirty years after the *Titanic*. In a macabre resemblance to the *Titanic* instance, one of these, the 72,000 ton aircraft carrier *Shinano*, was also sunk during her maiden voyage. This was the largest warship ever built.

[98] Mr. Roy Brander, Sr. Infrastructure Engineer at Calgary Waterworks. The author would like to thank Mr Brander for permission to draw from his thorough comparison of the *Great Eastern* and the *Titanic*.

[99] After hitting the iceberg, the *Titanic* had five bulkhead compartments flooded and a sixth leaking.

that sank the *Titanic*. To put things into perspective, the *Great Eastern*'s bulkheads were as many as 30 feet (10 metres) in the water *vis-à-vis Titanic*'s 10 feet (3 metres). By now, knowing how people weigh immediate out-of pocket costs *vis-à-vis* the costs of 'unlikely' accidents, you can easily guess how these engineering choices were made. In short, longitudinal bulkheads and the other compartments were costly to build and used precious space inside the ship. No expense, on the other hand, was spared in equipping the *Titanic* with sumptuous cabins and grand ballrooms to lure the rich and famous of the times. Immediately after the disaster, *Titanic*'s sister ship, the *Olympic*, was equipped with longitudinal bulkheads and an inner hull, increasing construction cost by a quarter of the original. These 'extravagances' and 'impossible costs' were suddenly affordable, after all. Doubts were also raised on the quality of the relatively cheap steel employed in the construction of the *Titanic*'s hull.

- The presence of lifeboats. Again, space on the upper decks was a scarce resource and lifeboats were far from the most profitable way of using it. Thus, the *Titanic*'s lifeboats could accommodate only 1,178 at most *vis-à-vis* the ship's potential population of 3,500 between passengers and crew. It did not help that the major line operators dominated the British body setting lifeboat regulations.

Ship collisions with icebergs were by no means new. Over the previous 60 years, icebergs had sunk 12 large transatlantic liners, at a cost of over 3,000 deaths. Despite this, 'Full Speed Ahead' was the standard practice for sailing through ice in the early 1900s. This industry practice was yet again driven by competition rather than by safety, as crossing the Atlantic in record time was highly visible from a marketing point of view.

Other aspects of the *Titanic* fatal maiden voyage are disquieting and illustrative of the atmosphere of complacency aboard the ship. For instance:

- The lookout's binoculars had not been seen since Southampton. It is worth noting that often no more than one-ninth of an iceberg is visible, as most of it is underwater. This makes it difficult to see one, especially at night and without binoculars.

- The normal route would take the ship to 42°N, 47°W, right into the middle of a vast field of ice signalled by other ships. This was located between 46°N and 31°3'N and stretched from 46°18'W to 50°40'W. 1912 would become the year in which more ice would be reported than at any time during the previous *50 years*.

- The presence of large icebergs in the ship's course was confirmed by as many as six ice warnings from other ships in the area. Unfortunately, the wireless operators were too busy sending personal messages for the passengers, and most warnings never reached the captain. When they did, as in the message from steamer *Caronia* at 1:42pm, they mostly remained in Captain E.J. Smith's pocket and did not result in any action. The last warning, from SS *Mesaba* at 9:40pm, reported ice in latitude 42°N to 41°25'N, longitude 49°W to 50°30'W. If these locations given had been charted, it would have immediately become apparent that the *Titanic* was heading straight for a vast belt of ice, stretching some 78 miles across her path. However, despite the deadly danger ahead in the dark night, only one person was manning the radio room.

Finally, at 11:40pm, one large dark shape was seen by lookouts on the bridge right ahead of the *Titanic*. Unfortunately, the ship was only 500 feet (150 metres) from the iceberg. It would have required 850 feet (250 metres) to stop. William Murdoch, the officer on the bridge, performed a quick manoeuvre that avoided head-on collision. It could not, however, avoid impact with the ship's side, which incurred a series of small holes. The iceberg scraped along the first 300 feet of the hull. Thereafter, another rudder manoeuvre had the iceberg clear the ship's stern. As Captain Smith and Thomas Andrews, the ship's designer, rushed below to inspect the damage, they saw mailbags floating in four feet of water. The *Titanic* was doomed and both of them gave the ship no more than two hours. Neither survived.

Confusion and poor ship abandonment procedures amongst the passengers compounded the disaster further, with many of the lifeboats leaving half empty. Indeed, only 705 survived. The *Titanic* finally sank at 2:20am the next morning.

PART III

Going forward

Only movement brings victory.
*(Colonel-General Heinz W. Guderian, father of modern
armoured warfare, German WWII general staff)*

CHAPTER 12

So, what now?

by Gilles Dufour

There is never a favourable wind for those who do not know where to go.

(*Socrates*)

All the charts and breadth indicators and technical palaver are statisticians' attempts to describe an emotional state. The first thing you have to know is yourself.
(*Edward C. Johnson, II, Founder of Fidelity Mutual Funds*)

7±2:

- Biases are not only 'bad'
- There is more hope for you than conventional behavioural finance says
- What kind of inner exploration should you consider?
- The five-minute pre-take-off checklist
- Could the re-programming rewrite history in some past mishaps?
- Your relationship with money
- A set of tools to work with

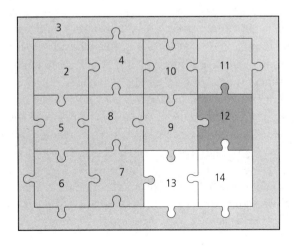

Abstract

The journey into the frames of risk began with you and cannot find a more worthy ending than yourself. OK, you have read all these chapters about biases. Behavioural finance says that you cannot do much about them. Is that the case? Let me argue that:

- First, you can be aware of them. You cannot deal with something that you cannot see! That's the ABC of Risk Management: the worst risk is the one that lurks in the deep.

- Secondly, there is scope to re-programme yourself and grow out of these biases. Your thoughts, language and behaviours are all areas of potential improvement. Various techniques and resources, such as coaching, are available to achieve that.

- While we are all conditioned to think that biases are necessarily 'bad', every behaviour performs some useful function for us. The trick is just recognizing which situations may be most suitable for certain biases and behaviours. Risk aversion, for instance, may become excessive and lead to underperformance if left without any control. With moderation, however, it helps preserve your precious trading risk capital for the next trade or project.

12.1 More on your beliefs and where they can lead you

Our decision processes cannot be free of bias. Everybody can find an instance in their own past in which he or she fell prey to overconfidence. Any trader or decision-maker had a situation of holding losses for too long and cutting profits too early. The key point here is mostly to understand the benefit of better and more thorough self-knowledge.

First of all, one should recognize how wonderful it is to commence the journey into a better understanding of one's needs, desires and, simply put, what is truly fulfilling. When you don't feel the thrill of the journey any more and can get any information about any part of the world in just a couple of clicks, the adventure of finding out more about yourself every day remains one of the most exciting ones. You will discover many new things about yourself while feeling quite safe from a physical standpoint. You will discover that you are much better than you think, but less than what you hope you are. At the same time, you will wonder what benefit you will get business wise. Being aware of certain biases that you have will help you in your decision process. It will help you understand why you always tend to repeat the same kind of error and, to a certain extent, prevent you from falling into it next time.

According to our experience, we can pinpoint certain elements that are very useful in better understanding yourself. The objective of this book is not to give you a guide about the human psyche but, rather, some tools that will be useful for you.

Just a little definition about beliefs or convictions: a belief is a generalization created in response to one or more significant experiences. Beliefs are the basic element of our identity consciousness. They are usually unconscious and determine whether we will succeed or fail in what we do. Usually we do not challenge our beliefs, as they feed and maintain the sense that we give to our lives. An example of beliefs is that we can make money only in a bull market, or in a volatile market. They can be, at the same time, the source of opening-up, or a limitation. The statement that 'very rich and successful people are not honest' can be a very limiting belief, especially if it remains in the unconscious. A belief does not have to be verbalized and conscious to operate: it is there and it can destroy your path to success – especially if your personal goal is to become rich and successful!

Another example of beliefs is that, according to medical doctors in the 1970s, it was impossible to climb Mount Everest without an oxygen tank, especially when one entered the 'death zone' above 7,600 m (about 25,300 ft). Two professional climbers, Reinhold Messner and Peter Habeler, were not aware of this limit in spite of their experience. Despite using no extra oxygen, they climbed Mount Everest (8,848 m) on 8 May 1978. At the time of writing, 66 other climbers have got to the summit without extra oxygen; they believed it was possible. This speaks volumes about the power of beliefs.

Let's go back to finance and some of its lessons. Consider the LTCM fiasco illustrated earlier in this book. Let's have a look at the set of beliefs held by three sets of actors in that instance:

- *Investors and counterparts* Who can manage money better than LTCM's dream team of star traders and academics? They cannot fail. And guess what happened? Markets are never a one-way street. The overconfidence of the LTCM managers got in the way of trading execution, always the most important contributor to performance.

- *LTCM academics and the traders influenced by them*
  - Markets have to revert to their fundamental values, best embodied by the mean. Mean reversion is still the most powerful force in finance. Noise trading and human irrationality do not matter and are welcome sources of potential arbitrage profits. In short, models, rather than human feelings, rule markets. And what happened and why: ... that's true but with the big EVENTUALLY word in front of it. You can profit from mean reversion only to the extent that your trading risk capital allows you to remain in the trade. Aggressive assumptions coupled with leverage tend to shorten that staying power. Eventually, as your equity drops relative to your risk inventory, you fall prey to gambler's fallacy and eventually run into gambler's ruin. Only with the FED-sponsored consortium of major dealers was LTCM able to gain some precious time to unwind its enormous positions.

  - Consistent with basic corporate finance assumptions, there are no limits to the availability of trading risk capital to correct mis-pricings. Unfortunately, margin calls may not be featured in finance books but they sure are a major factor in the real world!

  - Trading decision-makers behave independently of each other, and game theory has not enjoyed much attention from basic finance books. Nevertheless, LTCM was so large relative to the market as a whole that the other major players traded based on their expectations of LTCM's behaviour, accelerating its debacle.

- *Central banks and major market counterparts* No player is individually able to affect the stability of the world's global financial system. Alan Greenspan himself recognized that LTCM brought the world's financial system to the brink of collapse. Collateralizations and margins work fine in managing counterparty risk, except for the fact that every major dealer had them in place with LTCM!

Every day, we are living with beliefs that we are not aware of, and many of them are just creating our own reality. We tend to find justification with our brain for our beliefs in every new experience.

Happily, there are tools that allow us to uncover them, and to reassess them if we want to update or enhance our model of reality. But beliefs are by no means easy to change, as they often have their roots in one's family background and past experiences. And beliefs are at the heart of one of the recurrent themes in this book, framing and context dependence.

12.2 Your own mental computer – basics

The complexity of that incredibly powerful computer of yours which is called a brain is daunting at least. There is no way that this – or any – book could explain its workings without some major simplification and categorization. While individual differences are obviously enormous, there are five sets of standard elements that deserve a particular look in the life of a trader, or anybody who faces uncertainty in his own decisions. While everybody has to face these decisions, how we make them and how we manage their consequences is what makes the difference in performance and, in more general terms, between an exciting and a mediocre life:

- *Your decision-making process.* Behavioural psychology can help us to understand our decision process. In short, we can say that we are either risk orientated or process orientated in a scale that goes from very to little or right in the middle. If you are right in the middle, that does explain why you are slow to take decisions and why it can be a painful process. By knowing where you stand, you will better understand your biases and, for example, be able to take more into account process if you are risk driven and risk if you are process driven. We would emphasize that it is of key importance as a team leader to evaluate each member in that respect so that your total level of risk is acceptable.

- *Stress levels.* They can be quite high in the marketplace but are also key to your success. Everybody needs a certain level of stress or positive stress but the amount is different for everybody. One of the key errors of modern managers is that they put the amount of pressure which is 'right for them' on everybody's shoulders, whereas they should differentiate between the needs of each person. Stress can come from many different areas, and another source of stress comes when you try to adapt too much to what people are expecting from you, especially your boss. Quite often, people try to over-adapt themselves to what they perceive will be their key to success. Stress is often unconscious, and seldom discussed openly. One of the most important sources of stress comes from the inability to challenge authoruty as the main decision-making criterion.

■ *The ability to clean one's memory*. What was shown earlier about the power of one's beliefs demonstrates that one's past experience often resulted in beliefs that are inherited from a former job, childhood or even family experience. When a person wants to grow, his memory of past experience will often limit his climbing ability to move higher. This person has to be aware of such subconscious legacies and to erase them from memory to grow. This is similar to re-programming a computer with newer software. This, of course, is by no means as easy and linear but can help tremendously in certain circumstances. The ability to clean one's memory is both a psychological and a physical process.

■ *Recovery from losses*. This is simply one's skill in maintaining sufficient emotional detachment to avoid taking it too personally. Chapter 5 showed how traders who have incurred a loss will have difficulties entering a new position. Self-attribution bias will also lead them to blame others for losses and to congratulate themselves for gains. Personal development can help you tremendously in understanding in which way your decision process is wired to over- or underestimate certain flows or pieces of information. You will be in a better position to learn from your previous mistakes, and experience a little beep-beep in your ears when a certain scenario unfolds during the next decision.

■ *Alignment*. Feeling aligned with yourself means, for example, that your intuition (left brain) and your rational side (right brain) are well connected. Roger Sperry, a Nobel Prize winner, and Ned Herrmann studied the relationship in the brain between the right and the left hemispheres. They found that the left brain tends to function by processing information in an analytical, rational, logical, sequential way, while the right half of the brain tends to function by recognizing relationships, integrating and synthesizing information, and arriving at intuitive insights. In other words, the left side of your brain deals with a problem or a situation by collecting data, making analyses and using a rational thinking process to reach a logical conclusion. The right side of your brain approaches the same situation by making intuitive leaps to answers based on insights and perceptions. Of course everybody uses both parts of their brain, but Herrmann showed that people tend to be either left brain or right brain orientated when taking decisions. What is important in taking a trading decision, for example, is that you feel ok with both parts of your decision. You have to know that the left brain is very smart especially among well-educated traders and tends to overcome the intuitive self. Western education, and especially the European model, tends to favour dramatically the left brain. If one looks back at history, the last 300 years have created a strong disequilibrium in favour of the rational approach. Trading and risk decisions, however, are not so rational. Rather, they should be viewed as intuitions to be validated using one's analytical skills. And strong performers need both!

12.3 Moving forward

12.3.1 How to know yourself better and be more objective

Now that you are convinced that your career will benefit from knowing yourself better, you will probably ask yourself 'Well, how can I achieve this?' Should I read books, talk to my wife, husband, parents or friends, attend some special workshops, do it on my own? The answer is pretty straightforward: everything will help but, at some point, getting some help from a professional coach will be key to your success! Indeed, let me emphasize that knowing yourself on your own is an impossible task as you are, at the same time, your best friend and your worst enemy! As individuals, we tend to be either too complacent or too hard on ourselves and have very little objectivity.

Also, when you look at sport or movie stars, they all have their own 'mental' coach. This is somebody who helps them to feel better about their success, somebody who believes in them and knows them very well. They feel this person will give them a key to their development and show them how to deal with their success without falling into overconfidence. And who can help them achieve their own personal Everest! A couple of important things to know about coaches: they are there to help you accept your own reality, to help you define your goals or your 'realistic dreams', and then help you find the right path to get there. They then guide you along the process. You have to know the key assumptions about coaching:

- a person has all the resources in himself to do what he needs to do;

- a person knows everything he needs to know;

- you do not need to dig into the past to grow, but you have to accept where you are, what your present reality is;

- a coach will not give you advice, he is not a consultant, he will guide you along your path.

Finding the right coach is not an easy process, but this search will help you clarify your needs and objectives.

Tests provide another important set of tools: they give objective feedback as they are often statistics-driven. They can give you valuable feedback about your behavioural traits. Any results should be evaluated by a professional coach or a psychologist, as they are a tool to better understand yourself and an effective way to enter a deep discussion about yourself. Under no circumstances should they be viewed as an exact image of who you are. Rather, they tend to describe a set of your attributes and how you use the set of tools that everyone has at their disposal. These include:

- the way you answer to stimuli;

- your preferred way of communicating with others;

- your decision process;

- your energy level;
- your emotional intelligence;
- the amount of pressure you are comfortable dealing with;
- your inclination to teamwork;
- your values.

They describe you from a particular angle, which usually differs from the approach that you adopt when you think about yourself. For example, tests can help you understand your adapted behaviour, which we adapt to what we think are our boss's or colleagues' expectations of us. The natural one is the one when there are no consequences for us and where we feel we are ourselves. This is not the only instance in which our normal behaviour reasserts itself over our adapted one: extremely stressful situations provide another example. The ability to connect our two behaviours is of key importance, especially if you are a manager: your team members will always figure out a manager's true personality by seeing through his double language and double personality. That applies to both types of managers, the kind ones and the stressed-out ones!

Of course reading books, including this one, will help you. Let me emphasize, however, that self-knowledge is *not* a mental process. Indeed a lot of people know themselves quite well but they keep making the same mistakes again and again. So, the ability to change and enter a development path is more important than remaining unchanged but able to explain after the event why you failed or did not succeed in it. The path to transform you and grow is more a behavioural process that has to deal far more with your heart and body than with your mind: it is far better to grow and succeed without understanding the process, than to understand why you failed. Psychologically we are not predisposed to learn much from our mistakes. To change, we have to reprogramme our cells, our eprom, the very basic software of our right brain.

Workshops are also very effective in better understanding your team and the way you interact with others. It is a good way to experiment with different behaviour in a no-risk environment, and to start to reprogramme your behaviour. They are highly effective, as they will help you to change your reaction, to disconnect from your past and to be able to respond more accurately to your needs in the current context.

12.3.2 A couple of worthwhile tools

Let's be more practical: close your door, for just fifteen to twenty minutes, and take a pen and a sheet of paper.

We will study what we call the 'connection trees'. Write down all the professional relationships you have, including the one you feel is important in your bonus process. What is important in this exercise is the real organization chart, not the theoretical one. Please, write it down with different types of lines in between qualifying the quality of the relationship, for example:

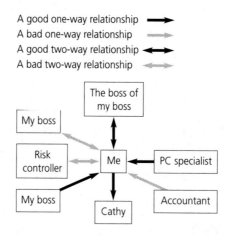

FIGURE 12.1 ▪ You, the surrounding relationships and their energy

You can qualify by good or bad what you think about the relationship. You can deem it good enough or inadequate based on what you think of the decision process, not according to how comfortable you feel with the person. After you have finished the graph, take a look at it, and write down where you think you should put more energy. Write down the precise action that you want to take in your communication with, for example, your boss, to enhance your relationship. This exercise will not take much of your time, and it can really increase your professional efficiency.

Another good practical tool is to work on what we would call the unofficial rules. They are the rules that are not communicated, but in fact are valid for the top managers. You understand them through the promotion process, the bonus and the hiring process.

Let's take the example of the Barings debacle. What was Barings' unofficial programme according to Nick Leeson in 1992?

▪ Do not ask questions that could make you or your boss look silly in front of other people.

▪ Think big to earn enough to pay bonuses to everybody in the firm.

▪ An earlier success in a position gives an individual the right to keep this position, even if there is a major obvious conflict of interest (for example, being responsible for back-office and trading at the same time).

▪ Success in a position (back-office in this case) should make you a successful head of a trading/brokers team.

Nick Leeson also had a strong belief of his own: a series of reverses (which, most likely, must have been ascribed to 'bad luck' rather than poor trading capabilities) did not prevent him from thinking he would make money in the future. Please note that his belief is reinforced by the fourth rule. This chapter will show how that kind of culture can be changed, and how you should be able to avoid such a huge debacle.

Answering those questions will not directly improve your P&L but it can improve the level of risk you are allowed to take, or the next position you would like to get, and consequently enhance your bonus, your career and your comfort in the medium term. This does not apply to traders only but, rather, to anybody facing uncertainty. A senior manager, regardless of whether or not he was promoted from trading, will often face investment decisions to expand or cut activities in a market, business line, product or location. While these decisions are unlikely to be marked to market daily in the same fashion as trading positions, their consequences can be at least as serious and costly if mistakes occur.

Understanding your relationship with money is another major challenge. You may not see what you trade as direct money, as the large amounts you deal with may affect your perception. If you want an example of this dissociation, consider the anecdotal evidence of professional derivative traders who manage huge portfolios for their banks and then leave their private savings in safe money-market deposits when the time comes to manage their own wealth. In short, your unconscious knows that you are dealing with money. In coaching experiences, they understand how family honesty can be a key limitation to your financial success.

Let's start with an exercise using six direct family members: your father, your mother and your grandparents from both sides. If you do not know one of them, imagine what they would do from what other members of your family have said about them. What is true is not important. The key in your beliefs and in your reality is what you have heard about them. So, take a pen and ask yourself three questions:

- What did your parents want as a job for you? What is their relationship with money, their beliefs?
- What are you trying to copy and to repeat in your family history?
- What are you trying to fix and to repair in it?

As an example, during one coaching session, there was a customer who was quite successful, but who was wondering why he was not more successful. This sounds like a familiar question, doesn't it? The coaching began with some exploratory work into his family background, in particular, his parents and grandparents. This provided major insights on the roots of some of his key beliefs and answered some of those questions:

- His mother believed that making money gives you independence and freedom, but too much money kills the family and people's integrity.
- His father believed that it is not worth working too much, because you have to keep some time for yourself and for fun.

The coaching then focused on improving the understanding of those unconscious beliefs that he accepted. On the one hand, he understood that working in the financial market was perfect unconscious honesty towards both parents. On the other hand, his limitation was that he did not want to be too successful financially and that he also did not want to work hard enough to make it to the next level. After some more coaching, he found out that he wanted to stay honest to his family values and accepted his position. As a result he had a better quality of life and released a lot of stress because he felt aligned between his own and his family's values. He did not want to change.

As money is a source of energy, it is key to let this energy keep flowing around you, do not block it. Also it needs to circulate between your past and your future. You all know that you have to give to the market from time to time to make money. Be generous and the universe will give it back to you. Accepting losses in the right amount is one of the major challenges confronting junior traders and risk-averse dealers: losses are a part of trading life.

Your reference points are also worth investigating. Another coaching session with a derivatives trader concentrated on his reference points. He found that he had grown up with a lot of animosity towards his parents, especially his father. He pointed out that he was trading most of the time against the trend or by following 'bad' traders. As an old trading adage states: the trend is usually your friend in the market. The trader was able to make money this way, but not as much as he thought he should. He felt that it was not any 'Peter's Principle' effect.[100] It finally dawned on him that what had worked for him as a child was now a limitation. So he changed this reference point to see other's people success. He became quite successful in his new assignment, at least much more than he had previously achieved. He was able for the first time to see and 'copy' successful colleagues.

12.3.3 How to communicate and take into account people's behaviour

How do you communicate verbally with your boss and your colleagues and members of your team? First, analyse how you communicate, and watch out if you think this way: if I was him (her), I would have liked or not liked to.... This can be very negative, as people are never like you. So should you concentrate more on what the person's needs are, regardless of his position? If you need to communicate more efficiently, watch carefully what kind of words he is using, what kind of metaphor he likes, what makes him alive, how you can connect with him. With this type of communication, you learn to express your feelings without attacking. This helps to minimize the likelihood of facing defensive reactions in others. This skill will help you make clear requests and will help you to receive critical and hostile messages without taking them personally, giving in, or losing self-esteem.

A couple of quick steps to enhance your communication:

- First, create your alliance with other people by telling them what they have achieved or succeeded in doing. Use their words, not your own. It has to make sense to them, not to you!

- Second, you can now start to be more critical, to express clear requests about specific actions and facts. Never blame the individual in front of you. You can of course blame his actions, what he has or has not done. It is vital that the person does not feel that they are

---

[100] By Peter's Principle, one means that everybody reaches their own level of incompetence.

being judged for who they are, for their identity. Of course, the more they feel safe with their individuality, the more they will accept criticism which diminishes the probability of a defensive reaction.

- If you can, add some specifics about what a good job they could have done: give them some positive objectives.

- Now you can finish by how you feel you can all work together to progress and get things done your way.

You should follow all those steps, even with someone you know very well and you see every day – the alliance has to be created each time you need to have a strong argument.

Another key to more efficient communication is to align your verbal and non-verbal communication. And that's a painful process. First, you need a mirror person or a tape recorder, or a video-camera. Then listen to yourself, look at yourself, especially when you are answering a difficult question. You will be amazed how much information you are giving away, both verbal and non-verbal. The more you align with yourself, the more efficient you will become!

12.3.4 You cannot change yourself, it is a matter of life

You might be afraid that coaching will change you. The answer is that you – and only you – can decide. Let me repeat it. You are the only one who can decide. To change, only some kind of personal development – such as coaching therapy – and life accidents can make you change, and only to a very limited extent. You will learn more about yourself, and work on accepting yourself rather than changing who you are. The easiest thing you can change is your behaviour in certain contexts. It will not change what you feel or what you think. However, by working on your personal development, it will help you adapt your own self to the present context in a way that respects your values, your own identity. Don't spend too much time trying to adapt to everybody's needs. It does not work in the long run and is very stressful and time consuming.

After reading this, a lot of people may see this as pure manipulation and feel the disgust that is often associated with it. Fear of manipulating oneself or others is indeed perfectly understandable. The first answer is affirmative, it is about manipulation, we are always manipulating or, in more politically correct terms, influencing each other. That's a fact of life, plain and simple. Just by the way we ask, our posture and body language, our convictions, and the conscious and subconscious responses that we send to the outside world, we keep on manipulating each other. But arguing about whether manipulation is moral or not misses the point and is yet another demonstration of the yes/no binary bias described earlier in this book. Becoming aware of that kind of manipulation, and understanding our bias, is what really matters. Are we into seductive manipulation, or into battle of wills? We all tend to have preferred scenarios that we use too often in an inappropriate environment. So, by using communication techniques already used by the advertising business, we will less unconsciously be manipulated. This will enable you to put yourself more often into the adult-to-adult relationship that should supposedly be the norm in the professional world!

12.3.5 But ... you can accept your growth or not!

The training process can be painful. But often, in psychology, the most painful step is the first one: when you discover something new in the past, of which you have never been aware. You find out that what you labelled as a 'rational process' is just a scenario from your childhood that you keep on repeating. It can be very painful, especially if the answer from the environment is negative to your stimulation. You feel bizarre, as if you have been driving a car at high speed in the highway without knowing the rules of the road. It was not so safe, but you made it through. The second step is usually easier, you just have to work and learn the way you learned it at school. But it is not finished yet, you now have to forget, to unlearn what you have just learned. Then it will become automatic, you will be able to integrate your change within you, without thinking about it. It is becoming your new scenario.

12.3.6 Opposition to change

It is normal for an individual or a team to resist change: at the beginning, it is the best way to keep your energy. For example, as you read these pages, your first reaction will probably be a refusal to understand. The sequence that most experience is articulated as follows:

- Every change is linked to a feeling of loss and a feeling of gain.

- You will mentally resist the change, with inertia, with argumentation, with revolt or with sabotage.

- You will feel the loss: decompensation, that's the starting point of the positive change. By decompensation, one means the instance in which active resistance against change has ceased but the latter has not been accepted yet.

- Then comes resignation, you do not put any more of your energy against the change so you start to accept it.

- By the end, you will integrate the change and feel satisfied; you feel the benefit of the change.

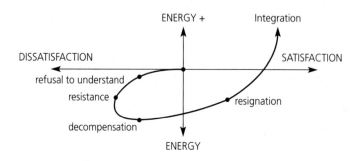

FIGURE 12.2 ▪ The five phases of change

You cannot avoid the first negative step. Use this to help you – and everyone else who is involved – to accept it. Just keep on communicating about the benefits and the usefulness of the change. Do not resist change by entering into opposition. Ensure that you let everyone involved know that you understand their pain, their negative feeling about the change. But keep communicating in a positive way about your objective, until most of those involved have left the resignation area, and entered the integration stage. Remember, everybody has his own rhythm, and some people may be more vulnerable than others.

12.3.7 Your vision and mission statement

Today most companies are writing their mission statement, especially at the creation process. But most individuals do not have any clue about their mission, their vision and how their career will fulfill their goal. To feel aligned, and be able to survive the difficult experiences that the universe sends you sometimes, the clearer you are about your own vision of your role, the better you will feel. Your vision can feature anything from feeding your family, helping others or embarking on a major project or endeavour. A link with other people and the purpose of helping others is its most critical ingredient. It can be religious or not, spiritual or material, but it has to be a positive, motivating, challenging and much more relevant role than just a mere material one.

12.3.8 The five-minute pre-flight checklist

So, let us assume that, after reading this chapter, you have developed a better awareness of all your biases. But before a big trade, or a big investment decision, what key questions should be asked? For just a few seconds, try to forget the trading room or the world of finance and picture yourself as the flight captain of a large airplane that is about to commence a long-haul intercontinental flight. You are in the cockpit and have this dazzling array of instruments, indicators and lights staring at you. You have only a few minutes to ask a small set of very important questions on your complex machine, such as fuel level, landing gear hydraulics, electrical power and so on. You want to ask as few as possible – if any – of those questions after take-off.

Many of your 'big' decisions will bear some resemblance to the complexity that confronts the flight captain. Your career, your firm and your colleagues are no less important than the large airplane of the example above. Let's have a look at some of these questions:

1. In what aspect should I favour this decision (circle no more than two of the following statements):

It makes my business 'big'	It makes me feel 'big', more important.	Our competitors are doing the same by venturing into this business/product/trade
It will make my business become more profitable	Because I/the firm have to do something, we cannot be seen as sitting still.	Because my short-term compensation may benefit, although I do not believe in this decision over the long term.
I am afraid of not taking a decision	I need to feel aligned with my own environment, feelings and values.	Other (please indicate) ....

2. In my listening process, what people and information sources did I listen to most attentively, and why?

3. In my decision process, what contrary evidence did I gather from people or other sources? Out of ten information elements that are used in the decision, how many do not support it?

4. In the past, did I enter a decision in the same way? What was the outcome?

5. What have my moods and energy levels been like lately? High, low or so-so? What is my bias right now?

6. If I knew nothing about it, as a layman, what would my intuition say? (Tip: Ask your taxi driver about the Stock Exchange!)

7. Finally, what will happen if I take my decision?

   – What will be the next step to confirm or deny it (continue or cut losses)?

   – What is the very worst case scenario that could materialize?

   – Is there a plan B/escape hatch that one can resort to in flight if my decision is wrong?

Answering these questions provides no guarantee against failure. Failure is a fact of life and has to be accepted as such. What this checklist does, however, is force you to crystallize your thoughts. That way, if things go wrong, you may have already an exit plan in place or, at least, know and document in advance the risk that you are taking and why. That will provide you with some immunization against regret. Regret, and especially the fear of it, often results in decision paralysis or can even drive disastrously wrong decisions in the future. If things turn sour, you will not be able to avoid it completely but can at least box it.

12.4 Re-programming the background of a risk problem

From a behavioural standpoint, what could the Barings management have done to avoid such a debacle? As a lot of study has already been done on the subject, we will concentrate on the personal, behavioural leadership and cultural issues. As the risk of hindsight bias in some of these remarks is real, this is just an example of a possible alternative course of action that could have been pursued with more conscious and thoughtful change management.

First, the top-down approach works best from a coach's point of view, as it provides immediate feedback on some of the personality tendencies and biases at the top. As the whole organization acts as a magnifying glass for these, a lot of intelligence can be collected fairly quickly. It is advisable to start a coaching/change consulting approach from the chairman or the general manager. If not possible, start with the head of a team.

Then one would suggest a survey[101] of the practice, malpractice of the management process with some interviews about the difficulties, the communication skills and the culture of the team. What belongs to the team? What belongs to the culture of the company? Quite often, when a company changes business model (in the specific case, from a classic investment bank to a capital markets boutique), the company has to reinvent itself and change all the best practices. This is true first and foremost for its management and leadership. So, a change in consulting assignment would be necessary to reveal the values of Barings in capital markets, more specifically in the arbitrage teams. With the help of internal communication managers, the consultants would have designed some specific seminar with the top management. This would have helped Barings create an environment where they:

- could creatively think together about the specifics of Barings and how it could create value in the market versus their competitors;
- could ask questions – even silly ones – without feeling stupid;
- could learn how to do business in a new environment without feeling in danger;
- could be granted the right and some tightly managed resources to fail, at least once, without being at risk. That is the price of learning!
- could probably get some training on how to better communicate in a difficult environment;
- would learn how to deal with conflict, and not avoid it;
- would learn how to express and receive feedback;
- would learn how to improve their listening skills, verbal and non-verbal;
- would learn to say no, even in a difficult environment.

Putting good practices under the spotlight is another strong source of information in a learning company. This aims to duplicate them in other businesses, desks, or locations. Barings' management could have asked someone, say another senior trader, to work with Nick's team and have him explain how he had found such a profitable niche. To report such strong results from a simple brokerage operation, he must evidently have been doing something of which competitors were not aware. Listening to Nick's answer would have been fun!

---

[101] Note the choice of the word instead of the more commonly used 'audit'. What matters here are not the poor processes in and of their own. There are plenty of auditors and consultants who can help you locate and fix them. Rather, what is important is what those flaws reveal about the personalities, assumptions and biases involved. The processes and poor results are *effects*. The focus here is on the *causes*.

In more general terms, change consultants would have helped the management to ask themselves some very basic questions. During phases of major change, these are often forgotten, especially if the change appears to be successful. Based on the previous paragraph, Barings' top managers could have asked themselves:

- Are we truly smarter than the competition?

- Do we have some personal interest in not enquiring/understanding about a specific situation?

- Did we listen enough to negative feedback given by controllers and treasurer, and are they asking the right questions?

- What is my intuition telling me about this free lunch?

- What decision should I take to create a more positive environment for this successful trading team?

- What decision should I take to duplicate this success to other parts of the firm?

The strategy of a change consultant or a coach is to focus on the process of leadership, and help people adapt their management style based on feedbacks, rather than on their wills or dreams!

In short, those issues would have put Barings' management into a learning path. The mission would have been conducted with a classic approach of a mix of interviews, seminar, team-building exercises and executive coaching.

Individual coaching is key in the process to help raise personal issues for those executives who are most at risk or feel the most concerned with the cultural and managerial change. Individual coaching is a safe place for an executive to understand his own behaviour and to help him adapt it to the context of his work environment in an efficient way. Also for top executives, learning fast and efficiently how to manage in a new business environment can be key to their success, especially if they are often afraid to do so in case they lose their image or status.

Team and individual coaching is an efficient, tailor-made answer to help people grow!

CHAPTER 13

The voice of wisdom: or is it?

Nuts!
(Brigadier General Anthony McAuliffe, Divisional Artillery Commander of the encircled US 101st Airborne Division: response to a formal surrender proposal by the German Panzer divisions, Batsogne, Belgium, 22 December 1944.)

7±2:

- Denial dies hard

- An evolutionary, rather than revolutionary, book

- Standard quantitative risk management is fine, this just complements it

- Nothing against salespeople, just setting the record straight

- The real risk is in the decision-maker's head, rather than in the results

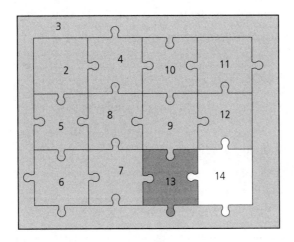

13.1 Word to the opposition

At this point, you might be justified in expressing some discomfort at seeing all the biases and their consequences and no hope or reference point. Some readers may also feel that their discussion has been quite one-sided and that 'rational' modern finance arguments or real-world considerations have not been taken into account .

I expect many people to disagree with me about remarks made in this book. After all, the tone is deliberately controversial. Taking a strong stance in favour of more behaviourally conscious risk management is more important than cookie-cutter politically correct statements. If making some waves and raising some eyebrows is a prerequisite of better risk management, so be it.

It is entirely understandable for others, leaving personal or corporate agendas aside, to oppose this book's call for embracing uncertainty and become truly responsible for the workings of one's brain. It is far easier to resist it and pretend you can control it. After all, achieving and maintaining awareness means quite a lot of work and involves substantial uncertainty, a far cry from lulling oneself into the comfortable belief that the standard quantitative risk management is adequate.

Upgrading risk management to a higher level, whereby the behavioural aspects are complemented and served by the standard quantitative toolkit rather than enslaved by it, is likely to encounter two sources of resistance:

- Passive resistance is best embodied by an attitude of denial and complacent dismissal of the importance of behavioural issues for decision-making.

- Active opposition takes the form of clinging to specific accepted principles, beliefs and ways of doing business that are standard in today's marketplace.

This brief account deals with each category in turn.

13.2 Denial = comfort

Some of the following arguments and rationalizations should sound familiar:

- 'Oh, that is just another trick, people will learn this one too and any of these inefficiencies and problems will disappear.'

- 'We have built an Artificial Intelligence system (or, equivalently, an e-trading platform), so that is immune from these biases.'

- 'We don't have time for this academic rubbish. We are here just to make money.'

Unfortunately, the nonchalance and dismissive attitude that underlie these statements are the very proof of biases and overconfidence:

- Biases are already consistent and difficult to eradicate with individuals, let alone with groups. People consistently underestimate their own biases and overstate their own objectivity and ability to learn from their own mistakes. There is a major difference between having a sense of these psychological problems and fixing them. Welcome to the knowledge-equal-solution fallacy, one of the biases described in Chapter 5.

- Systems, regardless of how intelligent they are, reflect the biases, assumptions and shortcuts of the people and groups who build them.

- Recent risk management disasters show how the neglect of these issues includes very tangible and monetary facets. Ignoring long-term consequences of short-term-orientated decisions may be a perfectly rational strategy from an individual point of view as long as one realizes that he or she is living on borrowed time. These biases – as clearly demonstrated by a substantial body of empirical evidence presented in this book – exist in reality, rather than just in academic theory. Recent regulatory practice and calls for better corporate governance emphasize individual responsibility and introduce heavier fines, career consequences and – possibly – criminal penalties. Anglo-Saxon policymakers and regulators have been at the forefront of this trend. The US Sarbanes-Oxley Act (2002) and UK FSA rules (SYSC[102]) concerning risk management and related systems pursue exactly this avenue.

13.3 Active resistance

Increasing specialization of roles amongst financial professionals is one, but by no means the only, result of heightened competition and industrialization in global capital markets. An important side effect is also the increasing focus that people display on the peculiar frames of risk that make them successful in their chosen field of specialization. The author is not exempt from this, as his own view of the importance of risk management is a by-product of his own work experience in trading and risk management. In very general terms, compare the following perspectives:

- A salesperson will put a premium on the ability to read between the lines of a client's mind and interpersonal skills. Attention to detail and the 'guts' to take risks are desirable but not necessarily the most important features necessary to succeed.

- At the opposite extreme of the spectrum, a spot FX trader has to decide which risks he wants to take very quickly. Even if his social skills are not particularly refined, he may still be able to earn profits, recognition and reward.

- A 'quant' is not automatically associated with developed social skills. However, his painstaking attention to detail is a critical feature of his profession. Omitting a tiny detail in his models or the computer code to run them can have disastrous consequences.

These descriptions may strike readers as somewhat abstract. Readers will forgive me for attributing some fantasy names to these characters, so that we can give them some life and make them look more real. Hopefully, in the case of readers who work in investment banks and trading rooms, this will play to their availability bias and help them recognize the attitude of some of their colleagues. Incidentally, people's language often provides a great lead into their biases and the auditory, visual and kinaesthetic mental programmes that they use in their decision-making.

---

[102] Under the UK Financial Services Authority (FSA), SYSC stands for SYStems and Controls, as part of the functions that fall under the responsibilities of Senior Management at a regulated firm.

In presenting some of the charges that will likely be moved against this book, scoring points is not my objective. My interest is only to provide you with different viewpoints from which you can choose. As F. Scott Fitzgerald neatly put it:

The test of first-rate intelligence is the ability to hold two opposed ideas in the mind at the same time, and still retain the ability to function.

13.3.1 Senior head of trading

Q: As is standard in risk management, this book is all about losses. Are you offering anything useful to actually *make* money?

A: As Chapter 8 reminds us, risk management awareness is one of the major contributors to strong trading performance. In addition, Chapter 5 has shown empirical evidence that losses provide between *two-and-a-half* and *three times* as much pain as the pleasure of a gain of equal amount. This principle is embodied by veteran traders' recommendation to strive for a three-to-one reward–risk ratio when evaluating a prospective trade. Of course, it is always easier and more politically correct only to show the bright side. So, by reducing losses, you have more risk capital available to run longer and greater winning trades.

13.3.2 Professor Ratyo Nall, PhD in finance, head of risk management

Q: In your book, you have done a lot of sniping at rational decision-making and modern finance, let alone conventional economics. But can you really offer a better model?

A: This book is not about sniping or creating some 'new-model' fetishes. No one has the time or interest in academic debate if it cannot be translated into results and performance. Besides, if that charge applied, what should one say of the decade-long battles in academia? If their advice was sufficiently practical, people should be learning and, over time, risk disasters should dwindle. But do they? The long list of losses from the last 15–20 years in Chapter 10 does not provide a lot of comfort. At the same time, let me distance myself from those academics, consultants and IT salesmen who are all too ready to offer ready-made – when not cookie-cutter – solutions. This book is not about creating a new sacred totem to replace the other ones. Far more modestly, my position is articulated as follows:

- Becoming aware of an organization's psychological frames of risk – and your own – is the starting point. It can undo any trade, business or risk project.

- No one can undertake that self-discovery process on your behalf. As any honest psychiatrist will tell you, the responsibility rests squarely on your shoulders. The poor track record of conventional psychiatric treatments should be sufficient to show you the consequences of neglecting this basic principle. Beware charlatans who offer you any shortcuts. This book does not claim to offer a model because you are the only one who can be in charge of the exploration of yourself and your biases.

- Standard behavioural finance claims that biases are a negative trait and there is nothing that can be done about them. Let me beg to differ. This book offers you a ray of hope but no shortcuts. Qualifying biases as 'good' or 'bad' is yet another example of context-dependence. Indeed, there can be some useful aspects in your biases provided that you recognize them and use them in the right context.

13.3.3 Mr O'Risk, operational risk consultant

Q: Operational risk – rather than your vaguely defined approach – is the way to deal with people's biases. It is a widely accepted practice that is also endorsed by international regulators and is well integrated with high-quality data provided by audit and a variety of other established internal processes. People's behaviours are not consistent. Trying to measure them, let alone manage them, is a waste of time. You cannot seriously believe that your approach can beat years of research and practice in operational risk. And, by the way, cooperating with traders can seriously jeopardize risk management's independence from them.

A: Again, this approach is *complementary* rather than *adversarial* relative to the established risk management toolkit. More conscious management of operational risk was indeed necessary and a welcome innovation for financial services firms. The progress in measuring the effects of operational risk is undeniable. At the same time, the empirical evidence presented in this book shows that human biases are far more tenacious and pervasive than most are willing to acknowledge. The results of the experiments by Kahneman and Tversky and their application in everyday trading mistakes should be a stern reminder against dismissing people's supposed lack of consistency in their behaviours. You may not *like* the fact that human biases are difficult to measure and quantify. That's hardly an argument to dismiss them as not 'consistent'. This book presents only a tiny subset of the hundreds of empirical studies on how people deal with risk and uncertainty.

With respect to standard practice in quantifying operational risk, let me add that the overwhelming majority of data collected for operational risk purposes is mostly about the *effects* of people's decisions. This information is indeed 'consistent' according to the definition that is close to the heart of controllers, auditors and accountants. Far too little has been done to dig deeper into the real *causes* that underpin people's decision-making. This book shows how complacency and overconfidence are the common denominators behind risk problems. Risk professionals should keep that in mind before using accounting consistency as grounds to brush aside people's psychological setup as the ultimate cause of mishaps. With refinements in their methodology, the psychometric tools that this book introduces in risk management can become a step towards a deeper understanding of operational risk. If the more refined operational risk assessment tools that have been around for at least five years work so well, why do risk disasters keep happening? Operational risk is just another variety of losses that, as market or credit risk, has human risk in common. *That* is the ultimate risk.

As for independence, it is undoubtedly necessary but not sufficient. There are already plenty of functions in a bank – such as product control or internal audit – that exclusively serve the board and ensure independence. Those – rather than risk management – are the most suitable areas for production functions. There is a real risk of overloading risk management with a variety of production responsibilities at the expense of the focus on the decision-making process. The emphasis mix between the former and the latter is what distinguishes risk reporting from risk management. A risk manager should not be subservient and his ultimate loyalty should be towards protecting his institution's risk capital. Simply put, there will always be instances and people requiring more sticks than carrots. Having said that, however, what drives an organization forward is making money. Nothing can beat that as an incentive towards better behaviours. Understandably, that's the traders' ultimate interest, too. They are far more likely to listen to and cooperate with someone who can help them make more money than to another number-crunching bureaucrat. Aside from the duplication with the functions above, if control – and the lack of trust that it implies – is the main objective of independence, why keep untrustworthy traders in the organization in the first place? Being able to see what people are doing is a necessary prerequisite for a good risk manager. That is a long way from saying that a controller's mindset is a necessary condition for him to get his job done.

13.3.4 Mr Gutsy, senior bond trader

(keeping his shirt neck unbuttoned and both feet on the table)

Q: According to this book, there are many problems and very few – if any – easy answers. Our job here is trading, rather than engaging in your risk philosophy. You talk about bloated egos, but what do they have to do with performance? It does not follow. Whether or not we have bloated egos does not affect my trading or my performance. We need answers and fast ones! By the way, what will be my bonus after reading this book?

A: The self-discovery process described in the previous point is by no means easy or quick. It is a continuous exploration that requires time, patience and commitment. If there is one message that you should take away from this book, it is to loathe easy answers. A total quality culture and commitment cannot be achieved overnight. This applies regardless of whether the topic of discussion is physical goods or the functioning of your brain and decisions. At the same time, this is an area of enormous potential exactly because so few are pursuing it. Veteran traders know how one's psychological state matters for performance. As for your bonus, top traders excel not because they trade for money but, rather, because they love trading, execute well and, as an inevitable consequence, improve their odds of making money.

13.3.5 Dr No, head of risk methodology

Q: You spend a lot of time blasting widely accepted risk management practices and models. You show such scepticism in quantitative risk management that you seem orientated to eliminate it to make room for your hazily defined psychological and behavioural tools. What's wrong with quantitative risk management and why are you mounting such a crusade against it?

A: This book is evolutionary, rather than revolutionary. There has been impressive progress in risk management over the last quarter-century. The next challenge for organizations is to integrate their conventional quantitative risk management toolkit with a behavioural overlay.

That should address the traditional Achilles' heel of standard risk management processes. As these depend on people and are context-dependent, it is just not prudent to ignore the way in which people frame problems and attempt to solve them.

The usefulness of today's highly sophisticated information is subject to the psychological biases of its users. Having information does not automatically imply that users understand it and know what to make of it. Insisting on the quantitative side alone and neglecting the psychological side is a path with diminishing marginal returns. The solution does not lie in adding more complexity, computers and PhDs. For most risks, the current degree of complexity already outstrips the information processing ability of common mortals anyway. The answer has to lie in developing better awareness and understanding of what is already there. In particular, risk managers ought to understand that the risk is at least as much in *who* trades as in *what* is traded. Simply put, one should have users' mindsets drive the development of tools rather than the other way around.

13.3.6 Dr Quantokrankivitch, senior quant

(in heavy Russian accent)

Q: You are an enemy of quants.

A: Quants have indeed provided a great service to financial institutions in devising novel ways and tools to summarize complex risks in elegant and concise relationships. At the same time, mostly due to their clients' and users' behavioural biases, they have unwittingly engendered an illusion of liquidity with respect to the ever more complex products and risks that they have made possible. Liquidity, or lack thereof, is always the dark side of more complex and particular products and strategies. The ability to slice and dice a product or risk analytically does not mean that one will be able to trade upon it. The fiascos of the 1987 stock market crash and LTCM – eleven (!) years later – should remind everybody of the consequences. Quantifying and reporting risks is not synonymous with being able to manage them!

13.3.7 Mr Structurator, head of sales & marketing

Q: Coming from a trading and risk management background, you dislike clients, marketing and relationships.

A: Banks exist to serve customers and these should always maintain a central position in their strategies. This book does not advocate turning them just into hedge funds! At the same time, the stability of financial institutions is too important for clients and for the whole macroeconomic pictures to be held hostage by dealmakers' ego trips. Let's face it, banks are by no means the low-cost producer of risk capital, as regulatory requirements surrounding them offer safety but involve costs. Under the current set of costs and incentives, keeping risk positions on one's balance sheet – first and foremost loans – is a widespread, but by no means rational, use of risk capital for society.

All that this book says is that the simplification process that is used around risk management may get deals done but is prone to cause problems in the long term. This book has shown practical examples of ways in which a nice-sounding 'neglible risk' frame can be constructed. It has also shown how the framing process can be used to hide wolves under sheep's clothes. From a systemic point of view, a healthy banking system matters mostly when it is time to support clients at or near the bottom of the economic cycle, rather than for financing stretched deals when the economy is firing on all cylinders.

Last, just to add one more frame of risk to the many in this book, it is interesting to note that many marketers' concern for their business with customers does not stretch beyond the short term. A bank that is too keen on getting short-term marketing business may unwittingly mortgage its long-term risk underwriting capability and be forced to downsize activities in the long run. Does this strike anyone as a sound marketing and customer service policy?

13.3.8 Mr Global, head of the global customer and trading division

Q: I hear you, but your recommendations are just not practical. The annual bonus cycle is structured in such a way that no one will be willing to make investments beyond that time horizon. You are offering more questions than answers.

A: If your timeframe extends only until the next bonus and you plan to jump ship, you can just save your time and skip the remainder of this book. Your producers do not qualify as hunter-gatherers, they are just predators and should be viewed and treated as such. Remember from Chapter 9 that the former are a bit more intelligent, as they ensure that the condition of their hunting grounds improves over time. Even so, understanding biases – other people's and your own – can make you a better manager, trader or structurer and, oh yes, get you a bigger bonus. Remember, there is a huge difference between *making money* and *building a business that makes money*! And, what is *practical*? Just making minor marginal increments to the existing setup? Watch out, that's status quo bias.

You are spot-on in stating that this book does not offer many ready-made answers. There are already too many advisers, consultants and yes-men in large organizations who offer just that. As a matter of fact, my intention is to help you ask yourself better questions. The answers are very much a by-product of your own personality and experiences.

CHAPTER 14

Epilogue

'I have a big budget to make, I need bigger limits.'
'Please lay on the couch first and tell me about your relationship with your parents.'
(Conversation between a trader and his risk manager–psychiatrist, circa 2020)

7±2:

- Individual frame of risk cheatsheet

- Organizational frame of risk cheatsheet

- Systemic frame of risk cheatsheet

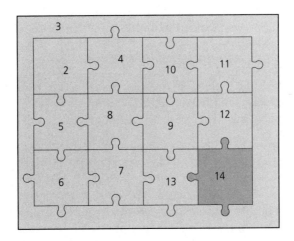

14.1 Wrap-up

As the end of this book is drawing close, let me thank you for taking all the time and effort to explore frames of risk and the behavioural side of risk management. It has been both a significant responsibility and a great honour to walk alongside you in this behavioural journey. This theme is seldom explored in risk management books. As a result, some readers may feel that many questions remain unanswered. This book lays no claim to offer answers to these complex behavioural problems – only charlatans could.

This book was never intended to demolish existing sacred totems and replace them with new ones. The fundamental issue remains how aware you are of the countless rules of thumb, mental shortcuts and circuit breakers that you use in your decisions every day, not only with respect to your career but also as someone who may be steering an organization or an entire system, such as a top manager, a regulator or a policymaker. Rising rapidly to the top does not free you from your biases! The higher you go, the more your increased responsibilities will magnify them.

Some general conclusions should be drawn from this book:

- *Few decisions, if any, escape context dependence*. Most 'truths' are just the most widely accepted frame of risk or model of reality. Understanding the context is the first step towards better risk awareness.

- *You reap the fruits of what you sow*. If your bank balance grows as a result of correct short-term decisions with adverse long-term consequences, make sure that your personality grows alongside. If your personality lags behind, your sub-conscious will eventually figure out a way to claw you back to your previous small reality – and drag your bank account down with it! Growth and risk are two sides of the same coin. The key is in the process of keeping them balanced.

- *The point is not simplicity-versus-complexity but, rather, the right balance of simplicity and complexity*. Here, again, we have a classic binary bias. The world is too complex to be reduced to complete, straightforward explanations or equations. At the same time, pouring in more physicists, PhDs and computers is hardly the way to improve common mortals' 'risk education'. People need to understand their biases, not hide them with the latest quantitative crutch.

As your career progresses, you may find yourself in all three frames risk explored in this book. As the last tribute to the 7±2 rule explored in several instances in this book, let me leave you with three sets of summary points for each frame of risk. Bearing these key principles in mind should help you in the many instances in which you will face risky decisions with little time.

14.2 Individual frame of risk summary points

You – not your boss, bank, broker or regulator – are responsible. If circumstances that create real or potential problems are really so beyond your control, at least say so. The path towards personal growth begins with the assumption of responsibility. While you cannot always choose the circumstances in which you find yourself in your career, you and only you can choose the responses.

It begins inside you. View your team, group and bank as a suit around the body of your personality. As inside, so outside. It is garbage in, garbage out. Work on your own weaknesses first. How could you credibly spread awareness in your organization if you have not even started asking questions about your own decisions?

You get the results that you want only in return for the effort and risks that you can bear. Resist the temptation to go for push-button fast answers or to skimp on quality. Cheap ingredients lead only to cheap results. Pursuing the fast buck may work in the short term but is no recipe for serious *real* personal growth. Remember, individuals' and groups' natural pain-avoidance, be-right biases make it safer to avoid the resistance and pain that are always involved in learning and experience. If an answer looks very easy, think again. It is probably *too* easy.

14.3 Organizational frame of risk summary points

Do not just talk about a commitment-based organization, do it! Manage people, do not just count them. How can you possibly ask your staff for trust, commitment and creativity if controls and fences are all you are putting around them? Leave the counting and controlling to your accountants and controllers and focus on putting people in the best position to maximize their psychological strengths. Remember, managers who are poor at putting people in the right place are as responsible for poor performance as poor performers themselves.

Beware tribal instincts in hiring and people management decisions. Modern risk management has taught people to take a hard look at concentrations in their financial portfolios. The evidence that the same attention is paid to their psychometric portfolio is scant at best. Put a crack team of 'corporate terrorists' in place and have them scout the organization for weaknesses and potential problems. These should balance any organization's penchant for the politically correct and popular sports of corporate entertainment and reassurance. Back whistleblowers as far as you can. The eyes and ears of these unsung heroes are amongst your most precious resources.

Product and organizational complexity beware. The sad ending of many banks that overcommitted in their lending decisions should remind people that more activity and size are not always synonymous with stronger performance. Compliance with fuzzily defined 'strategic' objectives may encourage going for size or getting engaged in product innovation beyond one's ability to manage it. More activity or increased product complexity may please inflated egos but is not synonymous with good management. More often than not, these ill-conceived expansionary targets test the scalability of an organization far more often than anybody would ever imagine. Remember, wherever there is an empire-builder, the odds are good of finding also his fair share of emotional baggage and self-delusions. Be suspicious of economy-of-scale arguments. These may work if your firm manufactured widgets, but do these feature in your financial institution's product line? As for complex products, they may – ah, again – please the corporate ego but do not, by virtue of their sophistication, automatically translate into profits. Remember from basic textbook marketing that product sophistication is only *one* of three possible means of competing.[103]

---

[103] Price competitiveness and service are the other two, best represented, respectively, by companies such as Sony and IBM. Sony would be an example of product-driven marketing. *The Discipline of Market Leaders* book was written in the mid-1990s on this precise topic.

14.4 Systemic frame of risk summary points

You get what you sow. Financial stability must be pursued as a means to support growth and development, rather than as an end in itself. Presenting people with a choice between higher or lower stability is the wrong way to frame the question, because anybody would opt for the safe alternative. The answer would probably be very different if people realized that the popular chimera of stability is not a freebie but carries a major cost in terms of missed development opportunities. Growth, jobs and development are only the bright side of a coin that has smart risk-taking on the flipside. Opportunity exists only in return for the intelligent risks that firms and individuals are allowed to run. You cannot get deep and liquid financial markets without creating incentives for someone to take the other side of the trade.

Diversification of behaviour, rather than diversification by type of investor or location, is what should be pursued and encouraged. As discussed in Chapter 7, having different types of investors makes no difference if one-size-fits-all metrics are then applied to all of them. Guess what, their behaviour is remarkably similar, particularly in exacerbating market volatility during turbulent periods!

Ensure that escalating complexity in products and organizational structure benefits the real economy rather than just their slick marketers. One of the favourite arguments of derivative products' salesmen is that there are no new risks, just new and more efficient combinations of products to manage old risks. But a basic law of derivatives states that each new generation of products is, by definition, less liquid than the original products from which it was created. If a bank takes a pool of credit instruments and segregates them into a better-quality tranche and an equity piece, the latter will absorb most of the illiquidity of the original credit instruments. The absolute amount of illiquidity in the system has not decreased at all. It has just been reapportioned to one tranche and somewhat buried in someone's portfolio of variable transparency. In another dramatic example in the US, mortgage-backed securities were split into two tranches labelled, respectively, interest-only (IO) and principal-only (PO). Each of these had an opposite sensitivity to interest rates and the expected effects on the prepayment speed of the underlying mortgages.[104] Two less liquid and more volatile products were born from an earlier-generation product. There will always be investors stretching for extra yield into less liquid and more volatile products and bans are out of question. By creating artificial barriers, these unwittingly induce greater complexity in the system. What policymakers can do, however, is to influence the price in these investors' decisions by granting more or less favourable capital requirements. These could depend on periodic assessments of how adequate are the systems and people who manage these funny risks for the investor or institution.

---

[104] So, if investors believed that interest rates would fall and the mortgage prepayments would soar, the price of the IO piece would drop. This is because the stream of their underlying interest payments on which the IO tranche was based would be expected to vanish as more and more of the underlying mortgages would be repaid. The opposite would apply to the PO, since the investor would receive the fixed (Principal) cashflow earlier.

'Serial financial killers' who threaten financial stability should never get a second chance to gamble. Unethical behaviours are as old as mankind and no sophisticated measurement or risk management process can eliminate them. After incurring large losses, their perpetrators should not just be terminated from their jobs; they should be banned from the financial services industry as a whole. In that respect, praise is in order for the efforts of the FSA, the UK financial services regulator, to introduce serious criminal and career consequences.

14.5 Farewell

Both in the professional and in the academic field, finance is associated far more often with cold numbers than with human feelings. Analytical reasoning and, in more general terms, the left side of the brain come to mind more often than emotions or human behaviours. All the quantitative arsenal notwithstanding, the many war stories, theories and empirical evidence presented in this book should tell you something about how important it is to respect the right side of the brain and harness its power. You have seen the consequences of breaching this rule. The author has experienced his fair share of sobering lessons in the marketplace and is the last to claim exemption from human biases.

How can we harness the power of our emotions and the right side of our brains? The usual law of nature applies:

Use it or lose it!

Appendices

Psychometric questionnaire

Section One

By taking the test, I understand that its primary purpose is to educate the reader and public about the five factor model of personality, and only secondarily, to estimate the respondent's standing within the five factor model. I understand that the program that generates the report is designed to produce estimates that are as accurate as possible, but that measurement error or improper responding can produce inaccurate results. If I think I have answered the items honestly and carefully but my results are inaccurate or not as pleasing as I would like them to be, I will have knowledgeable acquaintances – including qualified psychologists – evaluate the validity of the report before contacting either Mr Celati or Dr Johnson at IPIP. If I choose to critique the test or narrative report after receiving feedback from knowledgeable acquaintances, I will do so in a courteous and civil manner. I assume total responsibility for any adverse consequence – including but not limited to incurring trading losses – arising from the use of the Test's results, their disclosure to third parties or any legal or confidentiality issue associated with them. I hereby discharge Mr Celati and IPIP from any responsibility in connection with my use of the Test.

Instructions: Select the statement that best reflects your views with respect to each question below. After you have finished, turn to the answers in Section Two.

		Strongly Disagree	Disagree	Neither Agree Nor Disagree	Agree	Strongly Agree
		A	B	C	D	E
1	Worry about things.					
2	Make friends easily.					
3	Have a vivid imagination.					
4	Trust others.					
5	Complete tasks successfully.					
6	Get angry easily.					
7	Love large parties.					
8	Believe in the importance of art.					
9	Would never cheat on my taxes.					
10	Like order.					
11	Often feel blue.					
12	Take charge.					
13	Experience my emotions intensely.					
14	Make people feel welcome.					
15	Try to follow the rules.					
16	Am easily intimidated.					
17	Am always busy.					
18	Prefer variety to routine.					
19	Am easy to satisfy.					
20	Go straight for the goal.					
21	Often eat too much.					
22	Love excitement.					
23	Like to solve complex problems.					
24	Dislike being the centre of attention.					

	Strongly Disagree	Disagree	Neither Agree Nor Disagree	Agree	Strongly Agree
	A	B	C	D	E
25 Get chores done right away.					
26 Panic easily.					
27 Radiate joy.					
28 Tend to vote for liberal political candidates.					
29 Sympathize with the homeless.					
30 Avoid mistakes.					
31 Fear the worst.					
32 Warm up quickly to others.					
33 Enjoy wild flights of fantasy.					
34 Believe that others have good intentions.					
35 Get irritated easily.					
37 Talk to a lot of different people at parties.					
38 Like music.					
39 Stick to the rules.					
40 Like to tidy up.					
41 Dislike myself.					
42 Try to lead others.					
43 Feel others' emotions.					
44 Anticipate the needs of others.					
45 Keep my promises.					
46 Am afraid that I will do the wrong thing.					
47 Am always on the go.					
48 Like to visit new places.					
49 Can't stand confrontations.					
50 Work hard.					
51 Don't know why I do some of the things I do.					
52 Seek adventure.					

		Strongly Disagree	Disagree	Neither Agree Nor Disagree	Agree	Strongly Agree
		A	B	C	D	E
53	Love to read challenging material.					
54	Dislike talking about myself.					
55	Am always prepared.					
56	Become overwhelmed by events.					
57	Have a lot of fun.					
58	Believe that there is no absolute right or wrong.					
59	Feel sympathy for those who are worse off than myself.					
60	Choose my words with care.					
61	Am afraid of many things.					
62	Feel comfortable around people.					
63	Love to daydream.					
64	Trust what people say.					
65	Handle tasks smoothly.					
66	Get upset easily.					
67	Enjoy being part of a group.					
68	See beauty in things that others might not notice.					
69	Use flattery to get ahead.					
70	Want everything to be 'just right'.					
71	Am often down in the dumps.					
72	Can talk others into doing things.					
73	Am passionate about causes.					
74	Love to help others.					
75	Pay my bills on time.					
76	Find it difficult to approach others.					
77	Do a lot in my spare time.					

	Strongly Disagree	Disagree	Neither Agree Nor Disagree	Agree	Strongly Agree
	A	B	C	D	E
78 Interested in many things.					
79 Hate to seem pushy.					
80 Turn plans into actions.					
81 Do things I later regret.					
82 Love action.					
83 Have a rich vocabulary.					
84 Consider myself an average person.					
85 Start tasks right away.					
86 Feel that I'm unable to deal with things.					
87 Express childlike joy.					
88 Believe that criminals should receive help rather than punishment.					
89 Value cooperation over competition.					
90 Stick to my chosen path.					
91 Get stressed out easily.					
92 Act comfortably with others.					
93 Like to get lost in thought.					
94 Believe that people are basically moral.					
95 Am sure of my ground.					
96 Am often in a bad mood.					
97 Involve others in what I am doing.					
98 Love flowers.					
99 Use others for my own ends.					
100 Love order and regularity.					
101 Have a low opinion of myself.					
102 Seek to influence others.					
103 Enjoy examining myself and my life.					
104 Am concerned about others.					

	Strongly Disagree	Disagree	Neither Agree Nor Disagree	Agree	Strongly Agree
	A	B	C	D	E
105 Tell the truth.					
106 Am afraid to draw attention to myself.					
107 Can manage many things at the same time.					
108 Like to begin new things.					
109 Have a sharp tongue.					
110 Plunge into tasks with all my heart.					
111 Go on binges.					
112 Enjoy being part of a loud crowd.					
113 Can handle a lot of information.					
114 Seldom toot my own horn.					
115 Get to work at once.					
116 Can't make up my mind.					
117 Laugh my way through life.					
118 Believe in one true religion.					
119 Suffer from others' sorrows.					
120 Jump into things without thinking.					
121 Get caught up in my problems.					
122 Cheer people up.					
123 Indulge in my fantasies.					
124 Believe in human goodness.					
125 Come up with good solutions.					
126 Lose my temper.					
127 Love surprise parties.					
128 Enjoy the beauty of nature.					
129 Know how to get around the rules.					
130 Do things according to a plan.					
131 Have frequent mood swings.					
132 Take control of things.					

	Strongly Disagree	Disagree	Neither Agree Nor Disagree	Agree	Strongly Agree
	A	B	C	D	E
133 Try to understand myself.					
134 Have a good word for everyone.					
135 Listen to my conscience.					
136 Only feel comfortable with friends.					
137 React quickly.					
138 Prefer to stick with things that I know.					
139 Contradict others.					
140 Do more than what's expected of me.					
141 Love to eat.					
142 Enjoy being reckless.					
143 Enjoy thinking about things.					
144 Believe that I am better than others.					
145 Carry out my plans.					
146 Get overwhelmed by emotions.					
147 Love life.					
148 Tend to vote for conservative political candidates.					
149 Am not interested in other people's problems.					
150 Make rash decisions.					
151 Am not easily bothered by things.					
152 Am hard to get to know.					
153 Spend time reflecting on things.					
154 Think that all will be well.					
155 Know how to get things done.					
156 Rarely get irritated.					
157 Prefer to be alone.					
158 Do not like art.					
159 Cheat to get ahead.					

		Strongly Disagree	Disagree	Neither Agree Nor Disagree	Agree	Strongly Agree
		A	B	C	D	E
160	Often forget to put things back in their proper place.					
161	Feel desperate.					
162	Wait for others to lead the way.					
163	Seldom get emotional.					
164	Look down on others.					
165	Break rules.					
166	Stumble over my words.					
167	Like to take it easy.					
168	Dislike changes.					
169	Love a good fight.					
170	Set high standards for myself and others.					
171	Rarely overindulge.					
172	Act wild and crazy.					
173	Am not interested in abstract ideas.					
174	Think highly of myself.					
175	Find it difficult to get down to work.					
176	Remain calm under pressure.					
177	Look at the bright side of life.					
178	Believe that too much tax money goes to support artists.					
179	Tend to dislike soft-hearted people.					
180	Like to act on a whim.					
181	Am relaxed most of the time.					
182	Often feel uncomfortable around others.					
183	Seldom daydream.					
184	Distrust people.					
185	Misjudge situations.					
186	Seldom get mad.					

	Strongly Disagree	Disagree	Neither Agree Nor Disagree	Agree	Strongly Agree
	A	B	C	D	E
187 Want to be left alone.					
188 Do not like poetry.					
189 Put people under pressure.					
190 Leave a mess in my room.					
191 Feel that my life lacks direction.					
192 Keep in the background.					
193 Am not easily affected by my emotions.					
194 Am indifferent to the feelings of others.					
195 Break my promises.					
196 Am not embarrassed easily.					
197 Like to take my time.					
198 Don't like the idea of change.					
199 Yell at people.					
200 Demand quality.					
201 Easily resist temptations.					
202 Willing to try anything once.					
203 Avoid philosophical discussions.					
204 Have a high opinion of myself.					
205 Waste my time.					
206 Can handle complex problems.					
207 Laugh aloud.					
208 Believe laws should be strictly enforced.					
209 Believe in an eye for an eye.					
210 Rush into things.					
211 Am not easily disturbed by events.					
212 Avoid contact with others.					
213 Do not have a good imagination.					
214 Suspect hidden motives in others.					

		Strongly Disagree	Disagree	Neither Agree Nor Disagree	Agree	Strongly Agree
		A	B	C	D	E
215	Don't understand things.					
216	Am not easily annoyed.					
217	Don't like crowded events.					
218	Do not enjoy going to art museums.					
219	Pretend to be concerned for others.					
220	Leave my belongings around.					
221	Seldom feel blue.					
222	Have little to say.					
223	Rarely notice my emotional reactions.					
224	Make people feel uncomfortable.					
225	Get others to do my duties.					
226	Am comfortable in unfamiliar situations.					
227	Like a leisurely lifestyle.					
228	Am a creature of habit.					
229	Insult people.					
230	Am not highly motivated to succeed.					
231	Am able to control my cravings.					
232	Seek danger.					
233	Have difficulty understanding abstract ideas.					
234	Know the answers to many questions.					
235	Need a push to get started.					
236	Know how to cope.					
237	Amuse my friends.					
238	Believe that we coddle criminals too much.					
239	Try not to think about the needy.					
240	Do crazy things.					
241	Don't worry about things that have already happened.					
242	Am not really interested in others.					

	Strongly Disagree	Disagree	Neither Agree Nor Disagree	Agree	Strongly Agree
	A	B	C	D	E
243 Seldom get lost in thought.					
244 Am wary of others.					
245 Have little to contribute.					
246 Keep my cool.					
247 Avoid crowds.					
248 Do not like concerts.					
249 Take advantage of others.					
250 Am not bothered by messy people.					
251 Feel comfortable with myself.					
252 Don't like to draw attention to myself.					
253 Experience very few emotional highs and lows.					
254 Turn my back on others.					
255 Do the opposite of what is asked.					
256 Am not bothered by difficult social situations.					
257 Let things proceed at their own pace.					
258 Dislike new foods.					
259 Get back at others.					
260 Do just enough work to get by.					
261 Never spend more than I can afford.					
262 Would never go hang gliding or bungee jumping.					
263 Am not interested in theoretical discussions.					
264 Boast about my virtues.					
265 Have difficulty starting tasks.					
266 Readily overcome setbacks.					
267 Am not easily amused.					
268 Believe that we should be tough on crime.					
269 Believe people should fend for themselves.					
270 Act without thinking.					

	Strongly Disagree	Disagree	Neither Agree Nor Disagree	Agree	Strongly Agree
	A	B	C	D	E
271 Adapt easily to new situations.					
272 Keep others at a distance.					
273 Have difficulty imagining things.					
274 Believe that people are essentially evil.					
275 Don't see the consequences of things.					
276 Rarely complain.					
277 Seek quiet.					
278 Do not enjoy watching dance performances.					
279 Obstruct others' plans.					
280 Am not bothered by disorder.					
281 Am very pleased with myself.					
282 Hold back my opinions.					
283 Don't understand people who get emotional.					
284 Take no time for others.					
285 Misrepresent the facts.					
286 Am able to stand up for myself.					
287 React slowly.					
288 Am attached to conventional ways.					
289 Hold a grudge.					
290 Put little time and effort into my work.					
291 Never splurge.					
292 Dislike loud music.					
293 Avoid difficult reading material.					
294 Make myself the centre of attention.					
295 Postpone decisions.					
296 Am calm even in tense situations.					
297 Seldom joke around.					
298 Like to stand during the national anthem.					
299 Can't stand weak people.					
300 Often make last-minute plans.					

Section Two

Answer Key:

Your Answer		IPIP – 0	IPIP – C	IPIP – E	IPIP – A	IPIP – N
1	A=1, B=2, ---- E=5					
2	A=1, B=2, ---- E=5					
3	A=1, B=2, ---- E=5					
4	A=5, B=4, ---- E=1					
5	A=1, B=2, ---- E=5					
6	A=1, B=2, ---- E=5					
7	A=1, B=2, ---- E=5					
8	A=1, B=2, ---- E=5					
9	A=1, B=2, ---- E=5					
10	A=1, B=2, ---- E=5					
11	A=1, B=2, ---- E=5					
12	A=1, B=2, ---- E=5					
13	A=1, B=2, ---- E=5					
14	A=5, B=4, ---- E=1					
15	A=1, B=2, ---- E=5					
16	A=5, B=4, ---- E=1					
17	A=1, B=2, ---- E=5					
18	A=1, B=2, ---- E=5					
19	A=5, B=4, ---- E=1					
20	A=1, B=2, ---- E=5					
21	A=5, B=4, ---- E=1					
22	A=1, B=2, ---- E=5					
23	A=1, B=2, ---- E=5					
24	A=5, B=4, ---- E=1					
25	A=1, B=2, ---- E=5					
26	A=1, B=2, ---- E=5					
27	A=5, B=4, ---- E=1					

28	A=5, B=4, ---- E=1
29	A=1, B=2, ---- E=5
30	A=5, B=4, ---- E=1
31	A=1, B=2, ---- E=5
32	A=1, B=2, ---- E=5
33	A=1, B=2, ---- E=5
34	A=5, B=4, ---- E=1
35	A=1, B=2, ---- E=5
36	A=1, B=2, ---- E=5
37	A=1, B=2, ---- E=5
38	A=1, B=2, ---- E=5
39	A=5, B=4, ---- E=1
40	A=1, B=2, ---- E=5
41	A=1, B=2, ---- E=5
42	A=1, B=2, ---- E=5
43	A=1, B=2, ---- E=5
44	A=1, B=2, ---- E=5
45	A=1, B=2, ---- E=5
46	A=1, B=2, ---- E=5
47	A=1, B=2, ---- E=5
48	A=1, B=2, ---- E=5
49	A=5, B=4, ---- E=1
50	A=1, B=2, ---- E=5
51	A=1, B=2, ---- E=5
52	A=1, B=2, ---- E=5
53	A=1, B=2, ---- E=5
54	A=5, B=4, ---- E=1
55	A=1, B=2, ---- E=5
56	A=5, B=4, ---- E=1
57	A=1, B=2, ---- E=5
58	A=1, B=2, ---- E=5

59	A=1, B=2, ---- E=5
60	A=1, B=2, ---- E=5
61	A=1, B=2, ---- E=5
62	A=1, B=2, ---- E=5
63	A=1, B=2, ---- E=5
64	A=1, B=2, ---- E=5
65	A=1, B=2, ---- E=5
66	A=1, B=2, ---- E=5
67	A=1, B=2, ---- E=5
68	A=1, B=2, ---- E=5
69	A=1, B=2, ---- E=5
70	A=1, B=2, ---- E=5
71	A=1, B=2, ---- E=5
72	A=1, B=2, ---- E=5
73	A=1, B=2, ---- E=5
74	A=1, B=2, ---- E=5
75	A=1, B=2, ---- E=5
76	A=5, B=4, ---- E=1
77	A=1, B=2, ---- E=5
78	A=1, B=2, ---- E=5
79	A=5, B=4, ---- E=1
80	A=1, B=2, ---- E=5
81	A=5, B=4, ---- E=1
82	A=1, B=2, ---- E=5
83	A=1, B=2, ---- E=5
84	A=1, B=2, ---- E=5
85	A=1, B=2, ---- E=5
86	A=1, B=2, ---- E=5
87	A=1, B=2, ---- E=5
88	A=5, B=4, ---- E=1
89	A=1, B=2, ---- E=5

90	A=5, B=4, ---- E=1
91	A=1, B=2, ---- E=5
92	A=1, B=2, ---- E=5
93	A=1, B=2, ---- E=5
94	A=5, B=4, ---- E=1
95	A=5, B=4, ---- E=1
96	A=1, B=2, ---- E=5
97	A=1, B=2, ---- E=5
98	A=1, B=2, ---- E=5
99	A=1, B=2, ---- E=5
100	A=1, B=2, ---- E=5
101	A=1, B=2, ---- E=5
102	A=1, B=2, ---- E=5
103	A=1, B=2, ---- E=5
104	A=1, B=2, ---- E=5
105	A=1, B=2, ---- E=5
106	A=5, B=4, ---- E=1
107	A=1, B=2, ---- E=5
108	A=1, B=2, ---- E=5
109	A=1, B=2, ---- E=5
110	A=1, B=2, ---- E=5
111	A=5, B=4, ---- E=1
112	A=1, B=2, ---- E=5
113	A=1, B=2, ---- E=5
114	A=1, B=2, ---- E=5
115	A=1, B=2, ---- E=5
116	A=5, B=4, ---- E=1
117	A=5, B=4, ---- E=1
118	A=1, B=2, ---- E=5
119	A=1, B=2, ---- E=5
120	A=1, B=2, ---- E=5

121	A=1, B=2, ---- E=5
122	A=1, B=2, ---- E=5
123	A=1, B=2, ---- E=5
124	A=5, B=4, ---- E=1
125	A=1, B=2, ---- E=5
126	A=1, B=2, ---- E=5
127	A=1, B=2, ---- E=5
128	A=1, B=2, ---- E=5
129	A=5, B=4, ---- E=1
130	A=1, B=2, ---- E=5
131	A=1, B=2, ---- E=5
132	A=1, B=2, ---- E=5
133	A=1, B=2, ---- E=5
134	A=1, B=2, ---- E=5
135	A=1, B=2, ---- E=5
136	A=5, B=4, ---- E=1
137	A=1, B=2, ---- E=5
138	A=5, B=4, ---- E=1
139	A=5, B=4, ---- E=1
140	A=1, B=2, ---- E=5
141	A=5, B=4, ---- E=1
142	A=1, B=2, ---- E=5
143	A=1, B=2, ---- E=5
144	A=1, B=2, ---- E=5
145	A=1, B=2, ---- E=5
146	A=1, B=2, ---- E=5
147	A=5, B=4, ---- E=1
148	A=1, B=2, ---- E=5
149	A=5, B=4, ---- E=1
150	A=1, B=2, ---- E=5
151	A=5, B=4, ---- E=1

152	A=5, B=4, ---- E=1
153	A=1, B=2, ---- E=5
154	A=5, B=4, ---- E=1
155	A=1, B=2, ---- E=5
156	A=5, B=4, ---- E=1
157	A=5, B=4, ---- E=1
158	A=5, B=4, ---- E=1
159	A=5, B=4, ---- E=1
160	A=5, B=4, ---- E=1
161	A=1, B=2, ---- E=5
162	A=5, B=4, ---- E=1
163	A=5, B=4, ---- E=1
164	A=5, B=4, ---- E=1
165	A=5, B=4, ---- E=1
166	A=5, B=4, ---- E=1
167	A=5, B=4, ---- E=1
168	A=5, B=4, ---- E=1
169	A=1, B=2, ---- E=5
170	A=1, B=2, ---- E=5
171	A=1, B=2, ---- E=5
172	A=1, B=2, ---- E=5
173	A=5, B=4, ---- E=1
174	A=5, B=4, ---- E=1
175	A=5, B=4, ---- E=1
176	A=5, B=4, ---- E=1
177	A=5, B=4, ---- E=1
178	A=1, B=2, ---- E=5
179	A=5, B=4, ---- E=1
180	A=1, B=2, ---- E=5
181	A=5, B=4, ---- E=1
182	A=5, B=4, ---- E=1

183	A=5, B=4, ---- E=1
184	A=1, B=2, ---- E=5
185	A=5, B=4, ---- E=1
186	A=5, B=4, ---- E=1
187	A=5, B=4, ---- E=1
188	A=5, B=4, ---- E=1
189	A=5, B=4, ---- E=1
190	A=5, B=4, ---- E=1
191	A=1, B=2, ---- E=5
192	A=5, B=4, ---- E=1
193	A=5, B=4, ---- E=1
194	A=5, B=4, ---- E=1
195	A=5, B=4, ---- E=1
196	A=5, B=4, ---- E=1
197	A=5, B=4, ---- E=1
198	A=5, B=4, ---- E=1
199	A=5, B=4, ---- E=1
200	A=1, B=2, ---- E=5
201	A=1, B=2, ---- E=5
202	A=1, B=2, ---- E=5
203	A=5, B=4, ---- E=1
204	A=5, B=4, ---- E=1
205	A=1, B=2, ---- E=5
206	A=1, B=2, ---- E=5
207	A=1, B=2, ---- E=5
208	A=1, B=2, ---- E=5
209	A=5, B=4, ---- E=1
210	A=1, B=2, ---- E=5
211	A=5, B=4, ---- E=1
212	A=5, B=4, ---- E=1
213	A=5, B=4, ---- E=1

214	A=1, B=2, ---- E=5
215	A=5, B=4, ---- E=1
216	A=5, B=4, ---- E=1
217	A=5, B=4, ---- E=1
218	A=5, B=4, ---- E=1
219	A=5, B=4, ---- E=1
220	A=5, B=4, ---- E=1
221	A=5, B=4, ---- E=1
222	A=5, B=4, ---- E=1
223	A=1, B=2, ---- E=5
224	A=5, B=4, ---- E=1
225	A=1, B=2, ---- E=5
226	A=5, B=4, ---- E=1
227	A=5, B=4, ---- E=1
228	A=5, B=4, ---- E=1
229	A=5, B=4, ---- E=1
230	A=5, B=4, ---- E=1
231	A=1, B=2, ---- E=5
232	A=1, B=2, ---- E=5
233	A=5, B=4, ---- E=1
234	A=1, B=2, ---- E=5
235	A=5, B=4, ---- E=1
236	A=1, B=2, ---- E=5
237	A=1, B=2, ---- E=5
238	A=1, B=2, ---- E=5
239	A=5, B=4, ---- E=1
240	A=1, B=2, ---- E=5
241	A=5, B=4, ---- E=1
242	A=5, B=4, ---- E=1
243	A=5, B=4, ---- E=1
244	A=1, B=2, ---- E=5

245	A=5, B=4, ---- E=1
246	A=5, B=4, ---- E=1
247	A=5, B=4, ---- E=1
248	A=5, B=4, ---- E=1
249	A=1, B=2, ---- E=5
250	A=5, B=4, ---- E=1
251	A=5, B=4, ---- E=1
252	A=5, B=4, ---- E=1
253	A=5, B=4, ---- E=1
254	A=5, B=4, ---- E=1
255	A=5, B=4, ---- E=1
256	A=1, B=2, ---- E=5
257	A=5, B=4, ---- E=1
258	A=5, B=4, ---- E=1
259	A=5, B=4, ---- E=1
260	A=1, B=2, ---- E=5
261	A=1, B=2, ---- E=5
262	A=5, B=4, ---- E=1
263	A=5, B=4, ---- E=1
264	A=1, B=2, ---- E=5
265	A=5, B=4, ---- E=1
266	A=5, B=4, ---- E=1
267	A=5, B=4, ---- E=1
268	A=1, B=2, ---- E=5
269	A=5, B=4, ---- E=1
270	A=1, B=2, ---- E=5
271	A=1, B=2, ---- E=5
272	A=5, B=4, ---- E=1
273	A=5, B=4, ---- E=1
274	A=1, B=2, ---- E=5
275	A=5, B=4, ---- E=1

276	A=1, B=2, ---- E=5
277	A=5, B=4, ---- E=1
278	A=5, B=4, ---- E=1
279	A=1, B=2, ---- E=5
280	A=5, B=4, ---- E=1
281	A=5, B=4, ---- E=1
282	A=5, B=4, ---- E=1
283	A=5, B=4, ---- E=1
284	A=5, B=4, ---- E=1
285	A=5, B=4, ---- E=1
286	A=1, B=2, ---- E=5
287	A=5, B=4, ---- E=1
288	A=1, B=2, ---- E=5
289	A=5, B=4, ---- E=1
290	A=5, B=4, ---- E=1
291	A=1, B=2, ---- E=5
292	A=5, B=4, ---- E=1
293	A=5, B=4, ---- E=1
294	A=1, B=2, ---- E=5
295	A=5, B=4, ---- E=1
296	A=5, B=4, ---- E=1
297	A=1, B=2, ---- E=5
298	A=1, B=2, ---- E=5
299	A=5, B=4, ---- E=1
300	A=1, B=2, ---- E=5

Total by Psychometric Dimension

Brief explanation of the five dimensions of personality

The following excerpt provides some explanation of the basic five dimensions of personality. It is by no means omni-comprehensive. In addition, your absolute score gives you only a very rough estimate. The comparison between your scores and the population average is also very important. If, for argument's sake, each dimension has a possible score that ranges between 0 and 100, that does not mean that the others who take the test in the general population will have an average of 50. A 'high' score in one dimension may not necessarily put you above average. Likewise, a low score does not mean that you will be below population average in that dimension. If you are interested in these comparisons, please contact the author at info@riskandregret.com.

Openness to experience

Openness to experience describes a dimension of cognitive style that distinguishes imaginative, creative people from down-to-earth, conventional people. Open people are intellectually curious, appreciative of art, and sensitive to beauty. They tend to be, compared to closed people, more aware of their feelings. They tend to think and act in individualistic and non-conforming ways. Intellectuals typically score high on openness to experience; consequently, this factor has also been called *culture* or *intellect*. Nonetheless, intellect is probably best regarded as one aspect of openness to experience. Scores on openness to experience are only modestly related to years of education and scores on standard intelligence tests.

Another characteristic of the open cognitive style is a facility for thinking in symbols and abstractions far removed from concrete experience. Depending on the individual's specific intellectual abilities, this symbolic cognition may take the form of mathematical, logical, or geometric thinking, artistic and metaphorical use of language, music composition or performance, or one of the many visual or performing arts. People with low scores on openness to experience tend to have narrow, common interests. They prefer the plain, straightforward, and obvious over the complex, ambiguous, and subtle. They may regard the arts and sciences with suspicion, regarding these endeavours as abstruse or of no practical use. Closed people prefer familiarity over novelty; they are conservative and resistant to change.

Openness is often presented as healthier or more mature by psychologists, who are often themselves open to experience. However, open and closed styles of thinking are useful in different environments. The intellectual style of the open person may serve a professor well, but research has shown that closed thinking is related to superior job performance in police work, sales, and a number of service occupations.

A low score on openness to experience indicates that you like to think in plain and simple terms. Others would describe you as down-to-earth, practical and conservative.

Openness to experience has a number of key facets:

- *Imagination*. To imaginative individuals, the real world is often too plain and ordinary. High scorers on this scale use fantasy to create a richer, more interesting world. Low scorers on this scale are more oriented to facts than fantasy.

- *Artistic interests*. High scorers on this scale love beauty, both in art and in nature. They become easily involved and absorbed in artistic and natural events. They are neither necessarily artistically trained nor talented, although many will be. The defining features of this scale are *interest in*, and *appreciation of*, natural and artificial beauty. Low scorers lack aesthetic sensitivity and interest in the arts.

- *Emotionality*. Persons high on emotionality have good access to and awareness of their own feelings. Low scorers are less aware of their feelings and tend not to express their emotions openly.

- *Adventurousness*. High scorers on adventurousness are eager to try new activities, travel to foreign lands, and experience different things. They find familiarity and routine boring, and will take a new route home just because it is different. Low scorers tend to feel uncomfortable with change and prefer familiar routines.

- *Intellect*. Intellect and artistic interests are the two most important, central aspects of openness to experience. High scorers on intellect love to play with ideas. They are open to new and unusual ideas, and like to debate intellectual issues. They enjoy riddles, puzzles, and brain-teasers. Low scorers on intellect prefer dealing with either people or things rather than ideas. They regard intellectual exercises as a waste of time. Intellect should *not* be equated with intelligence. Intellect is an intellectual style, not an intellectual ability, although high scorers on intellect score *slightly* higher than low-intellect individuals on standardized intelligence tests.

- *Liberalism*. Psychological liberalism refers to a readiness to challenge authority, convention, and traditional values. In its most extreme form, psychological liberalism can even represent outright hostility toward rules, sympathy for law-breakers, and love of ambiguity, chaos, and disorder. Psychological conservatives prefer the security and stability brought by conformity to tradition. Psychological liberalism and conservatism are not identical to political affiliation, but certainly incline individuals toward certain political parties.

Conscientiousness

Conscientiousness concerns the way in which we control, regulate, and direct our impulses. Impulses are not inherently bad: occasionally time constraints require a snap decision, and acting on our first impulse can be an effective response. Also, in times of play rather than work, acting spontaneously and impulsively can be fun. Impulsive individuals can be seen by others as colourful, fun to be with, and zany.

Nonetheless, acting on impulse can lead to trouble in a number of ways. Some impulses are antisocial. Uncontrolled antisocial acts not only harm other members of society, but can also result in retribution toward the perpetrator of such impulsive acts. Another problem with impulsive acts is that they often produce immediate rewards but undesirable, long-term consequences. Examples include excessive socializing that leads to being fired from one's job, hurling an insult that causes the break-up of an important relationship, or using pleasure-inducing drugs that eventually destroy one's health.

Impulsive behaviour, even when not seriously destructive, diminishes a person's effectiveness in significant ways. Acting impulsively disallows contemplating alternative courses of action, some of which would have been wiser than the impulsive choice. Impulsivity also sidetracks people during projects that require organized sequences of steps or stages. The accomplishments of an impulsive person are therefore small, scattered, and inconsistent.

A hallmark of intelligence, what potentially separates human beings from earlier life forms, is the ability to think about future consequences before acting on an impulse. Intelligent activity involves contemplation of long-range goals, organizing and planning routes to these goals, and persisting toward one's goals in the face of short-lived impulses to the contrary. The idea that intelligence involves impulse control is nicely captured by the term prudence, an alternative label for the conscientiousness domain. Prudent means both wise and cautious. Persons who score high on the conscientiousness scale are, in fact, perceived by others as intelligent.

The benefits of high conscientiousness are obvious. Conscientious individuals avoid trouble and achieve high levels of success through purposeful planning and persistence. They are also positively regarded by others as intelligent and reliable. On the negative side, they can be compulsive perfectionists and workaholics. Furthermore, extremely conscientious individuals might be regarded as stuffy and boring. Un-conscientious people may be criticized for their unreliability, lack of ambition, and failure to stay within the lines, but they will experience many short-lived pleasures and they will never be called stuffy.

A low score on conscientiousness means you do not set clear goals to pursue with determination. People do not regard you as reliable and hard-working.

Conscientiousness articulates itself in the following facets:

- *Self-efficacy*. Self-efficacy describes confidence in one's ability to accomplish things. High scorers believe they have the intelligence (commonsense), drive, and self-control necessary to achieve success. Low scorers do not feel effective, and may have a sense that they are not in control of their lives.

- *Orderliness*. Persons with high scores on orderliness are well organized. They like to live according to routines and schedules. They keep lists and make plans. Low scorers tend to be disorganized and scattered.

- *Dutifulness*. This scale reflects the strength of a person's sense of duty and obligation. Those who score high on this scale have a strong sense of moral obligation. Low scorers find contracts, rules, and regulations overly confining. They are likely to be seen as unreliable or even irresponsible.

- *Achievement-striving*. Individuals who score high on this scale strive hard to achieve excellence. Their drive to be recognized as successful keeps them on track toward their lofty goals. They often have a strong sense of direction in life, but extremely high scorers may be too single-minded and obsessed with their work. Low scorers are content to get by with a minimal amount of work, and might be seen by others as lazy.

- *Self-discipline*. Self-discipline – what many people call will-power – refers to the ability to persist at difficult or unpleasant tasks until they are completed. People who possess high self-discipline are able to overcome the reluctance to begin tasks and stay on track despite distractions. Those with low self-discipline procrastinate and show poor follow-through, often failing to complete tasks–even tasks they want very much to complete.

- *Cautiousness*. Cautiousness describes the disposition to think through possibilities before acting. High scorers on the cautiousness scale take their time when making decisions. Low scorers often say or do the first thing that comes to mind without deliberating alternatives and the probable consequences of those alternatives.

Extraversion

Extraversion is marked by pronounced engagement with the external world. Extraverts enjoy being with people, are full of energy, and often experience positive emotions. They tend to be enthusiastic, action-oriented, individuals who are likely to say 'Yes!' or 'Let's go!' to opportunities for excitement. In groups they like to talk, assert themselves, and draw attention to themselves.

Introverts lack the exuberance, energy, and activity levels of extraverts. They tend to be quiet, low-key, deliberate, and disengaged from the social world. Their lack of social involvement should *not* be interpreted as shyness or depression; the introvert simply needs less stimulation than an extravert and prefers to be alone. The independence and reserve of the introvert is sometimes mistaken as unfriendliness or arrogance. In reality, an introvert who scores high on the agreeableness dimension will not seek others out but will be quite pleasant when approached.

A low extraversion score indicates that one tends to escape large crowds and has below-average levels of energy with people and activities.

Extraversion presents the following facets:

- *Friendliness*. Friendly people genuinely like other people and openly demonstrate positive feelings toward others. They make friends quickly and it is easy for them to form close, intimate relationships. Low scorers on friendliness are not necessarily cold and hostile, but they do not reach out to others and are perceived as distant and reserved.

- *Gregariousness*. Gregarious people find the company of others pleasantly stimulating and rewarding. They enjoy the excitement of crowds. Low scorers tend to feel overwhelmed by, and therefore actively avoid, large crowds. They do not necessarily dislike being with people sometimes, but their need for privacy and time to themselves is much greater than for individuals who score high on this scale.

- *Assertiveness*. High scorers on assertiveness like to speak out, take charge, and direct the activities of others. They tend to be leaders in groups. Low scorers tend not to talk much and let others control the activities of groups.

- *Activity level*. Active individuals lead fast-paced, busy lives. They move about quickly, energetically, and vigorously, and they are involved in many activities. People who score low on this scale follow a slower and more leisurely, relaxed pace.

- *Excitement-seeking*. High scorers on this scale are easily bored without high levels of stimulation. They love bright lights and hustle and bustle. They are likely to take risks and seek thrills. Low scorers are overwhelmed by noise and commotion and are adverse to thrill-seeking.

- *Cheerfulness*. This scale measures positive mood and feelings, not negative emotions (which are a part of the Neuroticism domain). Persons who score high on this scale typically experience a range of positive feelings, including happiness, enthusiasm, optimism, and joy. Low scorers are not as prone to such energetic, high spirits.

Agreeableness

Agreeableness reflects individual differences in concern with cooperation and social harmony. Agreeable individuals value getting along with others. They are therefore considerate, friendly, generous, helpful, and willing to compromise their interests with others'. Agreeable people also have an optimistic view of human nature. They believe people are basically honest, decent, and trustworthy.

Disagreeable individuals place self-interest above getting along with others. They are generally unconcerned with others' well-being, and are unlikely to extend themselves for other people. Sometimes their scepticism about others' motives causes them to be suspicious, unfriendly, and uncooperative.

Agreeableness is obviously advantageous for attaining and maintaining popularity. Agreeable people are better liked than disagreeable people. On the other hand, agreeableness is not useful in situations that require tough or absolute objective decisions. Disagreeable people can make excellent scientists, critics, or soldiers.

A low level of agreeableness indicates a limited interest in others' needs and well-being. This is associated with being unpleasant, unsympathetic, and uncooperative.

Agreeableness presents these facets:

- *Trust*. A person with high trust assumes that most people are fair, honest, and have good intentions. Persons with low trust scores see others as selfish, devious, and potentially dangerous.

- *Morality*. High scorers on this scale see no need for pretence or manipulation when dealing with others and are therefore candid, frank, and sincere. Low scorers believe that a certain amount of deception in social relationships is necessary. People find it relatively easy to relate to the straightforward high-scorers on this scale. They generally find it more difficult to relate to the un-straightforward low scorers on this scale. It should be made clear that low scorers are *not* unprincipled or immoral; they are simply more guarded and less willing to openly reveal the whole truth.

- *Altruism*. Altruistic people find helping other people genuinely rewarding. Consequently, they are generally willing to assist those who are in need. Altruistic people find that doing things for others is a form of self-fulfillment rather than self-sacrifice. Low scorers on this scale do not particularly like helping those in need. Requests for help will be perceived more like an imposition than as an opportunity for self-fulfillment.

- *Co-operation*. Individuals who score high on this scale dislike confrontations. They are perfectly willing to compromise or to deny their own needs to get along with others. Those who score low on this scale are more likely to intimidate others to get their way.

- *Modesty*. High scorers on this scale do not like to claim that they are better than other people. In some cases this attitude may derive from low self-confidence or self-esteem. Nonetheless, some people with high self-esteem find immodesty unseemly. Those who *are* willing to describe themselves as superior tend to be seen as disagreeably arrogant by other people.

- *Sympathy*. People who score highly on this scale are tenderhearted and compassionate. They feel the pain of others vicariously and are easily moved to pity. Low scorers are not affected strongly by human suffering. They pride themselves on making objective judgments based on reason. They are more concerned with truth and impartial justice than with mercy.

Neuroticism

Freud originally used the term *neurosis* to describe a condition marked by mental distress, emotional suffering, and an inability to cope effectively with the normal demands of life. He suggested that everyone shows some signs of neurosis, but that we differ in our degree of suffering and our specific symptoms of distress. Today neuroticism refers to the tendency to experience negative feelings. Those who score high on neuroticism may experience primarily one specific negative feeling such as anxiety, anger, or depression, but are likely to experience several of these emotions. People high in neuroticism are emotionally reactive. They respond emotionally to events that would not affect most people, and their reactions tend to be more intense than normal. They are more likely to interpret ordinary situations as threatening, and minor frustrations as hopelessly difficult. Their negative emotional reactions tend to persist for unusually long periods of time, which means they are often in a bad mood.

At the other end of the scale, individuals who score low in neuroticism are less easily upset and are less emotionally reactive. They tend to be calm, emotionally stable, and free from persistent negative feelings. Freedom from negative feelings does not mean that low scorers experience a lot of positive feelings; frequency of positive emotions is a component of the extraversion domain.

The score on neuroticism provides an indication of the intensity of one's level of emotional activity and of how well one is able to cope with stressful and frustrating situations. Neuroticism has these facets:

- *Anxiety*. The 'fight-or-flight' system of the brain of anxious individuals is too easily and too often engaged. Therefore, people who are high in anxiety often feel like something dangerous is about to happen. They may be afraid of specific situations or be just generally fearful. They feel tense, jittery, and nervous. Persons who score low in anxiety are generally calm and fearless.

- *Anger*. Persons who score high in anger feel enraged when things do not go their way. They are sensitive about being treated fairly and feel resentful and bitter when they feel they are being cheated. This scale measures the tendency to *feel* angry; whether or not the person expresses annoyance and hostility depends on the individual's level on agreeableness. Low scorers do not get angry often or easily.

- *Depression*. This scale measures the tendency to feel sad, dejected, and discouraged. High scorers lack energy and have difficulty initiating activities. Low scorers tend to be free from these depressive feelings.

- *Self-consciousness*. Self-conscious individuals are sensitive about what others think of them. Their concern about rejection and ridicule causes them to feel shy and uncomfortable around others. They are easily embarrassed and often feel ashamed. Their fears that others will criticize or make fun of them are exaggerated and unrealistic, but their awkwardness and discomfort may make these fears a self-fulfilling prophecy. Low scorers, in contrast, do not suffer from the mistaken impression that everyone is watching and judging them. They do not feel nervous in social situations.

- *Immoderation*. Immoderate individuals feel strong cravings and urges that they have difficulty resisting. They tend to be orientated toward short-term pleasures and rewards rather than long-term consequences. Low scorers do not experience strong, irresistible cravings and consequently do not find themselves tempted to overindulge.

- *Vulnerability*. High scorers on vulnerability experience panic, confusion, and helplessness when under pressure or stress. Low scorers feel more poised, confident, and clear-thinking when stressed.

Quite some pearls of wisdom…

Drill for oil? You mean drill into the ground to try and find oil? You are crazy.

(*Drillers who Edwin L. Drake tried to enlist to his project to drill for oil, 1859*)

They could not hit an elephant at this dist___.

(*Union Army General John B. Sedgwick's last words, uttered during the battle of Spotsylvania, 1864*)

Louis Pasteur's theory of germs is ridiculous fiction.

(*Pierre Pachet, Professor of Physiology at Toulouse, 1872*)

The device is inherently of no value to us.

(*Western Union's rationale for not buying the patent for Alexander Graham Bell's telephone, 1876*)

The Americans have need of the telephone, but we do not. We have plenty of messenger boys.

(*Sir William Preece, Chief Engineer of Britain's General Post Office, 1876*)

The radio craze … will die out in time.

(*Thomas A. Edison, 1892*)

Heavier-than-air flying machines are impossible.

(*Lord Kelvin, British mathematician and president of the British Royal Society, 1895*)

Everything that can be invented has been invented.

(*Charles H. Duell, Commissioner of the United States Office of Patents, recommending that his office be abolished, 1899*)

The horse is here to stay, the automobile is only a fad.

(*Potential investor in Ford Motor Company, 1902*)

Airplanes are interesting toys but of no military value.

(Marechal Ferdinand Foch, Professor of Strategy, Ecole Superieure de Guerre, 1910)

Babe Ruth made a big mistake when he gave up pitching.

(Tris Speaker, baseball player, 1921)

Get rid of that lunatic down there in reception who says he's got a machine for seeing by wireless. Watch him – he may have a razor on him.

(Editor of London Daily Express, 1922)

There is no likelihood man can ever tap the power of the atom.

(Robert Millikan, Nobel Prize winner for physics, 1923)

Who the hell wants to hear actors talk?

(H.M. Warner, Warner Brothers, 1927)

Can't act. Can't sing. Balding. Can dance a little.

(MGM executive, reacting to Fred Astaire's screen test, 1928)

Stocks have reached a permanent plateau.

(Irving R. Fisher, prominent Yale economist, a few days before the first Wall Street Stock Market Crash, 1929)

A severe depression like that of 1920–21 is outside the range of probability.

(Harvard Economic Society – weekly letter, 16 November 1929)

There is not the slightest indication that nuclear energy will ever be obtainable. It would mean that the atom would have to be shattered at will.

(Dr Albert Einstein, leading physicist and future father of the Theory of Relativity, 1932)

Hawaii Islands are over-protected. The entire Japanese Fleet and Air Force could not threaten them.

(Captain William Pulleston, former US Naval Intelligence Chief, August 1941)

Well, don't worry about it … It's nothing.

(Ltn. Kermit Tyler, Duty Officer of Shafter Information Center, Hawaii, upon being informed that a radar signal had picked up what appeared to be at least 50 planes soaring toward Oahu at almost 180 miles per hour, 7 December 1941)

We won't be at war with Japan within 48 hours, 48 days or 48 years.

(Wendell Wilkie [former Republican candidate for U.S. President], 7 December 1941)

I think there is a world market for about five computers.

(Thomas J. Watson, IBM Founder, 1943)

You'd better learn secretarial work, or else get married.

(Emmeline Snively, Director of Blue Book Modelling Agency, counselling would-be model Marilyn Monroe, 1944)

You ought to go back to driving a truck.

(Concert manager, firing Elvis Presley, 1954)

We don't like their sounds, and guitar music is on the way out.

(Decca Recording Co. rejecting the Beatles, 1962)

But what ... is it good for?

(Engineer at the Advanced Computing Systems Division of IBM commenting on the microchip, 1968)

No woman in my time will be Prime Minister or Chancellor or Foreign Secretary – not the top jobs. Anyway, I would not want to be Prime Minister.

(Margaret Thatcher, interviewed in the London Sunday Telegraph after being appointed Shadow Spokesman on Education, 26 October 1969)

There is no reason why anyone would want a computer in their home.

(Kenneth Olsen, founder of the computer firm Digital Equipment Corporation, 1977)

640K ought to be enough for anybody.

(Bill Gates, 1981)

This is battleship *Missouri* of the US Navy and, according to our radar, you are on collision course with us. We are escorted by three destroyers. Change direction immediately.

This is the lighthouse. Your call.

(Conversation near the Northfoundland Coast, North American Waters, 1985)

Based on our VaR, such a loss could happen less than once in a billion years.

(LTCM, August 1998)

Summary of key game theory models

1 Nash Equilibrium

You are a young graduate with an MBA from a prestigious Ivy League business school and have just joined the trading desk of a leading Wall Street firm. While the eighties and their fads are over, you have always dreamed of buying the 1970s version of a particular sports model of a famous European car. Now it's time to get even. You have been referred to a dealer that specializes in antique cars and triumphantly enter his shop. As luck would have it, he has exactly what you are looking for. By doing the deal, you would save at least $2,000 relative to those few shops where you have seen this model.

While the car is legendary, you know that their reputation for mechanical reliability is less than stellar. You know from the experience of another antique-car buff that a car in poor condition means about $3,000 of extra refitting. With over 120,000 miles on the clock, you want to be cautious and inquire about its condition with the salesman. The salesman wishes to sell the car. He will pocket a nice $2,000 profit – not bad considering it's only a couple of months since he bought it from another client who wanted to trade up.

However, the salesman also wants to preserve his strong reputation. He knows from experience that about one car in three of this model has some mechanical issue with the engine or the transmission. Everybody knows everybody, even more so in the small market for antique cars, and lying would seriously damage it. He knows from experience that enthusiastic young professionals such as this one bring in plenty of referrals. In addition, the dealer's company is carrying out an after-sales customer satisfaction survey and an extra bonus is awarded to those salespersons whose clients have both followed their recommendations and expressed a positive judgment on the salesperson's honesty.

What are the various outcomes of this situation?

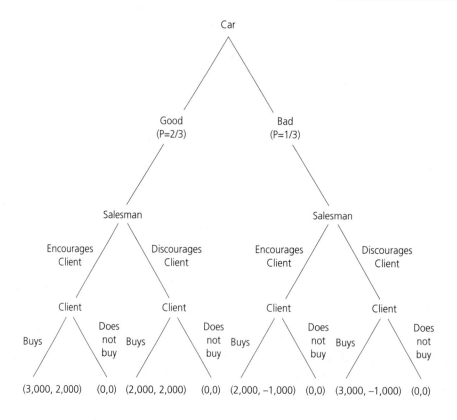

FIGURE A3.1 ■ Example of Nash Equilibrium

There are two states of nature here. Let's call them 'good car' and 'bad car', respectively. In addition, the salesman and you, the customer, can choose a variety of behaviours. The payoff matrix for the 'good car' scenario is:

	Customer behaviour >	Always buy	Trust	Distrust	Never buy
Salesman's behaviour:		1	2	3	4
Always say buy	A	(3000,2000)	(3000,2000)	(0,0)	(0,0)
Always tell truth	B	(3000,2000)	(3000,2000)	(0,0	(0,0)
Always lie	C	(2000,2000)	(0,0)	(2000,2000)	(0,0)
Always say don't buy	D	(2000,2000)	(0,0)	(2000,2000)	(0,0)

The shaded region of the table shows the payoffs for the salesman and for the customer, respectively. In cell C3, for instance, the salesman chooses to lie and discourages the customer despite the fact that this is a good car. The customer, however, has decided not to trust him and chooses the opposite course by buying the car, thereby achieving his $2,000 dollar savings. As he finds the salesman neither convincing nor trustworthy, the latter does not receive the $1,000 bonus following the survey and his payoff is limited to the profit on the car sale.

The payoff matrix for the 'bad car' scenario is:

	Customer behaviour >	Always buy	Trust	Distrust	Never buy
Salesman's behaviour:		1	2	3	4
Always say buy	A	(2000,–1000)	(2000,–1000)	(0,0)	(0,0)
Always tell truth	B	(3000,–1000)	(0,0)	(3000,–1000)	(0,0)
Always lie	C	(2000,–1000)	(0,0)	(0,0)	(0,0)
Always say don't buy	D	(3000,–1000)	(0,0)	(3000,–1000)	(0,0)

As the probabilities for the two scenarios are 2/3 and 1/3, respectively, the combined payoff matrix is then obtained by weighing the values in each cell accordingly. The results are:

	Customer behaviour >	Always buy	Trust	Distrust	Never buy
Salesman's behaviour:		1	2	3	4
Always say buy	A	(2667,1000)	(2667,1000)	(0,0)	(0,0)
Always tell truth	B	(3000,1000)	(2000,1333)	(1000,–333)	(0,0)
Always lie	C	2000,1000)	(0,0)	(1333,1333)	(0,0)
Always say don't buy	D	(2667,1000)	(0,0)	(2333,1000)	(0,0)

From the customer's point of view, Column 4 is almost always inferior to column 3, as only cell B4 shows a better payoff than B3. This is called *weak domination* of a strategy over another. He has an optimal payoff not in one but in two cells (B2 and C3) and cannot do anything to improve this equilibrium situation. The salesman, on the other hand, has his highest profit regions in areas in which the payoff is sub-optimal for the customer. His best strategy will be to try to inspire trust which will place him in cell B2. As neither player can do anything to improve his payoff by changing strategy unilaterally, the equilibrium between B2 and C3 is called Nash Equilibrium, after John Nash who developed the theory in the early 1950s.

2 A game theory classic: the prisoner's dilemma

You and your best mate have just got offers on Wall Street before the beginning of the last quarter at the business school. It's time to go out and enjoy the good life! It is Saturday evening and you find a quiet street in the city suburbs to test your new German car's capabilities. You and your friend agree that whichever one records the highest speed wins a bottle of champagne. Unfortunately, speed radars are operating even in the remote parts of the city and detect your speed. A couple of days later, you receive an unwelcome call from the policeman in charge. There's even worse news in store: the speed recorded by the radar was so far above the limit that whoever drove will serve a six-month sentence. The policeman knows from the picture that two people were in the car but not who was driving at the time. An investigation at your school, however, enabled the policeman to identify your mate.

Both of you are now in separate cells and are awaiting interrogation. The policeman goes into one cell and says:

'Come on, both of you guys have flashy professional jobs lined up so you'd better cooperate. If you tell me who was responsible and the other guy confirms, you may be free if you are innocent. If, however, each of you assumes responsibility, that is not going to be very helpful and we'll have to split the sentence between the two of you, since your cooperation will have provided no added value. If neither of you cooperates with us, we will have no basis to incriminate anybody for speeding. Nevertheless, I guarantee that both of you will still get a month's sentence for obstructing our investigation. This way you will not forget how costly it is to fool around with the law. By the way, I've made the same offer to your mate on exactly the same terms and conditions. You have until tomorrow morning to let us know.'

The following table summarizes the interaction between you two (with the two numbers within brackets referring to you and your mate, respectively) and the expected sentence – expressed in months:

	My mate confesses	My mate does not confess
I confess	(3,3)	(6,0)
I do not confess	(0,6)	(1,1)

This means that cooperating with your mate – by not revealing who was actually driving that night – is the alternative with the best expected outcome for both parties. If you or your mate confess, then either of you could suffer the maximum penalty. And if both of you confess, then you both suffer sentences that are longer than if neither of you had confessed.

3 The prisoner's dilemma with punishment

It's bonus time. The firm's frequent internal squabbles in recent years are no secret and have been the source of embarrassment for the Board and have provided a field day of guffawing for the press over the last two years. In the hope of assuaging bitter controversy, the Head of Corporate and Investment Banking is asking the two big chiefs of Equities, Investment Banking and Sales & Trading (comprising Equities, Fixed-Income, FX, Treasury and Commodities) to sit down and come back to him with a proposal. By passing the buck, he wants to avoid unpleasant one-on-one discussions and strengthen his reputation as someone who is effective at delegating.

Neither of the two divisional heads knows the total amount of the bonus pie. While the firm's overall profitability relative to peer industry competitors has been good, this has not been a great year for the industry. Rumours in the street say prospects for bonus payments do not look good. The common guess lies between $900 million and $950 million. The boss, however, has made no mystery of his eagerness to avoid yet another embarrassment with the Board and the two divisional heads fear that conflict may be punished with a cutback in the overall bonus pool to $800 million.

By absolute profit and loss after risk capital charges, the two divisions are quite similar. Absolute P&L was lower in investment banking than in the other division. The latter, however, recorded higher risk capital charges due to their reliance on trading revenue.

Each divisional head's situation can be summarized in the following table. Figures are expressed in millions of dollars. For the sake of understanding the main elements in the complex course of negotiations, let us assume that the process involves each divisional head making a proposal that is final and that the two add up their figures and submit them together to their boss. This means that no divisional head is able to retaliate and punish the non-cooperating colleague from the other division before the figures are submitted. The definition of retaliation includes both the ability to force the defecting head to cooperate and the ability to revise one's figures upward to match a non-cooperative proposal from the other.

The figures within brackets show, respectively, the bonus proposal from each division and the final amount awarded by the head of corporate and investment banking after reviewing the proposals. The figures in brackets represent the amount in thousands of dollars that 'my division' and the 'other division' receive, respectively.

	The other division cooperates	The other division does not cooperate
My division cooperates	(450,475)	(450,450)
My division does not cooperate	(500,500)	(500,400)

The situation captured in the first intersecting quadrant (where both divisions cooperate) shows the outcome that maximizes the bonus pool and obtains a bonus amount that is close to the high end of the range for each division. Given equal probabilities, the expected bonus value for the cooperating division is:

$$(475 \times 0.5 + 450 \times 0.5) = \$462.5 \text{ million}$$

Conversely, the expected bonus value for the non-cooperating division is:

$$(500 \times 0.5 + 400 \times 0.5) = \$450 \text{ million}$$

The situation in which all parties cooperate is a case of Nash equilibrium. This example does not consider collusion or retaliation but, if it did, it can be easily seen that the equilibrium that has been achieved is optimal. If in fact one divisional manager increased his request, the other one would likely retaliate by matching the increase by an equal amount. This would in turn prompt the drop in the bonus pool. Collusion, if admitted, would most likely encourage both divisional heads to split the $950 million expected bonus pool in equal parts. This is a prisoner's dilemma game with punishment, since the size of pie over which the two players are vying is subject to a feared cut by the head of corporate and investment banking in response to the two divisional bosses' conflict.

4 The winner's curse

You are the head of trading at a major international investment bank and are considering entering a new business, strengthening your emerging markets, sales and trading activity in a particular region. This region was very hot last year and both your tiny team and similar groups at major competitors achieved record revenues return on capital. The Board of Directors also strongly feels that your presence should be beefed up in light of that region's 'strategic' importance.

You enter into negotiation with a major team of professionals – regarded in the market as last year's superstars – from another street firm via your favourite headhunter. Your market intelligence reveals that three other investment banking firms, two mid-size shops and a global one, are eagerly talking to this group to secure their services for the coming year. You reckon that this activity will require approximately $250 million of economic risk capital. You estimate the revenue potential of these guys to exceed $50 million in extra revenue and, knowing that their activity is heavily sales-driven, you expect that they will about match the firm's 20 per cent return on capital yardstick after costs for this activity.

As your resources and reputation are about the same as your competitors', the negotiation boils down to the financial terms that you will offer to these guys. The magnitude of the guaranteed packages that the team requests through the headhunter is $10 million per year above the level that you had used to calculate the return on capital earlier. 'Hey,' you think, '40/250 is still a decent 16 per cent return on capital.' This is far less visible than the extra $50 million you expect the team to add to the revenue line, which, by the way, gives the firm more scale on their fixed costs. These guys are so good that they may well earn that extra $10 million, after all. And, anyway, top management's bonuses are only marginally affected by cost of economic capital. You ring the headhunter and gladly inform him of your acceptance.

Congratulations! You have just joined the ever-growing community of people who cannot swear to the rationality of their decision but somehow feel that they had little choice but to proceed. Overpaying to beat the competition in the quest for a particular goal is what the winner's curse is about. By definition, this situation does not occur when all players behave rationally. A corollary to this principle is that everybody has sufficient and fair information about everyone else's behaviour. The behavioural problems analysed in the previous chapters demonstrate how far-fetched management's rationality claim generally is. In addition, information is far from complete or correct in the real world. These issues surrounding overbidding are amongst the biggest anomalies that have escaped the neo-classical and modern finance formulation of rationality, and which were reviewed in Thaler's book on *Winner's Curse* (1992).

A subset of the winner's curse is the Atlantic Richfield case (Capen, Clapp & Campbell, 1971) concerning the value of oil drilling rights. In this situation, in which no firm would have achieved a special advantage over competitors had their auction been successful, firms relied on expert judgment to estimate the amount of oil in a given location. Understandably, a positive correlation was found between the firms' bids and the values attributed to the land by the experts that they had hired, so that increasing bids were generally submitted in instances in which the experts had higher estimates. Excessively high bids were an application of the winner's curse and resulted from two kinds of mistakes:

- You pay too much.

- You pay a fair amount but your experts' value estimate is too high.

Empirical evidence confirmed the fears of Capen, Clapp and Campbell. In the 1969 Alaska North Slope sale, the sum of the winning bids ($900 million) far outpaced the sum of the second-highest bids ($370 million). The winning bid exceeded the second bid by a factor of four in about one tract out of four, and by a factor of two in over three-fourths of the tracts. Additional analyses on the value of drilling rights in the Gulf of Mexico (Mead, Moseidjord & Sorensen, 1983) showed that only 22 per cent of the winning bids resulted in profitable investments. Five out of the eight drilling sites were found to be dry. Despite producing oil, the remaining (16 per cent) sites were not profitable. Other subsequent studies (Hendricks, Porter & Boudreau, 1987) also confirmed the trend towards overbidding for oil leases.

5 The ultimatum game

Suppose you wish to create a game to teach your children the value of sharing. Tom receives $10 and has to make an offer to Sheila. She can either accept or reject the offer. In the former case, she will receive whatever Tom offered her. If, on the other hand, she rejects, both will get nothing. What is the right amount that Tom should offer?

If the offer is unreasonably low and appears insulting, the odds are that Sheila will reject it. If, for instance, she received an offer for only one cent, that would be the maximum loss she would have to bear and her rejection would cost her little. Tom, on the other hand, would suffer a $9.99 loss. German economists Güth, Schmittberger & Schwarze (1982) carried out a test with 42 economics students and repeated it a week later. The mean offer with inexperienced students came out at 37 per cent of the total pool, which would translate to

$3.70 in our example. All offers for less than $1 and one of $1.2 were rejected. A week later, while the mean offer dropped to $3.2, only one offer was below $1 and it was duly rejected. Three more offers of $1 were turned down, as was one of $3. The intuition is that the recipient can inflict serious damage to the allocator at a small cost.

Two subsequent studies by Kahnemann, Knetsch & Thaler (1986) investigated the topic further. In the first one, 137 subjects at the University of British Columbia were posed a series of binary yes/no questions. When offered a given amount, would they accept or not? Twenty-two incorrect answers were excluded. The offers increased in $0.5 increments. Consistent with the previous study's findings, the mean minimum acceptable offer recorded in three different experiments ranged between $2 and $2.59. A subsequent study, conducted with students in a psychology class at Cornell University, investigated two questions:

- Will the allocators be fair even if their offers cannot be rejected?

- Will subjects sacrifice money to punish an allocator who behaved unfairly to *someone else*?

To answer the first question, each student was asked to split $20 between himself and a partner. He was asked to choose between only two alternatives. He could split the amount in half or keep $18 for himself and leave only $2 to his partner. Contrary to the previous experiments, though, the recipients could not refuse the offer. The answer was very generous, as 122 of the 161 respondents, or 76 per cent, decided for the 50–50 split. To answer the second question, the allocators were asked whether they would pay a dollar to split money with a stranger who had been generous rather than split it with a stranger who had been greedy. It is worth noting that the payoff from the latter alternative would be one dollar above the former. Nevertheless, about three-fourths of the respondents (74 per cent) opted to take the smaller reward and split with the generous partner.

6 Public goods game

This kind of situation provides a generalization to the cooperation issues involved in the prisoner's dilemma game that was discussed previously. While conventional utility theory and neo-classical economics would not deem this behaviour as rational (i.e., selfish), there are some concrete applications in real life, such as voluntary payment of taxes and contribution to teams and community goals. Compared to the prisoner's dilemma, this situation involves more than two players trying to out-guess each other. In addition, this game becomes more meaningful when it involves a series of interactions amongst the various players, whereas the classic prisoner's dilemma situation involves only a one-shot outcome.

Let's consider a situation in which ten subjects are told that $1 will be deposited in their private account as a reward for participating in each round of an experiment. For every $1 that a subject moves from his 'private account' to the 'public account', the experimenter will deposit one half-dollar in the private account of each of the subjects at the end of the game. This process can be repeated ten times and, at the end of the game, each participant can take home whatever he or she has in his or her private account.

If all ten subjects cooperate perfectly, each puts $1 in the public account at the end of each round, generating a public pool of $10, and the experimenter then puts $5 in the private account of each subject. After ten rounds of this, each participant will then have $50. If, by contrast, one subject is perfectly selfish while the others are cooperative, a different payoff would develop. The selfish one keeps $1-per-round in his private account, while the cooperative subjects continue to put $1 in the public pool. The selfish one would enjoy a free ride on the cooperative contributions of the others, concluding the game at $55, whereas all the others would end up with $45 each. If all players opted for the selfish payoff, no one would contribute to the public pool and each would end up with $10 at the end of the game. If only one was to contribute and all the others were selfish, that player would conclude the game with $5 while the others would have $15. The various behaviours and consequent outcomes are as follows:

- If others cooperate, it is best to take a free ride.
- If others are selfish, it is best to join them.
- However, if all players are selfish, all receive less than they would if they had all cooperated.

The experiments generally display a very instructive pattern, in that the selfish, rational behaviour predicted by conventional economics emerges only in the late stages of the game, after several rounds of contribution from the various players. Specifically, this rational behaviour would require contributions of zero. In the initial stages, however, their contributions are equal to approximately half of the worth of their private account. Some (Andreoni, 1995, 1998) explain this behaviour with a *homo reciprocans* approach: contributors in good faith want to retaliate against free-riders, and the only way available to them in the game is by not contributing themselves.

When subjects are given a more constructive way of punishing defectors, they use it as a means of sustaining cooperation. Studies by Dawes, Orbell & Van de Kragt (1986), Sato (1987) and Yamagishi (1988a, 1988b, 1992) have confirmed this effect. Ostrom, Walker & Gardner (1992) found that cooperation was significantly enhanced (to 93 per cent of the subjects) just by allowing subjects to communicate with each other, even in the absence of binding agreements. Sanctioning was required only in 4 per cent of the cases. Such communication is called *cheap talk*.

Further evidence on the cooperation benefit from the threat of punishing free-riders came from Fehr & Gächter (1999). In a repeated public goods game experiment, cooperation was found to improve even when costly punishments would not generate any monetary benefit for the subjects who would inflict it.

7 Bluff games

Bluffing does not enjoy the same status as other forms of interaction studied by game theory academics and, accordingly, does not appear in many game theory texts. It is nevertheless an important form of strategic interaction which players often use in both games and in business, and especially in finance and investment banking. A concrete example comes from negotiations between bank syndicates, clients and investors, whereby a bank may signal its ability to 'punish' a client or investor for not adopting a given behaviour without being really able to do so. For instance, the bank may signal that research coverage may be withdrawn for a defecting client, or may threaten to exclude an investor from allocations of future securities. In practice, commercial and legal reasons force dealers to use these threats sparingly. In addition, banks are often deluding themselves about the effectiveness of these signals and this is yet another widespread illusion of cognitive control in the industry. However, as internal behaviours are one of the key areas of interest of this book, bluffs are a relevant strategic behaviour to analyse.

Bluffs are a form of lying and deception for which the most classic application has been in poker games. Unlike lying, bluffing does not mean making false statements. Rather, it uses postures, facial expressions or other gestures to create a misleading impression in the counterpart's mind. It is the recipient's cognitive reactions to the unspoken message that matter the most. While liars, after being discovered, will never be believed again, bluffers will be able to confuse their counterpart on the next occasion, as there is no way to tell whether the bluff will be repeated or not. This has a major implication: a player may bluff once to create an impression of strength, be discovered and surprise their counterpart with a strong hand the next time.

Poker presents several points in common with the world of trading. First and foremost there is critical importance to risk management where in general there are lucky and less lucky short-term streaks, but the long-term outcome is rarely based on luck alone. Rather, long-term success crucially depends on how short-term losses are managed and how the staying power of risk capital is preserved. This is the genuine essence of risk management. If one loses too much in one hand, he will have to reduce the size of his bet next time or risk getting bankrupt.

One of the best analyses of bluffing is found in László Mérő's *Moral Calculations* (1998). Let's have a poker game that starts with two players, X and Y, putting respectively $10 and $30 on the table. The evolution of the game can be summarized as follows:

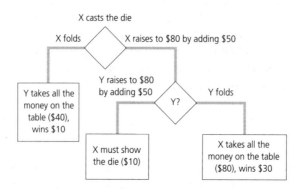

FIGURE A3.2 ■ Bluffing

Source: © Professor László Mérő and Springer-Verlag, reprinted with permission

From this game, one can understand that X's optimal strategy is to use bluffing sparingly, rather than in every round. Depending on his skill and experience, there are four different ways in which X can implement his bluffing strategy. Let us examine them:

(1) No bluffing

For instance, by acting as if he has not obtained a certain number when he has not will lead the counterpart to always believe him and result in a deficit. In this game, X wins $30 and loses $10 in successful and unsuccessful rounds, respectively. As there is a 1/6th chance that a certain number will be drawn, over the long run X will experience a win of only $30 for every five $10 losses.

(2) Poor bluffing

This occurs where Y can distinguish when X does not have a certain number. The outcome for X will be even worse, since a successful bluff will earn him only $30. This will be more than offset by the $60 that Y will earn when he calls X's bluff.

(3) Bluffing that is over-used

This will not earn X much, since Y will, after a while, never believe him. In Mérö's example, if X always raises, Y will soon stop believing him and will match the raise accordingly. He will then win five times $60, or $300, and lose $80 only once.

(4) Intelligent bluffing

For instance, establishing some quick-and-dirty mental rule would provide X with the best chance of long-term success. He may, for instance, decide to raise only when either there is a six or – and this is the bluff – the next number on the table is a nine. This is what is called a *mixed strategy*. Based on this strategy, there is a 1/9th chance that bluffing will occur and a 1/6th chance that raises will occur following a six that has already been drawn. If there are, for explanatory and computational simplicity, 54 rounds, X will expect to roll a six in (1/6 × 54) = 9 times. If Y accepts all the challenges, X will win $80 x 9 instances, or $720. In the remaining 45 rounds in which a six is not drawn, X will bluff in 1/9th of the instances (5 times), when the second number is a nine. He will lose $60 in each of these five times, or $300 in total. X will further lose $400, or $10 per time, by declining the remaining 40 rounds. In aggregate, this strategy will net him $(720 – 300 – 400) = $20.

The intuition of this theory – as confirmed by countless real life examples in banks and professional firms – is that bluffing adds a little 'salt and pepper' to your strategy by making it a bit less obvious and predictable to competitors and counterparts. Excessive use of this strategy, however, will defeat the purpose and jeopardize a player's reputation and trust-worthiness, as will poor execution skill. As usual, the trade-off between being reliable and becoming too transparent is a delicate balance to manage.

8 Political correctness

Academics have paid attention to this type of interaction only recently and mostly in the context of studies on *cheap talk* (see section 9), theory of conformity and the importance of reputation. Yet, this behaviour is frequently observed in business and finance and has major implications for decision-making, even more so in large and complex organizations. Political correctness is related to a number of other biases including status quo, complacent outside advisors, and other collective group biases, such as 'yes-men' (analysed in Chapter 5). It may also result in filters being applied to information that is conveyed in order to suit others' selective attention bias (see Chapter 4).

Morris (1999) provides one of the most comprehensive summaries on this topic. It is shown that this strategy makes sense only when two key conditions are met for the person who intends to adopt a politically correct strategy:

- the reputation in the eyes of his or her counterpart(s) is an important asset to preserve, and

- such reputation – often labelled influence within a group or organization – is deemed to be an important factor which may influence some future decisions that he or she cares to be a part of.

The corollary of this principle is that being politically correct matters only when a future relationship will be involved. Loury (1994, 1998) presents the following thought process to explain the motives behind political correctness:

- Within a given community or reference group, the people who are thought to be most faithful to communal values are – by and large – those who want most to remain in good standing with their fellows.

- Exclusion from the good standing in the community is one of the unwritten but oft-practised sanctions again those who speak in ways that offend the community.

- When one expresses himself in terms that the community deems offensive, the odds increase that otherwise informed listeners in that group will infer that such a person does not comply with communal values.

Two important cognitive issues are in action here. First, there is a misleading heuristic shortcut in the first step, 'if that person expresses a view that runs against the group common wisdom, he evidently does not subscribe to the group's values'. Without any other information, this absolute statement is obviously superficial. Second, there is an evident selective attention bias that is built into the inference drawn in point 3, namely overweighing the importance of the previous heuristic as the main or sole decision criterion.

The moral of this story for an intelligent manager, boss, or for an innovative organization is simple. If people are often navigating close to the coastline, they'd better be ready with an explanation as to what their future motives are. The act of preserving reputations may make the environment feel nicer and provide a false immediate sense of comfort and security. This safety, however, tilts the balance of decision-making towards complacency, self-promotion and self-congratulatory remarks for what has worked to date. It is not the best breeding ground for an aggressive and innovative risk-taking spirit. Even if your organization competes on service or price rather than on product technology and innovation, there is always a competitor lurking in the dark with some potential edge. Planning the obsolescence of your own products or services is a long-respected good practice in marketing. Tactical considerations notwithstanding, you are unlikely to pursue it by breeding and reinforcing yes-men behaviours in your organization.

9 Other important games

A wealth of additional game theory literature is available on other forms of strategic interaction. While they have real-life applications in business and finance, their discussion in detail is beyond the purpose of this book. Those interested are referred to the bibliography at the end of the book. Amongst the most important themes:

Procrastination

These are behaviours whereby a person might forego completing an attractive option because she plans to complete a more attractive but never-to-be-completed option. The intuition is that some find more pain in reaching decisions now than in the future and delay accordingly. A large body of empirical evidence (Ainslie, 1975, 1991, 1992; Ainslie & Haslam, 1992a, 1992b; Loewenstein & Prelec, 1992; Thaler, 1991; Thaler & Loewenstein, 1992) shows that intertemporal preferences take on a specific form of time inconsistency. Such inconsistency means that a person's relative preference for well-being at an earlier date over a later date gets stronger as the earlier date gets closer. This mental process is referred to as hyperbolic discounting. This behaviour challenges the standard economics assumption of time-consistent intertemporal preferences. These would imply that a person's relative preference for well-being at an earlier date over a later date is the same no matter when she is asked. In general, providing additional options to a non-procrastinator can induce procrastination. In addition, a person is more likely to procrastinate when pursuing important goals than unimportant ones.

Centipede games

These are interactions between a number (two or greater) of subjects who may defect or not in a series of repeated rounds. If a player defects, the game is over. If players otherwise cooperate by not stealing, 'Nature' gives them a certain positive payoff. The game continues until either one player defects or the value of the portfolio of each player reaches a given threshold amount. This often becomes a coordination game between several subjects. Some applications (Cassel Lab 2002) have been suggested for financial panics and pyramid schemes (commonly referred to as 'Ponzi schemes' in the US). It is easy to see the application of this type of interaction to currency speculations, whereby a speculator often holds a position – typically a deposit or a short-term fixed-income security – in a high-yielding currency and funds it with a liability in a low-yielding currency. In this instance, the speculator bets that the yield differential will more than offset any depreciation in the exchange rate between the two currencies in which he holds the position and related liability. The game continues until one player 'blows the whistle', for instance by highlighting the potential political and/or economic instability of the country with the high-yielding currency.

Common pool resource game

This is the situation in which subjects cooperate in the management of a commonly shared resource. The fact that the common resource continues to be shared indefinitely is what differentiates this form of interaction from the public goods game. To distinguish the latter from the former, the common pool is divided between the players at the end of the game. In a classic paper, Hardin (1968) provides an example of an English village where villagers are allowed to have their sheep or cows graze at a nearby area (denominated 'commons'). This is a n-person-repeated prisoner's dilemma game, in which each person hopes that the others will cooperate. They hope each will not take too much of the common resource. Relevant real-life examples in financial institutions are provided by an institution's creditworthiness or by the liquidity of its balance sheet, both of which allow more flexibility. Unfortunately, like many financial institutions, real-world communities often do not manage their shared resources well. Hackett, Schlager & Walker (1994) and Bardhan, Bowles & Gintis (2000) illustrate the case in which communities become so large that it pays to form a local coalition operating against the whole community. Large organizations and financial institutions often witness such turf wars. Their long-term benefits to the shareholders are questionable at best. The implication then becomes to create internal clients who will pay for the shared resource according to a fair transfer price. External market-based benchmarks for such services can be established.

Theory of cheap talk

This is previously referred to in the context of the public goods game. Ottaviani & Sørensen (2002) apply this type of interaction to instances of external professional advisers, such as analysts and consultants. Professional advisers are often notoriously far more concerned with their own reputation than with the decisions made on the basis on their recommendations. Within his own area of professional expertise, the expert would like to be deemed 'well-informed', since this favourable reputation influences his compensation. In the real world, no demonstrable proof can be given to substantiate the recommendation. It is shown that the expert has an incentive to deviate toward the neutral signal. Intuitively, a more conservative signal is less likely to deviate from the actual outcome, for instance by adding lots of caveats and assumptions. In turn, this results in a more favourable update on the ability of the 'expert'. Further, experts who provide their recommendations in equilibrium and who are motivated by the urge to preserve their good reputation as good forecasters are found to be less accurate than the information they possess. The study concludes that when the market evaluates performance in this naive way, excessive conformism results. Chapter 9 illustrates this issue in greater detail in the discussion of outside constituencies.

Additional tables for Chapter 7

TABLE A ▪ Source daily data for VaR and the other summary trading statistics

	Desk 1	Desk 2	Desk 3	Desk 4	Desk 5	Aggregate
02-Jan-02	(246,295)	647,007	446,160	439,582	2,128,866	3,415,320
03-Jan-02	(4,636,908)	249,982	113,070	262,542	619,990	(3,391,324)
04-Jan-02	(699,405)	395,096	479,050	350,436	(1,255,716)	(730,539)
07-Jan-02	(312,725)	962,322	(183,040)	531,802	(157,644)	840,715
08-Jan-02	757,715	(5,973,737)	2,957,380	144,478	843,939	(1,270,225)
09-Jan-02	(632,695)	(68,418)	807,950	(544,098)	(527,719)	(964,980)
10-Jan-02	(2,067,275)	1,942,007	(320,320)	2,145,652	(1,220,382)	479,682
11-Jan-02	(1,280,125)	404,197	(873,730)	378,102	3,841,893	2,470,337
14-Jan-02	(170,695)	(373,797)	642,070	205,958	(2,129,553)	(1,826,017)
15-Jan-02	1,832,507	2,007,917	223,642	(172,443)	80,752	3,972,375
16-Jan-02	514,080	331,949	803,660	418,064	3,056,600	5,124,353
17-Jan-02	(941,430)	(355,806)	(735,020)	310,474	1,424,232	(297,550)
18-Jan-02	(550,025)	(7,071,708)	882,310	89,146	298,773	(6,351,504)
21-Jan-02	(2,744,105)	490,025	(90,090)	(215,180)	(16,308)	(2,575,658)
22-Jan-02	576,520	117,675	244,530	(322,770)	3,544,272	4,160,227
23-Jan-02	259,105	(1,536,614)	(275,990)	(1,155,824)	(500,295)	(3,209,618)
24-Jan-02	915,180	(1,273,503)	(1,016,730)	(851,498)	3,012,903	786,352
25-Jan-02	(9,835)	(164,614)	1,430	250,626	(70,384)	7,223
28-Jan-02	(4,926,920)	(48,476)	2,156,470	233,624	(152,877)	(2,738,179)
29-Jan-02	(170,415)	1,028,515	(614,900)	15,370	5,460,462	5,719,032
30-Jan-02	2,191,805	(6,818,551)	210,210	393,472	1,094,772	(2,928,292)
31-Jan-02	(419,965)	(367,007)	1,487,200	(70,702)	(1,142,919)	(513,393)

	Desk 1	Desk 2	Desk 3	Desk 4	Desk 5	Aggregate
01-Feb-02	1,946,700	862,015	308,880	261,290	(1,194,561)	2,184,324
04-Feb-02	(6,801,870)	(555,212)	263,120	(132,182)	5,501,232	(1,724,912)
05-Feb-02	(370,510)	2,096,959	(856,570)	1,540,074	(260,928)	2,149,025
06-Feb-02	262,640	(1,340,674)	191,620	165,996	7,087,185	6,366,767
07-Feb-02	(1,029,630)	(76,170)	(763,620)	384,250	3,392,064	1,906,894
08-Feb-02	276,605	941,099	(853,710)	64,554	1,213,587	1,642,135
11-Feb-02	(90,580)	521,907	(497,640)	854,572	(176,431)	611,828
12-Feb-02	(252,000)	325,176	(732,160)	1,011,346	3,670,659	4,023,021
13-Feb-02	1,076,635	(41,549)	(7,547,660)	150,626	7,864,548	1,502,600
14-Feb-02	856,450	(325,077)	1,584,440	390,398	5,394,404	7,900,615
15-Feb-02	335,186	2,777,142	20,392	391,572	551,609	4,075,901
18-Feb-02	(612,539)	(851,675)	1,830,204	1,011,425	7,024,671	8,402,086
19-Feb-02	(1,153,992)	(621,711)	147,290	(304,326)	(360,135)	(2,292,874)
20-Feb-02	(902,067)	(340,504)	1,601,600	(3,074)	4,688,550	5,044,505
21-Feb-02	(8,124,102)	(23,318)	1,614,470	1,993,483	738,903	(3,800,564)
22-Feb-02	(449,435)	482,590	2,965,820	722,390	(543,600)	3,177,765
25-Feb-02	(1,079,575)	1,188,919	(513,370)	3,074	6,804,513	6,403,561
26-Feb-02	243,746	(883,441)	929,500	(18,444)	(247,338)	24,023
27-Feb-02	347,509	1,204,949	(311,740)	279,734	(1,601,574)	(81,122)
28-Feb-02	(205,693)	2,023,178	(813,670)	144,478	(853,664)	294,629
01-Mar-02	103,909	(5,874,073)	3,345,452	(21,518)	2,442,123	(4,107)
04-Mar-02	1,236,422	1,141,725	(34,320)	92,220	3,999,537	6,435,584
05-Mar-02	(8,367,185)	(944,901)	3,200,585	156,774	4,183,002	(1,771,725)
06-Mar-02	(441,000)	(4,396,227)	(353,210)	91,064	3,946,536	(1,152,837)
07-Mar-02	457,835	(737,997)	(101,407)	98,368	(941,990)	(1,225,191)
08-Mar-02	(239,557)	392,830	(642,070)	65,441	(326,160)	(749,516)
11-Mar-02	704,340	460,358	289,762	620,948	(451,884)	1,623,524
12-Mar-02	1,472,227	343,879	112,633	(77,401)	176,291	2,027,629
13-Mar-02	439,104	(101,472)	(61,339)	32,972	201,481	510,746

	Desk 1	Desk 2	Desk 3	Desk 4	Desk 5	Aggregate
14-Mar-02	341,006	284,590	120,725	68,402	142,064	956,787
15-Mar-02	(80,382)	90,261	(10,427)	111,527	237,482	348,461
18-Mar-02	(5,756,500)	(1,009,949)	(327,040)	2,635,066	(60,955)	(4,519,378)
19-Mar-02	1,073,491	(326,091)	80,531	291,723	(10,841)	1,108,813
20-Mar-02	391,956	172,443	280,041	(43,982)	44,272	844,730
21-Mar-02	(137,820)	403,928	600,583	60,267	25,084	952,042
22-Mar-02	873,203	(274,991)	193,457	(70,671)	381,824	1,102,822
25-Mar-02	(30,552)	(151,339)	(60,494)	81,123	339,080	177,818
26-Mar-02	(80,462)	345,548	51,920	(11,194)	(140,553)	165,259

TABLE B ▦ Source daily data for the portfolio decision problem

	<==== Monthly Returns ====>			<= Portfolio Cumul. Abs. Returns =>		
	Portfolio A	Portfolio B	Portfolio C	Portfolio A	Portfolio B	Portfolio C
January	−0.2	0.4	0.1	−0.200	0.400	0.100
February	−0.5	0.7	0.1	−0.699	1.103	0.200
March	0.2	0.2	0.2	−0.500	1.305	0.401
April	−0.1	0.5	0.2	−0.600	1.812	0.601
May	−0.4	0.2	−0.1	−0.997	2.015	0.501
June	−0.3	0.7	0.2	−1.295	2.729	0.702
July	−0.2	−0.4	−0.3	−1.492	2.318	0.400
August	0.4	0.5	0.45	−1.098	2.830	0.851
September	1.4	0.4	0.9	0.287	3.241	1.759
October	−0.6	0.4	−0.1	−0.315	3.654	1.657
November	−0.3	−0.1	−0.2	−0.614	3.551	1.454
December	−0.2	0.5	0.15	−0.813	4.068	1.606
January	−0.3	0.6	0.15	−1.110	4.693	1.759
February	−0.4	0.5	0.05	−1.506	5.216	1.809
March	1.1	−0.6	0.25	−0.422	4.585	2.064
April	−0.3	0.3	0	−0.721	4.899	2.064
May	−0.5	0.6	0.05	−1.218	5.528	2.115
June	−0.2	0.1	−0.05	−1.415	5.634	2.064
July	1.9	−1.7	0.1	0.458	3.838	2.166
August	−0.3	0.4	0.05	0.157	4.253	2.217
September	−0.2	−0.7	−0.45	−0.044	3.523	1.757
October	−0.3	0.1	−0.1	−0.344	3.627	1.655
November	−0.1	0.3	0.1	−0.443	3.938	1.757
December	−0.2	−0.3	−0.25	−0.642	3.626	1.503
January	−0.1	0.4	0.15	−0.742	4.040	1.655
February	−0.1	0.5	0.2	−0.841	4.561	1.858
March	−0.3	0.6	0.15	−1.138	5.188	2.011
April	1.1	−0.8	0.15	−0.051	4.347	2.164
May	−0.5	0.9	0.2	−0.551	5.286	2.368
June	−0.3	0.4	0.05	−0.849	5.707	2.420
July	−0.4	0.6	0.1	−1.246	6.341	2.522

Glossary

Term	Meaning
Alice-in-Wonderland	Creating an unrealistic mix of fantasy and reality.
Anchoring and adjustment	People's tendency to remain anchored to certain pieces of information, regardless of their relevance.
Arbitrage	Profit with limited or no downside risk.
Asian crisis	Currency crisis that began with the drop of the currency peg between the Thai baht and a basket of foreign currency (primarily US dollar, Japanese yen and German Mark). It lasted over one year and brought down in succession all major currencies in South-East Asia and the related stock markets.
Backwardation	Term of the futures markets that refers to the shape of the price curve. Under this condition, short-dated futures contracts trade at a higher price than longer-dated maturities. This condition is also labelled 'Inverted Market'.
Bayesian or conditional probability	Probability that depends on the probability of a prior event.
Behavioural finance	Alternative explanation of financial markets' behaviour, which uses empirical evidence collected by prospect theory proponents and insights from cognitive psychology to refute EMH investors' rationality assumptions of MFT.
Binary bias	Tendency to categorize problems in yes/no, black/white, good/bad tems.

Bottom up Decision-making process that starts from more detailed pieces of information and then consolidates them into a big picture. Many active equity managers prefer making stock-picking decsions first and then adding up the pieces. Preferred by people who are more detail-orientated.

Buridanic choice A situation in which the decision-maker cannot identify a strictly best option.

Calibration Process that uses prior statistical information to adjust models that will be used in future decisions. Vulnerable to confirmation bias.

Can't happen here bias Individual belief engendered by belonging to a large group. The size of the group or vehicle/body containing the group is thought to be a shelter. Watch for your thoughts on this next time you travel on a large airplane or ship!

Casuality Absence of *casual* link or relationship between two variables or financial products. The numbers and the statistics may mislead one into seeing non-existent relationships, thereby driving wrong decisions.

CDO See Collateralized debt obligation.

CDS See Credit default swap.

CMT See Constant-maturity T-note yield.

Cognitive dissonance Refers to the conflict between incoming information and feedback and one's own views. See also Dissonance.

Cognitive resonance Opposite of Cognitive dissonance (see Definition).

Collateral Amount of cash or risk-free securities that is pledged as a guarantee of a given future obligation. If the obligation is not fulfilled, the counterpart will be able to satisfy their claims on the collateral.

Collateralized debt obligation Pool of credit obligations from a set of obligors. These can be in cash (typically bonds) or synthetic form, such as credit default swaps. The investor receives an above-LIBOR interest rate in return for assuming the risk of default of each name in the pool. Is often subdivided in tranches based on the rating of the underlying names in each tranche.

Confirmation bias Setting fairly easy threshold conditions for the hypothesis under test such that the hypothesis cannot be falsified under those conditions.

Conservatism Analysts' tendency to delay the adjustment in their forecasts to reflect new incoming information.

Constant-maturity Treasury yield	Index published regularly by the Federal Reserve that refers to the yields on the US Treasury notes with a given maturity.
Contango	Term of the futures markets that refers to the shape of the price curve. Under this condition, short-dated futures contracts trade at a lower price than longer-dated maturities.
Context dependence	Situation in which the context affects the outcome of a decision. As shown by Kahneman & Tversky, the same bet may be accepted or rejected depending on the context or reference points around it. If I have made 10 in a previous bet, I will likely become risk-averse and not risk it all next time. If, on the other hand, I lost 10 last time, the odds are that I will increase the stakes next time to try to recoup the loss. Also very important in the visual field (see examples in Chapter 2).
Credit default swap	Financial derivative product whereby one party transfers the credit risk of a reference name (such as a country, company or other obligor with debt instruments) to another and pays a premium in return.
Credit matrices	See Statistical credit matrices.
Credit risk	The risk that a counterparty to a financial obligation – such as a loan, a bond or other contractual commitment – will default on repayments linked to the obligation.
Credit spreads	Spread between the yields offered by credit-risky bonds and those on riskless or near-riskless instruments, typically government bonds.
Cross-country skier's downhill run bias	Making unrealistically optimistic projections for the scenarios that will be faced to avoid the psychologically uncomfortable prospect of a laborious task ahead.
Currency peg	Parity set by a government or central bank between national currency and major global currencies (generally the US dollar).
Default risk	See Credit risk.
Denial	Disconfirming or ignoring information that conflicts with the decision-maker's opinions or actions. Frequently used to avoid negative feedback loops between reality and the subject's views.
Disposition effect	Tendency to hold on to losing positions and to realize gains quickly.
Dissonance	People's need to reduce or avoid psychological inconsistencies in their minds. It is further sub-divided into pre-decisional and post-decisional dissonance depending on whether the inner conflict occurs before or after a decision.

Doubling up	Progressively increasing the size of a position as market prices continue to move against its holder. This offers the psychological benefit of 'averaging down' the last of a position in the mistaken belief that the law of large numbers and probabilities will eventually drive the price up. See also Gambler's Fallacy.
Duration	Measures sensitivity of a bond's price to parallel shifts in the yield curve.
Efficient market hypothesis (EMH)	Key principle of modern finance theory (MFT). According to it, no riskless arbitrage is possible in financial markets, or, in layman's terms, there is no such thing as a free lunch (see related explanation). Investors are supposed to behave completely rationally and their behaviours are considered mostly irrelevant.
Ellsberg principle	Subjects' preference to bet on known rather than unknown probabilities.
EMH	See Efficient market hypothesis.
Endowment effect	Different treatment of wealth depending on the timing and ways in which it was acquired. Particularly relevant with inheritances or sudden windfall gains such as, for instance, winning a lottery.
Euroyen	Deposits or liabilities that are yen-denominated but made or assumed out of Japan. Colloquially, dealers refer to 'Euroyen contracts' to denote the future contracts on the three-month Euroyen LIBOR rate. This contract allows the parties to lock a set rate on the three-month Euroyen LIBOR starting at the contract maturity date.
Extrapolation bias	Tendency to predict the future by extrapolating from an existing trend.
Feedback trader	Trader who bases his decisions on prior price movements. It is sub-divided into positive and negative feedback trading depending on the decision to buy or sell, respectively, after price increases.
Frames of risk	Mental setup that creates a context surrounding a decision about uncertainty or information to be used in such decisions. Risk involves the possibility of loss, whether in financial or in real-world terms (accident possibly resulting in loss of human life). It refers to the way in which individuals, organizations and policymakers at the systemic level frame information concerning financial risk. See Individual, Organizational and Systemic frame of risk.

Framing	Refers to the process of creating a frame or a context around a risky decision or information associated with it. See also Context dependence.
Fungibility	Ability to exchange an asset or product for another at a given future date. Fungibility differs from liquidity, since one may have the latter without the former. In the case of a position composed of two or more legs, such as spreads between two products, one may indeed succeed in liquidating each leg but not necessarily be able to realize the value of the combination.
Gambler's fallacy	Decision-maker's misconceptions about probabilities and how they apply after a streak of outcomes. Results in oversizing bets too early and often causes Gambler's ruin (see definition).
Gambler's ruin	Unfortunate result of betting in increasing sizes, thereby rapidly burning one's risk capital. See also Gambler's fallacy.
Game theory	Theory that postulates that one's decisions on utility will not be independent of other's preferences (as assumed by conventional economics) but, rather, will take them into some account in formulating the choice. First developed by mathematician John Nash.
Get-even-itis	Introduced in Hersh Shefrin's *Beyond Greed and Fear*, it refers to an investor's tendency to hang on to losing positions and waiting to 'get even' relative to the original price at which the position was entered. Sometimes this may even degenerate into 'doubling-up' behaviours (see definition.)
Groupthink	Bias where group consensus results in decisions that are sub-optimal relative to individual suggestions, preferences or alternatives that may be otherwise desirable.
Hedonic framing	See Mental accounting.
Herd behaviours	Bias whereby one overweighs other people's views in forming his own. The conviction of group members increases as other members join that opinion. As a result, one ends up following the crowd.
Heuristics	Mental shortcuts to classify and categorize new information and situations.
Hindsight	Tendency to use the past to see one's own views confirmed after the fact.
Hindsight bias	This is sometimes called the I-knew-it-all-along effect.
Hot hands	Term from basketball that refers to people's belief that a successful shooter will have a higher probability of continuing his successful streak than an unsuccessful one.

I knew it all along	This is the definition used by Plous (1993).
Illusion of control	Belief that one has the means to control what is essentially a random process and outcome rules by chance.
Illusion of invulnerability	Group bias and over-optimistic self-assessment engendered by the reputation, competence and expertise of the group members.
Illusion of validity	See Confirmation bias.
Individual frame of risk	Frame of risk adopted by individuals in making decisions with uncertain (risky) outcomes and evaluating the information to reach such decisions.
Interest-only (IO)	Tranche derived from a mortgage-backed security whereby the interest is backed by the interest repayments from the underlying mortgage holders. Its price tends to rise when interest rates rise, since this is usually associated with slower prepayments in the underlying mortgages. Consequently, the set of interest cashflows accruing to the IO investor from the underlying mortgages PO investor will soar.
Inverted market	See Backwardation.
IO	See Interest-only.
JGBs	Japanese government bonds. These are Japan's sovereign bonds.
Knowledge-equal-solution fallacy	Assumption that action and solution will always automatically follow people's receipt of information.
Legal risk	Risk of loss resulting from legal controversy and/or application of contractual wording.
LIBOR	London Interbank Offered Rate, the floating rate rate charged by banks to Euromarket borrowers.
Loss aversion	Human aversion to incur a loss, meaning a diminution of one's personal wealth. Contrary to conventional economics' assumptions, this increases as one's wealth grows. Hence the popular saying that 'the poor take risks that they cannot afford while the rich don't take risks that they could bear'. Not to be confused with Risk aversion.
Lotto bias	See Gambler's fallacy
LTCM	Long-Term Capital Management, the hedge fund founded by John W. Meriwether.
Margin call	Cash or risk-free securities that are pledged as a guarantee of a given future obligation, generally in markets of listed derivative products, such as options and futures. It is divided into initial

	and variation margin, respectively calculated when the position is created and based on the daily change in value of the underlying position. If the party defaults, his contracts will be closed immediately and any losses arising from them will be met by the margin amount.
Market risk	Current or prospective risk to earnings and capital arising from adverse movements in bond prices, security and commodity prices and foreign exchange rates in the trading book.
Mean-reversion bias	See Gambler's fallacy
Mean-variance optimization (MVO)	In MFT, it refers to the process of combining assets into a portfolio in order to minimize risk for a given return target set by the investor. Alternatively, such combinations can be built by having the investor set his risk preference constraints and then seeking the portfolio that offers the highest expected return.
Mental accounting	Process of looking at one's portfolio and grouping its individual components in an inconsistent manner to treat gains and losses separately.
Metcalfe's Law	Refers to computer networks and states that a network gets stronger as the number of its members increases. The increase is calculated as the square of the number of participants.
MFT	See Modern finance theory.
Modern finance theory (MFT)	Dominant explanation of behaviour of financial markets and their securities to support the efficient market hypothesis (see explanation).
Mortgage-backed securities	Security where the cashflows are backed by the interest and principal payments of a pool of mortgages. As the mortgage holder pays interest and principal, these flows are passed to the investor.
MVO	See Mean-variance optimization.
No free lunch	Law number one of MFT. This means that an investor will earn excess returns only by assuming more risks.
Noise trader	Short-term trader who will use a variety of short-term rumours and other pieces of information other than fundamentals.
Not-me bias	Individual belief engendered by belonging to a large group. Results in beliefs such as 'why should I be the one suffering when there are so many others that could?'
Operating leverage	Measures the sensitivity of a business's profits to changes in revenues, typically sales. The steeper it is, the more sensitive the company gets to swings in sales volumes. Tends to be positively correlated with the level of fixed costs, whereby a business with

	a higher fixed overhead base will become more dependent on its sales than one with higher variable costs as a percentage of total costs.
Operational risk	According to the Basle Committee on Banking Supervision (Consultative Document, 31 May 2001), it is the 'risk of direct or indirect loss resulting from inadequate or failed internal processes, people and systems or from external events'.
Organizational frame of risk	Frame of risk adopted by companies, banks and organizations in evaluating and assessing decisions with uncertain (risky) outcomes.
Overconfidence	People's ignorance on their actual level of knowledge of a given situation, particularly when uncertainty is involved. Simply put, people cannot asses how much there is that they do not know.
PO	See Principal-only.
Portfolio insurance	Strategy that attempts to replicate dynamically the payoff of an option by having variable proportions of stock index futures in the portfolio.
Postdecisional dissonance	See Dissonance.
Predecisional dissonance	See Dissonance.
Prediction	See Extrapolation bias.
Present value (PV)	The process of discounting future cashflows and adding them up into a single (PV) figure.
Principal-only (PO)	Tranche derived from a mortgage-backed security whereby the principal is backed by the principal repayments from the underlying mortgage holders. Its price tends to rise when interest rates drop, since this is usually associated with faster prepayments in the underlying mortgages. Consequently, the PO investor will receive his PO cashflows earlier.
Principle of comparative ignorance	See Ellsberg principle.
Product control	Independent support area that validates traders' P&L and performs a variety of other checks to protect the integrity of a bank's risk books and records. In some organizations, product controllers also perform the independent risk checks required by financial regulators.
Program trading	Mass execution by computers of trading orders based on portfolio insurance strategies.

Prospect theory (PT)	Theory pioneered by Daniel Kahneman and Amos Tversky in the 1970s to explain people's shifting preferences when dealing with decisions concerning risk and uncertainty. PT showed that people have an S-shaped utility preference, with the flex set at people's reference point (see definition). This contrasts the stable risk preferences assumptions of traditional utility theory supported by conventional economics. People become risk-seeking below that reference point and risk-averse above it.
Quant	Colloquial expression to indicate staff with strong mathematical skills.
Recency bias	Tendency to overweigh recent information.
Reference point	Point where one finds oneself in a neutral situation between losses (below the reference point) and gains (above it). Key driver of prospect theory (see definition) and its S-shaped utility function.
Regret management	See post-decisional dissonance under Dissonance.
Relative-value trade	Trade in which one bets on the price of one security relative to another rather than on the absolute move magnitude of any of them. The latter would be an *outright* trade.
Repo	See Repurchase agreement.
Representativeness	Classification process whereby the mind uses a small sample to draw inferences and conclusions that will be used for a broad sample. The small sample is deemed to be representative of the behaviour of the large sample. It can be by retrieval, by construction or by information simulation.
Repurchase agreement	Agreement whereby a party finances the trading position for a pre-set period of time.
Risk aversion	Human aversion to incur risks (in the statistical sense, whereby one's wealth could either increase or decrease).
Risk buyer/ insurance seller	Someone who increases his risk.
Risk communication	Process of communicating information that will be used in risk decisions.
Risk management	In the financial context, it is the process of deciding how much risk capital should be allocated to the various trades, activities and businesses in an organization. Most common broad categories in financial services are market risk, credit risk and operational risk. Outside finance, most notably in engineering, it refers to the physical risk of collapse or accident of a major plant, project or device (such as an airplane, ship, nuclear power plant, spaceship or industrial process or operation).

Risk propensity	Tendency of a decision-maker to take or to avoid risks.
Risk reporting	Process of collecting the information supporting risk management decisions.
Risk seller/ insurance buyer	Somone who reduces his risk.
Risk transfer	Process of transferring risk from a risk seller to a risk buyer.
Salience	Features that will be most relevant in driving one's decision.
Sarbanes-Oxley Act 2002	US Act that increases financial and career consequences for Chief Executive and Chief Financial Officers who provide false or misleading financial statements.
Selective-attention bias	Tendency to select only those pieces of information that conform to the subject's views and opinions.
Self-attribution bias	Attribution of success to one's skill and ability and of failures to external causes.
Self-preservation bias	Set of biases that allows the subject to escape or minimize inner conflict with previously held views.
Sequential information processing bias	Tendency to analyse situations and problems as if they were a linear sequence of steps, regardless of correlations and inter-relationships with other contributing factors.
Similarity bias	Process of drawing conclusions by associating a given situation or decision to a previous one that is imprinted in the subject's memory. It relies on the connotative distance between the sample and the parent population.
Spread	See Relative-value trade
Square root rule	Simple trick to calculate the relative weight of standard-deviation relative to the mean and avoid popular probability misconceptions on the law of large numbers and mean reversion. See also Gambler's fallacy.
St Petersburgh paradox	Paradox of computing how much one should be willing to pay to take the other side of a gambler's bet. See also Gambler's fallacy.
Statistical credit matrices	Matrices that calculate the probability of migration of a given name (typically a sovereign or corporate obligor) across different rating buckets over a given time horizon.
Status quo bias	Bias whereby a subject chooses inaction as the best course of action going forward.
Stock index arbitrage	Arbitrage activity between the S&P500 stock-index futures contract and the cash market in New York. When the latter is

cheap, it involves buying a portfolio of stocks that make up the S&P500 Index and selling stock-index futures on the other side. The opposite is implemented when the latter side of the trade is cheap.

Sunk cost bias
Another form of mental accounting, whereby prior costs still weigh on present and future decisions irrespective of the subject's ability to reverse them.

Systemic frame of risk
Frame of risk adopted by policymakers, governments, regulators and supra-national organizations concerning how much risk the system can allow its participants to assume.

Thai baht
Currency of the Kingdom of Thailand.

Top down
Decision-making process that assembles information on the big picture first and then progressively drills down to increase the level of detail. Preferred by strategists and people who have limited interest in details. Well known in the field of portfolio allocation decisions, where one starts from a general decision of how much to allocate to the major asset classes (say, bonds, equities and cash) and then progressively refines the decisions with sub-allocations inside each asset class. Decisions on the geographical, credit or style limits are examples of this further sub-allocation.

Trading for time
Trading based on a longer-term fundamental or mean-reversion view.

Trading for timing
Trading with a small time horizon based on expected short-term moves. Very influenced by short-term noise, does not attribute excessive weight to long-term fundamentals.

Under- and over-reaction
… to new information, whereby prior information is either overweighted or underweighted, respectively.

Utility theory (UT)
Principle supported by conventional economics that states that people have stable risk preferences that do not take into account others' preferences. Both these assumptions have been under attack, respectively, by prospect theory and game theory.

Value-at-risk (VaR)
Indicator that is commonly used by financial risk managers to calculate the x-centile maximum loss that a risky position or portfolio may incur over a given time horizon. One uses a set of volatilities and correlations to compute the loss distribution of a portfolio. Historical simulation, Variance-Covariance (Riskmetrics™) and Monte-Carlo simulation are the three most common techniques to perform this computation.

| **Volatility** | Statistical definition based on the standard deviation of the price or returns of a financial security over a given time horizon. |
| **Wobegon, Lake** | Fictional Minnesota community in which all children are above average. |

References

Chapter 2

Cohen, D. (2001) *Fear, Greed and Panic*. Chichester: John Wiley & Sons.

Fiedler, P., www.youramazingbrain.com for several of the pictures used as examples of visual context dependence.

Friberg, L., Auditory and language processing, in D.H. Ingvar *et al* (eds), *Brain Work II, Abstracts*. Alfred Bengzon Symposium.

Friberg, L. and Roland, P.E. (1988) Functional activation and inhibition of regional cerebral blood flow and metabolism, in J. Olesen and L. Edvinsson (eds), *Basic Mechanisms of Headache*. Amsterdam: Elsevier, 1988, pp. 189–98.

Goldberg, L.R. (1972) Parameters of personality inventory construction and utilization: A comparison of prediction strategies and tactics. *Multivariate Behavioral Research Monograph*, 7, No. 72–2.

Goldberg, L.R. (1981) Language and individual differences: The search for universals in personality lexicons, in L. Wheeler (ed), *Review of Personality and Social Psychology. Vol. 2.* Beverly Hills: Sage, pp. 141–165.

Goldberg, L.R. (1990) An alternative 'Description of personality': The Big-Five factor structure. *Journal of Personality and Social Psychology,* 59, 1216–1229.

Goldberg, L.R. (1992) The development of markers for the Big-Five factor structure. *Psychological Assessment*, 4, 26–42.

Goldberg, L.R. (1993a) The structure of personality traits: Vertical and horizontal aspects, in D.C. Funder, R.D. Parke, C. Tomlinson-Keasey, & K. Widaman (eds), *Studying Lives Through Time: Personality and Development*. Washington: American Psychological Association, pp. 169–188.

Goldberg, L.R. (1993b) The structure of phenotypic personality traits. *American Psychologist*, 48, 26–34.

Goldberg, L.R. (1995) What the hell took so long? Donald Fiske and the Big-Five factor structure, in P.E. Shrout & S.T. Fiske (eds), *Personality Research, Methods, and Theory: A Festschrift Honoring Donald W. Fiske*. Hillsdale: Erlbaum, pp. 29–43.

Goldberg, L.R. (1999a) A broad-bandwidth, public-domain, personality inventory measuring the lower-level facets of several five-factor models, in I. Mervielde, I. Deary, F. De Fruyt, & F. Ostendorf (eds), *Personality Psychology in Europe*, Vol 7. Tilburg: Tilburg University Press, pp. 7–28.

Goldberg, L.R. (1999b) The curious experiences survey, a revised version of the dissociative experiences scale: Factor structure, reliability, and relations to demographic and personality variables. *Psychological Assessment*, 11, 134–145.

Goldberg, L.R. (in press) The comparative validity of adult personality inventories: Applications of a consumer testing framework, in S. R. Briggs, J. M. Cheek, & E. M. Donahue (eds), *Handbook of Adult Personality Inventories*. New York: Plenum.

Goldberg, L.R. Grenier, J.R., Guion, R.M., Sechrest, L.B., & Wing, H. (1991) Questionnaires used in the prediction of trustworthiness in pre-employment selection decisions: APA Task Force report. Washington: American Psychological Association.

Goldberg, L.R. & Strycker, L.A. (2002) Personality traits and eating habits: The assessment of food preferences in a large community sample. *Personality and Individual Differences,* 32, 49–65.

Goldberg, L.R., Sweeney, D., Merenda, P. F., & Hughes, J.E., Jr. (1996) The big-five factor structure as an integrative framework: An analysis of Clarke's AVA model. *Journal of Personality Assessment,* 66, 441–471.

Johnson, J.A. (2000) Predicting observers' ratings of the Big Five from the CPI, HPI, and NEO-PI-R: A comparative validity study. *European Journal of Personality,* 14, 1–19.

Johnson, J.A. (2001) Screening massively large data sets for non-responsiveness in web-based personality inventories. Invited talk to the joint Bielefeld-Groningen Personality Research Group, University of Groningen, The Netherlands. Available on: http://www.personal.psu.edu/~j5j/papers/screening.html.

Külpe, O. (1904) Versuche über Abstraktion, Bericht über International Kangress für experimentale Psychologie, 56–68.

Larssen, N.A., Ingvar, D.H. and Skinhøj, E. (1977) Brain function and blood flow. *Scientific American*, 239, 62–71.

Loewenton, I. (2003) Mastering and managing operational risks in banking and financial institutions & Basel II new Accord for Operational Risk. Dissertation thesis, Université de Lausanne.

Miller, G. (1955) The magical number seven plus or minus two: Some limits on our capacity for processing information. *Psychological Review*, 101: 2, 343–352.

Nørretranders, T. (1998) *The User Illusion: Cutting Consciousness Down to Size*. London: Penguin Books, p. 156.

Pollack, I. & Ficks, L. (1954) Information of elementary multi-dimensional auditory displays. *Journal of the Acoustical Society of America*, 26, 155–158.

Richmond, Alan www.eluzions.com for several of the pictures used as examples of visual context dependence.

Roland, P.E. and Friberg, L. (1985) Localization of cortical areas activated by thinking. *Journal of Neurophysiology,* 53, 1219–43.

Roland, P.E. *et al* (1987) Does mental activity change the oxidative metabolism of the brain? *Journal of Neuroscience*, 7, 2373–89.

Zimmermann, M. (1989) The nervous system in the context of information theory, in R.F. Schmidt and G. Thews (eds), *Human Physiology*, 2nd edn. Berlin: Springer-Verlag, p. 172.

Chapter 3

Murnighan, J.K. & Mowen, J.C. (2002) *The Art of High-Stakes Decision-Making,* New York: John Wiley & Sons, pp. 146–8.

Chapter 4

Barach, R. (1996) Mindtraps. Raleigh, NC 27606: Van K. Tharp Associates.

Black, F. and M. Scholes (1973) The pricing of options and corporate liabilities. *Journal of Political Economy*, 81, 637–654.

Cox, J.C., Ingersoll, J.E., & Ross, S.A. (1985) A theory of the term structure of interest rates. *Econometrica*, 53, 385–407.

Ellsberg, D. (1961) Risk, ambiguity and the savage axioms. *Quarterly Journal of Economics*, 75, 643–669.

Fox, C.R. & Tversky, A. (1991) Ambiguity aversion and comparative ignorance. *Quarterly Journal of Economics*, 110:3, 585–603.

Heath, C. & Tversky, A. (1991) Preference and belief: Ambiguity and competence in choice under uncertainty. *Journal of Risk and Uncertainty*, 4, 5–28.

Kahneman, D. & Tversky, A. (1979) Prospect theory. *Econometrica*, 47:2, 263–291.

Lintner, J. (1965) The valuation of risk assets and the selection of risky investments in stock portfolios and capital budgets. *Review of Economics and Statistics*, 47, 13–37.

Markowitz, H. (1952) The utility of wealth. *Journal of Political Economy*, 60, 151–158.

Markowitz, H. (1959) *Portfolio Selection: Efficient Diversification of Investment*. New York: Wiley.

Merton, R. (1973) An intertemporal capital asset pricing model. *Econometrica*, 41, 867–888.

Näätänen, R. & Summala, H. (1975) *Road User Behavior and Traffic Accidents*. Amsterdam: North Holland.

Rethans, A. (1979) An investigation of consumer perception of product hazards. Doctoral dissertation, University of Oregon.

Ross, S.A. (1976) The arbitrage theory of capital asset pricing. *Journal of Economic Theory*, 13, 341–360.

Russo, J.E. & Schoemaker, P.J.H. (1989) *Decision Traps*. New York: Fireside Publishing.

Sharpe, W. (1964) Capital asset prices: A theory of capital market equilibrium under conditions of risk. *Journal of Finance*, 19, 425–442.

Svenson, O. (1981) Are we less risky and more skilful than our fellow drivers? *Acta Psychologica*, 47, 143–148.

Tversky, A. & Kahneman, D. (1992) Advances in prospect theory. *Journal of Risk and Uncertainty*, 5, 297–323.

Weinstein, N.D. (1980) Unrealistic optimism about future life events. *Journal of Personality and Social Psychology*, 39, 806–820.

Chapter 5

Adler, A. (1930) Individual psychology, in Murchinson, C. (ed), *Psychologies of 1930*. Worcester: Clark University Press.

Albert, J. & Bennett, J. (2001) *Curve Ball: Baseball, Statistics, and the Role of Chance in the Game*. New York: Copernicus.

Albright, S.C. (1993) A statistical analysis of hitting streaks in baseball. *Journal of the American Statistical Association*, 88, 1175–1183.

Arkes, H.R., Wortmann, R.L., Saville, P.D. & Harkness, A.R. (1981) Hindsight bias amongst physicians weighing the likelihood of diagnoses. *Journal of Applied Psychology*, 66, 252–254.

Bachelier, L. (1900) *Theorie de la speculation*. Paris: Annales de l'École Normale Supérieure.

Bandler, R. & Grinder, J. (1984) *Reframing*. Moab: Real People Press.

Bandler, R. & Grinder, J. (1990) *Frogs into Princes*. New York: Eden Grove Editions.

Barraclough, G. (1972) Mandarins and Nazis. *New York Review of Books,* 19, 37–42.

Beckman, L. (1970) Effects of students' performance on teachers and observers' attributions of causality. *Journal of Educational Psychology*, 61, 75–82.

Bem, D. (1972) Self-perception theory, in L. Berkowitz (ed), *Advances in Personality and Social Psychology Vol. 6*. New York: Academic Press.

Bernoulli, D. (1738) Exposition of a new theory on the measurement of risk. *Econometrica,* 22 (1954), 23–36.

Carhart, M. (1997) On persistence in mutual fund performance. *Journal of Finance*, 52, 57–82.

Carpenter, G.S., Glazer, R. & Nakamoto, K. (1994) Meaningful brands from meaningless differentiation: The dependence on irrelevant attributes. *Journal of Marketing Research,* 31, 339–350.

Carpenter, J.N. & Lynch, A.W. (1999) Survivorship bias and attrition effects in measures of performance persistence. *Journal of Financial Economics*, 54, 337–374.

Christenfeld, N. (1995) Choices from identical options. *Psychological Science,* 6, 50–55.

Combs, B. & Slovic, P. (1979) Newspaper coverage of causes of death. *Journalism Quarterly*, 56: 4, 837–843, 849.

Daniel, K., Hirschleifer, D. & Subrahmanyam, A. (1998) A theory of overconfidence, self-attribution and security market under- and overreactions. *Journal of Finance*, 53, 1839–1886.

Danielsson, J. & Zigrand, J.P. (2003) On time-scaling of risk and the square-root-of-time rule. Department of Accounting and Finance, Financial Markets Group, London School of Economics, Working Paper.

Davis, W.L. & Davis, D.E. (1972) Internal – external and attribution of responsibility for success and failure. *Journal of Personality*, 40, 123–136.

Dembo, R.S. & Freeman, A. (1998) *Seeing Tomorrow: Rewriting the Rules of Risk*. New York: Wiley.

Doob, A.N., Carlsmith, J.M., Festinger, L. & Landauer, T.K. & Tom, S., Jr. (1969) Effect of initial selling price on subsequent sales. *Journal of Personality and Social Psychology*, 11, 345–350.

Dörner, D. (1996) *The Logic of Failure*. Boston: Perseus Books, Addison-Wesley, p. 30.

Edwards, W. (1968) Conservatism in human information processing, in B. Kleinmuntz (ed), *Formal Representation of Human Judgment*. New York: John Wiley & Sons.

Feather, N.T. (1969) Attribution of responsibility and valence of success and failure in relation to initial confidence and task performance. *Journal of Personality and Social Psychology*, 13, 129–144.

Festinger, L. (1957) *A Theory of Cognitive Dissonance*. Evanston: Row, Peterson.

Festinger, L. & Carlsmith, J.M. (1959) Cognitive consequences of forced compliance. *Journal of Abnormal and Social Psychology*, 58, 203–210.

Fischer, D.H. (1970) *Historians' Fallacies*. New York: Harper & Row.

Fischhoff, B. (1980) For those condemned to study the past: Reflections on historical judgment, in R.A., Schweder and D.W. Fiske (eds), *New Directions for Methodology of Behavioral Science: Fallible Judgment in Behavioral Research*. San Francisco: Jossey-Bass.

Fischhoff, B. & Beyth, R. (1975) I knew it would happen: Remembered probabilities of once-future things. *Organizational Behavior and Human Performance*, 13, 1–16.

Fischhoff, B. & Slovic, P. (1980) A little learning: Confidence in multicue judgment, in R. Nickerson (ed), *Attention and Performance*, 8, 779–800. Hillsdale: Erlbaum.

Fitch, G. (1970) Effects of self-esteem, perceived performance and chance on causal attributions. *Journal of Personality and Social Psychology*, 16, 311–315.

Freize, I. & Weiner, B. (1971) Cue utilization and attributional judgments for success and failure. *Journal of Personality*, 39, 591–606.

Gigerenzer, G. (2002) *Reckoning with Risk*. London: Penguin Books.

Gilovich, T.R. & Husted, Medvec, V. (1993) The experience of regret: What, when and why. *Psychological Review,* 102:2, 379–395.

Gilovich, T., Vallone, R. & Tversky, A. (1985) The hot hand in basketball: On the misperception of random sequences. *Cognitive Psychology*, 17, 295–314.

Goffman, E. (1967) *Interaction Ritual*. New York: Anchor.

Gross, A. (1966) Evaluation of the target person in a social influence situation. Unpublished doctoral dissertation, Stanford University, 1966.

Hendrick, I. (1943) The discussion of the 'instinct to master'. *Psychoanalytic Quarterly*, 12, 561–565.

Hendricks, D., Patel, J. & Zeckhauser, R. (1993) Hot hands in mutual funds: Short-run persistence of performance, 1974–1988. *Journal of Finance*, 48, 93–130.

Henslin, J.M. (1967) Craps and magic. *American Journal of Socialogy*, 73, 316–330.

Jennings, D.L., Amabile, T.M. & Ross, L. (1982) Informal covariation assessment: Data-based versus theory-based judgments, in D. Kahneman, P. Slovic, and A. Tversky (eds), *Judgment under Uncertainty: Heuristics and Biases*. Cambridge: Cambridge University Press.

Johnson, T.J., Feigenbaum, R. & Weiby, M. (1964) Some determinants and consequences of the teacher's perception of causation. *Journal of Experimental Psychology*, 55, 237–246.

Johnson, E.J., Hershey, J., Meszaros, J. & Kunreuther, H. (1991) Framing, probability, distortions and insurance decisions. *Journal of Risk and Uncertainty*, 7, 35–51.

Kahneman, D. & Tversky, A. (1971) Belief in the law of small numbers. *Psychological Bulletin*, 2, 105–110.

Kahneman, D. & Tversky, A. (1972) Subjective probability: A judgment of representativeness. *Cognitive Psychology*, 3, 430–454.

Kahneman, D., and Tversky, A. (1973) Availability: A heuristic for judging frequency and probability. *Cognitive Psychology*, 5, 207–232.

Kahneman, D. & Tversky, A. (1974) Judgment under uncertainty. *Science*, 185, 1124–1131.

Kahneman, D. & Tversky, A. (1979) The simulation heuristic, in D. Kahneman, P. Slovic & A. Tversky (eds), *Judgement under Uncertainty: Heuristics and Biases*. Cambridge: Cambridge University Press, pp. 201–210.

Kahneman, D. & Tversky, A. (1982) On the study of statistical intuitions. *Cognition*, 11, 123–141.

Kiell, G. & Stephan, E. (1997) Urteilprozesses bei Finanzanlageentscheidung von Experten. Abschlussbericht einer experimentellen Studie mit professionellen Devisenhändlern. Forschungsberichtdes Instituts für Wirtschafts- und Sozialpsychologie der Universität Köln.

Knapper, C.K., Cropley A.J. & Moore, R.J. (1978) Attitudinal factors in the non-use of seat belts. *Accident Analysis and Prevention*, 8, 241–246.

Knox, R.E. & Inkster, J.A. (1968) Postdecision dissonance at post time. *Journal of Personality and Social Psychology*, 8, 319–323.

Kritzman, M.P. (2000) *Puzzles of Finance*, New York: John Wiley & Sons, p. 51.

Kunreuther, H. (2001) Protective decisions: Fear or prudence, in S. Hoch, H. Kunreuther, and R.E. Gunther (eds), *Wharton on Making Decisions*. New York: Wiley.

Lakatos, I. (1970) Falsification and scientific research programmes, in Lakatos and A. Musgrave (eds), *Criticism and the Growth of Knowledge*, Cambridge: Cambridge University Press. Reprinted in Lakatos, *Philosophical Papers* Vol. 1, Cambridge: Cambridge University Press.

Langer, E.J. (1975) The illusion of control. *Journal of Personality and Social Psychology*, 32, 311–328.

Langer, E.J. & Roth, J. (1975) Heads I win, tails it's chance: The illusion of control as a function of the sequence of outcomes in a purely chance task. *Journal of Personality and Social Psychology*, 32, 951–955.

Leary, M.R. (1981) The distorted nature of hindsight. *Journal of Applied Psychology*, 115, 25–29.

Leary, M.R. (1982) Hindsight distortion and the 1980 presidential election. *Personality and Social Psychology Bulletin*, 8, 257–263.

Luce, R.D. (2000) *The Utility of Gains and Losses*. Mahwah: Lawrence Erlbaum Associates.

Luce, R.D. & Fishburn, P.C. (1991) Rank- and sign-dependent linear utility models for finite first-order gambles. *Journal of Risk and Uncertainty*, 4, 29–59.

Maki, D.M. & Palumbo, M.G. (2001) Disentangling the wealth effect: A cohort analysis of household saving in the 1990s. Board of Governors of the Federal Reserve System, Washington, DC.

Marzoni, P. (1971) Motivating factors in the use of restraint systems. Philadelphia National Analysts. (NTIS No DOT HS-80C 585).

Musgrave, A. (ed.) *Criticism and the Growth of Scientific Knowledge*. Cambridge: Cambridge University Press.

Nickerson, R. (ed.) (1980) *Attention and Performance VIII*. Hillsdale, NJ: Erlbaum.

Nisbett, R.E. & Ross, L. (1980) Human inference: Strategies and shortcomings of social judgment. Englewood Cliffs: Prentice-Hall.

Pennington, D.C., Rutter, D.R., McKenna, K. & Morley, I.E. (1980), Estimating the outcome of a pregnancy test: Women's judgment in foresight and hindsight. *British Journal of Social and Clinical Psychology*, 19, 317–324.

Plous, S. (1993) *The Psychology of Judgment and Decision-Making*. New York: McGraw-Hill.

Polefka, J. (1965) The perception and evaluation of responses to social influences. Unpublished doctoral dissertation, Stanford University, 1965.

Ross, L. & Anderson, C.A. (1982) Shortcomings in the attribution process: on the origins and maintenance of erroneous social assessments, in D. Kahneman, P. Slovic and A. Tversky (eds), *Judgment under Uncertainty: Heuristics and Biases*. Cambridge: Cambridge University Press, pp. 129–152.

Ross, S.A. (1976) The arbitrage theory of capital asset pricing. *Journal of Economic Theory*, 13, 341–360.

Russo, J.E. & Schoemaker, P.J.H. (1989) *Decision Traps*. New York: Fireside Publishing.

Samuelson, W. & Zeckhauser, R. (1988) Status quo bias in decision making. *Journal of Risk and Uncertainty*, 1, 7–59.

Shefrin, H. (1985) The disposition to sell winners too early and ride losers too long: Theory and evidence. *Journal of Finance*, 40, 777–790.

Shefrin, H. (2000) *Beyond Greed and Fear*. Cambridge: Harvard Business School Press, pp. 96–98, 101–102.

Shefrin, H. & Statman, M. (1995) Making sense of beta, size and book-to-market. *Journal of Portfolio Management*, 21, 26–34.

Slovic, P., Fischhoff, B. & Lichtenstein, S. (1976) Cognitive processes and societal risk taking, in J.S. Carroll and J.W. Payne (eds), *Cognition and Social Behavior*. Potomac: Lawrence Erlbaum Associates.

Slovic, P., Fischhoff, B. & Lichtenstein, S. (1978) Accident probabilities and seat belt usage: A psychological perspective. *Accident Analysis and Prevention*, 10.

Slovic, P., Fischhoff, B. & Lichtenstein, S. (1979) Rating the risks. *Environment*, 21: 3, 14–20, 36–39.

Solt, M. & Statman, M. (1989) Good companies, bad stocks. *Journal of Portfolio Management*, 15, 39–44.

Synodinos, N.E. (1986) Hindsight distortion: I knew it all along and I was sure about it. *Journal of Applied Psychology*, 16, 107–117.

Thaler, R.H. (1980) Towards a positive theory of consumer choice. *Journal of Economic Behavior and Organization*, 1, 39–60.

Thaler, R.H. (1985) Mental accounting and consumer choice. *Marketing Science*, 4, 199–214.

Thaler, R.H. (1993) *Advances in Behavioral Finance*. New York: Russell Sage Foundation.

Thaler, R.H. (1999) Mental accounting matters, in D. Kahneman and A. Tversky (eds), (2000) *Choice Values and Frames*. New York: Cambridge University Press, Russell Sage Foundation, pp. 241–268.

Thaler, R.H. & Johnson, E.J. (1990) Gambling with the house money and trying to break even: The effects of prior outcomes on risky choice. *Management Science*, 36, 643–660.

Tonks, I. (2002) Performance and persistence of pension fund managers. Working paper, Centre for Market and Public Organisation, University of Bristol.

Tversky, A. & Kahneman, D. (1986) Rational choices and the framing of decisions. *Journal of Business*, 59, S251–S278.

Walster, E. (1967) Second-guessing important events. *Human Relations*, 20, 23–249.

White, R.W. (1959) Motivation reconsidered: The concept of competence. *Psychological Review* 66, 297–333.

Wolosin R.J., Sherman, S.J. & Till, A. (1973) Effects of cooperation and competition on responsibility attribution after success and failure. *Journal of Personality and Social Psychology*, 220–235.

Yarrow, M., Campbell, J.D. & Burton, R.V. (1970) Recollections of childhood: A study of the retrospective method. *Monographs of the Society for Research in Child Development*, 35, 1970.

Chapter 6

Abel, A. & Mailath, G. (1994) Financing losers in financial markets. *Journal of Financial Intermediation,* 3, 139–165.

Acs, Z. & Audretsch, D. (1988) Innovation in large and small firms: An empirical analysis. *American Economic Review*, 78: 4, 678–690.

Ainslie, G. (1975) Specious reward: a behavioral theory of impulsiveness and impulse control. *Psychological Bulletin*, 82, 463–496.

Ainslie, G. (1991) Derivation of 'rational' economic behavior from hyperbolic discount curves. *American Economic Review*, 81, 334–340.

Ainslie, G. (1992) *Picoeconomics: The Strategic Interaction of Successive Motivational States Within the Person*. New York: Cambridge University Press.

Ainslie, G. & Haslam, N. (1992a) Self-control, in G. Loewenstein and Jon Elster (eds), *Choice Over Time*. New York: Russell Sage Foundation.

Ainslie, G. & Haslam, N. (1992b) Hyperbolic discounting, in G. Loewenstein and J. Elster (eds), *Choice Over Time*. New York: Russell Sage Foundation.

Allen, F. & Morris, S. (1998) Finance applications of game theory: Financial Institution Center, The Wharton School, University of Pennsylvania, in K. Chatterjee and W. Samuelson (eds) (2000) *Advances in Business Applications of Game Theory*, The Netherlands: Kluwer Academic Press.

Andreoni, J. (1995) Cooperation in public goods experiments: Kindness or confusion. *American Economic Review* 85, 891–904.

Andreoni, J. (1998) Why free ride? Strategies and learning in public goods experiments. *Journal of Public Economics,* 37, 291–304.

Aumann, R. (1998) Common priors: A reply to Gul. *Econometrica,* 66, 929–938.

Avery, C. & Zemsky P. (1996) Multi-dimensional uncertainty and herd behavior in financial markets. *American Economic Review*, 88: 4, 724–748.

Banerjee, A. (1992) A simple model of herd behavior. *Quarterly Journal of Economics,* 107, 797–817.

Bardhan, P., Bowles, S. & Gintis, H. (2000) Wealth inequality, credit constraints and economic performance, in A. Atkinson and F. Bourguignon (eds), *Handbook of Income Distribution*, Dortrecht: North-Holland.

Berger, P. & Ofek, E. (1995) Diversification's effect on firm value. *Journal of Financial Economics*, 37, 39–65.

Bhattacharya, S. & Thakor, A. (1993) Contemporary banking theory. *Journal of Financial Intermediation,* 3, 2–50.

Bieta, V. & Gelbhaar, S. (1998) Game-theoretical aspects of international lending and performance control. *Indian Economic Journal*, 58–66.

Bikhchandani, S. & Huang, C. (1993) The economics of Treasury securities markets. *Journal of Economic Perspectives,* 7, 117–134.

Bikhchandani, S. & Sharma, S. (2000) *Herd Behaviors in Financial Markets: A Review*. International Monetary Fund Working Papers 00/48, November 2000.

Bikhchandani, S., Hirshleifer D. & Welch, I. (1992) A theory of fads, fashions, customs and cultural change as informational cascades. *Journal of Political Economy,* 100, 992–1026.

Black, F. (1976) The dividend puzzle. *Journal of Portfolio Management,* 2, 5–8.

Brady, N. (1988) *Report of the Presidential Task Force on Market Mechanisms*. Washington: Government Printing Office.

Broecker, T. (1990) Credit-worthiness tests and interbank competition. *Econometrica,* 58: 2, 429–452.

Buzzell, R.D. (1983) *Is Vertical Integration Profitable?* Cambridge: *Harvard Business Review*.

Buzzell, R.D., Gale, B.T. & Sultan, R.G.M. (1981) 'Market share – a key to profitability'. Cambridge: *Harvard Business Review*.

Cammack, E.B. (1991) Evidence on bidding strategies and information in Treasury bill auctions. *Journal of Political Economy,* 99, 100–130.

Carlsson, H. & van Damme, E. (1993) Global games and equilibrium selection. *Econometrica,* 61, 989–1018.

CASSEL (California Social Science Experimental Laboratory) (2002) Laboratory experimentation in the social sciences. Presentation, Joint project of UCLA, Caltech, and the National Science Foundation, downloaded from http://research.cassel.ucla.edu/experimentation.pdf

Chari, V.V. & Kehoe, P.J.(2000) Financial crises as herds. Working Paper 600, Research Department, Federal Reserve Bank of Minneapolis.

Chen, Z., Lawson, R.B, Gordon, L.R. & McIntosh, B. (1996) Groupthink: Deciding with the leader and the devil. *Psychological Record,* 46, 581–590.

Damasio, A.R. (1994) *Descartes' Error: Emotion Reason and the Human Brain.* New York: Avon Books.

Dawes, R.M. & Orbell, J.M. & Van de Kragt, G.T. (1986) Organizing groups for collective action. *American Political Science Review,* 80, 1171–1185.

Devenow, A. & Welch, I. (1996) Rational herding in financial economics. *European Economic Review,* 40, 603–615.

DeYoung, R. & Hasan, I. (1997) The performance of De Novo Commercial banks. *Economics Working Paper* 97–3, Comptroller of the Currency, February.

Diamond, D. & Dybvig P. (1983) Bank runs, deposit insurance and liquidity. *Journal of Political Economy,* 91, 401–419.

Dörner, D. (1999) *The Logic Of Failure.* Reading: Perseus Books, p. 33.

Fehr, E. & Gächter, S. (2000) Cooperation and punishment. *American Economic Review,* 90: 4, 981–994.

Flowers, M.L. (1977) A laboratory test of some implications of Janis' groupthink hypothesis. *Journal of Personality and Social Psychology,* 35, 888–896.

Forsyth, D.R. (1999) *Group Dynamics,* 3rd edn. Belmont: Wadsworth Publishing Co.

Gigerenzer, G. & Selten, R. (2001) *Bounded Rationality – The Adaptive Toolbox.* Cambridge: MIT Press, p. 272.

Gillette, A.B., Noe, T.H. & Rebello, M.J. (2001) Corporate board composition, protocols and voting behavior: experimental evidence. University of Georgia. Sirif Behavioural Finance Conference, 3 September 2001, Edinburgh, Scotland.

Gintis, H. (2000) *Game Theory Evolving,* Princeton: Princeton University Press.

Gul, F. (1998) A comment on Aumann's Bayesian view. *Econometrica,* 66, 923–928.

Güth, W., Schmittberger, R. & Schwarze, B. (1982) Ultimatum bargaining for a shrinking cake: Experimental analysis. *Journal of Economic Behavior and Organization,* 3, 367–88.

Hackett, S., Schlager, E. & Walker, J. (1994) The role of communication in resolving common dilemmas: Experimental evidence with heterogeneous appropriators. *Journal of Environmental Economics and Management* 27, 99–126.

Halpern, J. (1986) Reasoning about knowledge: An overview, in J. Halpern (ed.), *Theoretical Aspects of Reasoning About Knowledge.* Los Altos: Morgan Kauffman.

Hardin, G. (1968) The tragedy of the commons. *Science,* 162, 1243–1248.

Harris, M. & Raviv, A. (1991) The theory of capital structure. *Journal of Finance,* 46, 297–355.

Heaton, J. & Lo, A.W. (1995) 'The Impact of a Securities Transaction Tax on Financial Markets and Institutions', in Suzanne Hammond (ed), Securities Transaction Taxes: False Hopes and Unintended Consequences. Chicago: Catalyst Institute.

Hedborg, A. (1997) Who is cursed in a Treasury securities auction? An empirical analysis of Swedish six-month Treasury bill auctions from 1991 to 1994, in G. Antonides, W. F. Van Raaij and S. Maital, *Advances in Economic Psychology.* Chichester: John Wiley & Sons, pp. 189–208.

Henrich, J., Boyd, R., Bowles, S., Camerer, C., Fehr, E., Gintis, R. & McElreath, R. (2001) *In Search of Homo Economicus: Behavioral Experiments in Fifteen Small-Scale Societies.* University of Michigan, Ann Arbor: School of Business Administration.

Henrich, J., Boyd, R., Bowles, S., Camerer, C., Fehr, E., Gintis, R. and McElreath, R. (2001) *Cooperation, Reciprocity and Punishment in Fifteen Small-Scale Societies*. University of Michigan, Ann Arbor: School of Business Administration.

Hermalin, B., & Weisbach, M. (1991) The effects of board composition and direct incentives on firm performance. *Financial Management,* 20,101–112.

Higgs, D. (2003) *Review of the Role and Effectiveness of Non-Executive Directors*. London: The Department of Trade and Industry. Available from www.dti.gov.uk/cld/non_exec_review.

Hirshleifer, D. (1995) Mergers and acquisitions: Strategic and informational issues, in Jarrow, Maksimovic and Ziemba (eds), 839–885.

Hodson, G. & Sorrentino, M. (1997) Groupthink and uncertainty orientation: Personality differences in reactivity to the group situation. *Group Dynamics: Theory Research and Practice*, 1, 144–155.

Janis, I.L. (1972) *Victims of Groupthink*. Boston: Houghton Mifflin.

Janis, I.L. (1982) *Groupthink: Psychological Studies of Policy Decisions and Fiascos*, 2nd edn. Boston: Houghton Mifflin.

Janis, I.L. (1983) Groupthink, in H.H. Blumberg, A.P. Hare, V. Kent and M.F. Davis (eds), *Small Groups and Social Interaction*, Vol 2, pp. 39–46. New York: Wiley.

Janis, I.L. (1985) International crisis management in the nuclear age. *Applied Social Psychology Annual*, 6, 63–86.

Janis, I.L. (1989) Crucial decisions: Leadership in policy making and crisis management. New York: The Free Press.

Janis, I.L. & Mann L. (1977) *Decision Making: A Psychological Analysis of Conflict, Choice and Commitment*. New York: The Free Press.

Kahneman, D., Knetsch, J.L. & Thaler, R.H. (1986) Fairness and the assumptions of economics. *Journal of Business*, 59, S285–S300.

Kraus, A. & Smith, M. (1989) Market created risk. *Journal of Finance,* 44, 557–569.

Kraus, A. and Smith, M. (1998) Endogenous sunspots, pseudo-bubbles, and beliefs about beliefs. *Journal of Financial Markets,* 1, 151–174.

Lee, I. (1993) On the convergence of informational cascades. *Journal of Economic Theory,* 61, 395–411.

Lee, I. (1997) Market crashes and informational avalanches. *Review of Economic Studies*.

Loewenstein, G. & Prelec, D. (1992) Anomalies in intertemporal choice: Evidence and an interpretation. *Quarterly Journal of Economics*, 107, 573–597.

Longley, J. & Pruitt, D.G. (1980) Groupthink: A critique of Janis's theory, in L. Wheeler (ed.), *Review of Personality and Social Psychology* (Vol. 1). Newbury Park: Sage.

Loomes, G. (1988) When actions speak louder than prospects. *American Economic Review,* 78, 463–470.

Loury, G. (1994) Self-censorship in public discourse: A theory of political correctness and related phenomena. *Rationality and Society,* 6, 428–461.

Loury, G. (1998) Strategic consultation and 'Yes Man' advisors. Princeton: Princeton University Press, Working Paper.

Manstein, E.V. (1995) *Lost Victories*. Novato: Presidio Press.

Mérö, L. (1998) *Moral Calculations*. New York: Copernicus, Springer-Verlag, pp. 63–72.

Monderer, D. & Samet, D. (1989) Approximating common knowledge with common beliefs. *Games and Economic Behavior,* 1, 170–190.

Moorhead, G. (1982) Groupthink: Hypothesis in need of testing. *Group and Organization Studies,* 7, 429–444.

Morris, S. (1995) The common prior assumption in economic theory. *Economics and Philosophy,* 11, 227–253.

Morris, S. (1999) Political correctness. Yale University, unpublished paper.

Morris, S. & Shin, H. (1997) Common knowledge and co-ordination: Recent lessons from game theory. *Journal of Logic, Language and Information,* 6, 171–190.

Morris, S. & Shin, H.S. (1998) 'Private versus public information'. Unpublished paper.

Morris, S. & Shin, H.S. (1999) *Risk Management with Interdependent Choice.* Oxford Review of Economic Policy, Special Issue on Financial Market Instability, Autumn 1999. Reprinted in the *Financial Stability Review*, Bank of England, November 1999.

Morris, S. & Shin, H.S. (1998) Unique equilibrium in a model of self-fulfilling currency attacks, *American Economic Review,* 88, 587–597. Available from http://nuff.ox.ac.uk/users/shin/working.htm.

Morris, S., Rob, R. & Shin, H. (1995) P-dominance and belief potential. *Econometrica,* 63, 145–157.

Nakamura, L.I. (1993) Loan screening within and outside of customer relationships. Federal Reserve Bank of Philadelphia Working Paper No. 93–15, June.

Osler, C.L. (2002) Stop-loss orders and price cascades in currency markets (forthcoming).

Ostrom, E., Walker, J. & Gardner, R. (1992) Covenants with and without a sword: Self-governance is possible. *American Political Science Review,* 86, 404–417.

Ottaviani, M. & Sørensen, L. (2002) *The theory of reputational cheap talk.* London Business School and University of Copenhagen. University of Copenhagen Discussion Paper No. 02–05.

Peterson, R.S. (1997) A directive leadership style in group decision making can be both virtue and vice: Evidence from elite and experimental groups. *Journal of Personality and Social Psychology,* 72, 1107–1121.

Rajan, R., Servaes, H. & Zingales, L. (1998) The cost of diversity: The diversification discount and inefficient investment. NBER Working Paper No. 6368.

Roth, A.E., Prasnikar, V., Okuno-Fujiwara, M. & Zamir, S. (1991) Bargaining and market behavior in Jerusalem, Ljubljana, Pittsburgh and Tokyo: An experimental study. *American Economic Review,* 81, 1068–1095.

Rubinstein, A. (1989) The electronic mail game: Strategic behavior under almost common knowledge. *American Economic Review,* 79, 385–391.

Ryan, C. (1999) *The Longest Day*. Ware: Wordsworth Editions Ltd.

Sato, K. (1987) Distribution and the cost of maintaining common property resources. *Journal of Experimental Social Psychology,* 3, 19–31.

Scharfstein, D. (1998) The dark side of internal capital markets II: Evidence from diversified conglomerates. NBER Working Paper No. 6352.

Scharfstein, D., & Stein, J. (1996) The dark side of internal capital markets: Divisional rent-seeking and inefficient investment. NBER Working Paper No. 5969.

Schlesinger, A.M. Jr. (1965) *A Thousand Days*. Boston: Houghton Mifflin, pp. 225 and 250.

Shaffer, S. (1997) The winner's curse in banking. Federal Reserve Bank of Philadelphia Working Paper No. 97–25, November.

Shiller, R. (1987) Investor behavior in the October 1987 stock market crash: Survey evidence. NBER discussion paper 2446, reprinted in *Market Volatility*, MIT Press, 1990.

Shin, H. (1996) Comparing the robustness of trading systems to higher order uncertainty. *Review of Economic Studies,* 63, 39–60.

Shin, H. & Stulz, R. (1997) Are internal capital markets efficient? Ohio State University Working Paper No. 97–4.

Silver, W.S. & Bufanio, K.A. (1996) The impact of group efficacy and group goals on group performance. *Small Group Research*, 27, 347–349.

Simon, D.P. (1994) Markups, quantity risk and bidding strategies at Treasury coupon auctions. *Journal of Financial Economics,* 35, 43–62.

Sucden, R. (1993) An axiomatic foundation for regret theory. *Journal of Economic Theory*, 60, 159–180.

Tetlock, P.E. (1979) Identifying victims of groupthink from public statements of decision makers. *Journal of Personality and Social Psychology*, 63, 403–425.

Thaler, R.H. (1992) *The Winner's Curse*. Princeton: Princeton University Press, pp. 21–25, 51 and 57–58.

Thaler, R. H. & Loewenstein, G. (1992) Intertemporal choice, in Richard Thaler (ed), *The Winner's Curse: Paradoxes and Anomalies of Economic Life*. New York: Free Press, pp. 92–106.

Turner, J.C. (1984) Social identification and psychological group formation, in H. Tajfel (ed), *The Social Dimension*. Cambridge: Cambridge University Press, pp. 518–538.

Umlauf, S.R. (1990) Uncertainty, collusion and returns in a multiple-bid auction with resale. London Business School: Working Paper.

von Neumann, J. & Morgenstern, O. (1947) *Theory of Games and Economic Behavior*, 2nd edn. Princeton: Princeton University Press.

Welch, I. (1989) Seasoned offerings, imitation costs, and the underpricing of initial public offerings. *Journal of Finance,* 44, 421–449.

Welch, I. (1992) Sequential sales, learning, and cascades. *Journal of Finance,* 47, 695–732.

Westrum, R. (1992) Cultures with requisite imagination, in J. Wise, D. Hopkin and P. Stager (eds), *Verification and Validation of Complex Systems: Human Factors Issues.* Berlin: Springer-Verlag, pp. 401–16.

Wheeler, D.D. & Janis, I.L. (1980) A practical guide for making decisions. New York: The Free Press.

Wulf, J. (2000) Influence and inefficiency in the internal capital market: Theory and evidence. The Wharton School, University of Pennsylvania, July 2000.

Yamagishi, T. (1988a) The provision of a sanctioning system in the United States and Japan. *Social Psychology Quarterly,* 51, 265–271.

Yamagishi, T. (1988b) Seriousness of social dilemmas and the provision of a sanctioning system. *Social Psychology Quarterly,* 51, 32–42.

Yermack, D. (1996) Higher market valuation of companies with a small board of directors. *Journal of Financial Economics,* 40, 185–212.

Chapter 7

Allen, L. & Saunders, A. (2002) *A Survey of Cyclical Effects in Credit Risk Measurement Models*. City University of New York and New York University.

Altman, E.I., Resti, A. & Sironi, A. (July 2002) The link between default and recovery rates: effects on the procyclicality of regulatory capital ratios. BIS Working Papers No. 113, Monetary and Economic Department.

Beach, L.R. & Mitchell, T.R. (1978) A contingency model for the selection of decision strategies. *Academy of Management Review*, July, 439–449.

Casey, C.J., Jr. (1980) Variation in accounting information load: The effect on loan officers' predictions of bankruptcy. *The Accounting Review*, 52: 1, 36–49.

Catarineau-Rabell, E., Jackson, P. & Tsomocos, D.P. (2002) *Procyclicality and the New Basel Accord – Banks' Choice of Loan Rating System*. Bank of England, March 2002.

Chervany, N.L. & Dickson, G.W. (1974) An experimental evaluation of information overload in a production environment. *Management Science*, 20: 10, 62–71.

Christensen-Szalanski, J.J.J. (1978) Problem solving strategies: A selection mechanism, some implications, and some data. *Organisational Behaviour and Human Performance*, 22, 307–323.

Connolly, T., & Thorn, B.K. (1987) Predecisional information acquisition: Effects of task variables on suboptimal search strategies. *Organisational Behaviour and Human Decision Processes*, 39, 397–416.

Davis, F.D., Lohse, G.L. & Kottemann, J.E. (1994) Harmful effects of seemingly helpful information on forecasts of stock earnings. *Journal of Economic Psychology*, 15, 253–267.

Dörner, D. (1996) *The Logic of Failure*. Boston: Addison Wesley, Perseus Books, p. 30.

Froot, K. & Dabora, E. (1998) How are stock prices affected by the location of trade? *Journal of Financial Economics*, 53, 189–216.

Handzic, M. (1997) Decision performance as a function of information availability: An examination of executive information systems. Proceedings of the Second New South Wales Symposium on Information Technology and Information Systems, Sydney, Australia.

Handzic, M. (2001) Does more information lead to better informing?, in A. Harriger, (ed.), Proceedings of the 2001 Informing Science Conference, 19–22 June, Krakow, Poland, pp. 251–256.

Levine, J.M., Samet, M.G. & Brahlek, R.E. (1975) Information seeking with limitations on available information and resources. *Human Factors*, 17: 5, 502–513.

Lo, A.W. & Repin, D.V. (2001) The psychophysiology of real-time financial risk processing, Cambridge, MA: MIT Sloan School of Management, Working Paper 4223-01. Available on http://papers.ssrn.com/abstract=282863.

Oskamp, S. (1965) Overconfidence in case-study judgments. *Journal of Consulting Psychology*, 29, 261–265.

Paese, P.W. & Sniezek, J.A. (1991) Influences on the appropriateness of confidence in judgment: Practice, effort information and decision making. *Organizational Behavior and Human Decision Processes*, 48, 100–130.

Payne, J.W. (1982) Contingent decision behaviour. *Psychological Bulletin*, 92: 2, 382–402.

Persaud, A. (2002) Where have all the risks gone? Lecture at Gresham College, 14 November 2002, London, England.

Peterson, D.K. & Pitz, G.F. (1988) Confidence, uncertainty and the use of information. *Journal of Experimental Psychology: Learning, Memory and Cognition*, 14, 85–92.

Schroder, H.M., Driver, M.J. & Streufert, S. (1967) *Human Information Processing*. Holt, Rinehart and Winston Inc.

Segoviano, M.A. & Lowe, P. (2002) *Internal Ratings, the Business Cycle and Capital Requirements: Some Evidence from an Emerging Market Economy*. London School of Economics and Bank for International Settlements, March 2002.

Wood, R.E. (1986) Task complexity: Definition of the construct. *Organisational Behaviour and Human Decision Processes*, 37: 1, 60–82.

Chapter 8

Antoniou, A., Koutmos, G. & Pericli A. (1999) Index futures and positive feedback trading: evidence from major stock exchanges. Working paper, University of Durham, United Kingdom.

Bandura, A. (1982) *The Biggest Game in Town*. Boston: Houghton-Mifflin.

Barber, B. & Odean, T. (2001) All that glitters: The effect of attention on the buying behavior of individual and institutional investors. Working Paper, University of California, Davis.

Bartram, D., Clough, P. & Williams, J. (1997) The relationship between personality, perceived risks and risk taking. Paper presented to the Academy of Management, Vancouver.

Biais, B., Hilton, D., Mazurier, K. & Sébastien Pouget, S. (2000) Psychological traits and trading strategies. C.E.P.R. Discussion Paper No. 3195.

Bjonnes, G.H. & Rime, D. (2001) *FX Trading ... LIVE! Dealer Behavior and Trading Systems in Foreign Exchange Markets*. Oslo Department of Economics, 13 September 2001.

Black, F. (1986) Noise. *Journal of Finance*, 41, 529–543.

Blake, D. & Timmermann, A., (2001) Performance benchmarks for institutional investors: Measuring, monitoring and modifying investment behaviour. London: The Pensions Institute, Birkbeck College, Discussion Paper PI-0106.

Blake, D., Lehmann, B. & Timmermann, A. (2000) Performance clustering and incentives in the UK pension fund industry. London: The Pensions Institute, Birkbeck College, Discussion Paper PI-9901.

Bodnar, G. & Gebhardt, G. (1999) Derivative usage in risk management by U. S. and German non-financial firms: A comparative survey. *Journal of International Financial Management and Accounting*, 10, 153–187.

Bodnar, G.M., Hayt, G. S. & Marston, R. C., (1996) 1995 Wharton survey of derivative usage by US non-financial firms. *Financial Management*. Winter.

Brennan, M.J. (1995) The individual investor. *Journal of Financial Research*, 18, 59–74.

Byrne, J.P., Miller, D.C. & Schafer, W.D. (1999) Gender difference in risk-taking: A meta-analysis. *Psychological Bulletin*, 125, 367–383.

Canoles, B.W. (1994) An analysis of the profiles, motivations, and modes of habitual commodity speculators. Doctoral dissertation, Department of Agricultural Economics, University of Illinois.

Cheung, Y.-W. & Chinn, M.D. (1999) Traders, market microstructure and exchange rate dynamics. Working Paper 7416, NBER. 2, 6, 11, 13.

Cheung, Y.-W., Chinn, M. & Marsh, I.W. (1999) How do UK-based foreign-exchange dealers think their market operates?, C.E.P.R. Discussion Papers 2230, Working Paper 7524, NBER.

Cutler, D.M., Poterba, J.M. & Summers, L.H. (1989) Speculative dynamics and the role of feedback traders. *American Economic Review*, 80, 63–68.

Draper, D.W. (1985) The small public trader in futures markets, in Anne E. Peck. (ed.), *Futures Markets: Regulatory Issues*. Washington: American Enterprise Institute for Public Policy Research.

Ersoy-Bozcuk, A. & Lasfer, M.A. (2001) *The Trading Behavior of UK Institutional Investors*. London: City University Business School.

Fenton-O'Creevy, M., Nicholson, N., Soane, E. & Willman, P. (2003) Trading on illusions: Unrealistic perceptions of control and trading performance. *Journal of Occupational and Organizational Psychology*, The British Psychological Society, www.bps.org.uk.

Fenton-O'Creevy, M., Nicholson, N., Soane, E. & Willman, P. (2004) *Traders: Managing Risks and Decisions in Financial Markets*. Oxford: Oxford University Press.

Friedland, N., Keinan, G. & Regev, Y. (1992) Controlling the uncontrollable – effects of stress on illusory perceptions of controllability. *Journal of Personality and Social Psychology*, 63: 6, 923–931.

Frino, A., Johnstone, D. & Zheng, H. (2002) The propensity for local traders in futures markets to ride losses: Evidence of irrational or rational behavior? Draft paper, University of Sydney.

Froot, K.A., Scharfstein, D.S. & Stein, J.C. (1993) Risk management: Coordinating corporate investment and financing policies. *Journal of Finance*, 1629–1658.

Gollwitzer, P.M., & Kinney, R.F. (1989) Effects of deliberative and implemental mind-sets on illusion of control. *Journal of Personality and Social Psychology*, 56: 4, 531–542.

Graham, J.R. & Smith, C.W., Jr. (1997) Tax incentives to hedge. Fuqua School of Business, Duke University, Unpublished manuscript, Financial Research (Fall), pp. 249–259.

Grant, K. & Marshall, P. (1997) Large UK companies and derivatives. *European Financial Management,* 3, 191–208.

Hakkarainen, A., Kasanen, E. & Puttonen, V. (1997) Interest rate risk management in major Finnish firms. *European Financial Management,* 3, 255–268.

Heisler, J. (1994) Loss aversion in futures markets: An empirical test. *The Review of Futures Markets*, 13: 3, 793–822.

Hilton, D.J. (1998) *Psychology and the City: Applications to Trading, Dealing and Investment Analysis.* London, UK: Centre for the Study of Financial Innovation.

Kahn, H. & Cooper, C.L. (1993) *Stress in the Dealing Room.* London: Routledge.

Kumar, A. (1999) Behavior of momentum following and contrarian market timers. Yale ICF Working Paper No. 99–01.

Kuserk, G.J. & Locke, P.R. (1993) Scalper behaviour in futures markets: An empirical examination. *Journal of Futures Markets*, 13, 409–431.

Langer, E.J. (1975) The illusion of control. *Journal of Personality and Social Psychology*, 32: 2, 311–328.

Langer, E.J. & Roth, J. (1975) Heads I win, tails it's chance: The illusion of control as a function of outcomes in a purely chance task. *Journal of Personality and Social Psychology*, 32, 951–955.

Locke, P.R. & Mann, S.C. (1999) Do professional traders exhibit loss realization aversion? Working paper, Texas Christian University, USA.

Lyons, R. K. (1995) Tests of microstructural hypothesis in the foreign exchange market. *Journal of Financial Economics*, 39, 321–51.

Manaster, S. & Mann, S.C. (1996) Life in the pits: Competitive market making and inventory control. *Review of Financial Studies*, 9, 953–975.

Mota, A.G. (2001) *Hedging, taking a view or speculating: Evidence from derivative US by large Portuguese non-financial firms*, CEMAF/ISCTE Working Paper, February 2001.

Nagy, R.A. & Obenberger, R.W. (1994) Factors influencing individual investor behavior. *Financial Analysts Journal,* July/August, 63–68.

Nance, D.R., Smith, C.W., Jr. & Smithson, C.W. (1993) On the determinants of corporate hedging. *Journal of Finance,* 48, 267–84.

Odean, T. (1998a) Are investors reluctant to realize their losses? *Journal of Finance, 53*:5, 1775–1798.

Odean, T. (1998b) Volume, volatility, price, and profit when all traders are above average. *Journal of Finance, 53*:6, 1887–1934.

Odean, T. (1999) 'Do investors trade too much?' *American Economic Review, 89*, 1279–1298.

Odean, T. & Barber, B. (1999) The courage of misguided convictions: The trading behavior of individual investors. *Financial Analyst Journal*, 41–55.

Odean, T. & Barber, B. (April 2000) Trading is hazardous to your wealth: the common stock investment performance of individual investors. *Journal of Finance,* 55:2, 773–806.

Odean, T. & Barber, B. (2000) Too many cooks spoil the profits: The performance of investment clubs. *Financial Analyst Journal,* 17–25.

Odean, T. & Gervais, S. (Spring 2001) Learning to be overconfident. *Review of Financial Studies,* 14:1, 1–27.

Odean, T. & Barber, B. (2001a) Boys will be boys: Gender, overconfidence, and common stock investment. *Quarterly Journal of Economics*, 116:1, 261–292.

Odean, T. & Barber, B. (Winter 2001b) The internet and the investor. *Journal of Economic Perspectives,* 15, 1.

Odean, T. & Barber, B. (2002a) Does online trading change investor behavior? *European Business Organization Law Review*, 3, 83–128.

Odean, T. & Barber, B. (2002b) Do the slow die first? *Review of Financial Studies,* 15: 2, 455–487.

Pennings, J.M.E. (2002) Pulling the trigger or not: Factors affecting behavior of initiating a position in derivatives markets. *Journal of Economic Psychology,* 23, 263–278.

Pennings, J.M.E. & Garcia, P. (2001) Measuring producers' risk preferences: A global risk-attitude construct. *American Journal of Agricultural Economics,* 83:4, 993–1009.

Pennings, J.M.E. & Leuthold, R.M. (2000) The role of farmers' behavioral attitudes and heterogeneity in futures contracts usage. *American Journal of Agricultural Economics,* 82:4, 908–919.

Powell, M. & Ansic, D. (1997) Gender differences in risk behavior in financial decision-making: An experimental analysis. *Journal of Economic Psychology,* 18, 605–628.

Sanders, D.R., Irwin, S.H. & Leuthold, R.M. (1996) Noise trader demand in futures markets. OFOR Paper Number 96-02.

Sanders, D.R., Irwin, S.H. & Leuthold, R.M. (1996) Noise traders, market sentiment and futures price behavior. Economics Working Paper, Washington University STL, Finance Series, No. 9707001.

Sentana, E. & Wadhwani, S. (1992) Feedback traders and stock return autocorrelations: Evidence from a century of daily data. *Economic Journal,* 102, 415–425.

Shapira, Z. (1995) *Risk Taking: A Managerial Perspective*. New York: Russell Sage Foundation.

Shefrin, H. & Statman, M. (1985) The disposition to sell winners too early and ride losers too long: Theory and evidence. *Journal of Finance,* 40, 777–790.

Shefrin, H. & Statman, M. (1999) Behavioral portfolio theory. Working Paper, Santa Clara, CA: Santa Clara University.

Silber, W.L. (1984) Marketmaker behavior in an auction market: An analysis of scalpers in futures markets. *Journal of Finance*, 39, 937–953.

Sitkin, S. & Pablo, A. (1992) Reconceptualizing the determinants of risk behavior. *Academy of Management Review,* 17, 9–38.

Slovic, P., Fischhoff, B. & Lichtenstein, S. (1980) Facts and fears: Understanding perceived risk, in R.C. Schwing and W.A. Albers (eds), *Societal Risk Assessment: How Safe is Safe Enough?,* 2nd edn. New York: Plenum Press, pp. 181–216.

Smidt, S. (1965) *Amateur Speculators*. Cornell University: Cornell Studies in Policy Administration.

Smith, C.W. & Stulz, R.M. (1985) The determinants of firms' hedging policies. *Journal of Financial and Quantitative Analysis*, pp. 391–405.

Smithson, C.W. (ed.) (1996) *Managing Financial Risk 1996 Yearbook*. New York: CIBC Wood Gundy.

Stulz, R.M. (1984) Optimal hedging policies. *Journal of Financial and Quantitative Analysis*, 127–140.

Stulz, R.M. (July 1990) Managerial discretion and optimal financing policies. *Journal of Financial Economics*, 3–27.

Stulz, R.M. (1996) Rethinking risk management. *Journal of Applied Corporate Finance*, 8–24.

Thompson, S.C., Sobolew-Shubin, A., Galbraith, M.E., Schwankovsky, L. & Cruzen, D. (1993) Maintain perceptions of control: Finding perceived control in low-control circumstances. *Journal of Personality and Social Psychology,* 64, 293–304.

Tufano, P. (1996) Who manages risk? An empirical examination of risk management practices in the gold mining industry. *Journal of Finance,* 1097–1137.

Tufano, P. (1998) Agency costs of corporate risk management. *Financial Management,* 27:1, 67–77.

Weber, M. & Camerer, C.F. (1998) The disposition effect in securities trading: An experimental analysis. *Journal of Economic Behavior and Organization,* 33, 167–184.

Willman, P., Fenton-O'Creevy, M.P., Nicholson, N. & Soane, E. (2001) Knowing the risks: Theory and practice in financial markets. *Human Relations*, 54:7, 887–910.

Willman, P., Fenton-O'Creevy, M.P., Soane, E. & Nicholson, N. (2002) Trader's tales: Agency, manager behaviour and loss aversion in investment banking. *Accounting Organizations and Society,* 27:1/2, 85–98.

Zuckerman, M. (1979) *Sensation Seeking: Beyond the Optimal Level of Arousal*. Hillsdale: Erlbaum.

Zuckerman, M., Ball, S. & Black, F. (1983) *Biological Bases of Sensation Seeking, Impulsivity and Anxiety*. Hillsdale: Erlbaum.

Zuckerman, M., Ball, S. & Black, F. (1983) Influences on sensation seeking, gender, risk appraisal and situational motivation on smoking. *Addictive Behaviors*, 15, 209–220.

Zurstrassen, P. & DeBondt, W. (2000) A portrait of European individual investors, in *11th Fund Forum 2001 Grimaldi Forum*. Monaco, France.

Chapter 9

Agrawal, A. & Chadha, S. (2002) *Who is Afraid of Reg FD? The Behavior and Performance of Sell-Side Analysts Following the SEC's Fair Disclosure Rules*. University of Alabama.

Allen L. & Saunders, A. (2002) A survey of cyclical effects in credit risk measurement models.

Altman, E.I., Resti, A. & Sironi, A. (2002) The link between default and recovery rates: Effects on the procyclicality of regulatory capital ratios. Monetary and Economic Department, Bank for International Settlements, Paper No. 113, Basel, July 2002.

Bradshaw, Moberg & Sloan (2000) *GAAP versus The Street: An Empirical Assessment of Two Alternative Definitions of Earnings*. Harvard Business School and University of Michigan.

Degeorge, F., Patel, J. & Zeckhauser, R. (1999) Earnings management to exceed thresholds. *Journal of Business,* 72, 1–33.

Dweck, C.S. (1999) *Self-Theories: Their Role in Motivation, Personality and Development*. Philadelphia: Psychology Press.

Fischhoff, B., Slovic, P., Lichtenstein, S., Read, S. & Coombs, B. (1978) How safe is safe enough? A psychometric study of attitudes towards technological risks and benefits. *Policy Sciences*, 9, 127–152.

Flynn J., Slovic, P. & Mertz, C.K. (1994) Gender, race and perception of environmental health risks. *Risk Analysis,* 14, 1101–8.

Hawken, P. (1994), Leave the world better than you found it. *The Ecology of Commerce*.

Huang P.H., Krawiec, K.D. & Partnoy, F. (2001) Derivatives on TV: A tale of two derivative debacles in prime time. USC Law School, Research Paper No. 01-1, NBER id 259854.

Koyluoglu, H. Ugur & Hickman, A. (1998) A generalized framework for credit risk portfolio models, published in abridged version as 'Reconcilable Differences'. *Risk*, pp. 56–62, October 1998.

Koyluoglu, H., Ugur, Bangia, A. & Garside, T. (1999) Devil in the parameters. July 1999.

Lewis, M. (1988) *Liar's Poker*. New York: Penguin USA.

Michaely, R. & Womack, K.L. (1999) Conflict of interest and the credibility of underwriter analyst recommendations. *Review of Financial Studies*, Special, 12:4, 653–686.

Murray D., Schwartz J. & Lichter, S.R. (2001) *It Ain't Necessarily So*. Lanham: Rowman & Littlefield.

Onge, J. (2003) Enron sues Citigroup, J.P. Morgan seeking $ 32.3 million. *Bloomberg LP*, 12 November.

Partnoy, F. (1998) *F.I.A.S.C.O.* London: Profile Books.

Stiles, P. (1988) *Riding the Bull*. New York: Random House.

Wattenberg, B. (1984) '*The Good News is the Bad News is wrong*'. New York: Simon & Schuster.

Wilson, T.C. (1997a) Portfolio credit risk (I). *Risk*, 10:9, 111–17.

Wilson, T.C. (1997b) Portfolio credit risk (II). *Risk*, 10:10, 56–61.

Wilson, T.C. (1998) Portfolio credit risk. Federal Reserve Board of New York, *Economic Policy Review*, 71–82, October.

Wood, R.E. & Bandura, A. (1989) Impact of conceptions of ability on self-regulatory mechanisms and complex decision making. *Journal of Personality and Social Psychology*, 56, 407–415.

Chapter 10

Bernstein, P.L. (1996) *Against the Gods*. New York: John Wiley & Sons, p.324.

Culp, C. & Miller, M.H. (1999) *Corporate Hedging in Theory and Practice: Lessons from Metallgesellschaft*. London: Risk Publications.

Cunningham, L. (2002) *Outsmarting the smart money*. New York: McGraw Hill Higher Education, p. 50.

Jacobs, B. (1999) *Capital Ideas and Market Realities*. London: Blackwell Publishers.

Krapels, E.N. (2001) Re-examining the *Metallgesellschaft* affair and its implications for oil traders. *Oil & Gas Journal*, 1–8.

Leeson, N. (1997) *Rogue Trader*. London: Warner Books.

Lowenstein, R. (2001) *When Genius Failed*. London: Fourth Estate, pp. 75 and 111.

Mello, A.S. & Parsons, J.E. (1994) Maturity structure of a hedge matters: Lessons from the Metallgesellschaft debacle. *Journal of Applied Corporate Finance*, pp. 106–120.

Nofsinger, J.R. (2002) *Investment Blunders of the Rich and Famous*. Upper Saddle River: Pearson Education Inc., Financial Times-Prentice Hall, pp. 193–249.

Partnoy, F. (2003) *Infectious Greed: How Greed and Risk Corrupted the Financial Markets*. London: Profile Books, p. 59.

Promontory Financial Group and Wachtell, Lipton, Rosen & Katz (2002) Report to the Board of Directors of Allied Irish Bank P.L.C., Allfirst Financial Inc., and Allfirst Bank concerning Currency Trading Losses, (Ludwig Report), March 12.

Shefrin, H. (2000) *Beyond Greed and Fear*. Cambridge: Harvard Business School Press, pp. 9, 119–126, 194–205.

Shiller, R. (2001) *Irrational Exuberance*. Princeton: Princeton University Press.

Shleifer, A. & Vishny, R.W. (1997) The limits of arbitrage. *Journal of Finance*, 52:1, 35–54.

Srivastava, S. (1998) Value at risk analysis of a leveraged swap. Paper for the Workshop on Risk Management, Isaac Newton Institute for Mathematical Sciences, Cambridge University.

Thackray, J. & Bere, C. (1995) The two faces of Kevin Hudson. *Derivatives Week*.

Weber, E. (1997) *Money, Misery, Madness: The Book of Financial Disaster Quotations*. London, England: Batsford Business Books, pp. 22–26.

Chapter 11

Aerospace Safety Advisory Panel (2002) Annual Report.

Brander, R. & Eng, P. (1995) The Titanic disaster: An enduring example of money management versus risk management, downloaded from www.cuug.ab.ca/~branderr.

Brander, R. & Eng, P. (1995) The RMS Titanic and its times: When accountants ruled the waves. Elias Kline Memorial Lecture, 69th Shock & Vibration Symposium, downloaded from www.cuug.ab.ca/~branderr.

Columbia Accident Investigation Board Report (August 2003). Available from www. caib.us.

Commodity Futures Trading Commission (1995) Order Instituting Proceedings Pursuant to Sections 6 and 8a of the Commodity Exchange Act and Findings and Order Imposing Remedial Sanctions, CFTC Docket No. 95-14, July 21.

Dörner, D. (1996) *The Logic of Failure*. Boston: Perseus Books, Addison-Wesley, pp. 28–34.

Glanz, J. & Schwartz, J. (2003) Dogged engineer's effort to assess Shuttle damage. *New York Times*, 26 September.

International Atomic Energy Agency (1999) Report on the preliminary fact finding mission following the accident at the nuclear fuel processing facility in Tokaimura, Japan, Vienna, Austria, November 1999.

Murnighan, J.K. & Mowen, J.C. (2002) *The Art of High-Stakes Decision-Making*. New York: John Wiley & Sons, Inc.

Perrow, C. (1990) *Normal Accidents*. Princeton: Princeton University Press, p. 358.

Plous, S. (1993) *The Psychology of Judgment and Decision-Making*. New York: McGraw-Hill, p. 217.

Reason, J. (1990) *Human Error*. Cambridge: Cambridge University Press, p. 255.

Rogers Commission (1986) Report of the Presidential Commission on the Space Shuttle Challenger Accident, May 1986. Available from: http://science.ksc.nasa.gov/shuttle/missions/51-l/rogers-commission/table-of-contents.html

Tenner, E. (1996) *Why Things Bite Back*. London: Fourth Estate.

Thaler, R.H. (1985) Mental accounting and consumer choice. *Marketing Science*, 4, 199–214.

Thaler, R.H. (1999) Mental accounting matters, in D. Kahneman and A. Tversky (eds.) (2000) *Choice Values and Frames*. New York: Cambridge University Press, Russell Sage Foundation, pp. 241–268.

USSR State Committee on the Utilization of Atomic Energy. The Accident at the Chernobyl Nuclear Power Plant and Its Consequences. Information compiled for the IAEA Experts' Meeting, 25–29 August, 1986. Vienna: IAEA, 1986.

Vaughan, D. (1989) *The Challenger Launch Decision*. Chicago: University of Chicago Press.

Weir, D. (1987) *The Bhopal Syndrome: Pesticides, Environment and Health*. San Francisco: Sierra Club Books, pp. 40–41.

Chapter 12

Carton, G.D. (1999) *Eloge du changement*, Paris: Edition Village Mondial, p. 212.

Herrmann, N. (1996) *The Whole Brain Business Book*, New York: McGraw-Hill Higher Education.

Senge P. M. (1993) *The Fifth Discipline: The Art & Practice of the Learning Organization*. New York: Century Business.

Skinner, B.F. (1976) *About Behaviorism*. New York: Vintage Books, Random House.

Further reading for practitioners

Finance

Advances in Behavioral Finance (Richard H. Thaler)

Beyond Greed and Fear (Hersh Shefrin)

Behavioral Finance (Joachim Goldberg & Ruediger Von Nitzsch)

Fooled by Randomness (Nassim Nicholas Taleb)

Investment Blunders of the Rich and Famous (John Nofsinger)

Infectious Greed (Frank Partnoy)

When Genius Failed (Roger Lowenstein)

Irrational Exuberance (Robert Shiller)

Framing and cognitive psychology

Why Smart People Make Big Money Mistakes & How to Correct Them: Lessons from the New Science of Behavioral Economics (Paul Belsky & Thomas Gilovich)

How We Know What Isn't So: The Fallibility of Human Reason in Everyday Life (Thomas Gilovich)

The Psychology of Judgment and Decision-Making (Scott Plous)

Randomness (Deborah J. Bennett)

Simple Heuristics that Make Us Smart (Gerd Gigerenzer)

Calculated Risk (Gerd Gigerenzer)

Decision-making

The Art of High-Stakes Decision-Making (J.K. Murnighan & J.C. Mowen)

The Logic of Failure (Dietrich Dörner)

Problems with technology and high-risk systems

Inviting Disaster (James R. Chiles)

Managing the Risks of Organizational Accidents (James Reason)

Normal Accidents (Charles Perrow)

Why Things Bite Back (Edward Tenner)

The Challenger Launch Decision (Diane Vaughan)

Human Error (James Reason)

... and, for some fun

The Worst-Case Scenario Survival Handbook (Joshua Piven & David Borgenicht)

The Experts Speak (Christopher Cerf & Victor Navasky)

www.boneheads.com: Great website on expert calls

www.youramazingbrain.com: Great website on visual illusions

www.eluzions.com: Another great website on visual illusions

Index